System Browser

Numeric Magnitude	-----------	accessing
Numeric-Numbers	Date	arithmetic
Collections-Abstrac	Magnitude	inquiries
Collections-Unorder	Time	converting
Collections-Sequenc	-----------	printing
Collections-Text		private

monthIndex
monthName
weekday
year

Instance   class

day

"Answer the day of the year represented by the receiver."

↑day

See Chapters 9, 10, 11, and 12

Senders of day

```
-----------
Date <
Date =
Date daysLeftInYear
```

< aDate

"Answer whether aDate precedes the date of the receiver."

```
    year = aDate year
        ifTrue: [↑day < aDate day]
        ifFalse: [↑year < aDate
year]
```

See Chapters 9 and 10

Implementors of day

```
-----------
Date day
-----------
```

day

"Answer the day of the year represented by the receiver."

↑day

See Chapters 9 and 10

Smalltalk–80

The Interactive Programming Environment

Adele Goldberg

Xerox Palo Alto Research Center

Addison-Wesley Publishing Company
*Reading, Massachusetts • Menlo Park, California
London • Amsterdam • Don Mills, Ontario • Sydney*

This book is in the
Addison-Wesley series in Computer Science
MICHAEL A. HARRISON
CONSULTING EDITOR

Library of Congress Cataloging in Publication Data

Goldberg, Adele.
    Smalltalk-80.

    Includes indexes.
    1. Smalltalk-80 (Computer system) I. Title.
II. Title: Smalltalk-eighty.
QA76.8.S635G638 1984   001.64   83-11856
ISBN 0-201-11372-4

ISBN 0-201-11372-4
BCDEFGHIJ-HA-8987654

Preface

The user interface to the Smalltalk-80 system is a multipurpose interface, designed to facilitate text and graphics creation and manipulation, program development, and information storage and retrieval. You, as the user create, manipulate, save, or retrieve, either a visual form or specific information within such a form. You interact with the system on a bitmapped display screen, using a typewriter keyboard and a pointing device.

The Smalltalk-80 system includes utilities typical of a computer's operating system: compiler, debugger, text editor. These are brought together on the display screen in the form of a collection of rectangular areas or *views* of information. One rectangular area might view the text of a program under development. Changing the text is accomplished by pointing to the parts to be changed, and typing new text or issuing an editing command such as delete. When the text is considered correct, an accept or compile command is issued. If any syntactic errors are detected, they will be indicated in the text in the window so that they can be corrected right away. Once all syntactic errors are corrected, the text is compiled into object code and linked into the system, as the system is running. The new code can then be tested by typing an appropriate expression, selecting it, and issuing an evaluate command. This process is immediate; no exchange of editing, compiling, filing, or executing "modes" is required.

Part One of this book is an introduction to the user interface to the Smalltalk-80 system. Part Two is an explanation of the support provided for finding information about objects that exist in the Smalltalk-80 system. Part Three is an illustrated description of how to explore the class descriptions available in the system, and of how to use the editors for implementing new class descriptions. Part Four presents the support available for finding and correcting errors, while Part Five introduces access to external files and system housekeeping support such as crash recovery and change management. Parts One through Five explain how to manipulate the components of the user interface. They are written to encourage specific practice and exploration; each section includes suggested exercises. A brief introduction to the Smalltalk-80 language is also provided in order to explain the ways in which the interface components provide access to the language components.

If you have access to a Smalltalk-80 system, you will need to read the book only once, after which you can rely on the on-line aids provided by the interactive system. The on-line aids consist of a menu-oriented interface to remind you of available functionality, comments for each class and method, an "explain" capability that can identify the tokens in a method, and a spelling corrector. This book is not intended as an introduction to programming in the Smalltalk-80 language. If an in-depth understanding of the language is desired, you should use this book in conjunction with *Smalltalk-80: The Language and its Implementation*, by Adele Goldberg and David Robson (Addison-Wesley, Reading, Mass., 1983), which includes reference material for the system classes. Because of the detailed scenarios and figures, this book can be used independent of a running system to learn about the components of the user interface, and about the process of working with a graphical-oriented, interactive system development environment.

About the Described System

The system described in this book was released for general licensing in May, 1983, by the Xerox Corporation as the "Smalltalk-80 System Version 2." Version 1 was a preliminary version of the system that was originally released to several companies participating in a review of the formal specification of the Smalltalk-80 virtual machine, and provided by Xerox Electo-Optical Systems (now Xerox Special Information Systems, Pasadena, Calif.) in 1981-1982 as one of their software offerings on the Xerox 1100 Scientific Information Processor. Version 2 added functionality to the system, notably the spelling correction used in compiling and debugging methods; special browser queries about instance and class variables, class references, and class hierarchies; and special inspectors. As a language, the Smalltalk-80 system Version 2 includes support for multiple inheritance and multiple language compilers. Some of the examples provided in this book use system user interface components from Version 2 that do not exist in the Smalltalk-80 System Version 1.

The larger examples of Smalltalk-80 definitions given in this book are provided to Xerox customers or system licensees as part of the files on their disk or magnetic tape. This includes the protocol and project browsers described in Chapter 15, the model for financial histories developed in Chapters 17, 18, and 19, and methods for viewing and interacting with financial histories listed in Appendix 1. Glenn Krasner and Evelyn Van Orden have been the main motivators and supporters in getting the system releases and examples completed for this kind of distribution.

Acknowledgments

As the Smalltalk-80 system evolved and was tested by nonXerox commerical organizations and universities, this book evolved from a user manual to a general description of the programming environment. The choice of content and organization benefited from review by many people. Norman Meyrowitz of Brown University was especially instrumental in pointing out omissions of detail. I wish also to thank Susanne Bodker, Glenn Krasner, Michael Madsen, Paul McCullough, Michael Rutenberg, Rachel Rutherford, and Evelyn Van Orden, (all of the Xerox Corporation); David Casseres (Apple Computer), Pavel Curtis (Cornell University), Steve Draper (University of California, San Diego), and Trygve Reenskaug (Central Institute for Industrial Design, Oslo, Norway).

The Smalltalk-80 System is the result of research and development of the Software Concepts Group of the Xerox Palo Alto Research Center. As the group manager, I took responsibility for documenting the system. It is not possible to identify the individual contributions made by each member of the group in the creation of the complete system. However, I would like to point to several aspects of the system documented in this book, and acknowledge several contributors: the system browser was first introduced by Larry Tesler and then enriched by Dan Ingalls, the debugger was introduced by Dan, the change manager by Peter Deutsch, the version handler by Steve Putz, the special inspectors and the file list view by Glenn Krasner, and the form and bit editors by Bob Flegal and Diana Merry. The first version of spelling correction was implemented by Steve and then incorporated into the system compiler by Dan. Ted Kaehler created the explanation utility on a suggestion by Ellis Cohen of Brandeis University. In addition, the example of a protocol browser given in Chapter 15 was suggested by Dave Wallace from the University of California, Berkeley, and that of the combinations of elements of a collection by Steve Putz. Many new ideas and bug fixes came from our colleagues at the Xerox Special Information Systems, including Evelyn Van Orden, who maintains the customer release version of the system (a system that includes network communication facilities), Rae Conrad, Bob Lansford, and Michael Malcolm (whose clever scrolling additions to the text editor are included in Version 2).

Glenn Krasner, Dave Robson, and Steve Putz helped me complete Version 2 of the Smalltalk-80 system, create the images of the display screen for the book figures, and produce the magnetic tapes for the typesetter. As in the other books in the Smalltalk-80 series, the original text for this book was supplied to the publisher on magnetic tape that included formatting codes identifying the various types of textual entity in the manuscript. The software for the conversion from the Xerox internal formats to that of the typesetter was written by Dave Robson. The timely manner in which the production process was handled was due both to Dave's software and personal support, and to the efforts of Eileen Colahan of the International Computaprint Corporation and Fran Fulton, the production editor.

The original syntax diagrams shown in Chapter 5 were prepared by Janet Moreland. All the figures that represent the Smalltalk-80 display screen graphics and the chapter opening artwork were created by me using the Smalltalk-80 system. They were printed on the Platemaker system developed by Gary Starkweather and the Imaging Sciences Laboratory of PARC. I would like to thank Gary, Eric Larson, and Julian Orr for making the Platemaker available.

Registered trademarks mentioned in this book are Lisa, (Apple Computer Inc.); VAX 11/780 and VAXstation (Digital Equipment Corp.); and Smalltalk-80 (Xerox Corp.).

Adele Goldberg

Palo Alto, California
October 1983

Contents

Appendixes

Indexes

PART ONE

The General System Interface

The Smalltalk-80 system consists of an object-oriented programming language and an integrated collection of tools for interacting with components of that language. In the Smalltalk-80 language, the fundamental way to indicate that something should happen is by sending a message to an object. An object is a representation of information consisting of private memory, and a set of operations to manipulate information stored in the private memory or to carry out some actions relative to that information. Sending a message is the Smalltalk-80 way of asking the object to carry out one of its operations.

All information in the Smalltalk-80 system is represented as an *object*. Each object knows the *messages* it can understand. Associated with each such message is a *method* that describes how the object should respond to the message. The user interface to the Smalltalk-80 system can be viewed as a graphical way in which to identify objects and to choose messages to send to objects. When an object is sent a message, the appropriate method is invoked and some action is taken. The purpose of this book is to describe the varied ways in which objects and messages can be identified and methods invoked; its purpose is also to describe some useful ways in which information about objects can be retrieved.

This book is written in a tutorial or "try and see" style. Each section describes the functionality of a part of the user interface and then encourages you to employ that functionality. Although this book does not substitute for a detailed exposition about the language, an overview is provided and a summary of the language syntax is included. The overview is sufficient information so that you can understand the chapters on evaluating expressions, on accessing objects already in the programming system, and on creating new objects.

The tutorials are presented in an order designed first to give you practice in controlling the hardware devices that support interaction with the graphical elements of the display screen, and in reading and responding to the visual cues. Visual cues include differently-shaped cursors, highlighted text, flashing rectangular areas of the screen, and prompters and confirmers. Next, the basic editing functions are introduced: creating rectangular areas on the screen, called *views*, in which to access information; and invoking *menus* in which to choose commands to send to objects, editing text, and editing pictures. Special views called *projects* allow you to manage several separate screens of information. Each project or screenful maintains its own history list of the views you have created and of the changes you have made to the system. After a description of how to create and edit projects, you are introduced to the Smalltalk-80 language, and how to evaluate expressions.

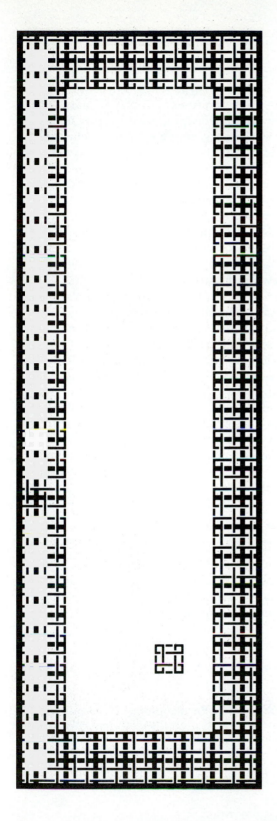

1

Introduction to the Book and the System

The Smalltalk-80 system runs on a microcomputer that includes a high-resolution bitmapped display screen, a typewriter keyboard, and a pointing device. The display is used to present graphical and textual views of information to the user. The keyboard is used to present textual information to the system. The pointing device is used to select information on the display screen. The pointing device controls the movement of a cursor on the screen; the cursor shows the location currently being selected. The pointing device can be, for example, a mouse, a graphics tablet, or function keys on a keyboard.

There are a variety of hardware configurations on which the Smalltalk-80 system runs. These configurations might have different resolutions for their display screens, different layouts of keys on their keyboards, and different types of pointing devices. Photographs of several Smalltalk-80 systems are shown in Figure 1.1.

Several sections of this book depend on the particular hardware configuration that you, the user, have available. These are Sections 1.1 and 1.2, on the hardware system and on how to get started, and the chapters of Part Five on the use of an external file system. Much of the interface to external files is the same for all hardware configurations, but the particulars of naming files and creating system back ups may differ. For a description of the hardware devices you have available, the initial start up sequence you must follow, and the file-naming and back-up conventions you should use, you must obtain information specific to your system that is not provided in this book.

Throughout the book, an indented paragraph of small print is used to provide information at a level of detail that may be of interest to you if you want to know a bit more about the structure of the Smalltalk-80 system.

> For example, the names of classes that support a user interface component may be given, along with messages that implement a particular user interface function.

You can skip over these comments without losing information needed to interact with the system. Also, alternate designs are given in small print as suggested exercises that you might try if you are proficient with the language and the programming environment.

Figure 1.1

Top: Tektronix Magnolia, experimental workstation (photo by Edward L. Reuss, courtesy of Tektronix Inc.), Apple Lisa, experimental software (photo courtesy of Apple Computer Inc.); middle: Hewlett-Packard Laboratories, development station (photo by Rich Marconi, courtesy of Hewlett-Packard), Digital Equipment Corp.,VAX-11/780 with VAXstation display (photo by Charles W. Gamage Jr., courtesy of Digital Equipment Corp.); bottom: Xerox Dorado and Xerox implementation on the SUN Microsystems Inc. workstation (photos by K. O. Beckman and Wes Dorman, courtesy of Xerox Corp.).

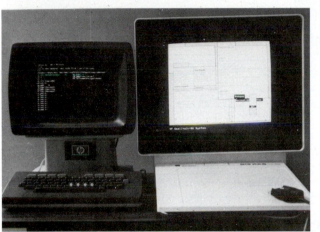

1.1

Appearance of the Hardware System

The significant parts of the hardware on which the Smalltalk-80 system runs are identified in Figure 1.2: the keyboard, the display screen, and a pointing device. These are the parts that play a significant role in the user interface of the system.

In Figure 1.2, keys that play a specific role in the Smalltalk-80 text editor are labeled. Henceforth, the names of the keys as indicated in the following keyboard map are used, rather than the key-cap label. To use the system, you must determine the correct mapping for the hardware system you have available.

Also in Figure 1.2, the coordinates of the corners of the display screen are marked. Notice that position 0, 0 is at the upper left corner of the screen, and that the y-coordinate increases as you move *down* the screen.

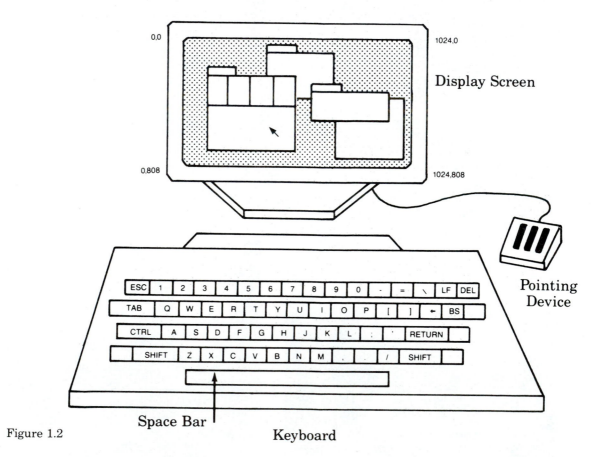

Figure 1.2

key names	key cap label
backspace	BS
carriage return	RETURN
control	CTRL
delete	DEL
escape	ESC
line feed	LF
space bar	no label (bottom row, large single key)

Appearance of the Display Screen

The display screen has a light gray background. White rectangular areas containing text and/or pictures are placed against this background. Each of these areas is called a *view*. The *content* of a view is the text and/or picture within its rectangular border that you can examine, create, store, and retrieve. A sample image of a Smalltalk-80 display is shown in Figure 1.3.

Most of the views on the Smalltalk-80 display screen are *standard system views*, meaning they provide some standard functions. In particular, you can

• visually identify a standard system view by a label

• change the screen location of a standard system view

• change its size

• replace it with an area containing only the label

• remove it from the screen

In Figure 1.4, there are several standard views. Each has a label in the upper left corner. Some, such as the two views in the center of the figure, consist only of a label. These are referred to as *collapsed* views. The views in the figure are in different locations and have different sizes. The view at the top of the figure consists of five parts or *subviews*. The content of a subview might depend on the content of one or more of the other subviews.

When you are working on several different tasks, the tasks can be presented in a variety of ways: with each in a different view, with some or all in the same view, or with some tasks, such as background processes, in no view at all. Views are known to a special system object called a *control manager*. This manager's job is to let you move the cursor within the border of a view, and to interact with either the view itself or with the information inside it.

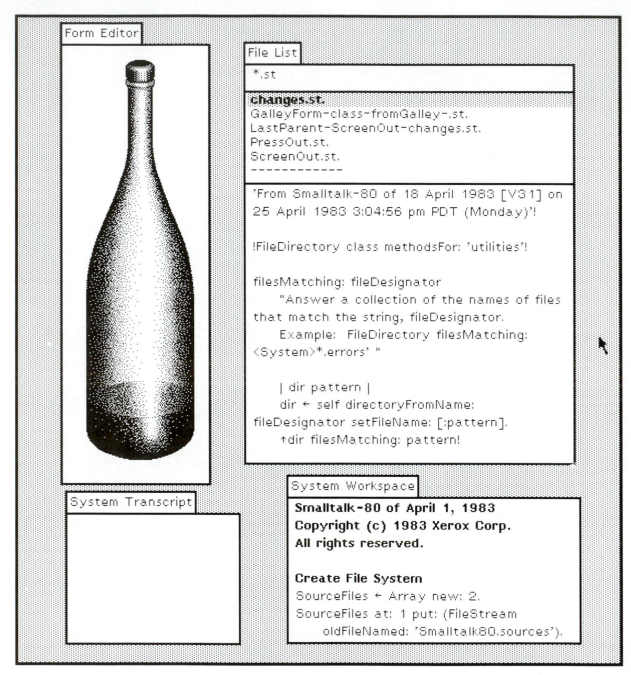

```
Form Editor

File List

*.st

changes.st.
GalleyForm-class-fromGalley-.st.
LastParent-ScreenOut-changes.st.
PressOut.st.
ScreenOut.st.
------------

'From Smalltalk-80 of 18 April 1983 [V31] on
25 April 1983 3:04:56 pm PDT (Monday)'!

!FileDirectory class methodsFor: 'utilities'!

filesMatching: fileDesignator
    "Answer a collection of the names of files
that match the string, fileDesignator.
    Example:  FileDirectory filesMatching:
<System>*.errors' "

    | dir pattern |
    dir ← self directoryFromName:
fileDesignator setFileName: [:pattern].
        ↑dir filesMatching: pattern!
```

```
System Transcript
```

```
System Workspace

Smalltalk-80 of April 1, 1983
Copyright (c) 1983 Xerox Corp.
All rights reserved.

Create File System
SourceFiles ← Array new: 2.
SourceFiles at: 1 put: (FileStream
    oldFileNamed: 'Smalltalk80.sources').
```

Figure 1.3

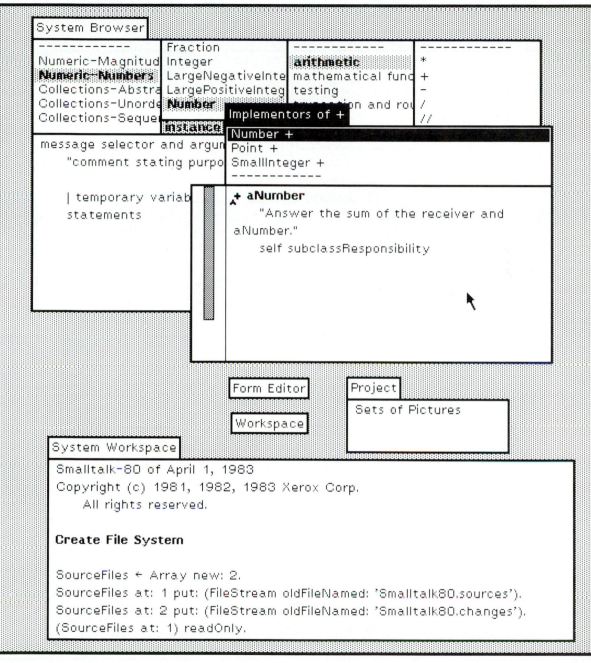

System Browser

```
------------     Fraction          ------------     -----------
Numeric-Magnitud Integer           arithmetic       *
Numeric-Numbers  LargeNegativeInte mathematical func +
Collections-Abstra LargePositiveInteg testing        -
Collections-Unorde Number                    ion and rou /
Collections-Seque              instance          //
```

```
                              Implementors of +
message selector and argu   Number +
    "comment stating purpo   Point +
                             SmallInteger +
                             ------------
    | temporary variab
    statements            + aNumber
                                "Answer the sum of the receiver and
                          aNumber."
                                self subclassResponsibility
```

Form Editor   Project

Workspace   Sets of Pictures

System Workspace

Smalltalk-80 of April 1, 1983
Copyright (c) 1981, 1982, 1983 Xerox Corp.
    All rights reserved.

Create File System

SourceFiles ← Array new: 2.
SourceFiles at: 1 put: (FileStream oldFileNamed: 'Smalltalk80.sources').
SourceFiles at: 2 put: (FileStream oldFileNamed: 'Smalltalk80.changes').
(SourceFiles at: 1) readOnly.

Figure 1.4

System Browser

------------ ------------ ------------ ------------
Numeric-Magnitud ------------ ------------ ------------
Numeric-Numbers
Collections-Abstr
Collections-Unord
Collections-Seque
Collections-Text

instance class

Workspace

bitmapped display screen, a typewriter
keyboard, and a pointing device. The display is
used to present graphical and textual views of
information to the user. The keyboard is used
to present textual information to the system.
The pointing device is used to select information
on the display screen. The pointing device
controls the movement of a cursor on the
screen; the cursor shows the location currently
being selected. The pointing device can be, for
example, a mouse, a graphics tablet, or function
keys on a keyboard.

There are a variety of hardware configurations
on which the Smalltalk-80 system runs. These
configurations might have different resolutions
for their display screens, different layouts of
keys on their keyboard, and different types of
pointing devices. Photographs of several
Smalltalk-80 systems are shown in Figure 1.0.

Several sections of this book depend on the

System Workspac

Create File Syste

SourceFiles ← Arr
SourceFiles at: 1
oldFileNamed:
'Smalltalk80.sour
SourceFiles at: 2
oldFileNamed:
'Smalltalk80.changes').

Figure 1.5

Available screen space has been optimized by allowing the views to overlap, partially or wholly. The *active view* (the view in which you are currently working) is automatically moved to the top of any stack of overlapping views. Since a view often contains more information than can be displayed at any given time within its boundaries, an additional *scroll bar* area is associated with each view, where appropriate. A scroll bar presents a method by which you can specify the part of the available information that you want displayed.

In Figure 1.5, a view of textual information is the active view, the one labeled Workspace. Its scroll bar area is shown at its left side. The fact that the gray area of the scroll bar fills only part of the scroll bar height indicates that you see only part of the information that can be accessed using this view.

Pointing Device "Buttons"

A likeness of a pointing device used by the Smalltalk-80 system developed at the Xerox Palo Alto Research Center is shown in Figure 1.6. It is called a *mouse*. The cursor on the display screen is moved by moving the mouse over a flat surface. The mouse has buttons on it which are used to make different kinds of selections.

Some hardware configurations for the Smalltalk-80 system have buttons on the pointing device that can be used to select display positions or to request the display of a particular menu. Other configurations use keyboard function keys for the same purpose. Each configuration shares an identical collection of techniques for accessing objects and messages, and an identical collection of tools for manipulating objects. For example, each system shares a common editor for creating and modifying text or pictures.

The Xerox mouse has three buttons on it. These buttons are identified in Figure 1.6 as *red button, yellow button,* and *blue button.*

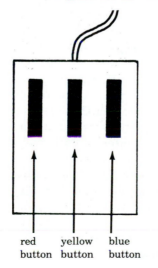

Figure 1.6

red   yellow   blue
button   button   button

The names are for historical, not visual reasons. Some of the original Xerox mice had colored buttons.

Throughout the standard Smalltalk-80 system,

- red button is used to SELECT information

- yellow button is used to get a menu for EDITING the CONTENTS of a view

- blue button is used to get a menu for EDITING the VIEW itself

In referring to the use of the buttons, we will use the following terminology:

press	push and hold the button down
release	remove finger from button, letting the button up
click	press button, then release it, without moving the cursor
double click	click two times in succession, without moving the cursor

Some people refer to selection using a click as *bugging*. Their expressions take the form of "bug that command" or "bug outside the view."

Note carefully that we distinguish between pressing the button down without releasing (press), and pushing the button down and releasing (click). Note also that a selected item is highlighted, typically by complementing it. To complement text, black characters on a white background are changed to white characters on a black background.

For many operations, pressing the button down is a separate action from releasing the button. Pressing down the yellow or blue button, for example, causes a list of items to appear on the screen; releasing the button chooses the selected item. This list of items is referred to as a *menu*. While the button is down, the system provides feedback about what can occur. For example, a menu item may be highlighted to indicate that it will be the one chosen if the button is released. This gives you a chance to confirm visually that it is the desired item, or to move the cursor to a different item and to see it selected (highlighted) before you release the button. Releasing the button chooses the item. The distinction between pressing and releasing a button is a significant one to learn in order to be able to interact with the Smalltalk-80 system. Most actions occur as a result of releasing a button. There are only two places in the system where the action is invoked when the button is pressed down: in controlling the scroll bar, and in selecting text.

In Figure 1.7, notice the image of the pointing device at the lower left side. The image consists of a rectangle with three subareas; one of the three subareas is filled with black, the others are white. Each area denotes one of the buttons you can press. In the picture, the image indi-

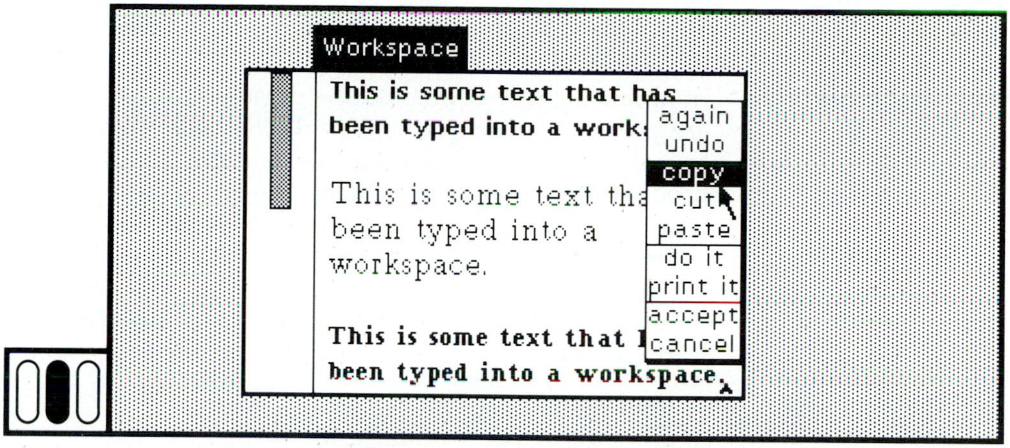

Figure 1.7

cates that the yellow button is currently being pressed, causing a menu to appear and an item in the menu to be highlighted. This image is used throughout this book in order to illustrate pressing a button, even though the three buttons on the hardware system you are using may not be grouped or packaged on a single rectangular-shaped device.

The four possible button images that may appear at the lower left side of a figure are shown in Figure 1.8. Each button image represents a press of one or no button. When we wish to denote "clicking" a button, two button images will be displayed at the lower left side of the screen image. The first button image designates the button to press, and the second indicates that a release should follow. Figure 1.9 shows the three possible images for button clicks.

denotes no
button pressed   denotes red
button pressed   denotes yellow
button pressed   denotes blue
button pressed

Figure 1.8

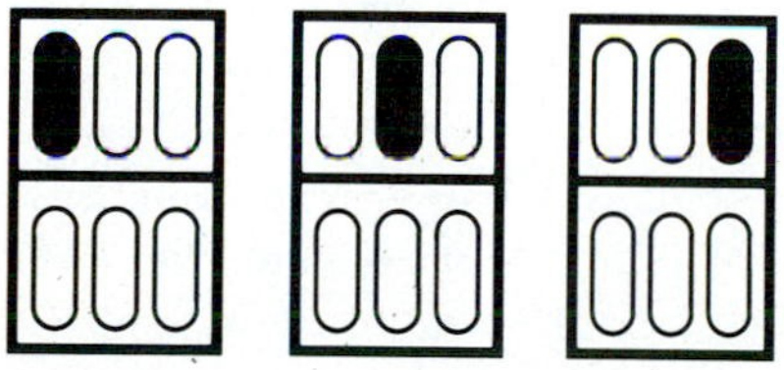

click red
button   click
yellow
button   click
blue button

Figure 1.9

1.2

Getting Started

In order to get your Smalltalk-80 system started, there should be a separate document for you to consult that describes your particular hardware system and file-naming conventions. It will identify the files you need, the procedure for turning the power on, and the commands or buttons to push in order to install the Smalltalk-80 system.

On most of the Xerox systems, for example, there is a small button located at the back of the keyboard that you push (called the "boot" button). A herald will appear announcing the Xerox Executive. If the Xerox Executive is installed with the proper files, you can then type

@st80.cm

and then press the "carriage return" key.

After a few moments, an image of the Smalltalk-80 programming interface should appear on the display screen.

System Files

Although different implementations may have different start up procedures, and perhaps require different sets of system files, the basic Xerox Smalltalk-80 system requires four significant files.

ST80 < Version > .im
This is the Smalltalk-80 system *image*. It contains the compiled form of each method, as well as the initial bitmap that appears on the screen when the system is installed, and all the other system objects.

ST80 < Version > .sources
This file contains the text for each method in the system. The compiled form of each method includes an index into this file so that the text can be retrieved upon user request. In the Xerox systems, when a network-based file server is available, this "sources" file resides on the file server and is shared by all Smalltalk-80 users.

ST80 < Version > .changes
Initially this is an empty file. When the user interacts with the Smalltalk-80 system, each action that involves evaluating an expression is stored in this file. If the system crashes, it is possible to recover your work by evaluating the expressions stored in this file. See Part Five for more details.

ST80 < Version > .run
This is the "run file" or virtual machine emulator for the Smalltalk-80 language. The system is invoked by executing this file with the name of the image file as its single argument. The file ST80.cm is a "command" file; it is an indirect way of naming the two files.

Wherever we have written <Version> in naming a file, we mean that the file name actually contains a date indicating a particular system release. Typically the date should be the same for all the files. In the Xerox systems, capitalization in file names is not meaningful.

1.3

Try It,
Just to See

The next chapters present details about the basic user interface components, the text editor, and how to evaluate Smalltalk-80 expressions. Before reading these chapters you might wish to try the system, just to see what you can do. This section illustrates an example interaction you can try in order to get an early introduction.

You already know that the display screen has a light gray background and that there may be one or more rectangular areas containing text. Move the cursor so that it is not inside any rectangular area, that is, move it so that it is over the light gray background. Press the yellow button; do not release the button. A menu appears (Figure 1.10a).

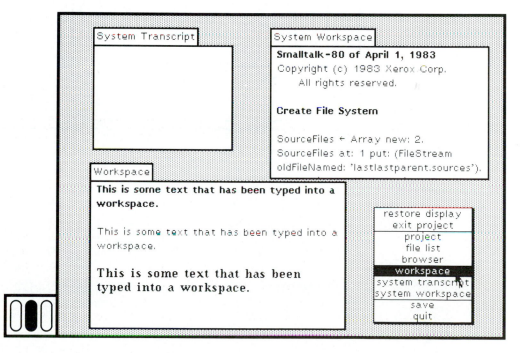

Figure 1.10a

Move the cursor up and down, noticing that different menu items are highlighted. Move the cursor so that the item workspace is highlighted. Release the yellow button.

The cursor changes shape (Figure 1.10b). Move the cursor anywhere towards the center of the screen and press the red button. You have selected the upper left corner of a rectangular area. The cursor changes shape again (Figure 1.10c). Move the cursor around to select the lower right corner of the area. Release the red button. You have now created a small workspace on the screen (Figure 1.10d).

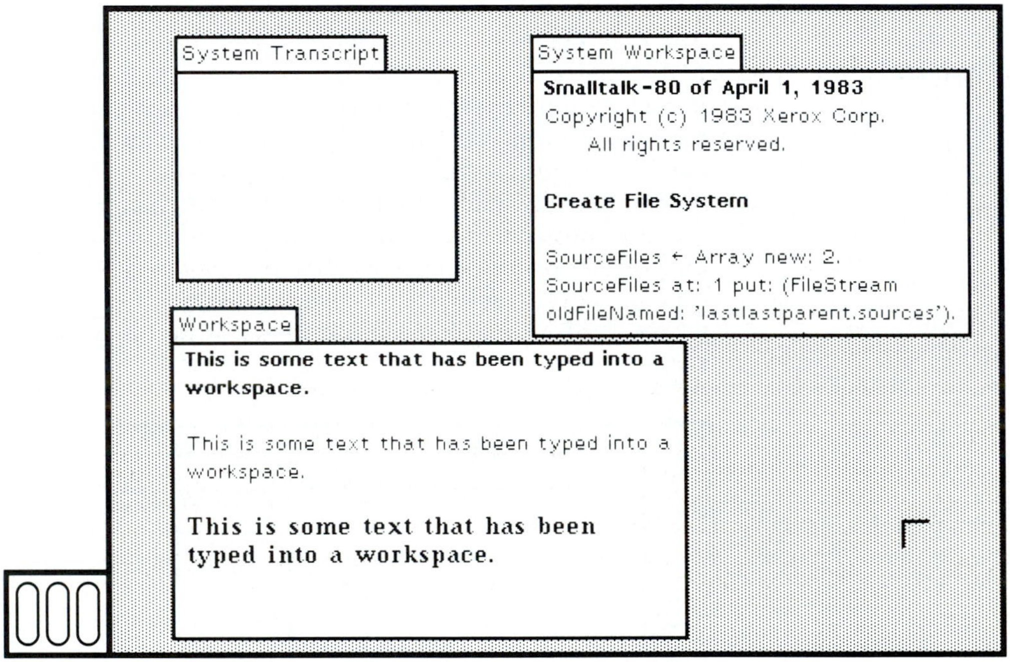

Figure 1.10b

System Transcript

System Workspace

Smalltalk-80 of April 1, 1983
Copyright (c) 1983 Xerox Corp.
All rights reserved.

Create File System

SourceFiles ← Array new: 2.
SourceFiles at: 1 put: (FileStream
oldFileNamed: 'lastlastparent.sources').

Workspace

This is some text that has been typed into a workspace.

This is some text that has been typed into a workspace.

This is some text that has been typed into a workspace.

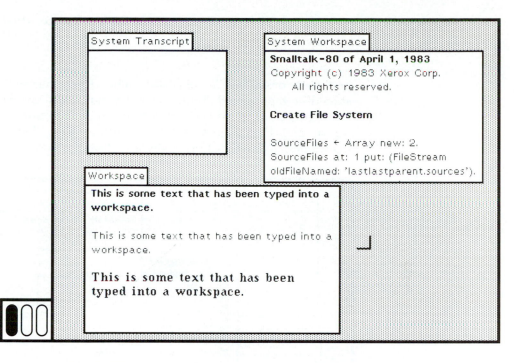

Figure 1.10c

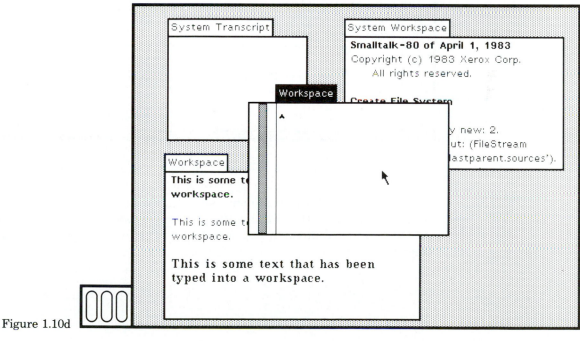

Figure 1.10d

Make certain the cursor is inside the workspace. Type

3+4

and then press the "escape" key. The three characters, 3, +, and 4 should be highlighted (Figure 1.11a). If not, place the cursor just before the character 3, press the red button, move the cursor past the character 4, and then release the red button. The characters should be highlighted. Note that they make up a Smalltalk-80 expression.

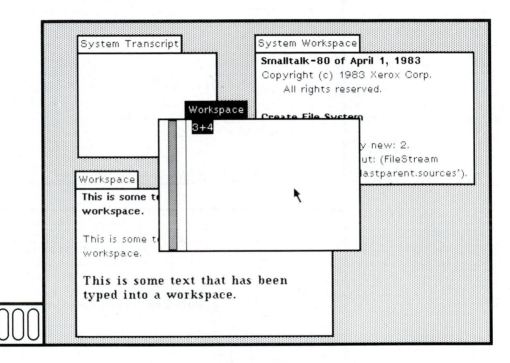

Figure 1.11a

Be sure that the cursor is still inside the workspace. Press the yellow button so that another menu appears (Figure 1.11b). Move the cursor so that the item print it in the menu is highlighted (Figure 1.11c). Now release the yellow button. Notice that the expression has been evaluated and the result printed in the workspace. The result 7 is highlighted (Figure 1.11d).

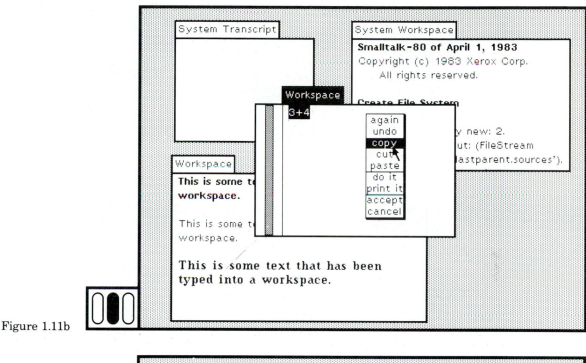

Figure 1.11b

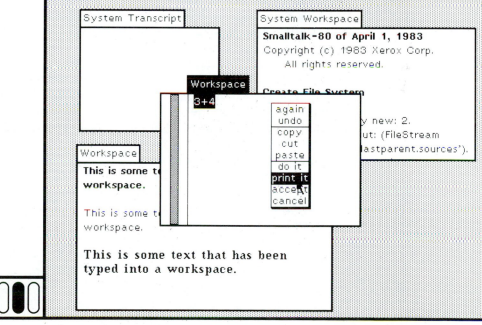

Figure 1.11c

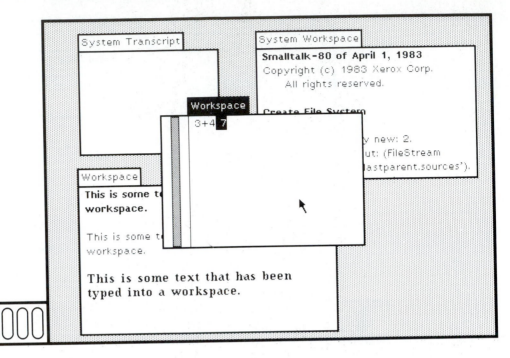

Figure 1.11d

Press the blue button so that another menu appears (Figure 1.12a). Move the cursor so that the item close is highlighted (Figure 1.12b). Release the blue button. A special menu called a *confirmer* appears. You have requested closing a workspace, but the contents have not been saved. This is acceptable to you. Notice that as you move the cursor around, the shape of the cursor changes. When the cursor is over the part labeled yes, it is shaped as a hand with a thumb pointing up; when the cursor is over the part labeled no, it is shaped as a hand with a thumb pointing down. If you move the cursor outside the confirmer, it will "flash" or "blink" to indicate that you must answer the confirmer's question before proceeding.

Move the cursor over the part of the confirmer that is labeled yes. Press the red button (Figure 1.12c). The item labeled yes is framed by a gray box as a way to indicate it is selected. Release the red button. The workspace will disappear.

If you were able to follow the example, you successfully created a new view on the screen, used the text editor, evaluated an expression, and closed the view.

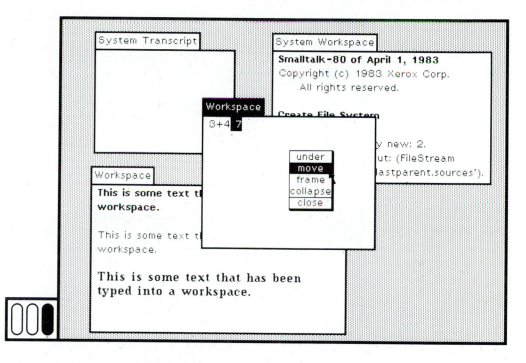

Figure 1.12a

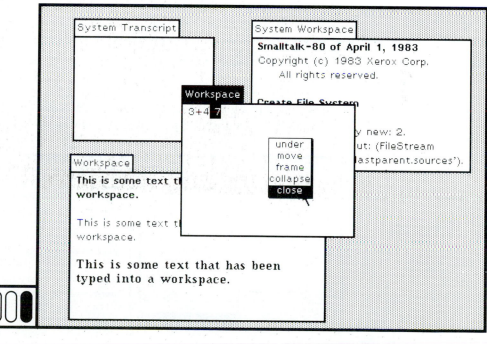

Figure 1.12b

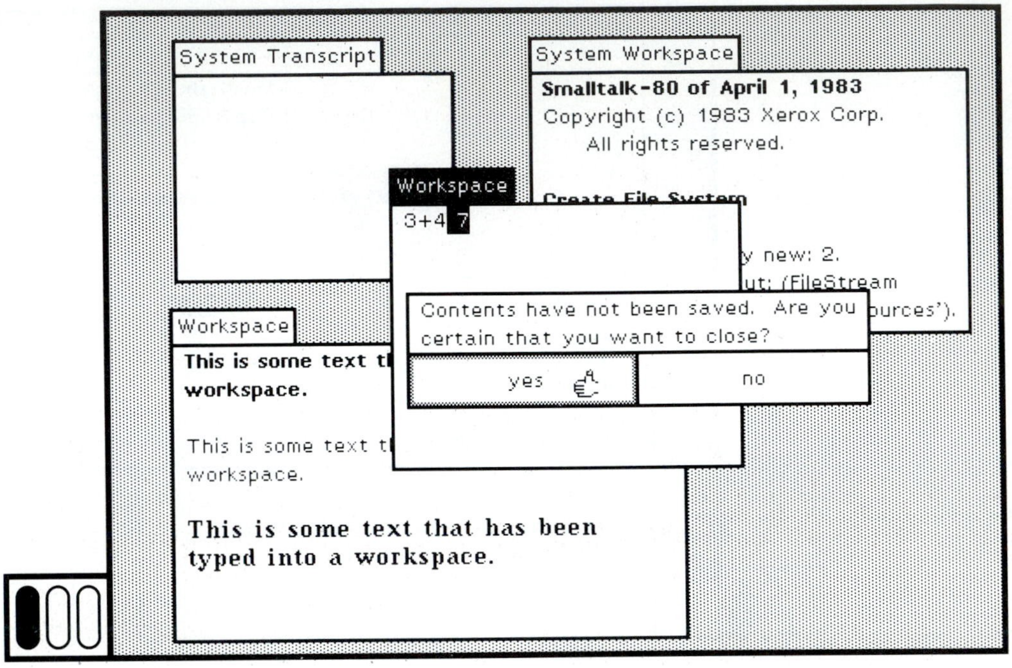

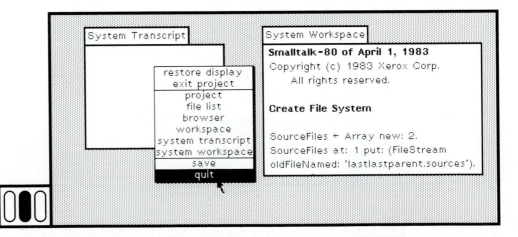

Figure 1.12c

1.4

**Stopping a
Work Session**

When you are ready to stop using the system, you choose a menu command quit.

Move the cursor so that it is over the light gray background. Press the yellow button to obtain the menu and move the cursor so that the item quit is highlighted (Figure 1.13a). Release the button.

Figure 1.13a

Another menu appears (Figure 1.13b), giving you three command choices.

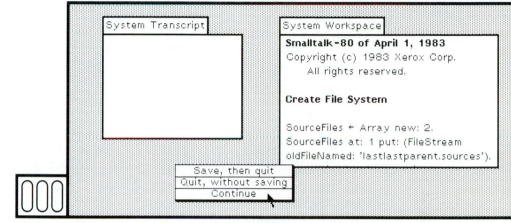

Figure 1.13b

Save, then quit	Creates a *snapshot* as described later in this section, and then takes you out of the system.
Quit, without saving	Takes you out of the Smalltalk-80 system. (Each implementation of the system will differ as to what happens next. In the Xerox systems, you are returned to the Xerox Executive. You then type quit followed by a "carriage return" to blacken the screen.)
Continue	Erases the menu and continues your use of the system.

Choose one of these commands by moving the cursor over the menu, press the red button, move the cursor until the item you prefer is highlighted (Figure 1.13c), and then release the button.

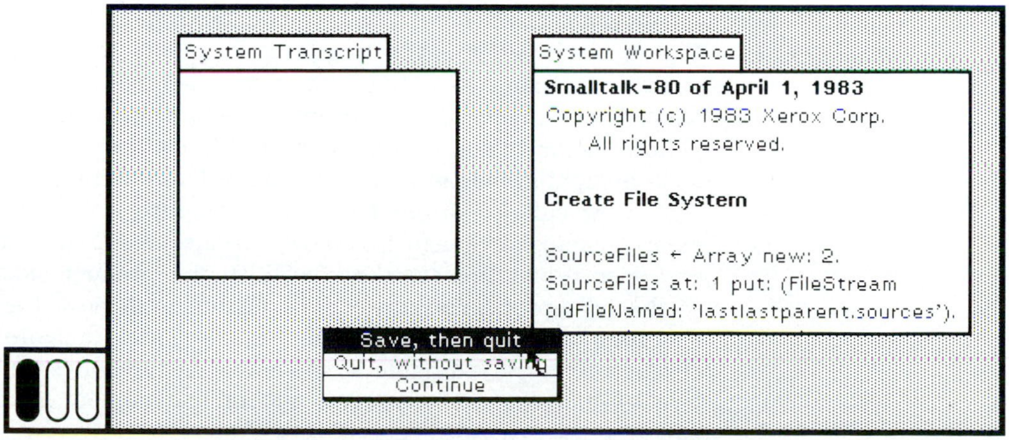

Figure 1.13c

Clicking the red button outside the boundaries of the menu will also erase the menu and allow you to continue your use of the system.

There are times when you will save the current state of your work using a command in the user interface to create a *snapshot*. What you save is a version of the system image, that is, the compiled methods (the system ones and any you may have added to the system), all other system objects, and a representation of your current display screen. This saved image is referred to as a *snapshot*, and is stored on a file named

snapshot.im

If you create a snapshot and then quit, you can use the saved version of the system, rather than the original image, by executing the run file with the name snapshot.im as its single argument. Most Xerox systems include a command file for this purpose, so that you simply type

@snap.cm

and then press the "carriage return" key.

Sometimes more than one user will share a computer and its disk space. Each may wish to maintain their own snapshot. Some care must be taken to manage this situation by maintaining both the "snapshot" file and "changes" file (backing up on a separate disk or changing the name on the current disk). Both files must be maintained in a coordinated way because the snapshot refers to source code written on the changes file. When you restart a snapshot, you must also be sure to use the same run file and the same sources file that were used when the snapshot was created. See Chapter 23 for more details about the coordination requirements.

☐ *Create a Snapshot*   Try to create a snapshot. There are two ways. Follow the instructions for stopping your work session given earlier and choose the menu item Save, then quit. Alternatively, choose the item save. That is, move the cursor over the light gray background, press the yellow button to obtain the menu, and move the cursor so that the item save is highlighted, as shown in Figure 1.14a. Release the button.

A view called a *prompter* appears (Figure 1.14b). The name of the current snapshot image file shows in the prompter. Let's assume that you wish to use this same name. With the cursor inside the lower half of the prompter, press the yellow button and move the cursor so that the item accept is highlighted (Figure 1.14c). Release the button to choose the displayed name as the name of the snapshot. As an alternative to choosing the command accept to complete your response, you can type the "carriage return" key.

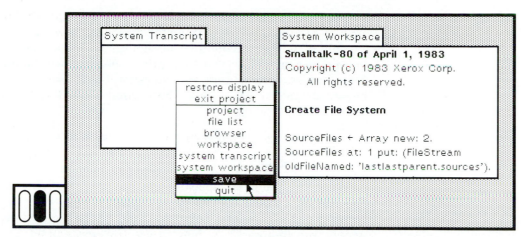

Figure 1.14a

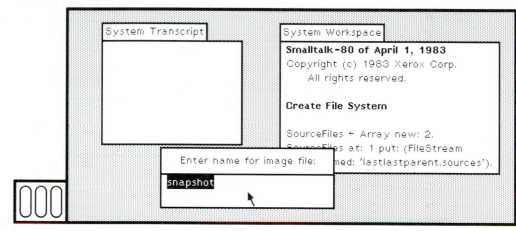

Figure 1.14b

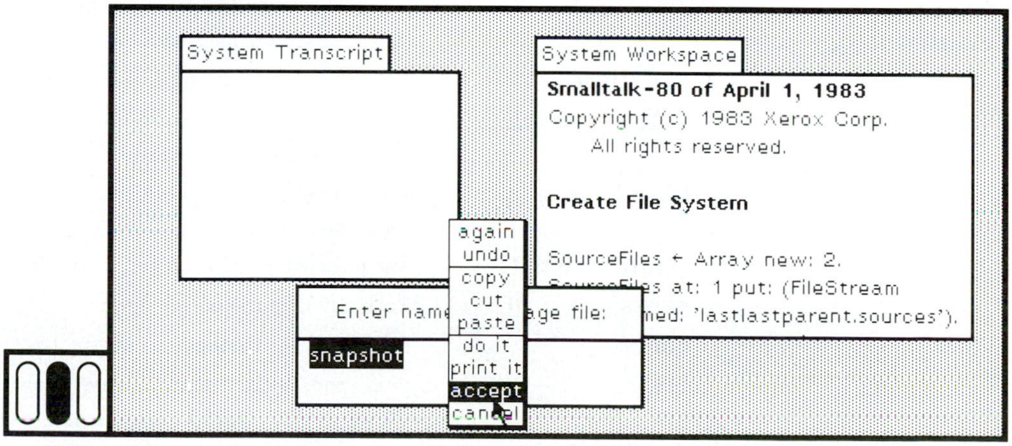

Figure 1.14c

The system now takes control to create the file. The cursor changes first to a slanted arrow with a star attached, meaning execution is taking place. It then changes to an hourglass shape, meaning "wait." If you make a snapshot prior to quitting, then you will be taken out of the Smalltalk-80 system once the snapshot file is created. Otherwise, the cursor shape changes back to the normal slanted arrow shape and you can continue working.

> In some of the Xerox systems, the screen turns to white while the snapshot file is being created. This is done to improve the speed with which the disk interactions are carried out.

When the prompter appears, you can choose to change the name of the file into which the image is copied. Simply edit the bottom text subview of the prompter before you choose the yellow button command accept (see Chapter 3 on how to use the text editor). The system will copy the existing changes file into a file whose name is the one you typed followed by a period and then the characters changes; the image file name is the name you typed followed by a period and then the characters im.

You must respond to the prompter. If you move the cursor outside the prompter boundaries, the prompter will "flash" or "blink" to indicate that a response is required. If you have changed your mind and do not want to create a snapshot, then delete all the text from the prompter response area and choose the yellow button command accept. The prompter will disappear and you can continue using the system.

1.5

Summary of Terminology

button	Button on a pointing device, or function key on a keyboard, that is used to request some action.
red button	Used to select information. (Left button in all illustrations.)
yellow button	Used to get a menu for editing the contents of a view. (Middle button in all illustrations.)
blue button	Used to get a menu for editing the view itself. (Right button in all illustrations.)
button action	The physical use of a button.
press	Push and hold the button down.
release	Remove finger from button, letting the button up.
click	Press the button, then release it, without moving the cursor.
double click	Click two times in succession, without moving the cursor.

confirmer	A "binary-choice" kind of menu, that is, a menu with two items from which to choose.
control manager	A system object that maintains a list of screen views; it lets you point to a view and interact with either the view itself or with information inside the view.
cursor	A locator of information on the display screen, presented as a small graphical image, superimposed on the screen and controlled by a pointing device.
file	Refers to a sequence of characters on an external storage device, such as a disk.
changes file	Initially an empty file; when the user interacts with the Smalltalk-80 system, each action that involves evaluating an expression is stored in this file.
image file	A file that contains the compiled form of each method and the initial bitmap that appears on the screen when the system is installed.
sources file	A file that contains the source text for each method in the system.
menu	A list or collection of selectable items; choosing an item from a menu invokes some action.
message	A request for an object to carry out one of its operations.
method	A procedure describing how to perform one of an object's operations.
mouse	A pointing device that the user manipulates in order to move the cursor.
object	A component of the Smalltalk-80 system represented by some private memory and a set of operations.
prompter	A "fill-in-the-blank" kind of menu in which you must type your choice.
scroll bar	A menu associated with a screen view; you use a scroll bar to specify which part of the available information you want displayed in the view.
snapshot	A file in which you save the current state of your Smalltalk-80 system image.
subview	A view contained as a subpart of another view.
system image	A set of compiled methods and global variables, and the initial display screen to be shown when the system is first installed.
view	A rectangular area on the display screen in which to access information.

active view	The view in which you are currently working.
collapsed view	A standard system view that displays only its label part, but can be selected and expanded to show the entire view.
standard system view	A view that provides standard interface functions for manipulating itself, for example, for moving, framing, collapsing, and closing.

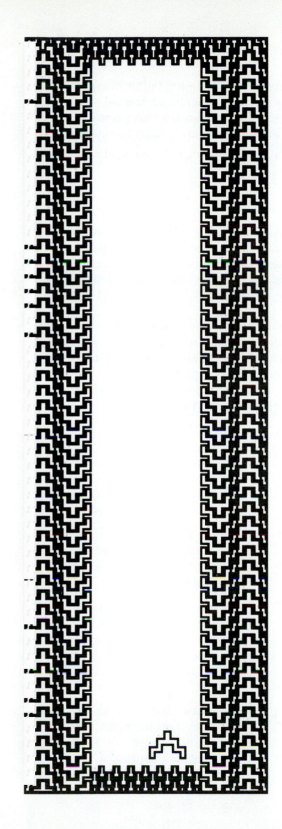

2

Basic User Interface Components

In the Smalltalk-80 programming environment, a bitmapped display screen is used to present to the user graphical and textual views of the information about objects. Menus and views are the primary ways in which objects are visually presented. A cursor is used to select items in menus or in parts of a view.

2.1

Display Screen Visual Cues

A cursor takes on different shapes in order to provide visual feedback about where you are pointing and what system activities you are currently doing. Highlighting is used to indicate menu, view, and text selections. Flashing screen areas draw your attention to attempts to initiate inappropriate actions.

Cursors

There is only one active cursor and it is controlled by the pointing device. In the following table, each cursor is listed with its name, its visual form, and its typical use in the system. The cursor takes on different shapes when it is used in editors for text, pictorial images (Form Editor), and magnified images (Bit Editor); in controlling the views on the screen; and in interacting with the external file system.

name	image	use
normal		The cursor looks like this most of the time. The point of cursor selection is at the upper left corner, at the tip of the arrowhead.
execute		Wait. The system is executing some time-consuming expression. During this time, you cannot do anything else.
origin		Indicates that you should designate the top left corner of a rectangular area by moving the cursor to where you want, and then pressing, but not releasing, the red button.
corner		Indicates that you should designate the bottom right corner of a rectangular area by keeping the red button depressed while you move the cursor to where you want the corner to be, then releasing the button.

read	👓	Wait. Information is being read from an external file.
write	✏	Wait. Information is being written on an external file.
crossHair	+	In the Bit Editor, indicates the location of the bit at which editing will occur.
down (previous information)	↓	In a scroll bar, indicates scrolling the text to see the preceding text.
up (next information)	↑	In a scroll bar, indicates scrolling the text to see the succeeding text.
marker (jump)	➡	In a scroll bar, indicates the proportional location to which you want to jump.
wait	⌛	Wait. The system is carrying out some file operation that is time consuming.
thumbs up	👍	Answer yes in the confirmer.
thumbs down	👎	Answer no in the confirmer.

The Form Editor prefers to let the cursor take on arbitrary shapes that depict the current painting tool. To do this, the cursor is made blank, and the editor itself provides an image of the painting tool at the location of the cursor. The confirmer uses the cursor in the shape of a hand with either thumb up or thumb down, depending on which item is selected.

Some versions of the system include storage reclamation in the form of a compactor; when compaction is taking place, an animated image of a cartoon character appears.

Class Cursor is defined in the Smalltalk-80 system as the representation of cursor forms. Cursor knows about several cursor forms that are predefined in the system and used in the interface. With the exception of the last two Cursors, the name of the cursor given in the preceding table is also the name of the unary message that should be sent to Cursor in order to gain access to the instance, for example, Cursor normal. Since a cursor is a kind of Form, it can be edited by sending it the message edit or bitEdit. See Chapter 7 "How to Make Pictures" to learn how to use the editors (the Form Editor and the Bit Editor) that you access in response to these messages.

Sending the message show to an instance of class Cursor sets the form of the visible cursor to be that of the instance. For example, sending the object, Cursor normal, the message show, makes the visible cursor look like a slanted arrow (as explained in Chapter 6, sending such a message directly involves typing the expression Cursor normal show in a workspace, selecting it using the red button, then choosing the yellow button command do it. The expression Cursor normal returns an instance of class Cursor; all instances of Cursor respond to the message show.) You can create cursors, instances of class Cursor, and use them as visual cues in your applications systems.

Highlighting

In using the Smalltalk-80 system, you will select various views or parts of views. For example, you will often select a sequence of characters using the text editor. When you do so, the system will highlight the sequence to indicate which one will be affected by the next editing command. Similarly, when you press a button to obtain a menu to choose one of its items, the system will highlight an item to indicate the current selection; the current selection is the one you choose by releasing the button. And when you select any standard system view, the system will highlight its label (located just above the view's top left corner) to indicate that it is the active view.

When you invoke a menu, the current selection is the item that you chose the last time you obtained this menu.

To highlight a selection, the system *complements* it. In complementing, the black bits on the screen are turned to white, and white bits to black. In particular, black text on a white background is turned to white text on a black background.

All views except the single active one are "inactive." Selections in inactive views are generally not shown. Selections in menus that are textual lists are still shown, but their visual emphasis is "toned down" a little—the background of the selection is changed from black to a gray tone.

As a design decision, standard system views allow for only one active view. Using the multitasking capabilities of the Smalltalk-80 system, you can create multiple simultaneous activities, including "active" views that operate in tandem with system views.

Figure 2.1 shows examples of highlighted text within a sequence of characters (in the active standard system view labeled System Workspace), several lists of items with highlighted selections (in the inactive standard system view labeled System Browser), an inactive standard system view (labeled Project), and an inactive standard system view labeled System Transcript. Menu items that appear in inactive standard system views are highlighted using a gray background.

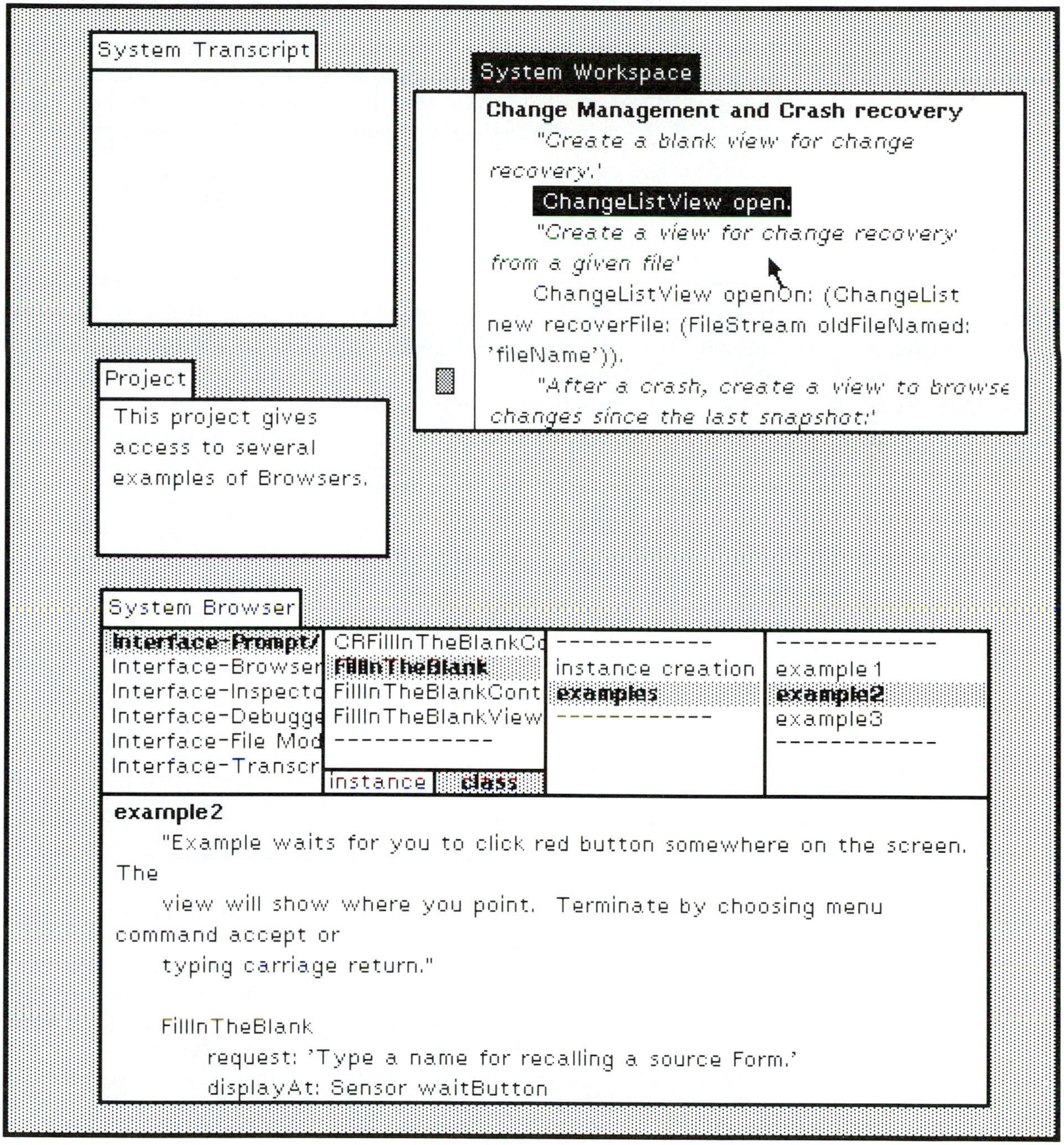

System Transcript

Project

This project gives
access to several
examples of Browsers.

System Workspace

Change Management and Crash recovery
   *"Create a blank view for change
recovery."*
   ChangeListView open.
   *"Create a view for change recovery
from a given file"*
   ChangeListView openOn: (ChangeList
new recoverFile: (FileStream oldFileNamed:
'fileName')).
   *"After a crash, create a view to browse
changes since the last snapshot."*

System Browser

Interface-Prompt/	CRFillInTheBlankCc	------------	------------
Interface-Browser	**FillInTheBlank**	instance creation	example 1
Interface-Inspecto	FillInTheBlankCont	**examples**	**example2**
Interface-Debugge	FillInTheBlankView	------------	example3
Interface-File Mod	------------		------------
Interface-Transcr	instance **class**		

example2
   "Example waits for you to click red button somewhere on the screen.
The
   view will show where you point. Terminate by choosing menu
command accept or
   typing carriage return."

   FillInTheBlank
      request: 'Type a name for recalling a source Form.'
      displayAt: Sensor waitButton

Figure 2.1

Flashing Screen Areas

A *flashing* area refers to an area of the display screen rapidly alternating its black and white bits so as to draw your attention to it. This is used in the programming interface to indicate that what you are trying to do is currently disallowed or not appropriate. Flashing will occur, for example, if you attempt to invoke a menu where no such menu is available, or if you do not complete a response to a confirmer or a prompter.

2.2

Designating Rectangular Areas on the Display Screen

Several interactions in the Smalltalk-80 system expect you to *designate* (to show location and size of) a rectangular area of the display screen. When this happens, the system will jog your memory by changing the cursor shape to look like the top left corner of a rectangle. A possible screen image is shown in Figure 2.2a.

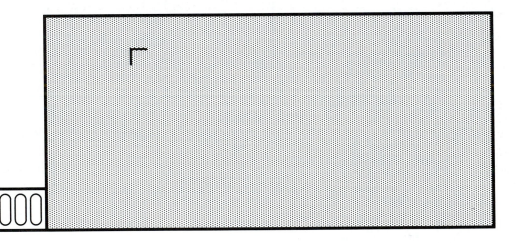

Figure 2.2a

After you have moved the cursor to where you want the top left corner of the rectangular area to be, press and *hold down* the red button. In response, the cursor will change shape again, this time to look like the bottom right corner of a rectangle. Where the corner first appears will delimit the minimum-sized rectangle for that particular kind of view. The cursor is shown on the screen in Figure 2.2b.

While still holding down the red button, move the cursor around. You will see that, as the cursor moves, a flashing image of the rectangular area changes correspondingly on the screen. The area shown always maintains any minimum size that may have been assigned by the constraints of the view that will fill the area. When you are satisfied that the selected area is the size you want it to be, release the red button. A possible resulting workspace is shown in Figure 2.2c.

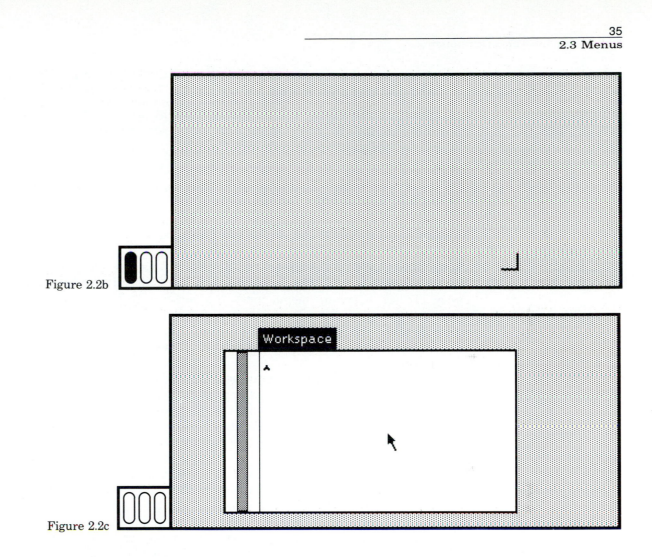

Figure 2.2b

Figure 2.2c

2.3

Menus

A menu on the display screen is similar to one in a restaurant: it shows you the available items from which to choose. An item in a menu represents a message. The item workspace in one of the menus you used in Chapter 1, for example, represents a message that creates a new view in which text can be created and edited. In the Smalltalk-80 interface, menus are displayed as lists of words or of phrases.

Menus come in several varieties, including *fixed* and *pop-up*. Examples of fixed menus were shown in the view labeled System Browser in Figure 2.1.

- To make a selection in a fixed menu, place the cursor over the desired item and press the red button; this will highlight the item.

- When you release the button, the system will carry out the action corresponding to the highlighted item, leaving the selection highlighted until you select a new item.

- To deselect the current selection without choosing another item, simply choose the same item again (that is, move the cursor over the item and click the red button).

To allow best utilization of space on the display screen, many menus in the Smalltalk-80 system have been designed to be *pop-up menus*. Fixed menus are already on the screen; pop-up menus appear when you press the appropriate button. The menu displays itself directly beneath the cursor. To see a pop-up menu, move the cursor into the background area of the display screen, outside the boundaries of any view. Press and hold down the yellow button. A pop-up menu will appear. (If you tried the various examples in Chapter 1, you have already seen several pop-up menus.)

In order to make a choice, continue to hold down the button, move the cursor around until the desired item is highlighted, and release the button. When you release the button, the menu will disappear. In order to make no choice, continue to hold down the button, move the cursor outside the menu area until no item is highlighted, and release the button.

Another variety of menu is one that appears in response to some user action. This kind of menu remains on the screen until you either choose an item using the red button, or until you click with the red button at a location outside the menu area. One example is a *confirmer*. This is a menu with a noneditable text subview that describes a binary choice, and two items: yes and no. If you create a workspace, type some text, and then try to close the workspace, a confirmer will appear to verify that you want to delete unsaved information. Recall that this example was presented to you in Chapter 1. Another example is the menu that appears when you decide to stop your work session. As described in Chapter 1, when you choose to stop a work session, a menu appears from which you can choose to create a snapshot, quit immediately, or change your mind.

A particular kind of fixed or pop-up menu is called a *list menu*. List menus appear as a sequence of lines, each one containing a menu item. For aesthetic purposes, and to help identify groups of items, lines of text in a list menu may be separated by a drawn line. Fixed list menus are used for choosing class names and messages in a system browser, for choosing class message pairs in a message-set browser or a debugger, and for choosing variable names in an inspector. (The different browsers, debuggers, and inspectors, will be described in detail in subsequent sections.) List menus appear in standard system views in response to your pressing the yellow or blue button. If you press the yellow button while the cursor is in the background gray area, the list menu we refer to as the *System Menu* will appear (see Section 2.4). You can create different standard system views by selecting items from the System Menu.

If a menu flashes when you try to make a selection, it has become *locked.* The system will lock a menu when you have not yet completed the activity associated with your current selection. This flashing is used as one of the ways to indicate that you have been editing text, but have not yet issued the command cancel or accept. (The use of a confirmer is another way the system indicates that text has not been saved.) The locked menu will become unlocked as soon as you properly complete the associated activity. Most of the subviews of the system browsers, which are the views for accessing class descriptions, fall into the category of lockable menus.

Whenever the user interface directions say that you should *choose an item from a pop-up menu,* the directions will state which button to press (yellow or blue) and which command to choose. Selection in fixed menus is done using a red button.

Scroll Bars

A view on the screen may not be large enough to display all the information appropriate to that view. Additional user interface control is given to such views in order to assist you in exploring all the information. Especially in views of textual information, this control is provided in the form of a *scroll bar.* Assume you wish to examine a large document of information, and that you have created a view on the screen for this purpose. The view is likely to be too small to display all of the document. So a rectangular area known as a *view* (or often called a *window*) is defined by mapping from the area allotted on the display screen to a corresponding-sized area of the document. The mapping determines how much document information can actually be displayed in the screen view. The purpose of a scroll bar is to change the area of the document that can be seen in the view.

A scroll bar is a rectangular area, displayed adjacent to the left side of the view it controls. The scroll bar appears in the active view only when the cursor is actually inside the view. If you move the cursor outside the view (without pressing a button), the scroll bar will disappear. It will appear as soon as you move the cursor back inside the viewing area. Thus the scroll bar is a useful visual cue that the view will notice your typing or button pressing. Scroll bars appear only in those views for which scrolling is appropriate, typically in any view in which text can be edited or in list menus.

The length of the scroll bar area is meant to represent the length of the entire document that can be examined. Inside the area is another rectangular area filled with a light gray tone. The length of this gray area represents the height of the window onto the document (as illustrated in Figure 2.3). The gray area is located within the scroll bar at a point relative to the location of the window: if the gray area begins at the top of the scroll bar, then the window is at the beginning of the document. If the gray area fills the entire scroll bar, then you can assume that all of the document is currently displayed (see Figure 2.4).

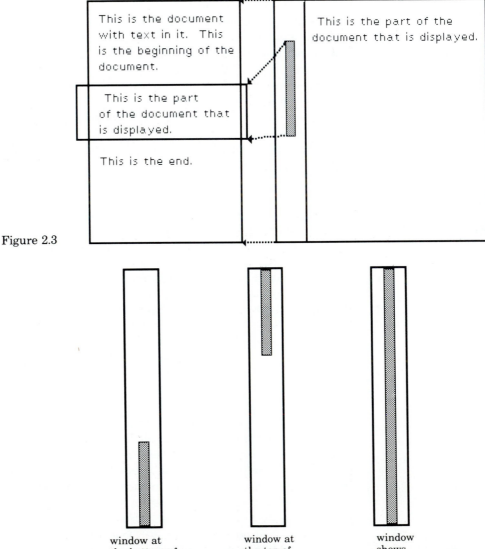

Figure 2.3

Figure 2.4

window at the bottom of document

window at the top of document

window shows entire document

You can change which part of the document is displayed by moving the window through the document. This action is called *scrolling*. It is done in one of three ways.

scroll next

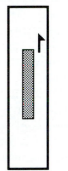

The line of text nearest the cursor is moved to the top of the view. Move the cursor into the scroll bar area, in the right one-third of the rectangle and outside of the gray area. The cursor shape becomes that of an up arrow. Click the red button. Scrolling occurs.

scroll previous

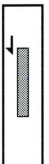

The line of text at the top of the view moves to become the line nearest to the cursor. Move the cursor into the scroll bar area, in the left one-third of the rectangle and outside of the gray area. The cursor shape becomes that of a down arrow. Click the red button. Scrolling occurs.

jump

Displays a view of the document beginning with a location in the document relative to the gray area in the scroll bar. Move the cursor into the scroll bar area, in the middle one-third of the rectangle and outside of the gray area. The cursor shape becomes that of a right arrow. Press the red button and hold. The gray area moves to the cursor location and then tracks the cursor until the red button is released. The displayed document jumps to the appropriate location. While the red button remains pressed, a lighter gray image is left in the scroll bar area to indicate the previous position of the gray area.

In an earlier design of the scroll bar, jumping was done by moving the cursor into the gray area. The cursor shape changed to a small dot. While the red button was pressed, you moved the gray area to the desired location. This design was abandoned because users found it difficult, if not impossible, to grab the gray bar when it was very small. Another design that has been used in an application was to divide the scroll bar into three parts horizontally, rather than vertically. When the cursor was in the small top part, the resulting action was to scroll next; when the cursor was in the small bottom part, the resulting action was to scroll previous. As programming exercises, you might like to experiment in creating different types of scroll bars.

☐ *Practicing* To start learning how to use the Smalltalk-80 system, try using the System Menu. Get the menu by first moving the cursor into the light gray background area, then pressing and holding down the yellow button. This will cause a pop-up menu to appear. As long as you keep the button down, you can move the cursor around in the menu, deciding between various selections.

You don't actually choose the highlighted item until you release the button, so be sure you have selected the item you want before you release the button. If you decide you don't want to make *any* choice, simply move the cursor out of the menu area completely (so no item is highlighted) and release the button. The menu will disappear.

Practice getting the System Menu and moving around in it. Become comfortable using the System Menu without making any selections, so that it becomes a habit to move the cursor outside the menu when you are undecided. Read the subsequent sections to find out what choosing each of the System Menu items will do.

Confirmers

A *confirmer* is a "binary choice" menu. That is, a confirmer is a menu with two items in it, where each choice represents opposing points of view. A confirmer consists of three parts, the top part is a statement or question; the other two parts are possible opinions about the statement or answers to the question.

An example is shown in Figure 2.5. It is a confirmer that appears when you choose the yellow button command close in a workspace, after you have typed some text without accepting it. Choose one of the answers, yes or no, by placing the cursor over the answer and clicking the red button.

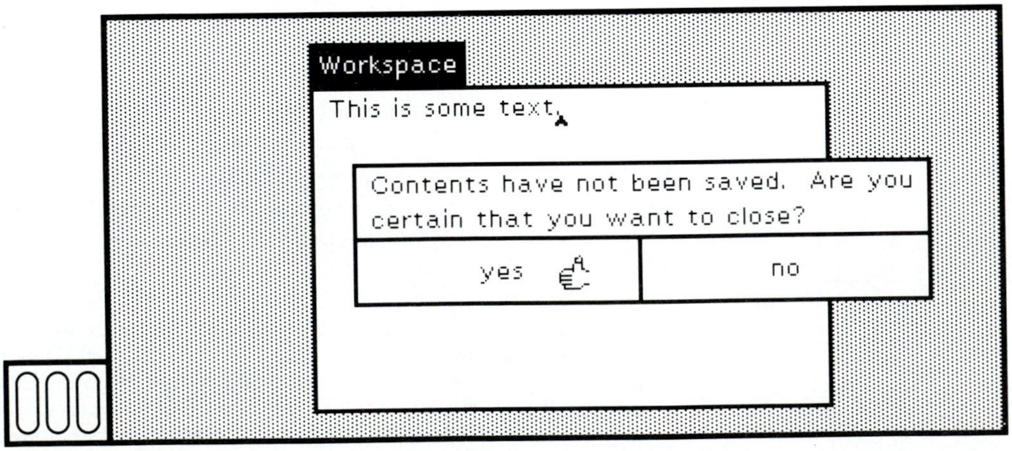

Figure 2.5

Prompters

A *prompter* is a "fill-in the blank" menu. That is, a prompter is a menu in which you must type your choice. It consists of two parts: the top part is a statement or question, and the bottom part is a workspace in which you type.

Two kinds of prompters are available in the system, as shown in Figure 2.6. One has a label and acts like a standard system view, with both yellow and blue button menus accessible. This kind of prompter is called a *scheduled prompter*. The other kind of prompter is *unscheduled*. It preempts activity and requires you to give a response. You press the "carriage return" key to indicate that your answer is completed. To give no response, type only the "carriage return" key. Unscheduled views like this prompter do not have a title label.

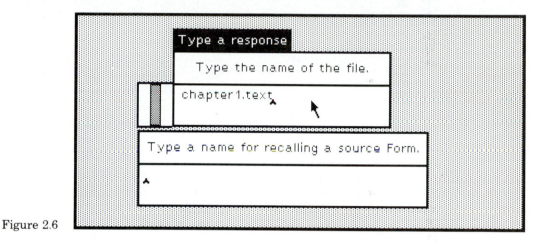

Figure 2.6

2.4

The System Menu

As noted earlier, the menu obtained by moving the cursor into the light gray background area and then pressing the yellow button is called the System Menu. It is shown in Figure 2.7. Each item or command in the System Menu is described briefly.

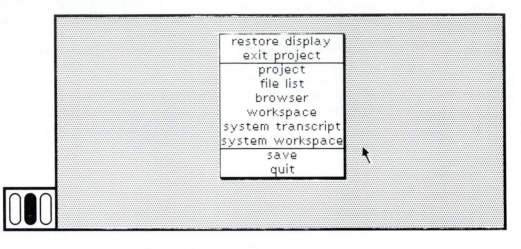

Figure 2.7

restore display

Redraws the display, getting rid of anything which is not known to the control manager. Often the display screen gets cluttered with the side effects of drawing or the results of erroneous actions. Whenever things look especially bad, you can redraw the views by choosing this command. Another effect of restoring the display is to reset the cursor to the slanted arrow (normal) cursor.

exit project

It is possible to create several different collections of views of information, each one called a *project*. Each project takes up an entire display screen for the presentation of its views. A project is accessed by creating a project view and then choosing the yellow button menu command enter. Once inside a project, it is possible to return to the project from which it was entered by choosing this command. At the topmost project, this command is equivalent to restore display. See Chapter 4 "How to Use Projects" for a more detailed description.

project

Creates a new project view. You are asked to designate a rectangular area in which the project view is to be displayed.

file list

Short files can be read, edited, updated, and evaluated, using a view that is created by choosing this command. You are asked to designate a rectangular area in which a *file list* view is to be displayed. See Chapter 22 "The File System" for a description of this view.

browser

A *browser* is a special view that allows you to access hierarchically-organized information. Choosing this command opens a system browser that allows you to traverse information about the Smalltalk-80 system itself. You are asked to designate a rectangular area in which the browser view is to be displayed. See Chapter 9 "Finding Out About System Classes" for a description of this view of system information.

workspace   Creates a blank area in which to edit text. You are asked to designate a rectangular area in which the workspace is to be displayed. See Chapter 3 "How to Use the Text Editor" for a description of how to use this view.

System Transcript   Most display screens in a Smalltalk-80 system have a special view known as a *System Transcript*. Because messages sent to the object Transcript affect this view, methods can contain expressions that print information in the System Transcript in order to create a form of user feedback. A view of the System Transcript is created by choosing this command. You are asked to designate a rectangular area in which the transcript view is to be displayed. See Section 3.4 "The System Transcript" for a description of this view.

system workspace   A special workspace is available that contains many useful message expressions that you can edit and evaluate, notably expressions about accessing files, querying the system, and recovering from a crash. You are asked to designate a rectangular area in which this special workspace is to be displayed.

save   Periodically you might decide that you have done a lot of work that you want to save. One way to save your work is to create a complete image of the system (see Section 1.4). A new system image is created in an external file whenever you choose this command.

quit   When you are done working, choose this command (see Section 1.4 "Stopping a Work Session").

☐ *Keep Practicing*   Several exercises are provided here so that you can practice with menus, scrolling, and creating workspaces.

Exercise 1: In the System Menu, choose **workspace** (Figure 2.8a). Designate a rectangular area in order to specify the location and size of a workspace (an example workspace is shown in Figure 2.8b). Do this several times so that there are three or four workspaces on the screen, some overlapping others (as shown in Figure 2.8c). The last workspace that you created is the active one. Notice that the label of this workspace is highlighted and that a scroll bar appears at its left side.

Basic User Interface Components

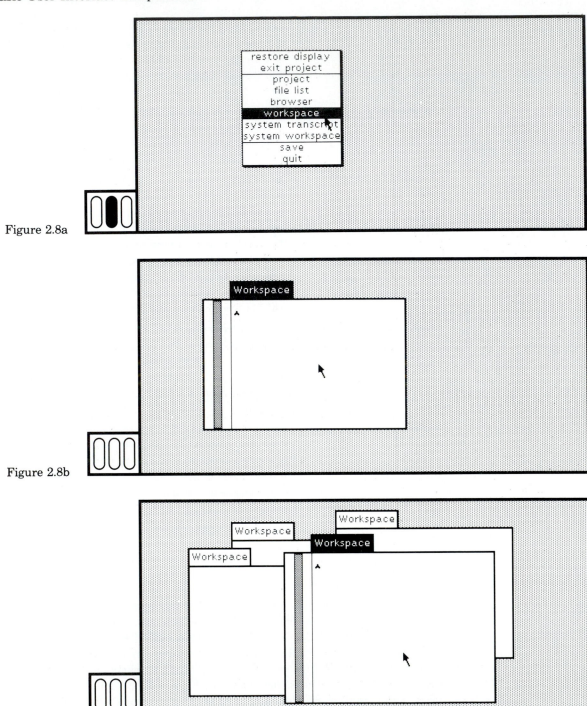

Figure 2.8a

Figure 2.8b

Figure 2.8c

Move the cursor outside the active view and into the gray background area. Click the red button. Notice, as shown in Figure 2.8d, that the workspace is no longer active, in particular, that its label is no longer highlighted. We refer to this action as *deselecting a view*. Typically, however, you do not explicitly deselect a view. Rather, the deselection takes place automatically when you select another view.

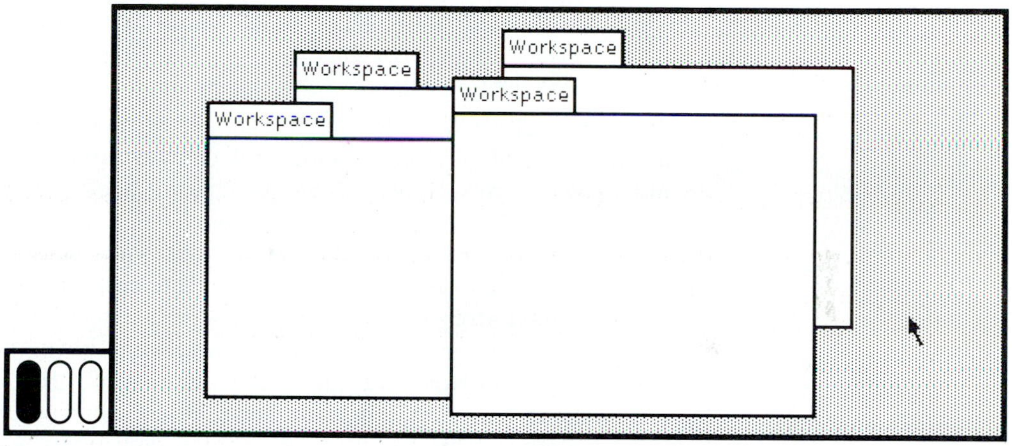

Figure 2.8d

Suppose no view is active (which would be true if you click the red button in the gray background area outside of all the views). Move the cursor into a workspace. Without your pressing a button, this workspace will become the active view. When all the views are inactive, whichever one you place the cursor into next becomes the active one.

Place the cursor in one of the other workspaces and click the red button. We refer to this action as *selecting a view*.

> A view can be deselected as described, or as a result of a message sent by selecting a menu item, or as a result of evaluating an expression. You can deselect a view by moving the cursor outside it, into the gray area or into another view, and then clicking the red button. Actually, you can press the yellow or blue button as well, which, in addition to deselecting the active view and selecting a new view if the cursor is inside one, may cause a menu to appear.

Exercise 2: To practice scrolling, choose the command System Workspace from the System Menu, or, if you have a workspace labeled System Workspace already open, select it. The System Workspace should have a lot of text in it. Try scrolling using it. Learn how to control the positioning of the cursor by watching for the change in cursor shape. Make the workspace larger by choosing the command frame from the blue button menu. You will be asked to designate a rectangular area. Notice the change in the scroll bar.

Exercise 3: Make an existing or new workspace active. Type a lot of keys on the keyboard and notice that the characters are displayed in the workspace; do not worry about typing correctly or meaningfully. Notice that the scroll bar does not change while you are typing. The scroll bar only changes (is updated) when you make a new selection, or you move the cursor into the scroll bar area or out of the view boundaries and back in again. Do not worry about editing the text just now.

> Deferred update of the scroll bar can be changed so that the update occurs while you are typing. Once you acquire Smalltalk-80 programming expertise, you might try to make this change to text views.

Move the cursor outside the workspace without pressing a button. Type some keys. The characters do not show up in the workspace; they do not show up anywhere. Move the cursor back into the workspace and notice that the characters now appear.

The cursor *must* be inside the active (text) view when you are typing keys on the keyboard in order to see the corresponding characters displayed immediately in the view.

Select a different workspace. Again, type some keys on the keyboard. Press the yellow button and notice the menu that appears. Release the button without choosing any command. Select another workspace. Obtain the yellow button menu; notice that it contains the same items in both workspaces.

2.5

Standard System Views

There are a number of kinds of views that can appear on the display screen of the Smalltalk-80 system. Most of these are standard system views, meaning, among other things, that they are seen as rectangular areas with labels above the top left corner. They become active when you place the cursor inside their bounded area and click the red button. Each standard system view provides a general interface accessed through a pop-up menu. Standard system views can be moved, stretched, and removed from the screen; other abilities depend on the particular kind of view. Abilities shared by all views are presented in the blue button menu; abilities of a particular kind of view are presented in the yellow button menu.

Access to the currently scheduled standard system views is maintained by a system component called the control manager. The references to views are stored in the control manager in a seemingly arbitrary order; ordering occurs as a by-product of the order in which the views are created and the order in which they become active. This ordering affects the way you can select views under one another.

This control manager is referenced by the system variable ScheduledControllers. This name reflects the fact that the control manager consists of references to kinds of Controllers that provide interfaces to Views. The active view is always the first element of ScheduledControllers.

Standard Blue Button Menu

When you press the blue button while the cursor is inside a standard system view, the pop-up menu shown in Figure 2.9 appears. Each of these menu items represents a message to the view. They are

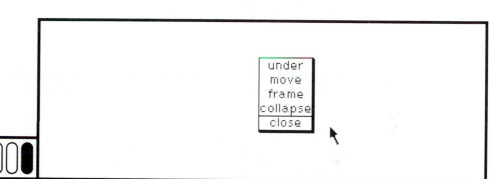

Figure 2.9

under
: Since standard system views can overlap, this menu item is a request to give control to (to make active) the view located underneath the currently active view and underneath the cursor location. A view can be overlapping several views—the one that appears on top when you choose under depends on the ordering of the references in the control manager; under might have to be chosen several times in order to locate the desired view. Also, a view might be underneath the currently active one and not underneath the cursor, in which case it will not be selected.

move
: The view disappears with only its label remaining, and the cursor changes to the shape of the origin cursor. Move the cursor around. The label of the view tracks the cursor. When you press the red button, the view reappears so that the label is at the last location to which you moved it.

When you move a view, space that is simply gray area appears in its place. The standard system does not try to keep a clean, refreshed display, since it assumes you can clean up by choosing the command restore display from the System Menu. Solutions to fix this problem of redisplaying hidden parts of overlapped views exist, but were not included in the standard Smalltalk-80 system.

frame
: The view disappears and the cursor changes to the shape of the origin cursor. You then designate a new rectangular area in which the view should reappear.

collapse   The view disappears with only its label remaining, and the origin cursor appears. Move the cursor around. The label of the view tracks the cursor. When you press red button, the label portion only of the view reappears on the screen at the last location to which you moved it. This considerably smaller area can be enlarged to show the full view by selecting it and choosing the blue button menu command frame.

close   The view disappears. Unless you have a reference to it, that is, it is referenced by some other object, it can not be made to reappear.

If the task in the view is not complete (typically completion is indicated by choosing the yellow button command accept), an attempt to close the view results in another view. This is a confirmer. The cursor moves automatically into the confirmer's area, and the confirmer becomes the active view. The message in the confirmer is a warning that a task or information will be lost by closing the view. If the view has several subviews, a gray box is drawn around any information that will be lost. An example is that a part of a system browser was changed but not saved before the close command was chosen. The gray box surrounds the lower part of the browser, and a confirmer appears. Choose yes to indicate that close is really intended; choose no to continue using the original view. If you close a view, it is irrecoverably gone.

> You can only recover it if you have made a snapshot and start over using the saved image, or if you have stored a reference to it. You can think of other messages to the view itself to put in the blue button menu. In some of the Xerox Smalltalk-80 systems, the message edit is available. When you choose edit, you can move the borders of the subviews (either up and down for horizontal lines, or left and right for vertical lines) in order to modify the layout of subviews within the view.

☐ *More Practicing*   Select different workspaces. Try the various blue button commands such as under, move, and frame. Try the command collapse and then frame again. Collapsed views save space on the screen yet allow direct access to the task represented in the view—simply select the view and choose the blue button command frame.

Try to close a workspace in which you have typed some characters. A confirmer view appears. Choose yes. The confirmer disappears and then the workspace disappears.

Again try to close a workspace in which you have typed characters. Before doing so, choose the yellow button command accept. Now try to close the workspace. No confirmer appears; the workspace disappears. Because you issued the command accept, the system believes you have "saved" your work.

2.6

Summary of Terminology

Bit Editor
A set of operations used to modify pictorial images that are presented in a magnified format (8 times original size).

browser
A view that allows you to access hierarchically organized and indexable information.

confirmer
A "binary-choice" menu, that is, a menu with two items from which to choose.

cursor
An image on the display screen that is used to select information such as text, menu items, or parts of a view.

file list
A view that provides access to short files of text.

flashing area
Rapidly alternating the black and white bits of an area of the display screen (black to white, white to black).

Form Editor
A set of operations used to modify pictorial images.

menu
A list or collection of selectable items.

fixed
A menu, typically associated with a view, that remains displayed on the screen as long as the view is displayed.

list
A menu appears on the screen as a sequence of lines, each containing an item; it can be of the fixed or pop-up variety.

locked
A menu that is in a state such that you are not allowed to change the current selection.

pop-up
A menu that appears when you press a button, and disappears when you release the button.

system
A pop-up list menu that is obtained by pressing the yellow button while the cursor is located over the gray background area.

project
A collection of views of information that takes up an entire display screen for the presentation of its views.

prompter
A "fill-in-the-blank" menu, in which you must type your choice.

system transcript
A workspace. Text in a transcript can be edited as in any workspace. In addition, text can be printed in a transcript as the result of expression evaluations.

system workspace
A workspace that contains many useful message expressions that you can edit and evaluate, notably expressions about accessing files, querying the system, and recovering from a crash.

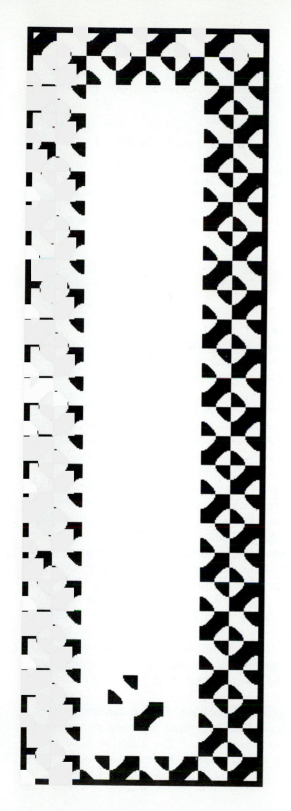

3

How to Use the Text Editor

The same text editor is used everywhere in the Smalltalk-80 system views. Learning how to use the text editor involves learning how to:

- make a text selection

- issue an editing command using a menu or the keyboard

> Note that this is a text editor for a single paragraph of text, not for a large document. Paragraphs have extensive format and style knowledge; however, the generally-used text editor is a simple one that does not provide a menu-based interface for changing the format nor the style. More sophisticated document-creation systems can be created that provide function-key or menu-based access to these aspects of a paragraph.

3.1

Text Selection

Text is selected using the pointing device and the red button. Text editing can be carried out in those system views in which the information is textual. Examples are a workspace, a transcript, a project, a file list, and the parts of browsers that provide editing areas for Smalltalk-80 methods.

Select a view that contains text, such as a workspace. A small caret (an inverted "v") appears near the point you selected in order to make the view active. If there is no text in the view, then the caret will appear in the top left corner. Figure 3.1a shows a workspace containing text. The caret appears at the end of the first sentence.

Type some text. Move the cursor somewhere else in the view, either *at* one of the characters or between characters or at the end of the passage of text. Click the red button. The caret appears at the cursor location or at the gap just before the character. Notice that you are asked to point *at* a character or between characters, not under a character.

Move the cursor to one end of the passage of text and press the red button (as shown in Figure 3.1b). Hold it down while moving the cursor to the other end of the passage (Figure 3.1c). The text that is traversed is highlighted. This activity is called *draw through*. It is not necessary to traverse intermediate characters en route to the destination (that is, when drawing through several lines). When the cursor reaches the other end of the passage, release the button (Figure 3.1d). The selected passage remains highlighted. The highlighted text is called the *text selection*.

Pointing to a place in the text and clicking the red button creates a zero-width selection. The method of clicking once between characters is the one to use if you want to insert text. The method of drawing through a passage of text is the one to use if you want to replace, copy, delete, or change the font or emphasis (bold or italic face) of the text.

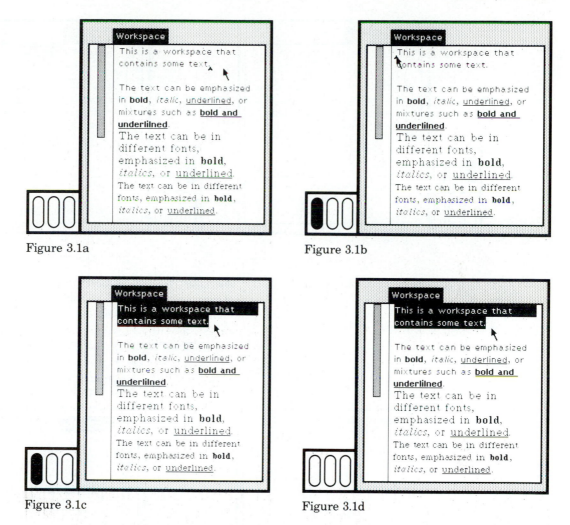

Figure 3.1a

Figure 3.1b

Figure 3.1c

Figure 3.1d

Clicking the button twice with the cursor in the same location selects different passages, depending on the cursor location.

To select	Double click
a whole word	Within a word, or just before or just after the word if the word is not just inside a delimiter (as demonstrated in Figure 3.2a, first click, and Figure 3.2b, second click).

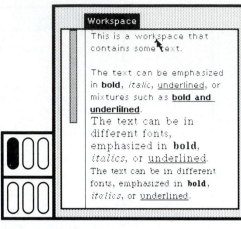

Figure 3.2a

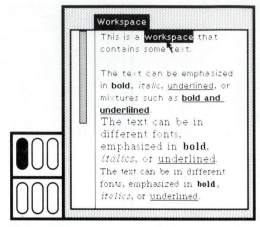

Figure 3.2b

a delimited text

Just after the left member of a pair of delimiters or just before the right member (the delimiters themselves are not selected); recognized delimiters are parentheses, square brackets, angle brackets, braces ("curly brackets"), single quotes, and double quotes (see Figures 3.3a and 3.4a, first clicks, and Figures 3.3b and 3.4b, second clicks).

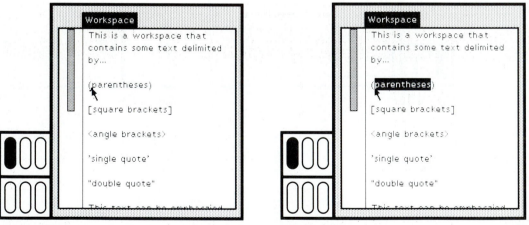

Figure 3.3a

Figure 3.3b

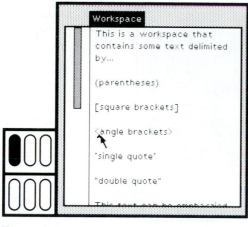

Figure 3.4a

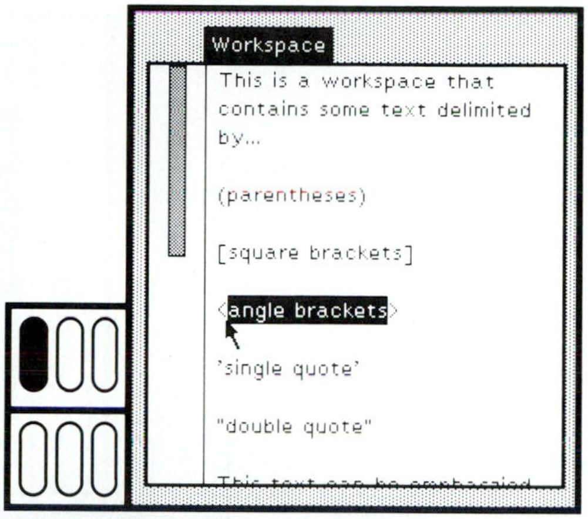

Figure 3.4b

all text in the view

At the beginning or the end of everything in the view (as demonstrated in Figure 3.5a, first click, and Figure 3.5b, second click, and Figure 3.5c, scrolling to see the rest of the text).

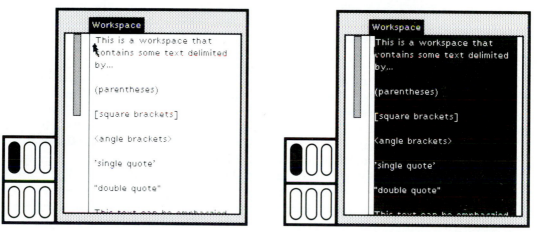

Figure 3.5a

Figure 3.5b

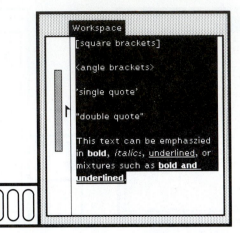

Figure 3.5c

a line of text	(If the line is delimited by carriage returns) at the beginning of a line (just after a carriage return), or at the end of a line (just before a carriage return).

Double clicking provides a faster way to make a text selection. Because double clicking will always select the designated text, it makes it possible to select text that is not visible on the screen.

Extending Text Selection Beyond the Visible Text

Suppose you wish to select text that is not visible on the screen, but that the text is not delimited in such a way that double clicking will support selection. Try the following technique. Move the cursor to either end of the passage of text that you want to select. Press the red button. Hold the red button down while moving the cursor to the other end of the passage. So far, this is the usual way to select visible text. But the other end of the passage is not visible. You have to move the cursor outside the boundaries of the text view (either above or below the view). As long as you hold down the red button, the text in the view will be scrolled (to the previous text or to the next text), and the text that becomes visible will be selected. Keep holding down the red button until you see the end of the passage. Don't worry about scrolling past the end, because you can always move the cursor back into the view. When you move the cursor back into the view, the scrolling stops. You can then position the cursor at the desired end of the passage and release the red button.

The distance that you move the cursor outside the view affects the speed at which the text scrolling takes place. The further outside the view you move the cursor, the faster the scrolling.

*Selecting Text
with the Escape
Key*

The "escape" key on the keyboard can be used to select text that was typed since the last mouse click. Simply press the "escape" key when you have finished typing. The characters you just typed will be highlighted.

This is especially useful if, after typing in some text, you wish to make it the current text selection so you can copy the text to another place, or cut it, and so on.

> The purpose of invoking this selection command from the keyboard rather than from a menu is to support the fast typist who wishes to select a passage of text that was just typed in order to issue a cut, a font, or an emphasis change command, which may also be invoked from the keyboard. Perhaps you prefer to have an item in the text editor yellow button menu that selects the most recently typed characters; changing the menu is an exercise you can try once you know enough about the Smalltalk-80 system.

3.2

Inserting Text

Pressing a key on the keyboard always replaces the current selection by the typed character and automatically selects the gap following that character. If nothing is selected, the "zero-length selection" at the caret is replaced.

To replace a passage of text, first select it and then type the replacement. The first keystroke deletes the original text. To insert between characters, select the gap between those characters and then type the insertion. Essentially, you are replacing nothing with something. The destructive backspace function always deletes the character preceding the selection, even if that character was there before the selection was made.

3.3

Issuing an Editing Command

When you issue a text editing command, you are sending a message to the text about the current selection. Selection always precedes commands. Every command is executed immediately when you issue it. No confirmation is required. Commonly-used editing commands are found in the yellow button menu. A brief description of each follows.

again

This command attempts to repeat the last replace, copy, or cut edits you do.

undo

The main purpose of undo is to reverse the effects of the last issued command. For example, paste in the last text cut out; cut out the last text pasted in; delete the last text inserted; or, if a text selection was replaced, paste it back. (Issuing two undo commands in sequence should leave you in the state you were in prior to the first undo.)

copy

Place a copy of the current text selection into a buffer.

cut

Delete the current text selection; save the text in a buffer. This command is illustrated in Figures 3.6a and 3.6b.

paste

Text is remembered in a buffer. Replace the current text selection with the remembered text. Assuming the text remembered is the text cut in Figure 3.6a, then the next sequence of figures illustrates the use of the paste command. Select the destination location (Figure 3.7a), select the command paste (Figure 3.7b), and then the inserted text becomes the selection (Figure 3.7c).

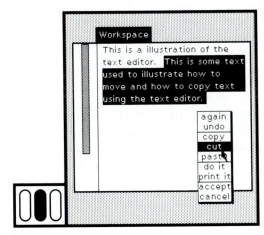

Figure 3.6a

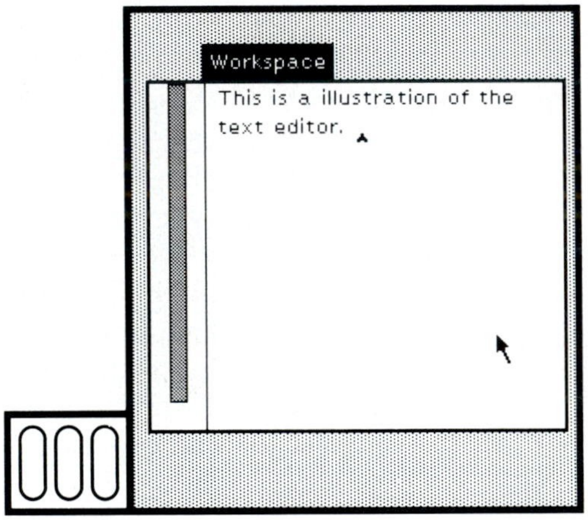

Figure 3.6b

Suppose you just selected some text (text A, such as demonstrat as shown in Figure 3.8a) and replaced it with other text (text B, such as illustrat as shown in Figure 3.8b). The command again will find text occurring after the caret that is just like text A and will replace it with text B (as shown in Figures 3.8c and 3.8d on page 60). By holding down the "shift" key on the keyboard while selecting again, the replacements will be done as many times as is possible.

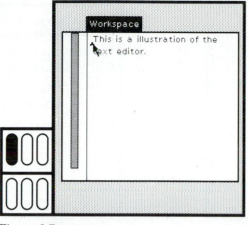

Figure 3.7a

Figure 3.7b

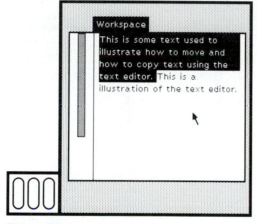

Figure 3.7c

Suppose you just selected some text A and cut it out. The command again will find text occurring after the caret that is just like text A and will select it. You can then decide to cut it. Similarly, if you copy some text A, the command again will find text occurring after the caret that is just like text A and will select it (thus providing a text search capability in the editor).

The again command is shared across views so that you can move into several views in order to do the same replacement in each.

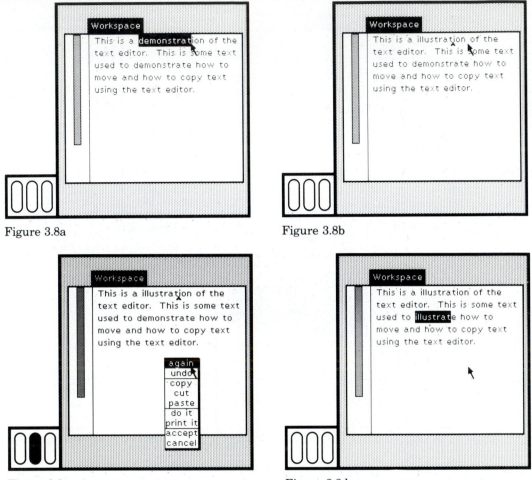

Figure 3.8a

Figure 3.8b

Figure 3.8c

Figure 3.8d

From the menu description, you can see that there is a "buffer" of information into which text that is typed, cut, or copied is stored. The contents of the buffer changes whenever you type new text, or you issue the cut or copy commands. It is possible to take information from one view and paste it to another view because this buffer is shared across views.

> Some people refer to this buffer as the *scrap*. The text editor in the standard system does not provide a way to view the information in the buffer; you can treat viewing the buffer as a possible exercise.

Moving and Copying Text

Some common editing commands such as "move text from here to there" and "copy text from here to there" cannot be issued by a single menu command because they require two parameters: the source selection and the destination selection. They may even involve more than one view. A "move" is done by cut and paste. First, you select the source text and choose cut. The cut command deletes the selected text but leaves it in the hidden buffer where it can be retrieved by paste. Then you select the destination and choose the paste command to complete the move. This process was illustrated in Figures 3.6a and 3.6b.

The destination can be in a different view than the source. A copy move is done by copy and paste, which is completely analogous to cut and paste, but does not delete the original text.

Searching for Text

There is no command for "searching for a sequence of characters." A search can be done as follows. Type the sequence of characters you wish to find, then select it and choose the cut command. Now choose the again command. If the sequence appears anywhere after the current selection (after the caret), it will become the text selection.

If one instance of the text you want to find is already visible, select it, and choose the copy command. Then choose the again command.

Issuing Editing Commands Using Keys and the "Control" Key

Various text editing commands can be issued by pressing the "control" key simultaneously with another key from the keyboard. When the "control" key is combined with a number, it means change the font of the current text selection. Conditional statements in the Smalltalk-80 language consist of the keywords ifTrue: and ifFalse:. Since these are frequently needed, "control" combined with "t" or "f" effectively types the keyword ifTrue: or ifFalse:, respectively.

A summary of the special editing keys is shown next. The symbol ctrl denotes the "control" key on the keyboard.

type keys	action
ctrl 0	Change the font of the text selection. The system default is sans-serif 12-point font. Changing a text selection to bold, italic, or underline is considered a change in font and is done by selecting the appropriate font number. The numbers depend on the current style being used.
ctrl 1	Change the font of the text selection. The system default is sans-serif 10-point font.
ctrl 2	Change the font of the text selection. The system default is sans-serif 10-point font, bold.
ctrl 3	Change the font of the text selection. The system default is sans-serif 10-point font, italic.
ctrl 4	Change the font of the text selection. The system default is serif 12-point font.
ctrl 5	Change the font of the text selection. The system default is serif 12-point font, bold.

ctrl 6	Change the font of the text selection. The system default is serif 12-point font, italic.
ctrl 7	Change the font of the text selection. The system default is serif 10-point font.
ctrl 8	Change the font of the text selection. The system default is serif 10-point font, bold.
ctrl 9	Change the font of the text selection. The system default is serif 10-point font, italic.
ctrl t	Insert the text ifTrue:.
ctrl f	Insert the text ifFalse:.
ctrl w	cut the text selection and the word preceding the caret (typically used while typing and while there is no text selection simply to delete the last word typed).
"delete"	cut the current text selection.
"backspace"	cut the text selection and the character before the selection.
ctrl -	Underline the selected text.
ctrl b	Make the selected text boldfaced.
ctrl c	This is the system interrupt and should not be typed while text editing unless a process interrupt is desired (for details on such user interrupts, see Chapter 20).
ctrl shift -	Remove any underline from the selected text.
ctrl shift b	Make the selected text not boldfaced.
ctrl shift c	This is a special system interrupt, used when the system seems dead and everything else fails (see Section 20.4).

Note that ctrl w and "backspace" do a cut of the current text selection and of the word or character preceding the text selection. The undo command is supposed to be able to reverse the effects of a cut by pasting the saved information. However, in using ctrl w or "backspace," two cut actions are really taken and only the last, the word or character deleted, is remembered. Therefore, undo will only paste the deleted word or character.

All fonts are instances of class StrikeFont and are stored as an array in an instance of class TextStyle. The system default is accessible by sending TextStyle the message default. The message fontAt: can be sent to a TextStyle to access the fonts. The default TextStyle has 24 fonts. Fonts are indexed from 1 to 24, where the first 9 are the ones listed earlier; the one numbered 0 is actually font 10. Fonts are stored in triples—base, bold, and italic. The system includes

fonts 10, 11, and 12—sans-serif 12 point

fonts 13, 14, and 15—serif 10 point underlined

fonts 16, 17, and 18—serif 12 point underlined

fonts 19, 20, and 21—sans-serif 10 point underlined

fonts 22, 23, and 24—sans-serif 12 point underlined

Suppose you want typing the "control" numbers to change the text font to a sans-serif 10 point underlined, rather than a serif 12 point. You can change the affect of the text editor keyboard controls by evaluating the following expressions.

```
TextStyle default fontAt: 4 put: (TextStyle default fontAt: 19)
TextStyle default fontAt: 5 put: (TextStyle default fontAt: 20)
TextStyle default fontAt: 6 put: (TextStyle default fontAt: 21)
```

Now when you type ctrl 4 or ctrl 5 or ctrl 6, sans-serif 10 point fonts, underlined, will display. Typically you should also store the fonts you replace so that you can get them back again; either create a global variable or copy the TextStyle.

Inserting Delimiters About a Selection

Make a text selection (including a zero-width selection), then type one of the following control combinations in order to insert delimiters about the text. The control combinations are toggles, that is, if the selected text is already surrounded by the indicated delimiter, then the command removes it.

type keys	*insert delimiters*
ctrl [	[and]
ctrl (	(and)
ctrl <	< and >
ctrl "	" and "
ctrl '	' and '

An example of first delimiting some text using double quotes, and then removing the delimiters, is shown in the next sequence of figures. Text is selected in Figure 3.9a; in Figure 3.9b, the user types ctrl " to delimit the selected words. The text selection is the sequence of delimited characters, as shown in Figure 3.9c; in Figure 3.9d, the user types ctrl " again to remove the delimiters.

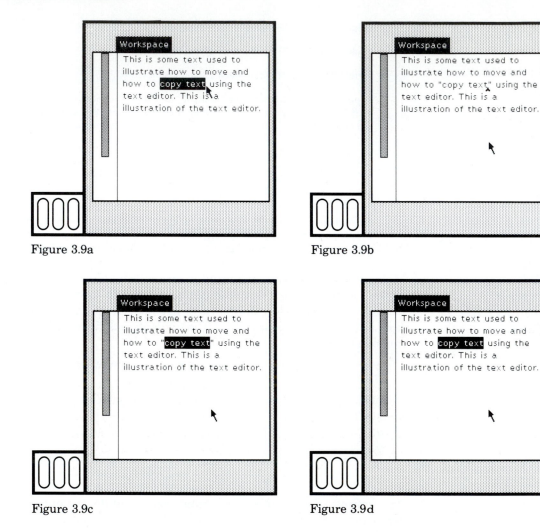

Figure 3.9a

Figure 3.9b

Figure 3.9c

Figure 3.9d

Clearly these kinds of commands could be placed on the pop-up menu as well, especially if you find it cumbersome to move from the mouse to the keyboard. There is a tradeoff, however, in the size of the menu. Cascaded menus, where selecting an item invokes a related menu, could be used. For example, the main text editor yellow button menu might include the item delimiters. Choosing this command would invoke a new menu whose items were each of the possible delimiters. The first menu could be left on the screen or not; leaving the first on the screen allows the user to change his or her mind by returning to it to select another item, rather than by aborting all action.

3.4

The System Transcript

A "transcript" is a special kind of workspace known as a *text collector*. It is basically the same as a workspace in that you can use the text editor in it. In addition, it is possible to write and evaluate expressions in which messages to store characters are sent to a text collector.

There is one special text collector that we refer to as the System Transcript. It typically appears at the top left corner of an initial Smalltalk-80 display. It is a standard system view, so it can be moved, framed, collapsed, and closed. If it is open on the screen, you will sometimes see text appear, informing you of some system event. You can use the System Transcript in the Smalltalk-80 methods that you write, sending the System Transcript messages to store descriptions of objects you create.

For example, type, select, and evaluate the expression

    Transcript show: 'some text' ; cr

For information on how to send messages by evaluating a typed expression, see Chapter 6. The System Transcript for the current project is referred to by the system global variable Transcript.

The system transcript is primarily used as the place where comments to the user appear as a form of feedback when other visual feedback techniques are not available. For example, if the system scheduling mechanism fails, a message stating the problem and what to do about it is displayed in the System Transcript. When users are debugging methods and it is desirable to print periodic messages indicating the state of evaluation (rather than to interrupt execution), the System Transcript is a useful place in which to display the messages. When categories of classes are filed out or classes are recompiled, the name of each class appears in the transcript so you can tell what kind of progress is being made.

If you do not already have a System Transcript on your display screen, you can obtain one by choosing the System Menu command system transcript.

3.5

Summary of Terminology

text collector

A workspace; the System Transcript is a kind of text collector. Whereas most workspaces are used for editing text directly, text collectors are primarily used for displaying information determined in print messages included in class methods.

text editor	A set of operations for creating and modifying a paragraph of characters.
caret	A symbol used to denote a text selection that contains no characters.
draw through	The activity of selecting a passage of text by pointing to one end of the passage, pressing the red button, and then moving to the other end of the passage before releasing the red button.
text selection	The sequence of characters of a paragraph that is currently highlighted.

4

How to Use Projects

Projects support your ability to manage several programming tasks at a time, without getting your work space too cluttered. You use projects the way you might use several desks in an office or several offices in a building—that is, as spaces in which to manage related information or activities. You might, for example, be working on two applications programs at one time. So you might have two projects, the top one and another; each application is developed in a different project so that you can create workspaces with information related to just the one project. Each project maintains information about the changes you make to class definitions and methods while you are working in its views. Thus you can use projects to keep separate records of the methods you develop for each application. Or, you might use projects in order to keep programming tasks separate from access to mundane daily work (letter writing, receiving and sending mail, retrieving an address from a database).

Any classes created in one project are immediately available to all projects in the system. The global name space for variables is also shared across all projects. Thus if you create a variable in one project and change it in a second project, it will be changed as well in the first project. The primary support provided by projects is

1. maintenance of separate lists of changes to classes, and

2. visual layout of a set of views.

The separate list of changes is a useful way to distinguish the changes to the shared classes that were needed to support the application in an individual project. (For information about how the system maintains references to the changes you make, see Chapter 23.)

To practice creating and using projects, try the following sequence of actions. Choose the System Menu command project (Figure 4.1) and create the project view (Figure 4.2). You can type characters in the project view that describe the project; this is a way of documenting the purpose of the project.

In the project view, select the yellow button command enter. The yellow button menu is shown in Figure 4.3. The result of choosing the command enter is shown in Figure 4.4.

The display screen is now blank—no views are displayed. No activity has yet occurred in this project. Choose the System Menu command workspace and the System Menu command system transcript. The two views are shown in Figure 4.5. The views in the current project are not immediately accessible from other projects.

Now choose the System Menu command exit project as shown in Figure 4.6.

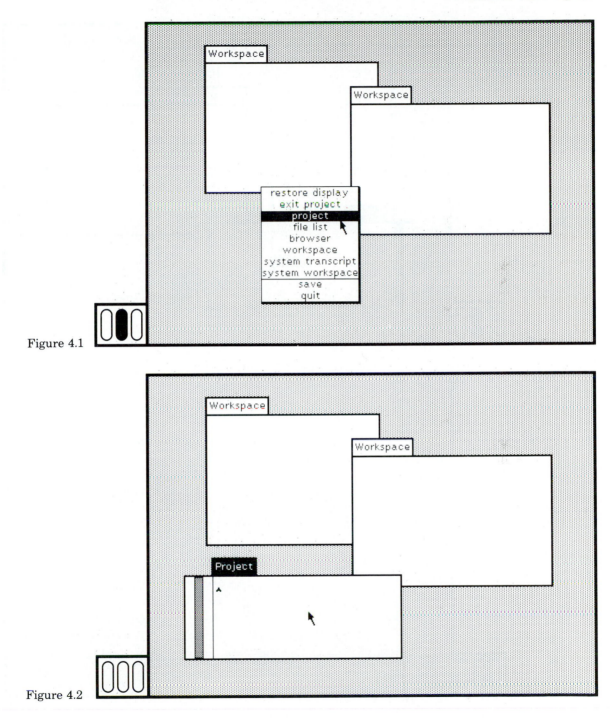

Figure 4.1

Figure 4.2

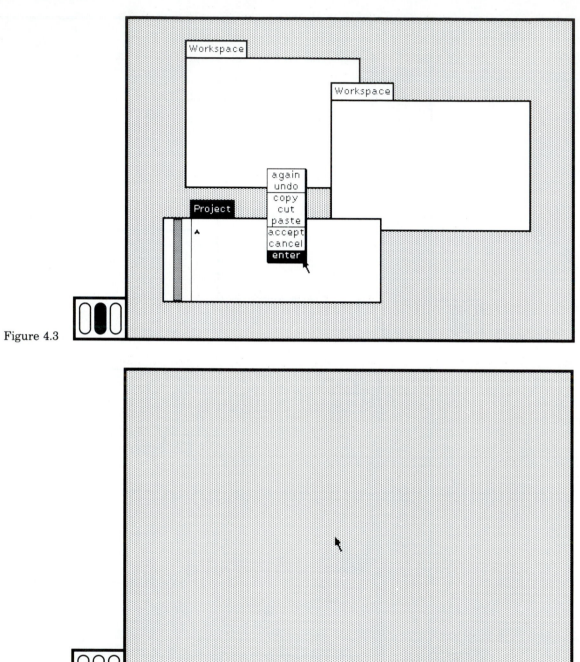

Figure 4.3

Figure 4.4

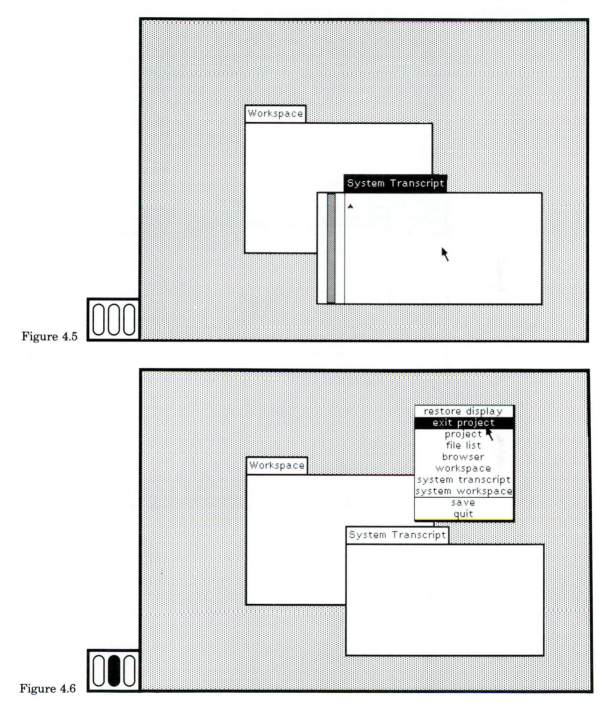

Figure 4.5

Figure 4.6

The display screen clears and the first collection of views reappears, including the project view (Figure 4.7). You can now do your work in this (top) project. Or you can re-enter the other project as you did before. Try re-entering, then return to the top project. Select the project view and then choose the blue button command close (Figure 4.7). Since there are views open in the project you are trying to close, a confirmer appears to warn you that you might be irreversibly destroying information (Figure 4.8). If it is okay, choose yes. The project view disappears and, with it, your access to the project's views and changes, if any.

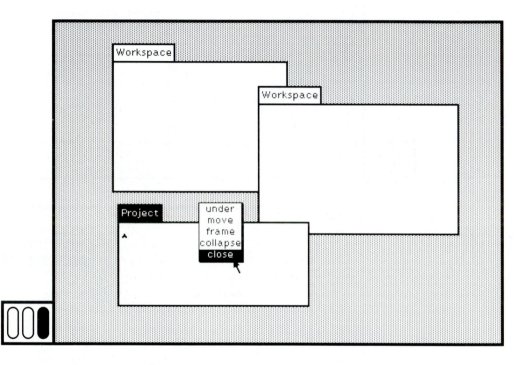

Figure 4.7

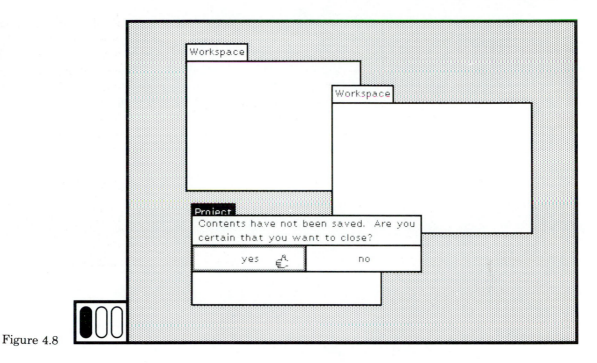

Figure 4.8

This particular implementation of projects creates a hierarchical organization, where the path to projects is through a view that exists in the "parent" project; each parent can have several "children" projects. The analogy is to workrooms whereby each room has several doors into other workrooms. For this reason, some people call project views "doors."

An alternative design is to create a project browser that can be opened in any project by choosing an appropriate command from the System Menu. A project could be named, described, and accessed by choosing items in a project browser, in a way analogous to the way classes are named and described in a system browser. Creating a project browser is an exercise you might try to do when you are proficient in Smalltalk-80 programming. It is given as an example in Section 15.2.

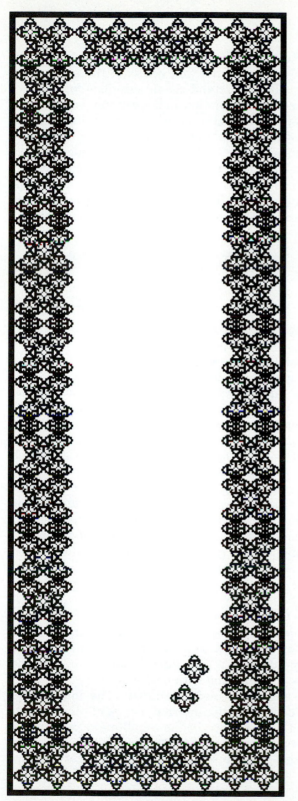

5

Fundamentals of the Smalltalk-80 Language

The particular kinds of user interface components provided in the Smalltalk-80 system are designed to give you access to the elements of the Smalltalk-80 language. To understand the descriptions for evaluating expressions and for finding information in the system, you need an introduction to the concepts of object-oriented programming and the syntax for expressions in the Smalltalk-80 language, and you need an overview of the programming process. Subsequent sections suggest various expressions to try and describe the system components that support program development. You should turn to the companion book, *Smalltalk-80: The Language and its Implementation* by Adele Goldberg and David Robson, for a more thorough presentation of the programming language.

5.1

Objects, Messages, and Methods

The Smalltalk-80 language is based on a uniform use of objects and messages. An *object* is a uniform representation of information that is an abstraction of the capabilities of a computer. The two capabilities of a computer that are of interest in the language are the capability to store information and the capability to manipulate information. An object has the capability to store information. We say that an object has "private memory." An object also has the capability to manipulate its stored information or to carry out some activity. These are called the operations of an object. The set of operations is referred to as the object's *message interface* or *message protocol*.

An object carries out one of its operations when an object sends it a message to do so. Each object knows the messages it can understand; associated with each such message is a procedure or *method* that describes how the object should answer the message. A crucial property of an object is that its private memory can only be manipulated by the operations in the object's interface. Computing is viewed as an intrinsic capability of objects that can be uniformly invoked by sending messages.

Linking these concepts to ones more familiar to you, an object is like a computer consisting of data and procedures that operate on that data. An operation is invoked by calling on some procedure. Sending a message is the Smalltalk way to invoke a procedure; Smalltalk is a simulation of many computers communicating with one another.

Objects and messages encourage modular design. The implementation of one object cannot depend on the internal details of other objects, only on how they respond to messages. In the Smalltalk-80 system, objects and messages are used to implement the entire programming environment. Objects are used to represent numbers, lists, text strings, dictionaries, spatial locations, areas, text editors, processes, compilers, debuggers, and all other system components. Once objects and messages are understood, the entire system is accessible.

The messages an object understands depend on what the object represents. Objects representing numbers understand messages that request arithmetic functions to be computed and their results returned. Objects representing lists and dictionaries understand messages requesting that information be stored or retrieved (in the form of other objects, naturally). Objects representing spatial locations and areas understand messages inquiring about their relation to other locations and areas.

In many respects, you can think about real-world situations and identify the parts or components that play a role in these situations. These are the objects. These objects act out their roles by communicating with the other objects; that communication takes the form of a language of words—commands or informational data. These are the messages that make up the interface to the objects.

A basic problem in designing Smalltalk programs is determining which kinds of objects should be described and what message names provide a useful language of interaction among these objects. In Smalltalk, the choice of message names is arbitrary, although there is a concrete syntax that must be followed. Appropriate choice of objects depends, of course, on the purposes to which the application will be put and the granularity of information to be manipulated. For example, if a simulation of an amusement park is to be created for the purpose of collecting data on queues at the various rides, then it would be useful to describe objects representing the rides, the waiting lines, workers who control the rides, and the people visiting the park. If the purpose of the simulation does not include monitoring the consumption of food in the park, then objects representing these consumable resources are not required. If the amount of money exchanged in the park is not to be monitored, then details about the cost of rides do not have to be represented.

Classes, Instances, and Subclasses

There are many objects in the Smalltalk-80 system. Objects that respond to the same messages in the same way are grouped together. When they are grouped together, their private memory is represented in the same way and their methods refer to their data with the same set of names. A group of objects related in this way is called a *class*. Objects in a group are called *instances* of the class. Programming in the Smalltalk-80 language consists of creating new classes, creating instances of classes, and specifying a sequence of message exchanges among all of these objects.

Every object in the Smalltalk-80 system is an instance of a class. All instances of one particular class represent the same kind of system component. Classes have names that describe the kind of component their instances represent. Instances of a class named Point represent spatial locations. Instances of a class named Rectangle represent rectangular areas. Instances of a class named Process represent independent processes.

Refining existing class descriptions is a powerful way in which to approach Smalltalk-80 programming. Such refinement is supported by the ability to create a *subclass* of an existing class. A subclass describes a group of objects that inherit information from an already existing description. A subclass can add new functionality or private memory, and modify or prohibit existing functionality.

Consider the amusement park example. Suppose we wish to create a simulation of this park. The first task is to determine the objects involved in the park. What do you think of when considering an amusement park? There is a merry-go-round, cotton candy, ferris wheels and roller coasters, tickets to buy, souvenirs to buy, a fun house, games, side shows (animals, strange people), a train ride, ice cream booth, cafeteria, sit-down restaurant, animal rides, lines of people waiting to get on a ride or to get a ticket, someone selling balloons, and so on. Oh yes, there are crying kids and crying parents, dizziness, stomach aches, and sunburn.

Focusing our attention on the kinds of places, rather than the people or animals, we can organize the parts of an amusement park into rides, game booths, and places to buy things. One organization might divide the parts into places where you buy things and places where you do not buy things. Places where you buy things include rides, food vendors, and nonfood vendors. To create a Smalltalk-80 simulation, classes must be described for each of these kinds of objects. For example, we might create the class Ride; instances of Ride may be ferrisWheel or merryGoRound.

Each Ride has a waiting line of some kind made up of customers waiting for service. This means that the private memory of each kind of Ride includes a reference to a waiting line. This line must be an instance of a class that describes the appropriate kind of data structure that can reference an ordered sequence of customers. Since everything is an object, and each object is an instance of a class, then a customer must be an instance of a class, perhaps of class ParkVisitor.

At some time, a worker assigned to the ride announces "next, please" to the line; the next customer waiting is given service. At various times, customers arrive and enter the line, or they get tired of waiting and leave. The customers in the waiting line can be different kinds of objects. However, they all must be able to carry out the behavior appropriate to waiting in line and getting out of the line. So customers might be instances of ParkVisitor or they might be instances of a special kind of visitor, say an ElderlyParkVisitor, who gets preferential treatment at the park. ElderlyParkVisitor could be created as a subclass of ParkVisitor so that all of the capabilities given a ParkVisitor are inherited by ElderlyParkVisitor as well. In addition, ElderlyParkVisitor might act differently—always entering a waiting line at the front instead of the rear.

To create the Smalltalk-80 simulation, we will have to decide what messages the ParkVisitor, and thereby ElderlyParkVisitor, will understand —perhaps

goToNextRide

and

buyTicket

Advantages of Object-Oriented Programming

Programming in the Smalltalk-80 language consists of identifying objects, classifying them according to similarities and differences, and designing a language of interaction among these objects. These are important organizing skills and communication skills that can be taught using this form of computer programming.

What are the advantages of this form of programming?

1. The information known privately to an object is protected—this information can only be accessed directly by the methods of the object. This means that the structure of an object (the representation of the information of an object) can be changed without affecting interactions with instances of other classes. This ensures that there is a structure or discipline by which objects interact and that a user can make changes or additions to very complex systems without getting caught in a maze of interdependencies.

2. The user accesses existing objects as well as creates new ones or modifies existing ones. Modification is done by adding a new message and its method to a class description, or by adding new data slots to the private memory of all the objects in a class. This means that the Smalltalk-80 language provides a simple and expressive model for the relationship among parts and wholes so that the process of building a system can draw on one's intuitive ability to synthesize and analyze.

3. The Smalltalk-80 system is built on the model of communicating objects. Large applications are viewed in the same way as the fundamental units from which the system is built. The interaction between the most primitive objects is viewed in the same way as the highest-level interaction between the computer and the user.

4. Objects support modularity. The complexity of the system is reduced by a minimization of interdependencies of system parts.

Complexity is further reduced by grouping together similar parts, where this grouping is achieved through classes. Classes are also the chief mechanism for extension in the system. And subclasses support the ability to factor the system in order to avoid repetitions of the same concepts in many different places. Managing complexity is a key contribution of the Smalltalk-80 approach to software.

5.2

Expression Syntax

The syntax of the Smalltalk-80 language is simple, providing a way to refer to objects and messages and arguments using alphanumeric names. There is no restriction in the language on the length of a name; there are some restrictions on the use of special symbols.

In this section, syntax diagrams for the language are presented. The diagrams are like those used, for example, in the *Pascal User Manual and Report*, Kathleen Jensen and Niklaus Wirth, Springer Verlag, 1978. The term being defined is shown at the left margin; each term is defined with respect to other terms (shown in boxes) or literals (shown in ovals or circles) in the language. The diagram helps determine whether an expression is syntactically correct.

An *expression* is a sequence of characters that describes an object called the value of the expression. The four kinds of legal expressions are *literals*, *variable names*, *message expressions*, and *block expressions*.

□ *Literals*   Literals are *numbers*, *symbol constants*, *character constants*, *strings*, and *array constants*, as shown in Figure 5.1.

literal

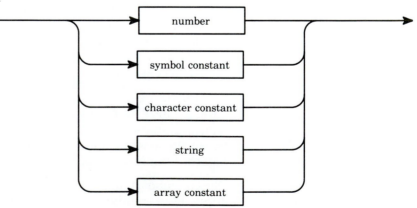

Figure 5.1

☐ *Numbers*   The diagram for numbers is shown in Figure 5.2.
Example numbers are

```
3
30.45
-14.0
13772
8r153
16rAC.DC
1.586e-3
16r1e10
```

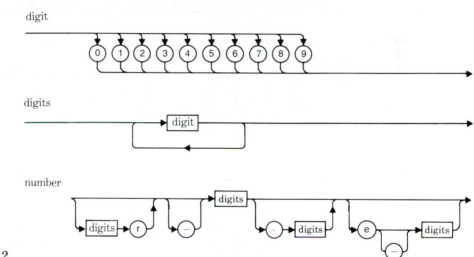

Figure 5.2

☐ *Characters*   The diagram for characters and character constants is
shown in Figure 5.3. Note that in the syntax diagrams, a character is
defined as any element from the ASCII character set other than double
quote (″) or single quote (′); the definition of character constant is a
character or a double quote or a single quote.
Example character constants are

```
$a
$M
$-
$$
$[
$@
```

Fundamentals of the Smalltalk-80 Language

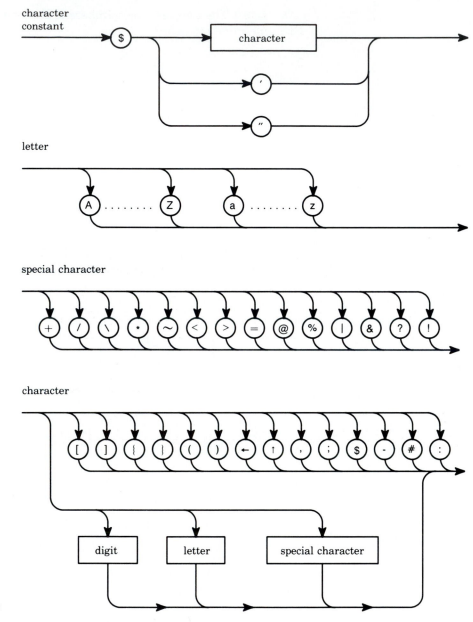

Figure 5.3

☐ *Strings*   Figure 5.4 is the diagram for strings. Example strings are

'hi'
'the Smalltalk-80 system'
'can''t'

string

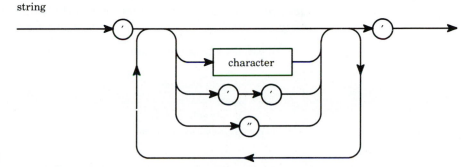

Figure 5.4

☐ *Symbols*   Figure 5.5 is the diagram for symbols.

identifier

symbol

symbol constant

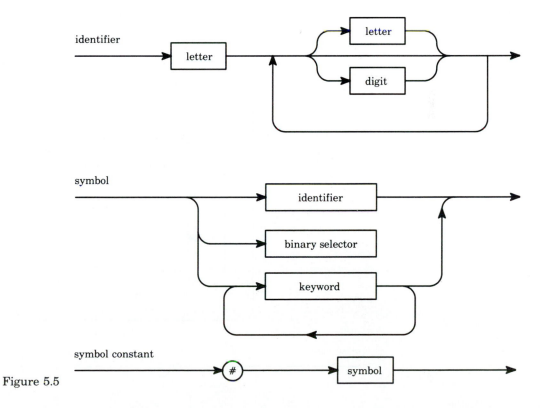

Figure 5.5

Example symbol constants are

#bill
#M63

There will never be two symbols with the same characters; each symbol is unique—that is, any reference to a symbol made up of the same sequence of characters is a reference to the same symbol. Examples of binary selectors and keywords are given in subsequent sections.

If you do look ahead, you will notice that the following are symbols.

Smalltalk is an identifier
* is a binary selector
// is a binary selector
at:put: is a keyword selector

☐ *Arrays*   An array is a simple data structure whose contents can be referenced by an integer index from 1 to a number that is the size of the array (Figure 5.6).

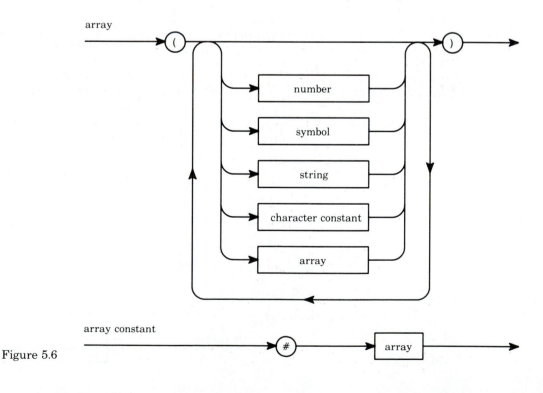

Figure 5.6

Example array constants are

```
#(1 2 3)
#('food' 'utilities' 'rent')
#(('one' 1) ('not' negative) 0 -1)
```

☐ *Comments*   In addition, comments can be placed anywhere within an expression or sequence of expressions (Figure 5.7).

comment

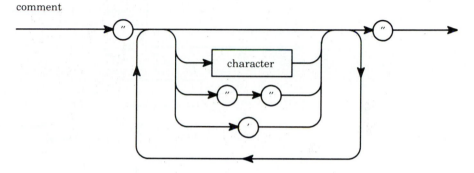

Figure 5.7

Example comments are

```
" This is a comment "
" with an embedded quote " " symbol "
" and an embedded single quote ' symbol "
```

☐ *Variables*   The memory available to an object is referenced by the use of variable names. A variable name is simply an identifier (Figure 5.8).

variable name

Figure 5.8

By convention, when identifiers are created by concatenating words, the first letter of each additional word is capitalized. For example

```
BicPen
redButtonPressed
totalSpentOn:
```

☐ *Message Expressions*   Messages represent interactions between the components of the Smalltalk-80 system. A message requests an operation on the part of the receiver. A message expression describes a receiver, a selector, and possibly some arguments. The receiver and

arguments are described by other expressions; the selector is specified
literally. A unary selector is simply an identifier, and a binary selector
is either a minus sign or one or two consecutive special characters. A
keyword is an identifier with a trailing colon; the keyword selector is a
concatenation of the keywords in a message. The diagrams for unary
selector, binary selector, and keyword are shown in Figure 5.9.

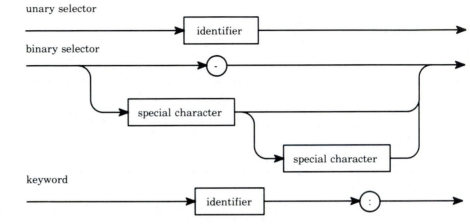

Figure 5.9

In the message expression

    ages at: ′James′ put: 25

there are two keywords, at: and put:. The keyword selector, that is, the
literal part of the message expression, is at:put:. The two arguments of
the expression are ′James′ and 25; the receiver is ages.

> Keyword selectors do not show up in expressions; hence there is no diagram for
> them independent of the diagram for symbol. However, they are the symbols stored
> as the keys of a class's message dictionary; they can be seen, for example, in one of
> the subview's of the system browser as described in Chapter 9.

There are three kinds of message expressions: *unary*, *keyword*, and
binary. Diagrams for message expressions are shown in Figure 5.10.
The following are unary expressions.

    theta sin
    BicPen home
    Pen new home

In the third example, a unary expression (Pen new) is parsed as a unary
object description that is sent a unary message (home).

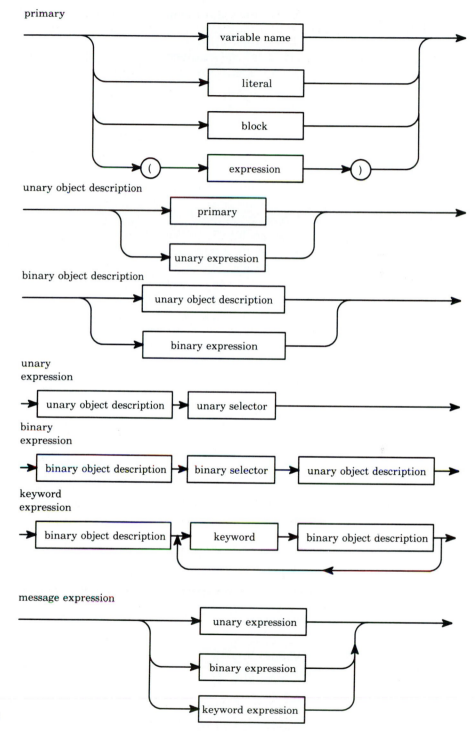

Figure 5.10

The following are binary expressions.

```
3 + 4
previousTotal - expenditure
(sum / count) * reserve amount
```

In the third example, the binary expression is formed as a binary object description ((sum   count)) followed by a binary selector (*) followed by a unary object description (reserve amount). The binary object description is itself a unary object description that, as a primary, is a parenthesized expression.

The following are keyword expressions.

```
3 max: 2
finances totalSpentOn: 'food'
anArray at: 3 put: 100
HouseholdFinances expenditures totalSpentOn: (reasons at: i)
```

In the fourth example, the keyword expression is formed as a binary object description followed by a keyword (totalSpentOn:) followed by a binary object description. The first binary object description is a unary expression that is the variable HouseholdFinances followed by the unary selector expenditures. The second binary object description is a primary, the parenthesized keyword expression reasons at: i.

☐ *Parsing*   When the receiver or argument of a message expression is described by another message expression, the issue of how the expression is parsed arises. Parentheses can be used to indicate the order of evaluation when that order is different from the ordinary parse. The parsing rules are:

1. Unary expressions parse left to right

2. Binary expressions parse left to right

3. Binary expressions take precedence over keyword expressions

4. Unary expressions take precedence over binary expressions

5. Parenthesized expressions take precedence over unary expressions

For example,

expression	parses as
4 + 5 - 3	(4 + 5) - 3
2 * theta sin	2 * (theta sin)
frame width: otherFrame width * 2	frame width: ((otherFrame width) * 2)

☐ *Cascaded Messages*   Cascading specifies multiple messages to the same object. A cascaded message expression consists of one description of the receiver followed by several messages separated by semicolons. The diagram for a cascaded message expression is shown in Figure 5.11.

cascaded message
expression

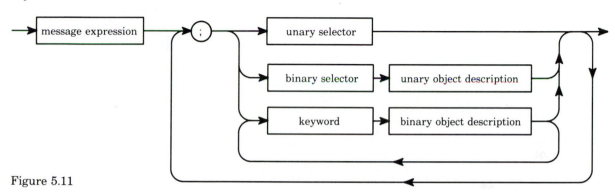

Figure 5.11

For example, a cascaded message expression is

BicPen home; up; turn: 89; go: 50+i; turn: 91; go: 200

which is equivalent to

BicPen home.
BicPen up.
BicPen turn: 89.
BicPen go: 50+i.
BicPen turn: 91.
BicPen go: 200

☐ *Assignments*   A literal constant will always refer to the same object, but a variable name may refer to different objects at different times. The object referred to by a variable is changed when an assignment expression is evaluated. Any expression can become an assignment by including an assignment prefix, that is, a variable name followed by a left arrow. For example

quantity ← 19
index ← initialIndex
name ← 'Chapter 1'
flavors ← #(vanilla chocolate strawberry rootbeer)
foo ← array at: 4
BicPen ← Pen new home; turn: 89

Thus the definition of an expression is a primary, a message expression, a cascaded message expression, or an assignment, as shown in Figure 5.12.

expression

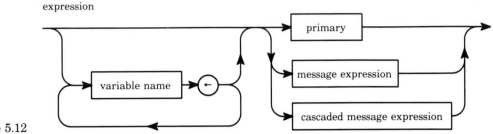

Figure 5.12

☐ *Block Expressions* Blocks are objects used in many of the Smalltalk-80 control structures. A block represents a deferred sequence of actions. A block expression consists of a sequence of expressions separated by periods and delimited by square brackets (Figure 5.13).

statements

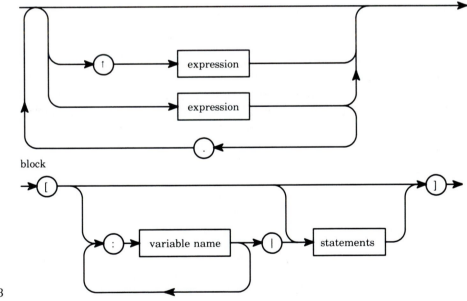

block

Figure 5.13

Blocks may take one or more arguments. Block arguments are specified by including identifiers preceded by colons at the beginning of a block. The block arguments are separated from the expessions that make up the block by a vertical bar.

For example,

```
[ quantity + 19]
[ index ← initialIndex. index ← index + 1]
[ :array |  total ← total + array size]
[ :x :y |  BicPen goto: x @ y]
```

Since a block is a primary, the following assignments are expressions.

```
savedAmount ← [ quantity + 19]
incrementer ← [ index ← initialIndex. index ← index + 1]
sum ← [ :array |  total ← total + array size]
```

A block without any arguments is evaluated by sending it the message value. A block with one argument is evaluated by sending it the message value: anArgument. Blocks with multiple arguments are evaluated by sending messages with a value: keyword and argument for each of the block arguments.

For example,

```
[ quantity + 19] value
[ :array |  total ← total + array size] value: #(a b c d e f)
[ :x :y |  BicPen goto: x @ y] value: 100 value: 250
```

☐ *Control Structures* Two kinds of control structure found in most programming languages are provided in the Smalltalk-80 system: conditional selection and conditional repetition. *Conditional selection* consists of a message to a Boolean object with block expressions as the arguments. There are four such messages whose keyword selectors are ifTrue:ifFalse:, ifFalse:ifTrue:, ifTrue:, and ifFalse:. For example,

```
number < 0
        ifTrue: [ absValue ← number negated]
        ifFalse: [ absValue ← number]
number < 0
        ifFalse: [ absValue ← number]
        ifTrue: [ absValue ← number negated]
number < 0
        ifTrue: [ number ← number negated]
number > = 0
        ifTrue: [ number ← number negated]
```

Conditional repetition is provided by a message to a block with the keyword selector whileTrue: or whileFalse:, and another block as an argument. Evaluation of the argument continues until the receiver evaluates to true or to false, respectively. These are like the Algol "while" and "until" statements. Examples of two expressions that carry out the same actions are

```
[index < = list size]
        whileTrue: [ list at: index put: 0. index ← index+1]
```

and

```
[index > list size]
        whileFalse: [ list at: index put: 0. index ← index+1]
```

In each case, the idea is to put the value 0 in each position in an array list, starting with some value of variable index and continuing until index exceeds the size of the array.

☐ *Methods*   A method describes how an object will perform one of its operations. A method is made up of a message pattern and a sequence of expressions separated by periods. A message pattern contains a message selector and a set of argument names for each argument that a message with that selector would have. A method may obtain some other variables for use during its execution. These are called *temporary variables*. A temporary variable declaration consists of a set of variable names between vertical bars.

The default value of a method is the receiver itself. When another value is to be specified, one or more *return expressions* are included in the method. Any expression can be turned into a return expression by preceding it with an up arrow. The diagrams for a method are shown in Figure 5.14. Note that the up arrow is specified in the diagram for "statements."

An example method in which a counter is incremented until the user presses the red button, and in which the final count is returned, is

```
| tempVar |
tempVar ← 0.
[Sensor redButtonPressed]
        whileFalse: [ tempVar ← tempVar + 1].
↑tempVar
```

The temporary variable is tempVar. It is initially assigned to the value 0.

```
tempVar ← 0
```

Then the expression

```
Sensor redButtonPressed
```

temporaries

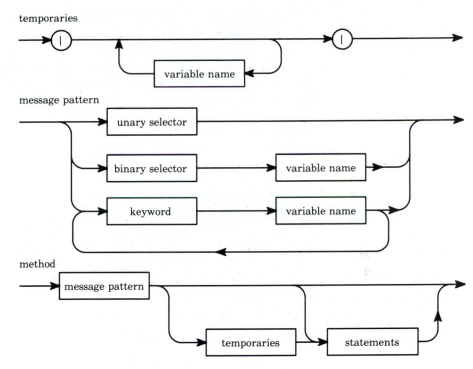

message pattern

method

Figure 5.14

is evaluated. This is a test of the hardware pointing device. As long as the red button is not pressed, the expression

tempVar ← tempVar + 1

is evaluated. This assignment changes the value of tempVar, incrementing it by 1. When the user presses the red button, the current value of tempVar is returned.

Class Descriptions

Each class has a name that describes the type of component its instances represent. A class name serves two purposes; it is a simple way for instances to identify themselves, and it provides a way to refer to the class in expressions. Since classes are components of the Smalltalk-80 system, they are represented by objects. A class's name automatically becomes the name of a globally shared variable. The value of that variable is the object representing the class. By convention, the first letter of names of shared variables are capitalized.

A description of a class has four parts.

1. A class name.

2. The superclass of the class.

3. A declaration of the variables available to instances.

4. The methods used by instances to respond to messages.

The methods in a class description are divided into categories; the categories have names that indicate the common functionality of the methods. The classes in the Smalltalk-80 system are also grouped into categories. These two kinds of categorizations in the system are orthogonal to the semantics of the language; they are used to document the intended use of classes and methods, and they are useful in providing a way to index the system's functionality.

The methods in a class have access to five different kinds of variables. These kinds of variables differ in terms of their scope, and how long they persist.

1. Instance variables exist for the entire lifetime of the object. They represent the current state of an object.

2. Temporary variables are created for a specific activity and are available only for the duration of the activity. They represent the transitory state necessary to execute a method.

3. Class variables are shared by all the instances of a single class.

4. Global variables are shared by all the instances of all classes.

5. Pool variables are shared by the instances of a subset of the classes in the system.

The majority of shared variables in the system are either class variables or global variables, most of which refer to the classes in the system.

> Names of global variables are stored as the keys in a special dictionary named Smalltalk. In order to declare a new global variable, you evaluate an expression of the form
>
> Smalltalk at: #VarName put: varValue
>
> To evaluate an expression, you type the appropriate expression in a workspace, select the text of the expression, and then choose the yellow button menu command do it. You can then use VarName in expressions that you evaluate in a workspace.

We said earlier that all Smalltalk-80 system components are represented by objects and all objects are instances of a class. Therefore, the classes themselves are represented by instances of a class. A class whose instances are themselves classes is called a *metaclass*. In the description of a class, it is necessary to distinguish between the messages sent to the instances of a class and those sent to the class itself. Messages sent to the class itself are stored in the message dictionary of the class's metaclass.

A class's metaclass is automatically created whenever the class is created. In the programming interface to the system, a menu in the system browser supports the user in specifying whether a message is to be sent to instances or to the class itself. The programming interface also supports creating class and message categories.

Method Determination, self *and* super

When a message is sent, the methods in the receiver's class are searched for one with a matching selector. If none is found, the methods in that class's superclass are searched next. The search continues up the superclass chain until a matching selector is found.

The search for a matching selector follows the superclass chain and terminates at the root of the class hierarchy, which in the Smalltalk-80 system is class Object. If no matching selector is found in any class in the superclass chain, the receiver is sent the message doesNotUnderstand: with an argument that is the offending message selector (the one that could not be found). The response to the message doesNotUnderstand: is found in class Object; the result is to report an error to the programmer or user.

A pseudo-variable name is similar to a variable name, however, the value of pseudo-variable name cannot be changed by an assignment. The names of variables in a message pattern are pseudo-variable names. In addition, there are special pseudo-variable names in the system. The pseudo-variable self refers to the receiver of a message. When a method contains a message whose receiver is self, the search for the method for that message begins in the instance's class, regardless of which class contains the method containing the pseudo-variable self. The pseudo-variable super is also available for use in a method's expressions. The pseudo-variable super refers to the receiver of the message, just as self does. However, when a message is sent to super, the search for a method does not begin in the receiver's class. Instead, the search begins in the superclass of the class containing the method. The use of super allows a method to access methods defined in a superclass, even if the methods have been overridden in subclasses.

5.3

System Components

The Smalltalk-80 system includes a set of classes that provide the standard functionality of a programming language and environment: arithmetic, data structures, control structures, and input/output facilities. The system includes objects representing both real and rational numbers. There are also classes for representing linear magnitudes (like dates and times) and random number generators.

Most of the objects in the Smalltalk-80 system function as data structures of some kind. While most objects also have other functionality, there are a set of classes representing more or less pure data structures. These classes represent different types of collections. Objects and messages implement the standard control structures found in most programming languages. They provide conditional selection similar to the "if-then-else" statements of Algol and conditional repetition similar to its "while" and "until" statements. Two classes are provided to support these control structures. Booleans represent the two truth values and blocks represent sequences of actions. Booleans and blocks are used to create new kinds of control structures. Objects representing independent processes and mechanisms for scheduling and synchronous interaction are also provided.

There are several classes in the Smalltalk-80 system that assist in the programming process. There are separate classes representing the source (human-readable) form and the compiled (machine-executable) form of methods. Objects representing parsers, compilers, and decompilers translate between the two forms of method. Objects representing classes connect methods with the objects that use them (the instances of the classes). Objects representing organizational structures for classes and methods help the programmer keep track of the system, and objects representing histories of software modification help link the efforts of other programmers. Even the execution state of a method is represented by an object. These objects are called *contexts* and are analogous to stack frames or activation records of other systems.

Classes helpful for presenting graphical views represent points, lines, rectangles, and arcs. Since the Smalltalk-80 system is oriented toward a bitmapped display, there are classes for representing and manipulating bitmapped images. There are also classes for representing and manipulating the more specific use of bitmapped images for character fonts, text, and cursors. Built from these graphical objects are other objects representing rectangular windows, command menus, and content selections. There are also objects that represent the user's actions on the input devices and how these relate to the information being viewed. Classes representing specific viewing and editing mechanisms constructed from these components provide views for classes, contexts, and documents containing text and graphics. The views of classes provide the fundamental mechanism to interact with the software in the system.

The Smalltalk-80 system allows communication with external media. The standard external medium is a disk file system. Objects represent individual files as well as directories. If a connection to a communications network is available, it can be accessed through objects as well.

The System Class Hierarchy

Figure 5.15 is of the system classes that are presented in the companion book *Smalltalk-80: The Language and its Implementation*. Lines are drawn around groups of related classes; the groups are labeled to indicate the numbers of the chapters in which specifications of the classes can be found.

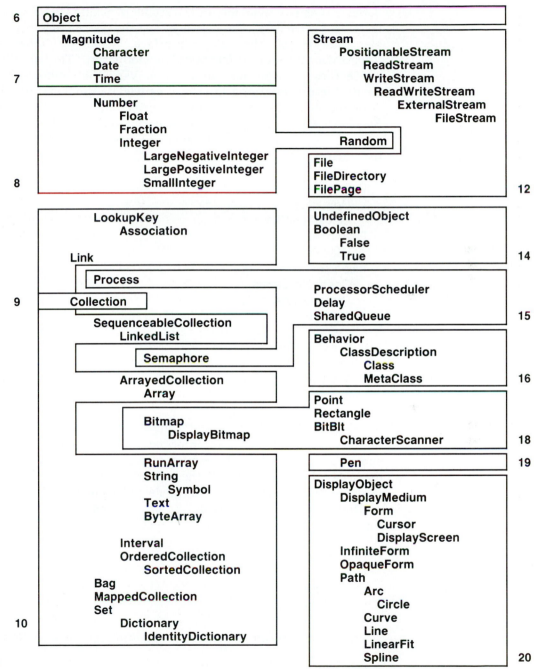

6 — Object

7 — Magnitude / Character / Date / Time

Stream / PositionableStream / ReadStream / WriteStream / ReadWriteStream / ExternalStream / FileStream

8 — Number / Float / Fraction / Integer / LargeNegativeInteger / LargePositiveInteger / SmallInteger

Random

12 — File / FileDirectory / FilePage

LookupKey / Association / Link

UndefinedObject / Boolean / False / **14** — True

9 — Process / Collection / SequenceableCollection / LinkedList / Semaphore / ArrayedCollection / Array / Bitmap / DisplayBitmap

ProcessorScheduler / Delay / **15** — SharedQueue

Behavior / ClassDescription / Class / **16** — MetaClass

Point / Rectangle / BitBlt / **18** — CharacterScanner

RunArray / String / Symbol / Text / ByteArray / Interval / OrderedCollection / SortedCollection / Bag / MappedCollection / Set / **10** — Dictionary / IdentityDictionary

Pen — **19**

DisplayObject / DisplayMedium / Form / Cursor / DisplayScreen / InfiniteForm / OpaqueForm / Path / Arc / Circle / Curve / Line / LinearFit / Spline — **20**

Figure 5.15

Several classes available in the standard Smalltalk-80 system are not listed in Figure 5.15. Some of these are the classes that support the implementation of the user interface, including View, Controller, ControlManager, and WindowingTransformation. The specific way in which these classes and subclasses of View and Controller are used to create the programming interface, as well as graphical and interactive interfaces to applications, will be described in a future companion book, *Smalltalk-80: Creating a User Interface and Graphical Applications.* Some of the classes that describe the standard program development tools are

Browser
   Debugger
   MethodListDebugger
FileModel
   FileList
Inspector
   ContextInspector
   DictionaryInspector
StringHolder
   ChangeList
   FillInTheBlank
   Project
   TextCollector
SyntaxError

There is a subclass of View and Controller for each of these; the subclass of View supports the way information about the development tool should be presented on the display screen, and the subclass of Controller describes the way in which the pointing device, menus, and the keyboard are used to interact with the development tool.

There are classes for organizing classes and messages, and for keeping track of changes to classes and methods; these are

ChangeSet
ClassCategoryReader
ClassOrganizer
   SystemOrganizer

There are classes that describe parsing, compilation, and decompilation.

Compiler
ParseNode
   AssignmentNode
   BlockNode

CascadeNode
Decompiler
Encoder
LeafNode
    LiteralNode
    SelectorNode
    VariableNode
MessageNode
MethodNode
ReturnNode
ParseStack
Scanner
   Parser

And there is a class that describes creating a new version of the system.

SystemTracer

5.4

Overview of the Programming Process

Programming in the Smalltalk-80 system involves the specification of one or more class descriptions, creating instances of classes, and sequencing messages to the instances. In the course of using the system, you interact with various views that give you access to the classes in the system, messages, methods that implement messages, expressions in which messages are sent to objects, and intermediate execution states.

The programming environment supports describing classes in an incremental fashion. The "class editor" is presented in the form of a *browser*, which is a way to present a hierarchical index to classes and to messages. Browsers are set up to help you find classes either by name or by category. You can find a message name under the class that uses it, and, given the name, you can find its implementors or senders.

> To determine the class of an instance, you send the instance the message class. To determine the category of a class, you send the class the message category.

The browser is used to retrieve descriptions of existing classes. It also provides a structure within which new classes are defined and existing classes are modified. When you use a browser to examine existing class descriptions, the source code for each method is retrieved from a special file.

Some hardware/software configurations of the Smalltalk-80 system might not have sufficient local or remote secondary storage space for this file. In such cases, attempts to retrieve the source code will fail. In order to view the method, you must use the system decompiler. You decompile the resident compiled code by holding down the "shift" key on the keyboard while selecting the message selector to be retrieved. Alternatively, set the value of SourceFiles to be nil (that is, evaluate the expression SourceFiles ← nil), indicating that no sources and no changes files are available. Decompiling loses comments and the names of temporary variables.

A system browser looks like a rectangular area on the screen that is divided into five parts. The parts either indicate a categorization for classes or a categorization for the methods of a particular class. These categorizations are orthogonal to the language itself; they provide a way in which to organize and document the class description. Parts Two and Three describe the system browsers in detail.

Classes are created by editing templates that are accessed via the system browser. The template for defining a new class as a subclass of an existing class, and for declaring the private and shared variables is

```
NameOfSuperclass subclass: #NameOfClass
    instanceVariableNames: 'instVarName1 instVarName2'
    classVariableNames: 'ClassVarName1 ClassVarName2'
    poolDictionaries: ''
    category: 'Category-Name'
```

In order to create a new class, you edit this template. You specify the names of classes (replacing NameOfClass and NameOfSuperclass), and you replace or delete the place holders for variable names, e.g., instVarName1 or ClassVarName1. The result is a Smalltalk-80 expression. For example

```
View subclass: #FinancialHistoryView
    instanceVariableNames: ''
    classVariableNames: ''
    poolDictionaries: ''
    category: 'Financial-Histories'
```

When you evaluate the preceding expression, you create the new class whose name is FinancialHistoryView as a subclass of View. It has no new variables declared. The yellow button menu associated with the part of the browser in which the template is displayed includes the command accept. When accept is chosen, the expression is evaluated. If there are no errors in syntax, then the new class is added to the system. If the class already exists, then it is redefined (its superclass or its variables may be changed); in this case, all existing methods of the class and its subclasses are recompiled so that references to variables can be rechecked.

The template for defining new methods is

message selector and argument names
    "comment stating purpose of message"

    | temporary variable names |
    statements

It is displayed in a part of the system browser as a result of your selecting a class category, a class, and a class message category. The yellow button menu associated with the part of the browser in which the template is displayed includes the command **accept**. When **accept** is chosen, the method is compiled. If there are no syntax errors, the compiled method is stored in the selected class's method dictionary.

You can develop your class description in parts. Each time you wish to add a method, you use the system text editor (as described in Chapter 3) and edit the method template. In order for the system to store the text as an actual method, you have to compile it. You compile the text by choosing the yellow button command **accept**. Compilation is done incrementally, method by method.

> Compilation is from Smalltalk-80 expressions into a bytecode instruction set which is interpreted by the Smalltalk-80 virtual machine.

As expressions are evaluated in a workspace, or as class descriptions are developed using a browser, information pertaining to each action is saved on a special disk file that we refer to as the "changes file." In this way, there is a file that represents an audit trail of each of your actions; this file can be used to recover your work in case of a system failure. A description of the recovery process is provided in Chapter 23. Your changes are also monitored in a kind of dictionary. We refer to this dictionary as the system "Change Set." It is useful as a reference for writing out a description of your final work (any class changes) onto a disk file. Typically, users share information, such as method descriptions, by sharing files of incremental changes or files of complete class descriptions. The system Change Set is documented in Chapter 23.

The process of developing class descriptions is supported by the browser. Using it you can ask questions about existing classes. You can find out which methods in which classes send a particular message. And you can find out which classes implement a particular message. Support for finding out such information is described in Part Two; support for programming is described in Part Three.

An execution interrupt occurs when you encounter a runtime error, you evaluate a breakpoint that you inserted in a method, or you type **ctrl c** (the "control" key and the "c" key concurrently). You can create a debugging view onto the context of that interrupt. Notifiers for interrupts and the debugger are described in Part Four. Note that you can edit a method within the debugger, compile it by choosing the yellow button command accept, and proceed with testing your work (without explicitly reloading the system).

Changes you make are local to your copy of the system. When you have completed your work, you can save it in one of two ways. You can either save a textual description of your class descriptions by using the "file out" command available in the system browsers (see Chapters 9 and 22), or save a new image of the entire system by creating a snapshot (see Chapters 1 and 23). It is useful to keep a snapshot of your work, expecially if you have created several kinds of objects that have information state that has evolved during your work session. Files created using the first approach can be shared with other users (they can file in the descriptions) so that your class descriptions can become part of their personal systems.

5.5

Summary of Terminology: General Concepts

argument name   Name of a pseudo-variable available to a method only for the duration of that method's execution; the value of the argument names are the arguments of the message that invoked the method.

class   A description of a group of similar objects. An object that describes the implementation of a set of similar objects.

class variable   A variable shared by all the instances of a single class.

global variable   A variable shared by all the instances of all classes.

instance   One of the objects described by a class; it has memory and responds to messages.

instance variable   A part of an object's private memory. A variable available to a single object for the entire lifetime of the object.

interface   The messages to which an object can respond.

message   A request for an object to carry out one of its operations.

message pattern   A message selector and a set of argument names, one for each argument that a message with this selector must have.

method   A description of one of an object's operations; it is made up of a message pattern, temporary variable declaration, and a sequence of expressions. A method is executed when a message matching its message pattern is sent to an instance of the class in which the method is found.

object	A component of the Smalltalk-80 system represented by some private memory and a set of operations.
pool variable	A variable shared by the instances of a subset of the classes.
primitive method	An operation performed directly by the Smalltalk-80 virtual machine.
protocol	Is a term used interchangeably with "interface," as in message protocol or message interface.
receiver	The object to which a message is sent.
subclass	A class that inherits variables and methods from an existing class.
superclass	The class from which variables and methods are inherited.
system classes	The set of classes that come with the Smalltalk-80 system.
temporary variable	A variable created for a specific activity and available only for the duration of that activity.

5.6

Summary of Terminology: Syntax

array	A data structure whose elements are associated with integer indices.
assignment	An expression describing a change of a variable's value.
binary message	A message with one argument whose selector is made up of one or two special characters.
block	A description of a deferred sequence of actions.
block argument	A parameter that must be supplied when certain blocks are evaluated.
cascading	A description of several messages to one object in a single expression.
expression	A sequence of characters that describes an object; the object is called the value of the expression.
keyword	An identifier with a trailing colon.
keyword message	A message with one or more arguments whose selector is made up of one or more keywords.
literal	An expression describing a constant, either a number, symbol constant, string, or array constant.
message argument	An object that specifies additional information for an operation.
message selector	The name of the type of operation a message requests of its receiver.

pseudo-variable name	An expression similar to a variable name. However, unlike a variable name, the value of a pseudo-variable name cannot be changed by an assignment.
symbol	A string whose sequence of characters are guaranteed to be different than those of any other symbol.
unary message	A message without arguments.
variable name	An expression describing the current value of a variable.
↑	When used in a method, indicates that the value of the next expression is to be the value of the method.
self	A pseudo-variable referring to the receiver of a message. Responses to messages to self are found by starting the method search in the class of the receiver, continuing up the superclass chain, and terminating at class Object.
super	A pseudo-variable referring to the receiver of a message. Responses to messages to super are found by starting the method search in the superclass of the method in which super appears, continuing up the superclass chain, and terminating at class Object.

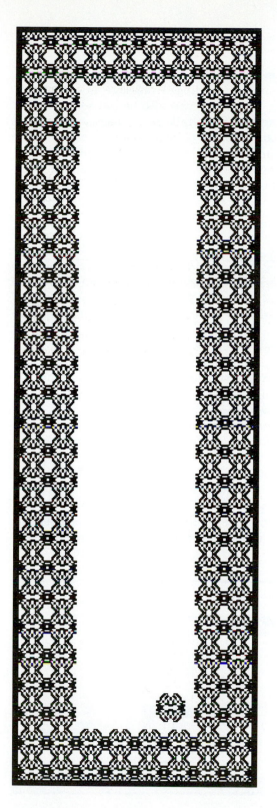

6

How To Evaluate Expressions

Commands or items in menus correspond to messages for an object. Choosing a command corresponds to sending a message to the object. Messages are also sent, that is, commands can also be issued, by evaluating Smalltalk-80 expressions. Any Smalltalk-80 message can be sent simply by typing the appropriate expression in a view that can contain text, selecting the expression, and choosing the yellow button command do it or the yellow button command print it. You select text representing a Smalltalk-80 expression to be evaluated in the same way you select any text to be edited.

6.1

The do it
Command

Whenever evaluation of expressions is possible, the item do it will appear in the yellow button menu; choosing do it provides immediate execution of any Smalltalk-80 expression or sequence of expressions that is selected.

It is common practice to keep around a workspace in which to type expressions that can be selected and evaluated, or from which to select previously typed expressions. Whenever you want to reevaluate an expression evaluated earlier, simply select the appropriate text in the workspace and choose the yellow button command do it.

You may of course edit some of the existing text before you select and evaluate it. In a sense, text left in workspaces form templates for commands.

When you choose the do it command (Figure 6.1), the selected expression is compiled. If an expression is not syntactically correct, a message to that effect will be inserted in the text (Figure 6.2). The point of location will precede the erroneous place in the expression. The insertion will be selected so that you can cut it out or replace it as soon as the error is understood.

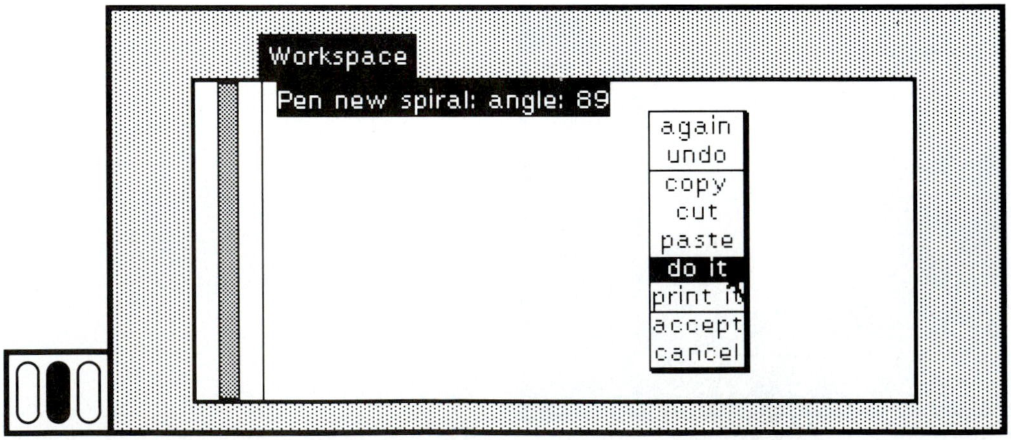

Figure 6.1

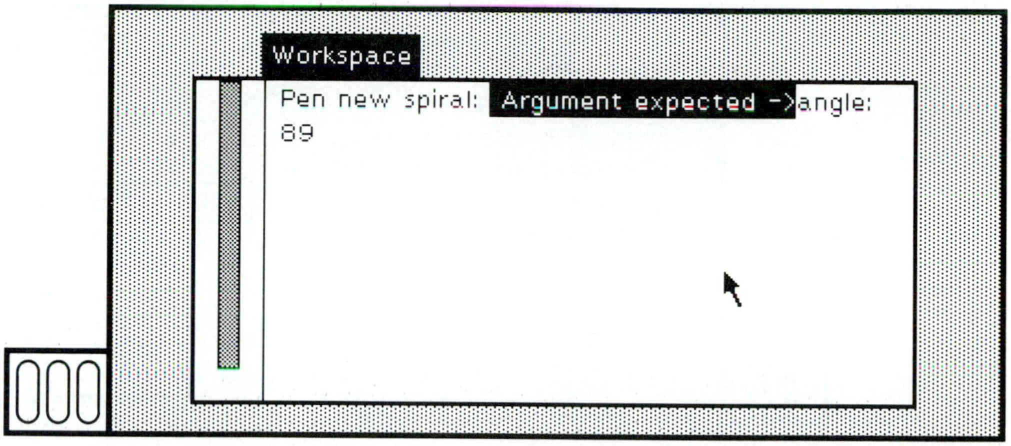

Figure 6.2

As another example, the error might be that a term in the expression is not a variable that has been declared at a global level or as a temporary variable of a sequence of statements. If you evaluate an expression with a variable that is not recognized (Figure 6.3), a menu appears (Figure 6.4). It gives you the option to declare the variable, to call on a spelling corrector to help you determine the correct variable name, or to cancel the evaluation. One of the items must be chosen (Figure 6.5). Spelling correction is explained in Chapter 16.

Evaluation is always carried out in the context of the view in which the do it command is issued. This is especially useful in a view of an interrupted process in which you are able to carry out debugging activities. In such a view, there is a menu from which you choose an interrupted message sent to an object, usually referred to as a *message-send*; evaluation within the view is carried out in the context of the selected message-send. It is also useful in a view for inspecting the internal state of an object. In such a view, evaluation is carried out in the

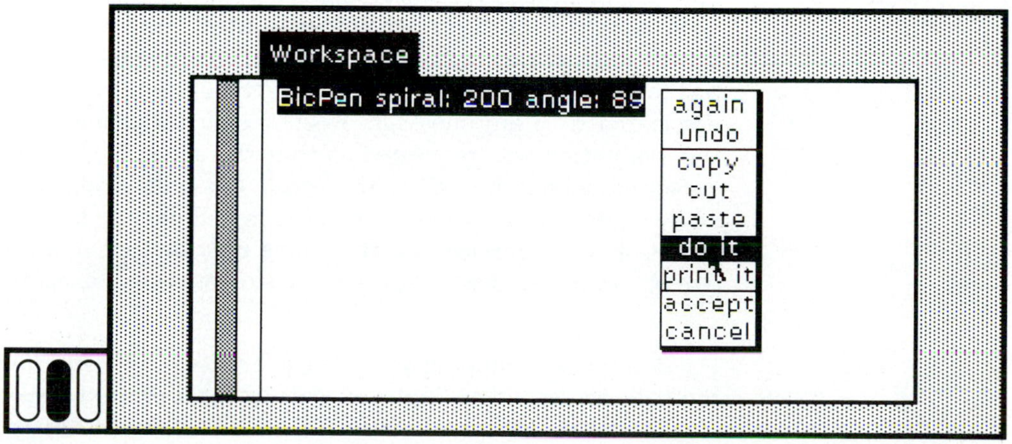

Figure 6.3

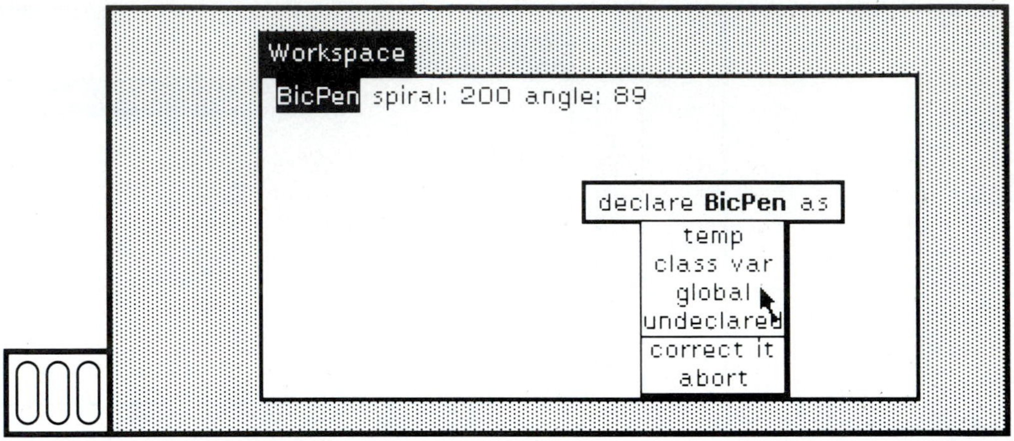

Figure 6.4

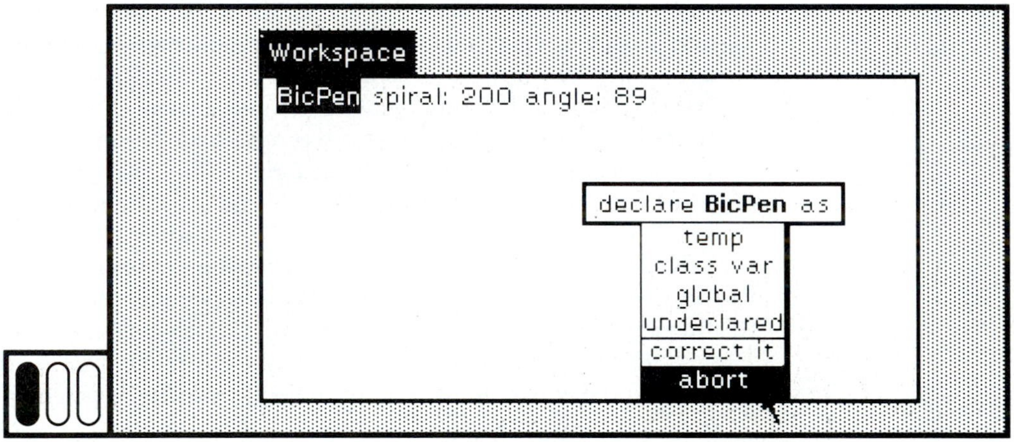

Figure 6.5

context of the variables of the object under inspection. An example of a view for inspecting an object is given in Chapter 8.

While the expression is being evaluated, the scroll bar will disappear. It will reappear as soon as evaluation is completed. This is a useful signal to you that you have to wait for the system to complete the actions associated with any message. Keep the cursor inside the view in which the evaluation was requested so that the scroll bar can reappear. If the cursor is outside the view, the scroll bar will reappear but quickly go away again. In many cases, the cursor will change shape while an evaluation is being carried out; the shape may be that of an hourglass (wait cursor) or of a slanted arrow with a star attached (execute cursor).

☐ *Practicing* Suppose you wish to create a new variable name that is globally accessible so that you can assign different values to the variable. First you have to store the new variable name in the dictionary Smalltalk. In the following example, the variable named is Frame.

Smalltalk at: #Frame put: nil

The above expression declares that Frame is a global variable name; its value is the object nil. Type the expression in a workspace, select it, and then choose the yellow button command do it (Figure 6.6). Now let's assign a new Rectangle to be its value. Type, select, and evaluate the expression (Figure 6.7)

Frame ← Rectangle fromUser

or

Frame ← Rectangle origin: 200@300 extent: 150@200

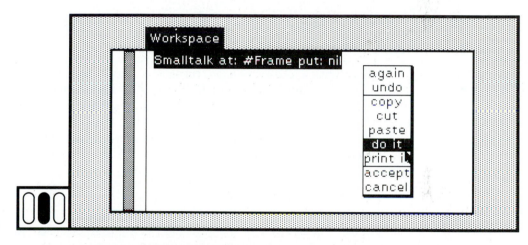

Figure 6.6

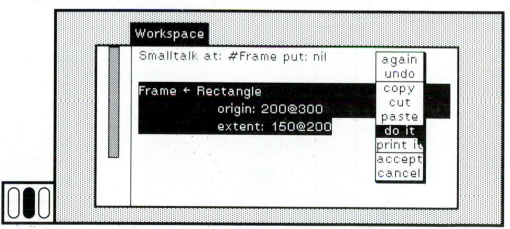

Figure 6.7

Both expressions are used to create new instances of class Rectangle. The expressions are well-formed because you declared the name Frame in advance.

> The system includes a dictionary named Undeclared. If you try to evaluate an expression that contains an undeclared variable name, then the name is stored in this dictionary. Before you can successfully declare it (that is, store it in the dictionary Smalltalk), you must remove it from Undeclared. You can remove it from Undeclared by evaluating
>
> Undeclared removeKey: #VariableName
>
> where VariableName is the name that was used without prior declaration. Alternatively, you can use one expression to remove the variable from Undeclared and store it in Smalltalk by evaluating
>
> Smalltalk declare: #VariableName from: Undeclared

6.2

The print it **Command**

Evaluating an expression returns a result that is an object that can print a description of itself. The result obtained by choosing the do it command is not printed. The command print it is identical to do it with the exception that the object resulting from evaluation prints its description after the text selection. The description then becomes the text selection.

In a workspace, type the expression

    3+4

Type the escape key. This selects the expression. Now choose the yellow button command print it (Figure 6.8a).

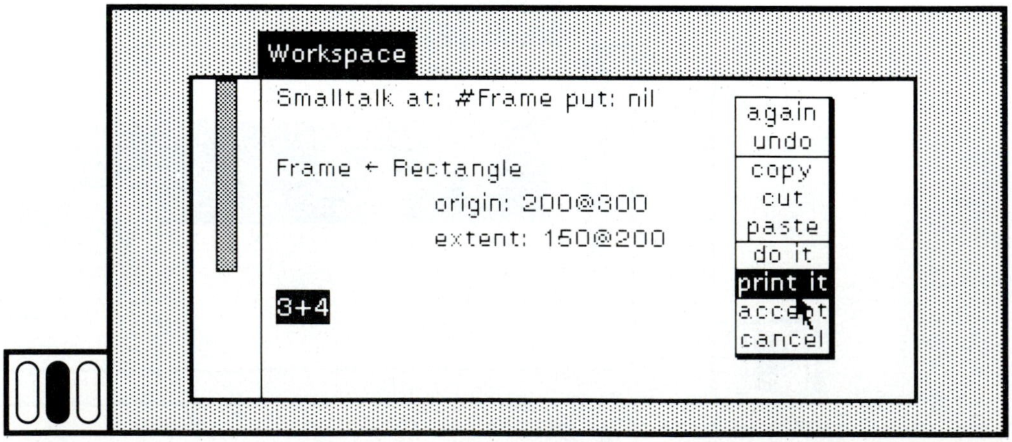

Figure 6.8a

The expression is compiled, evaluated, and then the result, 7, is inserted after the expression in the workspace (Figure 6.8b).

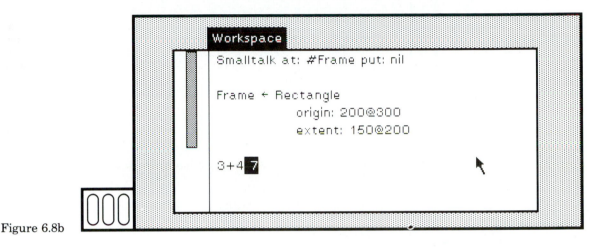

Figure 6.8b

6.3

The System Workspace

A special workspace labeled the System Workspace is available in the system. Its purpose is to provide documentation or templates for some of the common expressions you might need to evaluate. Most of these expressions pertain to activities common to an operating system, activities such as opening or editing a file, reading a file, resetting the size of the display screen, or accessing the audit of changes you have made so far. There are also expressions for inquiring about methods, messages, and literals in the system. These expressions form templates for operations that you may wish to invoke. By editing the expressions in the System Workspace, you specify, for example, a particular file or a particular size for the screen.

The System Workspace usually appears in the upper right screen area of an initial Smalltalk-80 system display. An image of a typical System Workspace is shown in Figure 6.9.

An index of the use of expressions found in the System Workspace is provided in the back of the book. Notice that the System Workspace includes a template for declaring global variable names. You can find and edit it rather than typing the entire expression yourself (as suggested in Section 6.1).

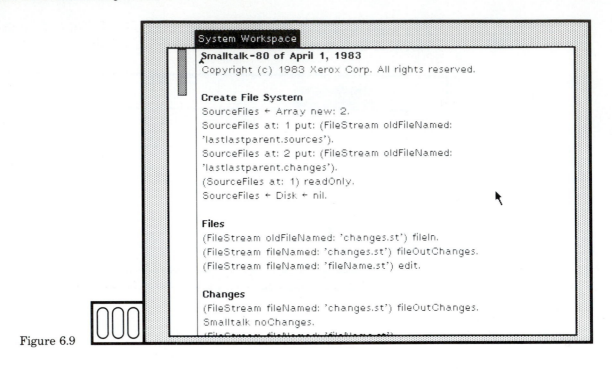

Figure 6.9

6.4

Examples

In order to give you some practice evaluating expressions, some examples of system variables and messages you can send to them are given in this section.

Exercise 1: In a workspace, type the expression

Transcript show: ′hello′

Select the expression and then choose the yellow button command do it (Figure 6.10a). The special System Transcript is referred to by the global variable name Transcript. This expression is a message to Transcript to insert the characters in the string ′hello′ (Figure 6.10b). The System Transcript usually appears at the upper left part of the initial Smalltalk-80 display screen. If one does not appear, you can create it by choosing the System Menu command system transcript.

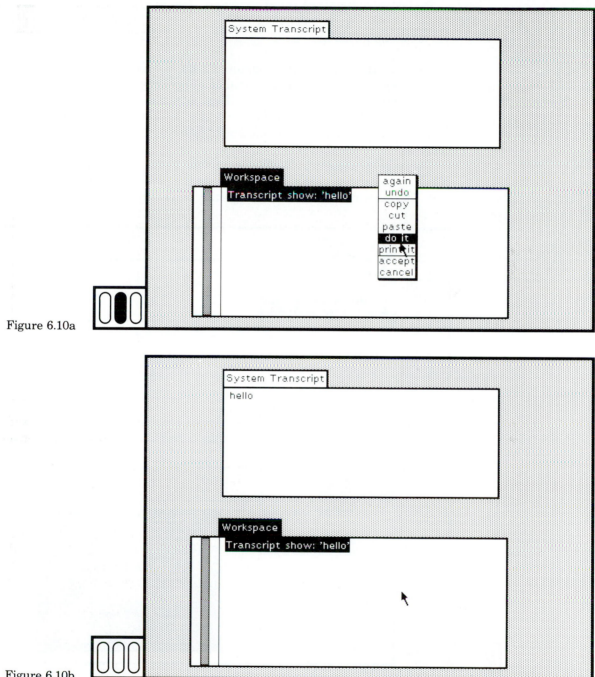

Figure 6.10a

Figure 6.10b

Exercise 2: Type and select the expression

Rectangle fromUser

and choose the yellow button command do it. The expression is a message to Rectangle to create an instance of itself by having you designate a rectangular area of the screen. Evaluate the same expression with print it this time (Figure 6.11a). Specify a rectangular area (Figure 6.11b). A description of the Rectangle prints in the workspace (Figure 6.11c).

Exercise 3: Display is a global variable name that refers to the display form that represents all the bits on the screen. It is an instance of class DisplayScreen. You can change the size of the full screen by send-

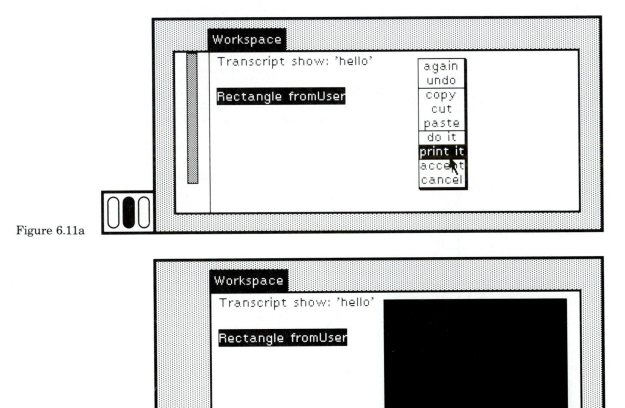

Figure 6.11a

Figure 6.11b

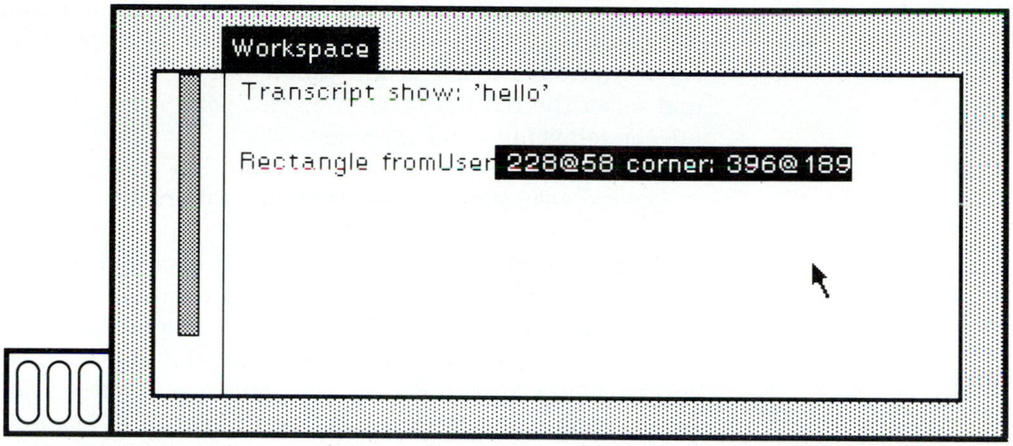

Figure 6.11c

ing a message to DisplayScreen, telling it the new coordinates. For example,

DisplayScreen displayExtent: 512 @ 640

will modify the layout to be 512 dots wide by 640 dots high. An expression of this form is provided in the System Workspace. The width and height you try should not exceed the actual limits of the hardware you are using.

You can change the image of the current display by sending messages to Display. For example, the expression

Display gray

will clear the screen to a gray tone.

Suppose you type this expression in a workspace and then evaluate it using the command do it. There may be a side effect if you keep the cursor in the active workspace—in particular, the workspace's scroll bar will probably display itself after the expression is successfully evaluated.

Exercise 4: You can access the cursor display coordinates by sending a message to Sensor (which is an instance of InputSensor), as shown in the following sample messages.

Sensor cursorPoint	Will determine the screen coordinates of the cursor.
Sensor waitButton	Will wait until any button is pressed and then determine the current cursor point.
Sensor redButtonPressed	Will determine whether only the red button is pressed.

Try these expressions using the yellow button command print it. Trying the third expression by evaluating it in a workspace is a bit tricky because you have to press the yellow button, release it to choose print it, and select the red button in the same time frame. It is simpler to evaluate the following two expressions

Sensor waitButton. Sensor redButtonPressed

The first expression will wait until you choose a button before evaluating the second expression. Thus you can use these expressions to experiment with testing pressing one of the three buttons.

More information about controlling the objects Display and Sensor can be found by examining the definitions of their respective classes, DisplayScreen and InputSensor. See Chapter 9 to learn how to find these definitions.

Exercise 5: You can create an infinite recursion by evaluating a message that simply calls on itself. For example, suppose Pen responded to the message go by evaluating

self go

If you sent a Pen the message go, you might notice right away that nothing is happening the way it should. Or you might not notice until your system starts running out of space and a notification, such as "low storage indicator," is displayed on the screen. In the first case, you can stop the recursion by typing ctrl c, the system interrupt request. A view that is a notification that a process was interrupted appears. Chapter 18 describes how to handle notification views.

6.5

Summary of Terminology

compiling	Checking for correct syntax and then translating into executable form.
Display	A global variable name that refers to the display form that represents all the bits on the display screen. It is an instance of class DisplayScreen.
message-send	A message sent to an object. In a view of an interrupted process, the term message-send usually refers to a message from which a response has not yet been received.
nil	The only instance of class UndefinedObject; it is typically the value of variables that have not been assigned as yet.

Sensor

A global variable name that refers to an instance of class InputSensor. User interactions with the system input/ output devices are tested by sending messages to an InputSensor.

Smalltalk

A global variable name that refers to the dictionary of all variable names known globally in the system, in particular, the names of all classes.

System Workspace

A special workspace containing expressions or templates for expressions that are useful for such operating system activities as opening and editing files, resetting display screen size, and accessing the references to any system changes.

Transcript

A global variable name that refers to a text collector, the System Transcript.

7

How to Make Pictures

Now that you know how to evaluate expressions, you can try creating some graphical images. The Smalltalk-80 system provides support for creating graphical images by freehand drawing using the display screen as the *canvas* and the pointing device as the *brush*, and by writing methods in which graphical objects are sent messages to construct an image.

Simple images are represented by instances of Form. A Form has height and width and an array of bits (a bitmap) that indicates the white and black regions of the particular image being represented. A complex image can be represented in either of two ways: by a very large Form or by a structure that includes many Forms and rules for combining and repeating them in order to produce the desired image. An image that is drawn as a sketch (in a freehand manner) is an example of the first; text is an example of the second.

Two sections of this chapter focus on how to make Forms by "painting" with a "brush" on the display screen using the pointing device to specify brush positions. These sections present the two interactive editors that are available in the Smalltalk-80 system: a Form Editor, which is a general set of tools for creating graphical forms; and a Bit Editor, which focuses on creating and modifying forms by selectively making each point (bit) of the form either black or white. A third section of this chapter discusses messages you can send to instances of Pen in order to create images on the screen. Chapters 18, 19, and 20 of the companion book, *Smalltalk-80: The Language and its Implementation*, provide further explanations and examples of methods for creating graphical images.

7.1

Making Pictures with the Form Editor

The basic idea of the Form Editor is to provide a *canvas*, an area of the screen in which drawings can be created, and a set of tools for placing *paint* on the canvas. All or part of the drawings can be saved on an external file and retrieved at later times. Figure 7.1 shows the canvas of the Form Editor on which some drawing has been done, and the menu of editing commands. The items in this menu are graphical images rather than text; as such, the menu is called an *iconic* menu. When the view for the Form Editor is not active, the iconic menu is hidden; when you select the view to make it active, the menu appears along the bottom edge of the view.

Five tool functions comprise the basic graphical form vocabulary. These are: single-copy, repeat-copy, line, curve, and block. Each of these tools can be modified in its use by four variables that modify its effect on the screen: form source, color tone, grid spacing, and painting mode.

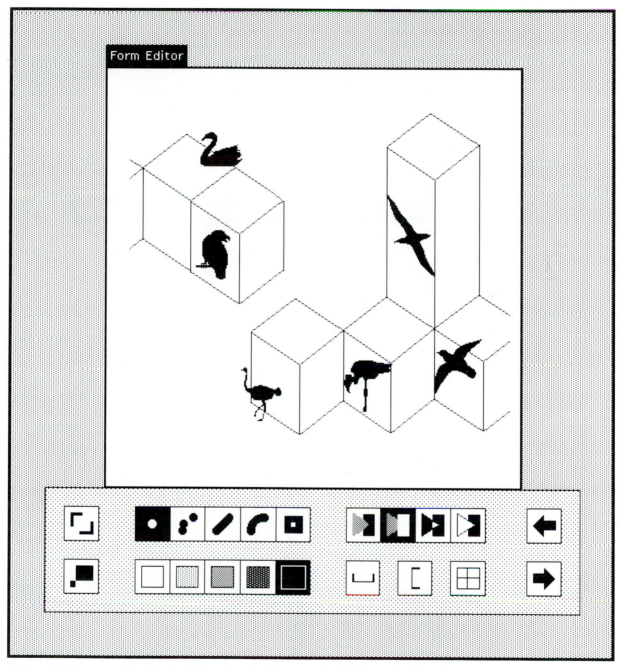

Figure 7.1

The functions are represented in the iconic menu that appear when the Form Editor is invoked.

To choose any tool or variable in the Form Editor, either move the cursor over the icon representing the desired action and click the red button, or type a corresponding key on the keyboard. You can press the red button and move the cursor over the icons; the current selection is highlighted by displaying a gray box within the icon. Releasing the red button chooses the current selection.

> The use of a gray box rather than complementing the icon was the aesthetic choice of the graphics artist who was involved in designing the editor.

The Form Editor is in a standard system view so that the standard blue button menu is available. However, the size of the viewing area can not be changed. A full screen editor can be created as well.

Create a Form Editor by evaluating an expression of the form

```
(Form new extent: 300 @ 400) edit
```

or

```
FormEditor openFullScreenForm
```

The message edit can be sent to any instance of Form. The system prompts you to choose the upper left corner of the viewing area. Note that the numbers you choose for the size of the Form should not exceed the width and height of your display screen. Moreover, in determining the height of the entire viewing area, you should allow for at least 112 pixels for the height of the menu.

The second expression creates a new Form the size of the display screen and then creates the editor for it.

The menu accessed by pressing the yellow button while you are in a Form Editor has two commands: accept and cancel. As in text editing, the picture being created does not modify the original Form unless the accept command is chosen. If at some stage of drawing you wish to experiment with different changes to a Form and you do not want to save versions on an external file, you can choose the accept command to store the current version, make some changes, and then choose the cancel command to restore the image to the earlier accepted version.

An iconic menu appears at the bottom of the Form Editor view whenever the view is active. A labeled image of the menu is shown in Figure 7.2. The corresponding keys on the keyboard are shown in Figure 7.3. Notice that the keyboard arrangement lines up with the icon positions. A description of each icon follows. You can try each one. A suggested exercise follows the description of the editor.

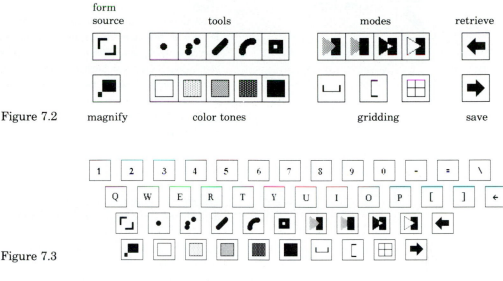

Figure 7.2

form source   tools   modes   retrieve

magnify   color tones   gridding   save

Figure 7.3

Form Source

(Key a)

Used to select or specify a Form that is used as the "brush" for painting. You are asked to designate a rectangular area of the screen. The image within that area becomes the new brush. You are then asked to designate a rectangular area whose contents become the new brush shape. You can designate this area from anywhere on the display screen.

Magnify

(Key z)

Used for detailed editing of an area of the display screen. You are asked to designate the rectangular area within the canvas that is to be edited in its magnified form. Then you designate the upper left corner of the editing area in which each screen dot is magnified eight times its normal size. The upper left corner can be anywhere on the display screen such that the editing area fits on the screen. See the description of the Bit Editor later in this chapter.

Single-copy Tool

(Key s)

When this tool is selected, the form source is copied onto the display screen at the position of the cursor whenever the red button is pressed.

Repeat-copy Tool

(Key d)

When this tool is selected, the form source is copied onto the display screen at the positions of the cursor, as long as the red button is pressed.

Line Tool

(Key f)

Used to specify lines between two points. The form source is used as the "pen" to connect the end points. Move the cursor to the position of one of the end points and press red button. Keep the button pressed and move the cursor to the other end point. The line image "drags" along. Release the button to specify the second end point. The line appears. (Note that when this tool is used with gridding assistance, graphs of horizontal and vertical lines can be easily created.)

Curve Tool

(Key g)

Used to specify a curve defined by three points (1, 2, 3). The curve begins and ends on points 1 and 2, and is tangent to the directed line segments formed by 1,3 and 2,3. As in the line tool, the form source is used as the "pen" to draw the curve. The three points for defining the curve are indicated by first moving the cursor to the desired position of point 1 and pressing the red button. Keep the button pressed and move the cursor to point 2. Release the button. Now move the cursor, essentially "dragging" out the curve to whatever shape is desired, and then click the button. The location of point 3 is implied by the positioning of the cursor. This technique implements a kind of "rubberband" approach to specifying the curve, similar to that used in specifying a line.

Block Tool

(Key h)

Used to fill rectangular areas on the display screen with color tone. Designate the rectangular area. It fills with the current tone using the current painting mode.

Color tones are set by choosing one of the five colors; each is shown in the menu as an icon that is a square of the tone.

 White Tone

(Key x)

 Light Gray Tone

(Key c)

 Gray Tone

(Key v)

Dark Gray Tone   (Key b)

 Black Tone   (Key n)

The form source is copied to the display screen according to one of the four modes that can be set. These are

 Over Mode   (Key j)

Copy both the black and white portions of the form source onto the display. The result is to replace the currently displayed image with the form source.

 Under Mode   (Key k)

Copy only the black portions of the form source onto the display.

 Reverse Mode   (Key l)

Copy such that wherever the form source is black and the display is black, the display turns to white.

 Erase Mode   (Key ;)

Copy such that the black portions of the form source appear as white on the display.

The painting area has a grid associated with it in both the x and y directions. You can set the size of the gridding. When gridding is not used, the brush can place paint anywhere in the canvas. The horizontal and vertical gridding can be used separately or together. When gridding is used, the paint is aligned on the grid boundaries. That is, the x (when horizontal gridding is used) or y (when vertical gridding is used), or both x and y (if both horizontal and vertical gridding are used) positioning of the source upper left corner is forced to align with the grid boundaries. Three icons represent the gridding controls. They are

 Horizontal Grid   (Key m)

A toggle for turning the horizontal grid on and off. When the grid is on, the icon is highlighted.

Vertical Grid   (Key ,)

A toggle for turning the vertical grid on and off. When the grid is on, the icon is highlighted.

 Set Gridding   (Key .)

Specify the horizontal and vertical grids. The integers represent the bits of the display screen. The initial value of

both grids is 8 bits. A prompter appears, first for the horizontal and then for the vertical grid. Type the number, not to exceed the screen width or height, followed by a carriage return key. Type only the carriage return to keep the value shown in the prompter.

The image in the entire painting area is not saved on an external file. Rather, the current form source is saved. To save everything, select everything as the form source. When a Form is retrieved from an external file, it becomes the current form source.

Retrieve Form Source

(Key ')
Change the form source to be the Form found on an external file. A prompter appears. Type the file name followed by a carriage return key. If no file name is given or if the name is not a well-formed file name, a confirmer appears stating that the file name is illegal, or the file was not found. You choose the menu item yes if you want to try another file name; choose no if you want to cancel the retrieve request. If the retrieval is unsuccessful, the form source does not change.

Save Form Source

(Key /)
Write a description of the current form source on an external file. A prompter appears. Type the file name followed by a carriage return key. If no file name is given, does nothing.

Note that it is possible to choose whether you want the paint brush/cursor to flash or not while you are "painting." The initial system arrangement is that the cursor flashes. To change it, evaluate the following expression before opening the Form Editor.

FormEditor flashCursor: false

The argument is true if the cursor should flash, false otherwise.

☐ *Default Setting*   When you first create the Form editing area, the settings for the tools and variables are

- Form Source—a small, 8 x 8 black square
- Tool—Repeat-copy
- Mode—Over
- Horizontal and Vertical Grids—both off
- Grid setting—8 by 8

☐ *Practice Painting*   Create a standard system view in which you can use the Form Editor by typing and evaluating the following expression (Figure 7.4)

    FormEditor openFullScreenForm

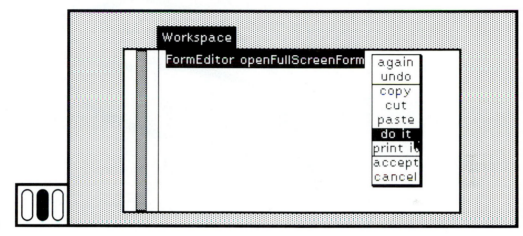

Figure 7.4

This will create an editor for a Form that uses the entire display screen, with the exception of the space needed for the iconic menu. The initial painting brush is a small 8 x 8 square with black tone. The tone is placed on the screen using the over mode. The painting tool is repeat-copy. Try it by moving the cursor around the canvas area, holding down the red button. You can draw a sketch. When the button is not pressed, no tone is placed on the screen.

If you want to start over, choose the yellow button command cancel.

Try the different color tones. Move the cursor into the iconic menu area. Notice that the shape becomes a normal cursor rather than the painting brush shape. Place the cursor over one of the gray tones and click the red button. Now move back to the canvas and sketch some more. Do this for each tone. Notice that white tone is useful for erasing.

The speed with which you move the cursor makes a difference as to the smoothness of the sketching line.

Try the different modes. Choose black tone. Choose the yellow button command cancel so that the painting area is clean. Place a thick stroke of black across the canvas. You have been using over mode. Now choose dark gray tone. Paint over some of the black on the canvas. Choose under mode and again paint over some of the black area already on the canvas. Notice that the tone is placed under the black strokes, not over. Try reverse and erase modes as well. A possible image resulting from following these instructions is shown in Figure 7.5.

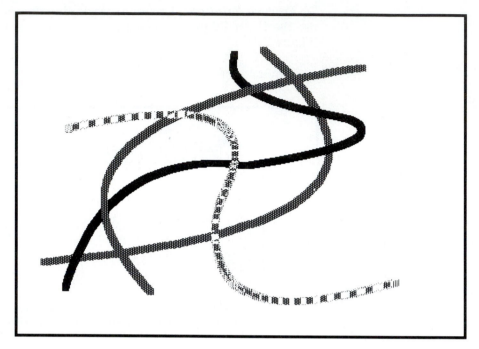

Figure 7.5

You should try each tool as well, changing paint tones and modes to test the various effects. For now, choose black tone and over mode. Now select line tool. Draw lines. You have no assistance with respect to gridding. Choose the yellow button command cancel so that the painting area is clean again. Choose horizontal grid and vertical grid. The gridding is now 8 by 8. That is, the lines you draw can be lined up on every 8 pixels, horizontally and vertically. It is, of course, possible to use only one of the grids at a time. Draw some vertical or horizontal lines to see how you can make use of the gridding (Figure 7.6).

Choose set gridding and set each grid to 32 (Figure 7.7).

Choose repeat-copy tool. Now try to paint (Figure 7.8).

Choose horizontal grid and vertical grid again. These items are toggles so that the gridding will no longer be used when you are painting. Try the curve and block tools with different tones and modes (Figure 7.9).

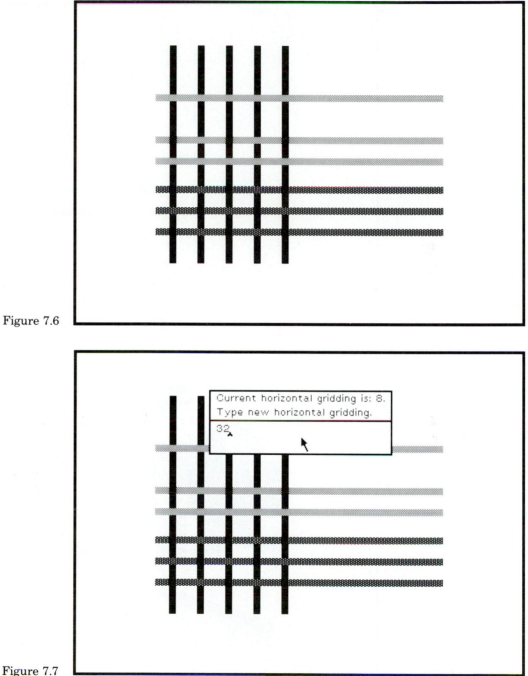

Figure 7.6

Figure 7.7

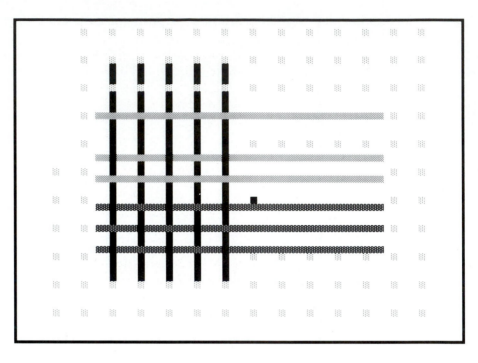

Figure 7.8

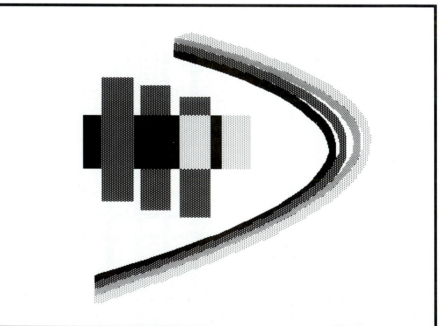

Figure 7.9

So far you have only used one brush shape (the default small square). Choose form source and designate an area from which to select a new brush shape. Try painting with it. Be careful to select something, i.e., do not select an all white area, else there will be no brush shape and you will see nothing for a brush on the canvas. If you do, simply type the key labeled a in order to select a brush again.

Try making a brush that is a horizontal or vertical line and paint using the repeat-copy, line, or curve tools. Set the grids and try these brushes. You can make grid paper this way. Be sure that the mode is over when you try these experiments.

Now choose the yellow button command cancel and start a fresh canvas. Choose a small square or circle for a brush. Choose black tone and over mode. Draw a simple little sketch, of a flower with a bee on it, perhaps. You probably had some trouble getting it just right--the pointing device is not, after all, a fine pen for sketching. It would be better if the bits on the screen were much larger.

Choose magnify, designating the area around the bee (not too much) and then designating the origin so that a magnified view of all or part of the bee can be displayed. The view area for the magnified version of the bee should not overlap the original image on the screen. An example is shown in Figure 7.10.

> Note that you can not have a Form that contains more than 1024K bits. Since magnification is 8-fold, you should not select an area to be magnified that is larger than about 128 bits x 128 bits.

Figure 7.10

You are now using the Bit Editor (see the next section for details). While doing so, notice that the original bee changes while you are editing the enlarged bee. Click the red button outside the editor's area in order to exit the Bit Editor. Now make the bee your brush (choose form source) and turn the griddings on (choose horizontal gridding and vertical gridding). Choose repeat-copy and black tone and under mode and paint a swarm of bees, as shown in Figure 7.11.

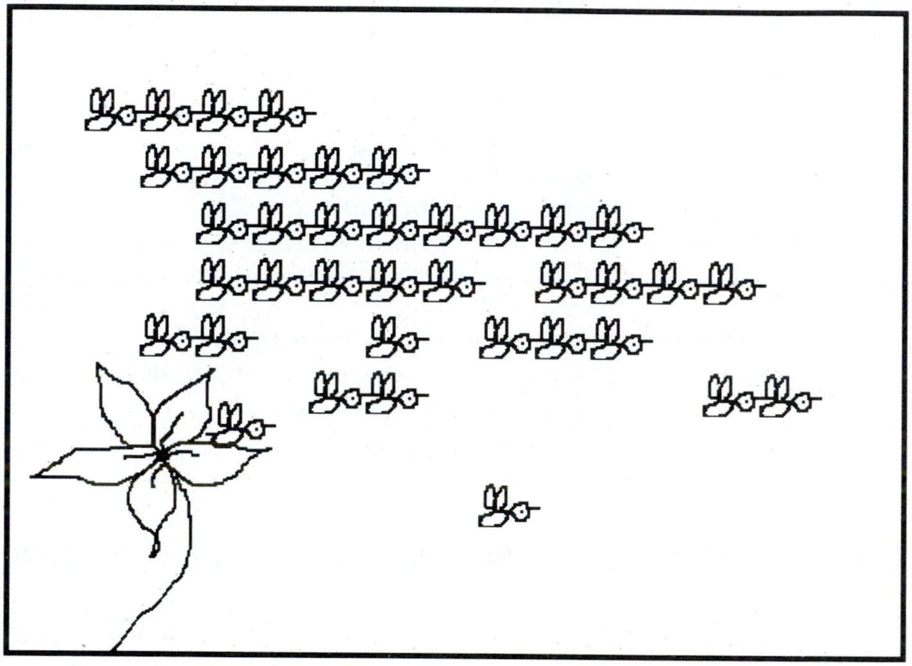

Figure 7.11

You can save your work using save form source. Remember that the image you want to save must be the current form source (brush). Close the Form Editor by choosing the blue button command close.

In using the Form Editor, there are some simple tricks to remember:

1. The under mode is preferred to over, especially when you want to place an image onto the canvas without erasing any portion of the neighboring image.

2. Modes reverse and erase are useful for obtaining interesting affects with mixing images. Using reverse, block tool, and black tone, you can reverse the video of all or parts of an image.

3. It is often easier to make straight lines by making the border of a view the paint brush and copying it to the canvas using under mode and the single-copy tool.

7.2

Making Pictures with the Bit Editor

Typically, the Bit Editor is invoked from the Form Editor as described in the previous section, or by evaluating an expression such as

> Form fromUser bitEdit

In each case, you designate the rectangular area on the screen from which the Form is defined. Then you designate the top left corner of the area in which the magnified view of the Form is to be displayed. This area is a view containing both the magnified view and a view of the actual image. Editing takes place in the magnified view (Figure 7.12). The view of the Form for editing obtained using the message bitEdit is contained in a standard system view, so that the blue button menu can be invoked for closing the view.

Figure 7.12

Note that there are only two things you can do in the Bit Editor, choose black tone so that you can turn dots to black, or choose white tone so that you can turn dots to white. Availability of some of the Form Editor tools would be useful in the Bit Editor. Adding these tools to the Bit Editor is an exercise you might try. Also, showing grid for the bits is useful visual information.

Entering the magnified area, the cursor shape changes to the crossHair cursor. The red button is used for setting dots in the magnified view to either black or white. A menu of colors appears below the magnified form. Choose one with the red button or by typing a key on the keyboard. The keyboard correspondences, which are aligned with the keys in the Form Editor, are

color	key
black	n
white	x

The yellow button is used for the commands accept and cancel in a way analogous to the use of these commands in the Form Editor. The blue button brings up the standard blue button menu.

You can also create the Bit Editor by specifying an existing Form and sending it the message bitEdit. For example, Figure 7.13 shows the magnified image of the read-a-file cursor (eyeglasses). The cursor is obtained by sending the message read to class Cursor. Thus, the Bit Editor on it is obtained by evaluating the expression

Cursor read bitEdit

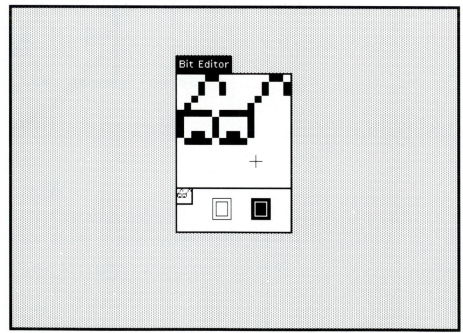

Figure 7.13

As another example, the result of evaluating

(Form new extent: 64 @ 64) bitEdit

is an editor on a newly created Form whose bits are all initially white.

It is possible to create a Bit Editor that does not appear in a standard system view. Rather, the editor grabs complete control until you click any button outside the bit-editing area. This is the Bit Editor as it is accessed from the Form Editor.

☐ *Opaque Forms* The Smalltalk-80 system also includes a class named OpaqueForm that stores one of three colors, black, white, or transparent ("gray"). These Forms are especially useful in creating animations since any image that is underneath the transparent part of an opaque form will be visible. The message bitEdit is understood by an OpaqueForm to create a Bit Editor whose menu of colors includes a gray tone representing "transparent paint" (Figure 7.14). The keyboard correspondences are

color	key
black	n
gray	v
white	x

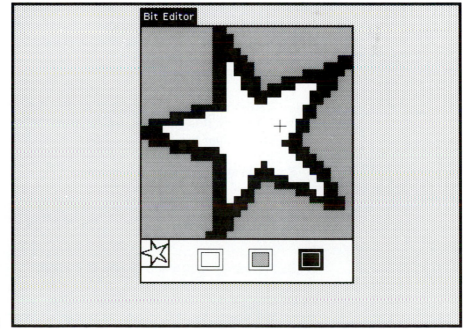

Figure 7.14

7.3

Making Pictures with Expression Evaluation

Pictures can be made by direct drawing using the Form Editor or the Bit Editor. Alternatively, pictures can be made by sending messages to graphical objects. Generally, pictures made this second way are constructed in a highly structured manner by creating instances of class View or one of its subclasses. The Smalltalk-80 system has many examples of such views: BrowserView, InspectorView, and NotifierView are the primary components of the user interface. These views, in turn, contain subviews that are CodeViews, ListViews, SwitchViews, FormViews, DisplayTextViews, or StringHolderViews. Examples of StringHolderViews are ProjectViews, TextCollectorViews, and FillinTheBlankViews. A StringHolderView is a way of creating an image of any object that can present itself using information stored as a string.

Primitive graphical objects are instances of Pen, Rectangle, and Quadrangle. We have already referred to Rectangle; you create a rectangle whenever you designate a rectangular area of the screen in which a view is displayed. The scroll bars are examples of the use of Quadrangle in the system. The next section explains how to use a Pen. In addition, the system includes the class DisplayObject; instances of subclasses of DisplayObject can be used in creating structured pictures. Example subclasses are Arc, Curve, Line, LinearFit, and Spline.

Pens

A Pen is used for line drawing. It consists of a position on the screen, a direction in which to move, a Form that it uses for creating images, and a mask and a rule for combining the Form with its destination area on the display screen. A Pen is created by sending a message of the form

    BicPen ← Pen new

Here we refer to the new instance of the Pen as BicPen. Recall that if you wish to try this example, BicPen must be declared as a global variable. Rather than use the above assignment, you can evaluate

    Smalltalk at: #BicPen put: Pen new

We can constrain BicPen to draw only within a fixed boundary, which we call its clipping rectangle, by sending it the message frame: aRectangle. For example,

    BicPen frame: (200@200 extent: 300@300)

According to the above expression, BicPen will only draw in a square area 300 pixels by 300 pixels, starting at location 200, 200. Without such a constraint, BicPen could have drawn anywhere on the screen. The center of a Pen's drawing area is known as its home. We can place BicPen at its center by sending it the message home.

BicPen home

Initially, the tip or nib of BicPen is a 1 by 1 black dot with which we can draw thin lines. We can change the size of this nib by sending the message defaultNib:. The argument is an Integer, and the resulting nib is a square with length of side Integer.

BicPen defaultNib: 8

The nib of BicPen is now an 8 by 8 black square. Alternatively, we can send BicPen the message sourceForm:. The argument is a Form.

BicPen sourceForm: Cursor normal

The nib of BicPen is now the shape of the normal cursor, i.e., a slanted arrow.

A Pen can receive messages asking it to change the state of its mask.

black	Set the mask to black.
white	Set the mask to white.

And a Pen can receive a variety of messages asking it to change its position, the state of its ability to draw, and its direction. These consist of

home	Go to the center of the Pen's frame.
down	The ink form with which drawing is done should be positioned for drawing when the pen moves.
up	The ink form with which drawing is done should be positioned so that no drawing is done when the Pen moves.
turn: anInteger	Change the direction in which the Pen will move by the amount, anInteger, measured in degrees.
north	Orient the Pen towards the top of the display screen.
go: anInteger	Move a distance equal to anInteger pixels; draw using the source form if the ink form is positioned down.
place: aPoint	Place the Pen at location aPoint regardless of orientation; do not change the current direction, and do not draw.
goto: aPoint	Move the Pen to location aPoint, ignoring the current direction, but drawing if the ink form is positioned down.

As described in subsequent chapters, you can see various ways to make designs with Pens by browsing to the examples in the instance or class methods. Two examples for you to try are given here.

Pen new mandala: 30 diameter: 300

and

Pen new spiral: 200 angle: 89

The result of the first is shown in Figure 7.15, and of the second in Figure 7.16. After trying each example, you will want to choose the System Menu command restore display.

Pen is the Smalltalk-80 version of the "turtles" designed many years ago at MIT's Logo laboratory and described in Seymour Papert's book *MindStorms: Children, Computers, and Powerful Ideas* (Basic Books, New York, 1980). Another excellent reference on the use of turtles is by Hal Abelson and Andrea diSessa, *Turtle Geometry: The Computer as a Medium for Exploring Mathematics* (Cambridge, MIT Press, 1981).

Figure 7.15

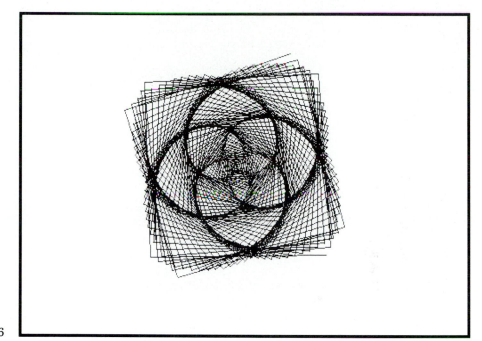

Figure 7.16

7.4

Summary of Terminology

DisplayObject	A system class whose subclasses represent the graphical objects in the system, such as lines, circles, arcs, and splines.
Form	A system class that represents simple images. Instances of Form have height and width and an array of bits that indicate black and white regions of an image.
iconic menu	A menu whose items are presented as graphical images rather than as text.
opaque form	A Form that represents an array of bits each of which can indicate a black, a white, or a transparent region of the image.
Pen	A system class that represents a form source, a current display screen position, and a current direction in which to move. Instances of Pen are used to draw lines on the display screen.

PART TWO

How to Find Information in the System

All information that you can seek about the Smalltalk-80 system involves information about existing objects or about objects that can be created. You can find out information about the internal state of an object using a system view called an *Inspector*. You can find out about the message interface to an object using a system view called a *Browser*. A *System Browser* gives you access to all the class descriptions available in the system, including comments about the classes, comments about the methods, and examples of how to use many of the classes. Other ways to find out about messages and methods involve creating system views called *Message-Set Browsers*. These views are created in response to queries to determine which methods send a particular message, which classes implement a particular message, or which methods reference a particular variable or literal.

This part includes an introduction on how to find out about a running process, in particular, how to interrupt an activity to find out which objects are interacting to create that activity. The system views used in this exploration are *Notifiers* and *Debuggers*. More details about notifiers and debuggers are provided in Part Three.

Several forms of on-line documentation and assistance will be identified: comments, explanations, templates, examples, and menus. In addition, the spelling correction capabilities of the Smalltalk-80 system are explained in Part Three.

Comments. Each class description includes a command about the purpose of the class. A class comment is obtained (for reading or for editing) by choosing the yellow button command comment in the class-names subview of the browser. Other comments document the purpose of a method. These are found by choosing a message selector; the comment is the text within double quotes at the beginning of the method definition. Programmers can also document the design of a method by interspersing quoted text within the method itself.

Explanations. Suppose you want to understand an existing method. One form of explanation could be explanation about the tokens that appear in the method. You can select any token and then choose a command to obtain a short description of the role of the token.

Because of the class and message structure of the system, it is possible to provide explanations about which messages are sent in a particular method, and to obtain browsers to answer queries as to which methods send a particular message, which classes implement a particular message, and which messages are sent in a particular method. These are the kinds of queries that a programmer must be able to make to determine the structure of the Smalltalk-80 system. The system browser as the program editing interface provides the framework for both the incremental development of class descriptions, as well as the context for accessing information about classes. Each new class added to the system by the programmer is accessible via a browser and can be queried in the same way as all system-provided classes.

Templates. Whenever the system "knows" something about the form in which information should be provided, a template or a default solution is provided. The user edits the template, replacing descriptive words with the actual desired text. This means that the user does not have to remember syntax and can be prompted on the kind of information that is required. Templates are used to assist in defining classes and methods, and in commenting the system.

Examples. In many of the descriptions of classes in the system, there are messages that consist of examples of how to interact with instances of the class. Examples show how to create a new instance or how to use an instance. These examples are typically messages to the class itself, where the method includes documentation comments and expressions to be evaluated. Since you can add your own methods, a strategy for learning how to use the system is to work out examples of your own that you store with the associated class.

Menus. Menus are a form of assistance in the system. The items in a menu denote and remind you of the kinds of activities you can do. You choose an activity by pointing to the menu item, rather than having to remember the correct key words and having to type the words correctly. Items in a menu represent the behavior of an object; most likely, there is a message in the class description of the object that carries out the behavior represented by the menu item. You can learn about programming in the system by searching for these menu item/message correspondences.

☐ *Please Note* The tutorial presentations in this part of the book assume that the system sources are available to you and accessible from your system. Without them, you can still use the system and access system class descriptions. However, you will not be able to access class and method comments nor actual method argument names.

8

Finding Out About Instances

In developing definitions or learning about the system, you can examine the named or indexable instance variables of an object. The message inspect can be sent to any object. The result is an inspector view of the object.

8.1

The Structure of an Inspector

An inspector is a view made up of two parts: one is a list menu of the names of the instance variables; the other is a text view in which the value of the selected variable is shown. As an example of using an inspector, try evaluating the expression

(Rectangle origin: 10 @ 10 corner: 60 @ 60) inspect

The result of evaluating the parenthesized expression is an instance of class Rectangle with origin at screen location 10, 10 and corner at 60, 60. Recall that 0, 0 is at the upper left corner of the display, and that x increases to the right and y increases to the bottom of the screen. A message expression of the form aNumber1 @ aNumber2 denotes an instance of class Point; the Point represents a location on the display screen whose Cartesian coordinates are aNumber1, aNumber2.

This new Rectangle is then sent the message inspect. The result is that you are asked to designate a rectangular area in which the inspector will appear. An example inspector on this Rectangle is shown in Figure 8.1.

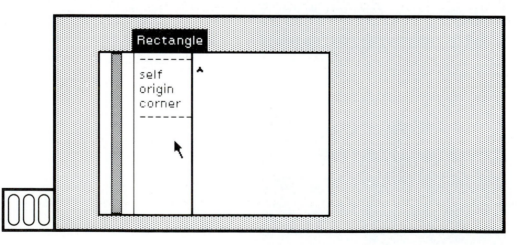

Figure 8.1

The left subview of the inspector is the list menu. The menu contains the pseudo-variable name self, which refers to the inspected object. It also contains the instance variable names origin and corner. You choose items in the list menu by placing the cursor over the item and clicking the red button.

Choose one of the variable names; a description of the value of the variable prints in the right subview (as shown in Figure 8.2a). Choose self from the list menu. A description of the Rectangle prints in the right subview (Figure 8.2b). Note the special print format for Rectangles that is displayed in the right text subview.

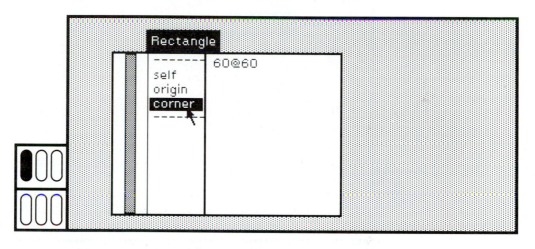

Figure 8.2a

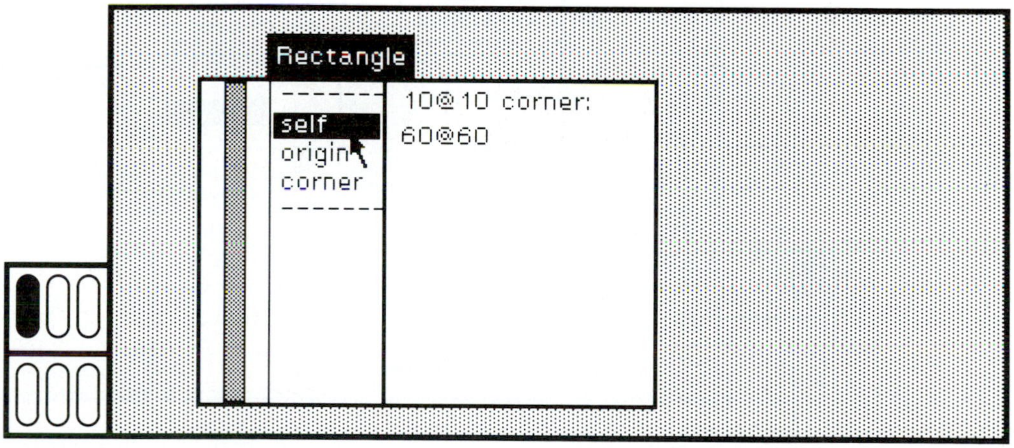

Figure 8.2b

Choose the instance variable name corner. Press the yellow button. The pop-up menu that appears contains the single command inspect (Figure 8.3a). Choose inspect. You are asked to designate another rectangular area in which to display an inspector for the object referred to by corner. This object is an instance of class Point. Notice that the label of the inspector contains the name of the class of the inspected object (Figure 8.3b).

Close this second inspector by choosing the blue button command close.

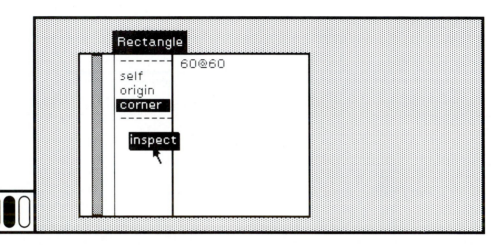

Figure 8.3a

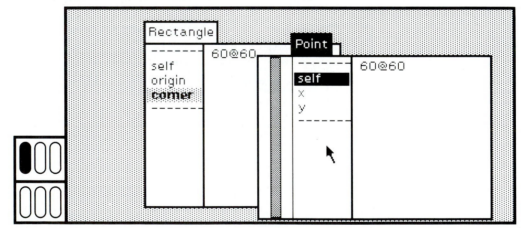

Figure 8.3b

8.2

Changing the Values of Variables

You can change the value of an inspected object's variables by typing an expression for the new value in the right subview and then choosing the yellow button command accept.

Choose origin from the list menu of the inspector for the Rectangle you created earlier. Change the value 10 @ 10 to be 20 @ 15 simply by editing the text and choosing the yellow button command accept in the right subview of the inspector (Figure 8.4a). Now choose self in the list menu to see that the current description of the Rectangle has changed (Figure 8.4b).

> The private memory of an object is supposed to be protected from such direct manipulation. However, for testing or for debugging purposes, the ability to directly set the values of instance variables is very useful.

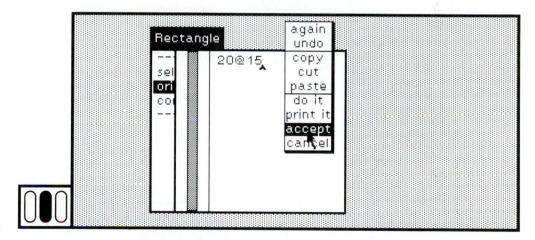

Figure 8.4a

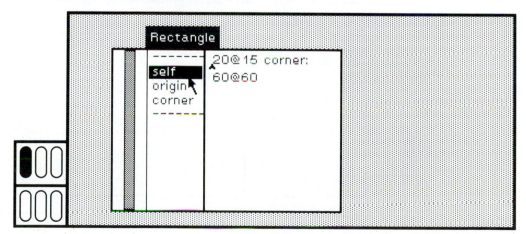

Figure 8.4b

Try another example. Create an array of arrays by typing and selecting the following expression in a workspace, and choosing the yellow button command do it.

#(($a $b $c) $d ($e $f)) inspect

The first inspector presents an instance of class Array (Figure 8.5a). The object has three indexed variables. If you choose the first item in the list menu, self, a description of the instance is printed (Figure 8.5b). Choose item 1 in the menu of the inspector (Figure 8.5c). A description of the first element of the Array prints. Choose the yellow button command inspect (Figure 8.5d). Another inspector is created; it presents another instance of class Array, this time one with the three characters as its elements. Try inspecting the different variables. Item 2 in this second inspector is a Character (Figure 8.5e).

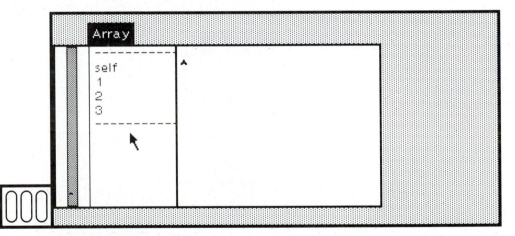

Figure 8.5a

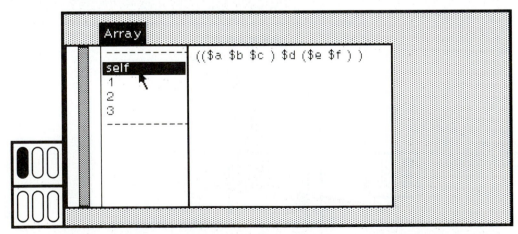

Figure 8.5b

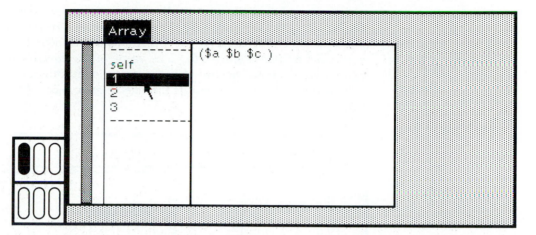

Figure 8.5c

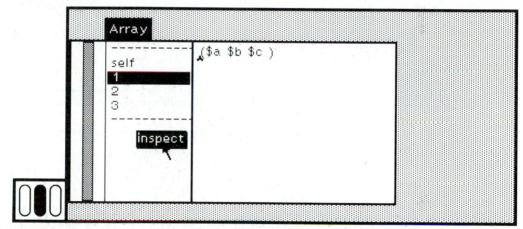

Figure 8.5d

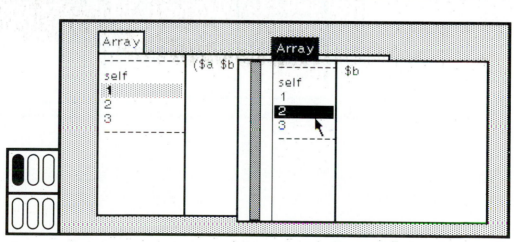

Figure 8.5e

Choose the first element of the array in the second inspector (item 1 in the list menu) (Figure 8.5f). Now edit the text view so that it contains the text #(1 2) instead of the Character $a. Choose the yellow button command accept (Figure 8.5g). The value of the first element of the current array is now the two-element array of numbers 1 and 2. Choose self in the list menu to see the change (Figure 8.5h). Close both inspectors.

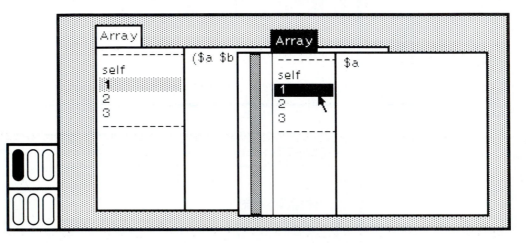

Figure 8.5f

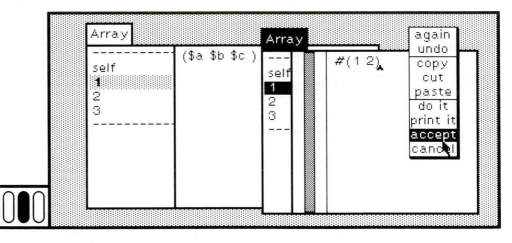

Figure 8.5g

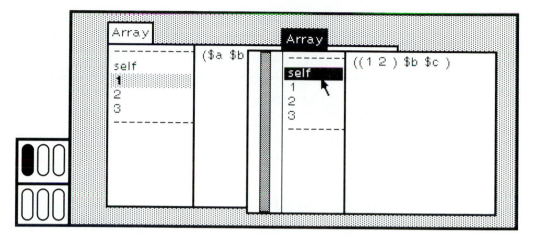

Figure 8.5h

To see how the information about an object can be multiply-viewed by the system views, create two inspectors on the same object. For example, try to inspect another instance of Rectangle by evaluating the expression

Rectangle fromUser inspect

You will first designate the area for the Rectangle and then the area for the inspector. Choose the item self in the list menu (Figure 8.6a). (Your rectangle will probably have different coordinates.)

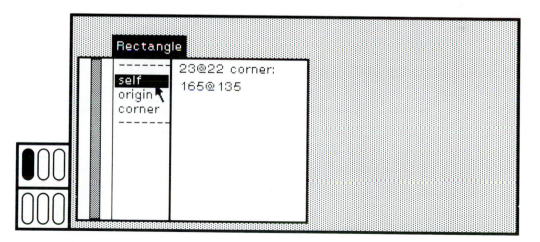

Figure 8.6a

Choose the yellow button command inspect (Figure 8.6b) to create a second inspector (Figure 8.6c). Choose origin in both inspectors (Figure 8.6d).

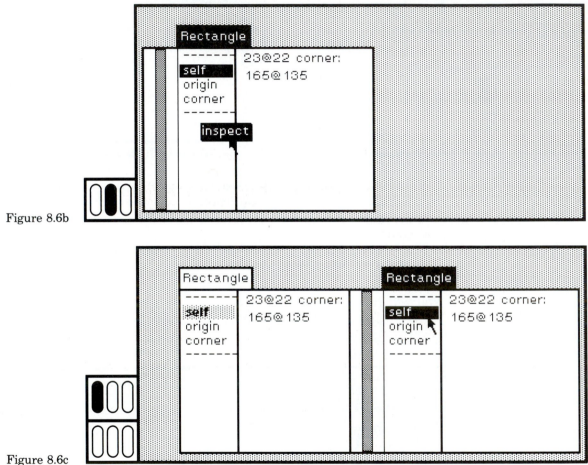

Figure 8.6b

Figure 8.6c

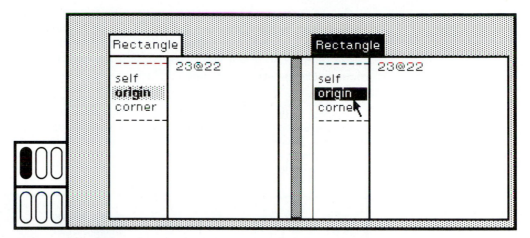

Figure 8.6d

You cannot use a more direct approach to creating the two inspectors, such as evaluating

```
| rect |
rect ← Rectangle fromUser.
rect inspect.
rect inspect
```

because as soon as the first message, inspect, is sent to the rectangle instance, rect, the workspace loses control to the newly created and scheduled inspector. The last expression is never evaluated.

Change the value of one of the variables in one inspector (Figure 8.6e).

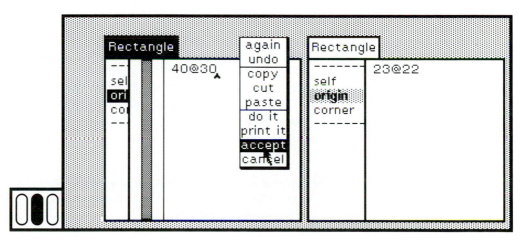

Figure 8.6e

See that the other inspector knows about the change (Figure 8.6f). If the variable is already selected in the second inspector when its value was changed in the first, you will have to reselect it to see the changed value. Similarly, if self was selected, you must choose it again to see the change. Close both inspectors.

The yellow button menu of the inspector's left subview contains only one item, inspect. Only the instance variables of the object are shown. As an alternative design, a command to inspect the class variables could be added. In some variations of the Smalltalk-80 system used within Xerox, this command is called classVars; it creates an inspector on a Dictionary whose keys are the class variable names and whose values are the values of the named variables.

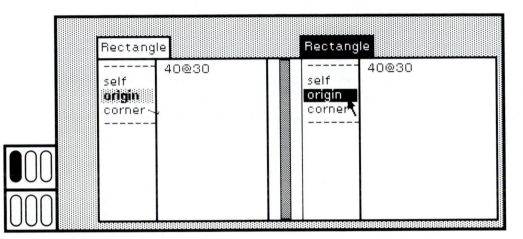

Figure 8.6f

8.3

Sending Messages to an Object

Another use of the right subview of an inspector is to test sending messages to the inspected object, or to test evaluating message expressions. For example, Rectangles understand messages for determining width, height, and area. In the right subview of the inspector for the first Rectangle that was created in an earlier example, type and select the following expression

    self area

Note that in this example we assume the origin is at 20, 15 and the corner at 60, 60. Choose the yellow button command print it (Figure 8.7a). The result is printed (Figure 8.7b).

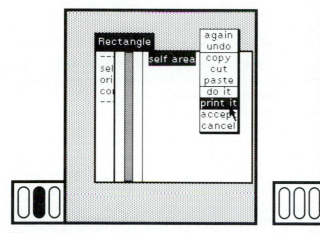

Figure 8.7a

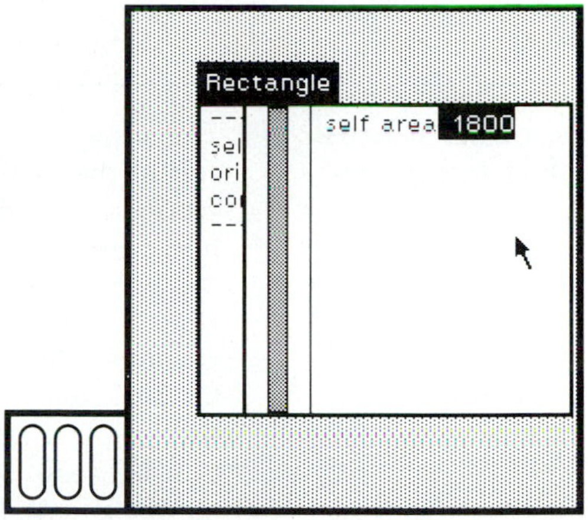

Figure 8.7b

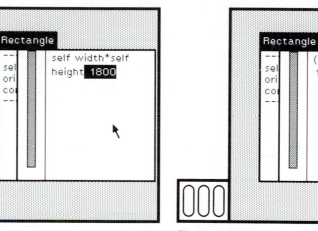

Figure 8.7c

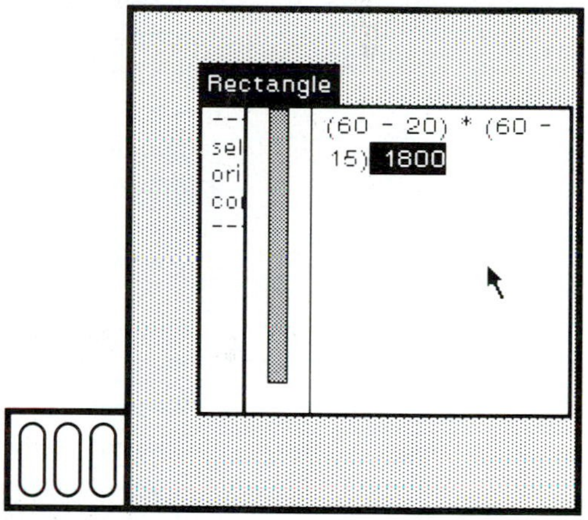

Figure 8.7d

Is the result correct? Type and evaluate either

self width * self height

or

(60 - 20) * (60 - 15)

as shown in Figures 8.7c and 8.7d. Both expressions compute the area and show that the result from evaluating the expression self area was correct.

All evaluation in the inspector is done within the context of the inspected object's variables. Thus the expression

corner - origin

can be selected and successfully evaluated in the Rectangle's inspector because the variable names are known to the inspected object.

8.4

Special Kinds of Inspectors

The message inspect is implemented in class Object. Typically, the result of the method is to create the inspectors described in the preceding sections. In addition, the system includes two special inspectors, one for instances of class Dictionary and the other for instances of class View.

Dictionary Inspector

Objects such as Dictionaries are represented with indexable instance variables. As demonstrated for an Array, the list menu of an inspector for such objects contains indices referring to the indexed variables. In the case of a Dictionary, the value of one of these variables is an association between a Dictionary key and a value. Figure 8.8a shows an example Dictionary. The special inspector for a Dictionary shows the Dictionary keys in the list menu, rather than the indices; choosing a key causes the associated value to display. Figure 8.8b shows this inspector for the example Dictionary. Editing the value and choosing the yellow button command accept stores a new value for the selected Dictionary key (Figure 8.8c).

Since the system supports the special form of inspector for a Dictionary, you have to do something special to obtain the default kind of inspector. To create the examples, first create the Dictionary Test by evaluating the following expressions.

```
Smalltalk at: #Test put: Dictionary new.
Test at: #first put: 1.
Test at: #second put: 2.
Test at: #third put: 3.
Test at: #fourth put: 4.
Test at: #fifth put: 5.
```

Now create an inspector for Test.

```
Test inspect
```

The inspector will be like the one shown in Figure 8.8b. In the text part of this inspector, evaluate the expression

```
super inspect
```

The new inspector that you create will be like the one shown in Figure 8.8a.

Besides the command inspect, the yellow button menu of the left subview of a Dictionary inspector provides commands for adding and deleting elements from the Dictionary, add field and remove. Only add field shows when no item is selected. Certain Dictionaries in the Smalltalk-80 system are used for storing references to pooled variables; the keys of such Dictionaries are variable names that can be referenced in the methods of one or more classes in the system. The yellow button menu also provides a command, references, to search for and to create a message-set browser for all methods that contain references to the selected Dictionary key. Figure 8.8d shows the yellow button menu for the Dictionary inspector. Message-set browsers are described in Chapter 10.

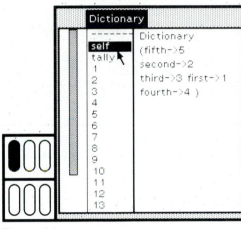

Figure 8.8a

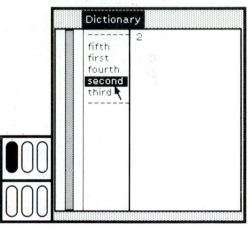

Figure 8.8b

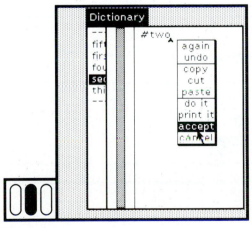

Figure 8.8c

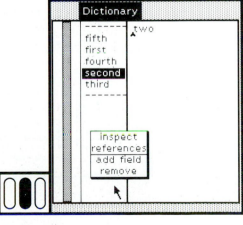

Figure 8.8d

Model-View-
Controller
Inspector

Many objects in the Smalltalk-80 system are closely related to one another. In particular, the user interface of the system is implemented using subclasses of two classes, class View and class Controller. A View represents ways of presenting information on the screen; a Controller represents ways in which the user interacts with a screen view. Any View is related to a Controller and to another object, the object whose information is accessed in the View. This other object is referred to as a "model." Whenever you inspect a View, you typically want to inspect its related model or Controller. There is a special inspector in the system for inspecting the two main objects related to a View, as well as the View, whenever a View is sent the message inspect. An illustration of this inspector is shown in Figure 8.9. It is an inspector containing three subviews, each of which is itself an inspector—one for the model, one for the View, and one for the Controller. In the figure, the model is a system browser.

In order to try to create a special inspector for a View, evaluate the expression ChangeListView new inspect. Very few of this View's variables will be initialized as yet, but you can at least explore the structure of the special inspector.

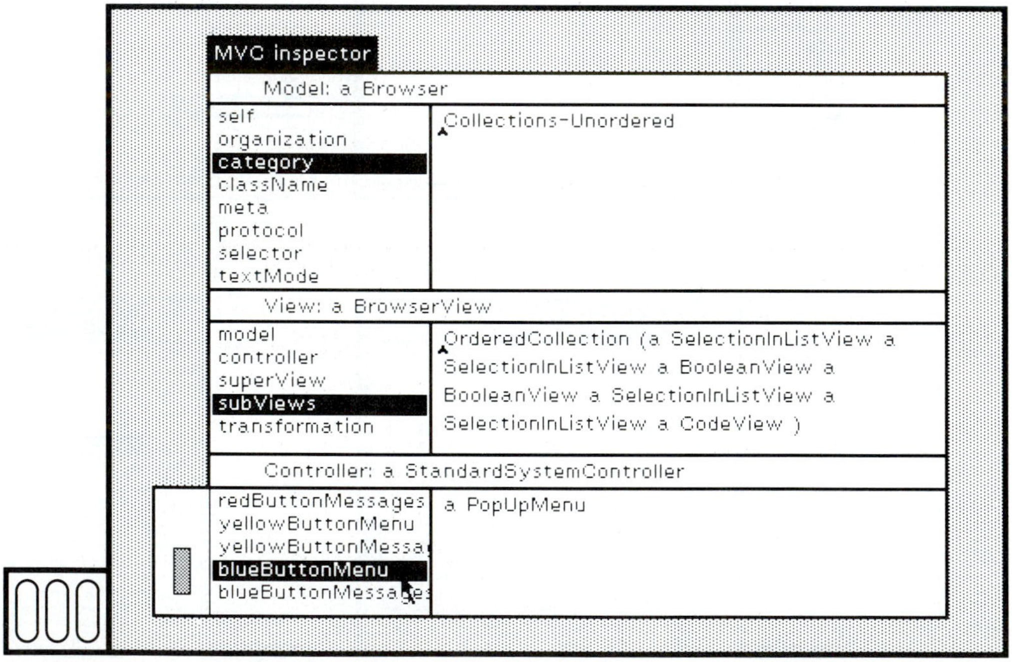

Figure 8.9

8.5

Finding Out About a Running Process

A notifier provides a simple description of an activity or *process* at the time that the activity was interrupted. Interruption can occur because of a runtime execution error, or because you purposefully cause such an interruption. This purposeful interruption is accomplished by typing ctrl c on the keyboard (that is, type "control" and the "c" keys at the same time). The notifier displays the reason for the interruption in the label of the view, and displays the sequence of messages that were invoked but not yet completed.

Try to create a notifier by typing ctrl c. The currently running process is interrupted. The notifier appears centered on the display screen. A possible interruption is shown in Figure 8.10a. Choose the yellow button command proceed in order to continue the process; when you choose proceed, the notifier is automatically closed.

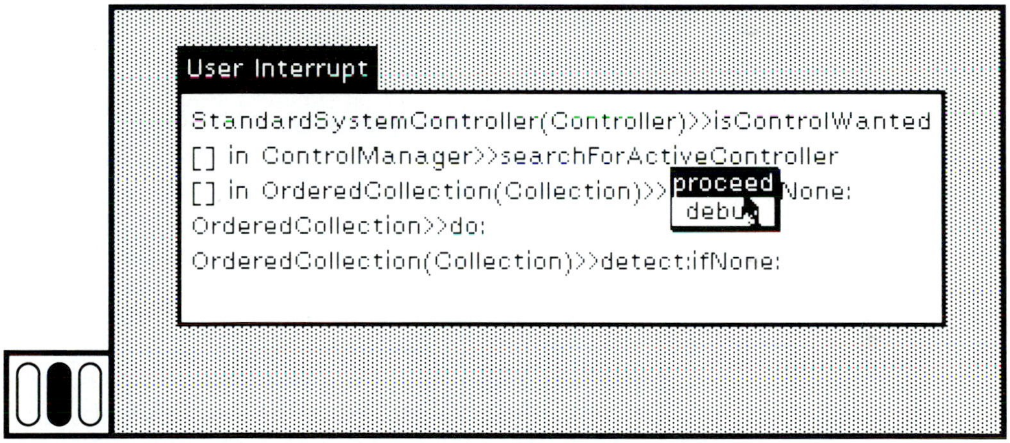

User Interrupt

StandardSystemController(Controller)>>isControlWanted
[] in ControlManager>>searchForActiveController
[] in OrderedCollection(Collection)>> proceed None:
OrderedCollection>>do: debug
OrderedCollection(Collection)>>detect:ifNone:

Figure 8.10a

Typing ctrl c can be used to interrupt a successfully running process that you wish to explore, perhaps to change the part of the system that supports the running process. Suppose you wish to know where text selection highlighting takes place in the system so that you can change the style of highlighting. While you are making a text selection, type ctrl c (Figure 8.10b).

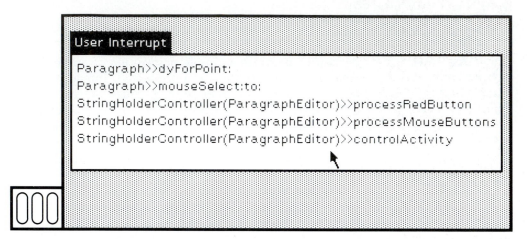

Figure 8.10b

The label of the notifier that appears indicates the reason for the interruption.

User Interrupt

The view displays a sequence of class names and message selectors whose method activations were interrupted. The notifier only displays the most recent class/message selectors of the interrupted execution.

You can choose the yellow button command debug to obtain another view of the interrupted process. This view is called a debugger. It lets you explore the methods associated with the interrupted activity, to make needed changes, and then to proceed. Further details about the debugger are given in Part Three.

A reason to interrupt a running process is to stop what appears to be a nonterminating process. When some activity seems to be taking too long, you can type ctrl c, and then determine whether to proceed or to terminate the activity. To terminate, choose the blue button command close.

The notifier view is non-preemptive. You can just leave it on the screen and do something else, returning to deal with the interrupted situation at a later time.

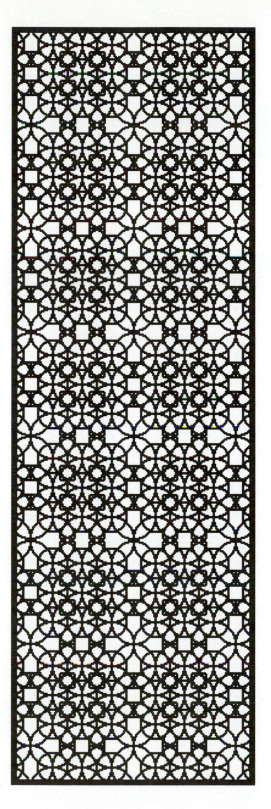

9

Finding Out About System Classes

The main way to find out about classes in the system is to use a system class browser. A browser presents a hierarchical index to information. A Smalltalk-80 class browser presents a hierarchical index to classes in the system. This index is independent of programming logic; it is designed solely for user access to class descriptions via subject categories. The browser presents categories that organize the classes within the system, and categories that organize messages within each class. The information about a class that you can retrieve using a browser includes

- a comment about the role of the class in the system

- a description of the part of the system class hierarchy in which the class is found

- a description of the variables of a class

- a description of the messages and methods of the class, including comments about the use of the message and the design of the method

- a classification of the class with respect to other classes

- a classification of the messages of the class

- access to all methods in the system that send a particular message

- access to all methods in the system that implement a particular message

- a list of all messages sent in a particular method

The system browser also provides access to templates for defining new classes and templates for defining new messages, as introduced in Section 5.4.

There are a number of class browsers in the Smalltalk-80 system, distinguished by the particular subset of classes that can be accessed. You obtain the browser for all of the classes in the system on the display screen by choosing the System Menu command browser. The browser that you see takes the form shown in Figure 9.1.

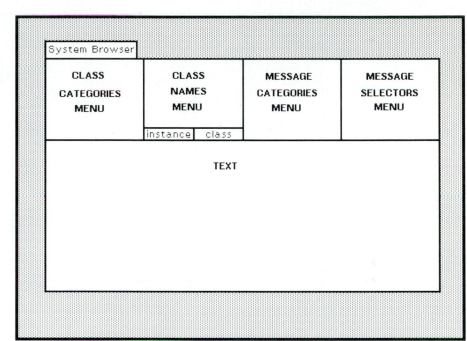

Figure 9.1

9.1

The Structure of a System Browser

The browser is made up of five subviews and two menu items labeled class and instance. When you first create a browser, the menu item instance is selected. This means that the messages you are able to retrieve are the ones sent to instances of the class, rather than to the class itself. When the menu item class is selected, the messages you are able to retrieve are the ones sent to the class itself.

Four of the subviews are fixed list menus; the fifth is a view in which methods can be defined and modified using the text editor. We will refer to the various subviews of the browser by their labels in Figure 9.1. There is a yellow button menu associated with each subview of the browser, as shown in Figure 9.2. The commands in each menu are described in this chapter.

Classes in the system are organized according to categories. In the full system browser, these categories are seen in a list menu in the first subview, which is labeled class categories menu in Figure 9.1.

Choosing an item in the class-category subview causes a list of class names to appear in the adjacent subview. This adjacent subview is labeled class names menu in Figure 9.1. For example, if you choose the item Graphics-Primitives in the class-categories subview of the class

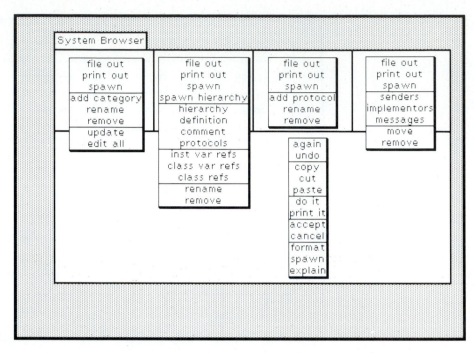

Figure 9.2

browser, a list menu of four class names appears in the adjacent subview (Figure 9.3). One of the items that appears is the class name Pen.

In addition, when a class category is selected, a template for defining a new class appears in the subview that is labeled text in Figure 9.1. The template is shown in Figure 9.3. You can edit this template in order to substitute proper names for the various parameters so that a well-formed expression is created that defines a class. When you choose the yellow button command accept, and if the edited information is syntactically correct, a new class is created (or an old one modified). The class is categorized under the class category selected in the first subview.

The subviews of the browser are thus dependent on each other. A selection in one subview specifies the information for another subview. When a class is selected in the class-names subview, its list of categories of messages appears in the adjacent subview. This subview is labeled message categories menu in Figure 9.1. In addition, when a class is selected, the class definition appears in the text subview. An example in which the class name Pen is selected is shown in Figure 9.4. By choosing yellow button commands in the class-names subview, comments about the class and the class hierarchy of the selected class can be explored, and, if appropriate, modified.

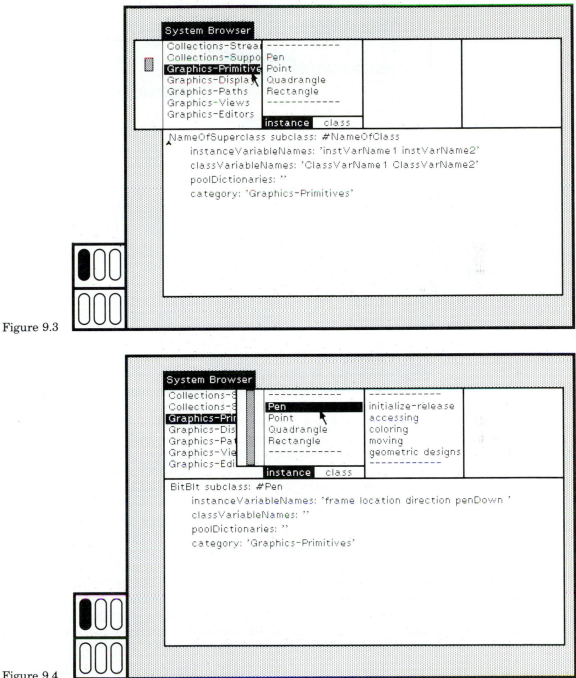

Figure 9.3

Figure 9.4

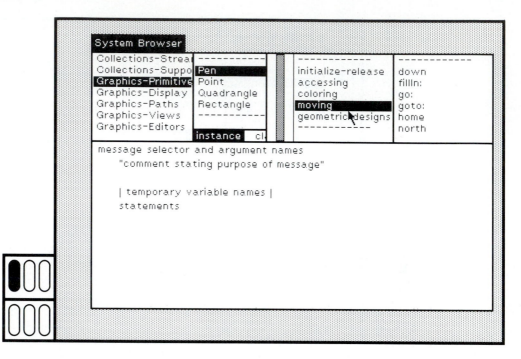

Figure 9.5

When a message category is selected, a list of messages in that category appears in its adjacent subview. The subview is labeled message selectors menu in Figure 9.1. An example is shown in Figure 9.5. In addition, when a message category is selected, a template for defining a new method appears in the text subview. You can edit this template, specifying the message pattern, a comment, and the sequence of statements. When you choose the yellow button command accept, and if the method is syntactically correct, a new method is created. It is added to the description of the selected class, categorized in the selected message category.

Choose a message selector. Its method appears in the text view. An example appears in Figure 9.6. You can edit the method using the text editor. You then recompile it and reinstall it automatically in the system by choosing the yellow button command accept in the text subview. Information about the method is provided in comments that also appear in the text view, usually at the beginning of the method. You can use the browser to find a message and its associated method in order to read the comments and to learn about the intended use of the message.

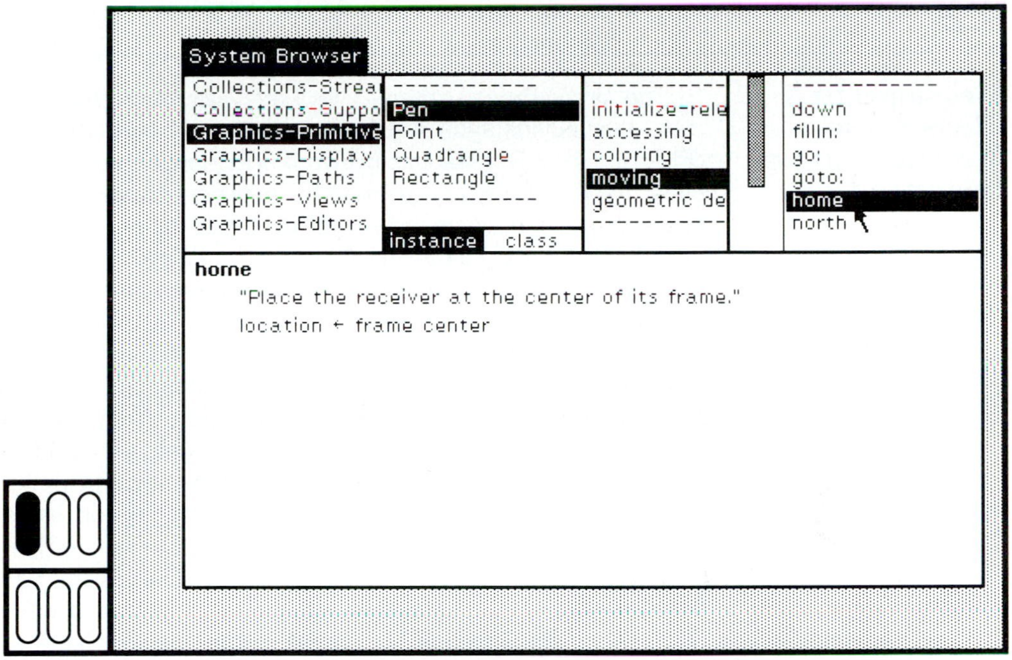

Figure 9.6

The browser search approach implies that you need to know the category of a class in order to find it in the browser. Besides exploring in the browser, you can find out the category of a class by sending it the message category. For example, the answer from the message category to the class object Pen

Pen category

is Graphics-Primitives. Type this expression in a workspace, select it, and then choose the yellow button command print it. The category name is printed. Also, as will be described at the end of this chapter, it is possible to create a browser for a subset of the information in the system. To get a browser for a single class, you create an instance of class Browser, specifying the class. For example, try evaluating the expression

Browser newOnClass: Pen

to get a browser just for class Pen.

Another approach might be to add a subview to the browser in which you can type a keyword, like a class name, to get the browser to automatically select the correct subview menu items, thus showing you the index hierarchy. Another possible feature is to be able to save the selected "query path" (the one, two, three, or four selected indices) in an additional menu so that the path can be selected directly.

9.2

Messages to a Class versus Messages to an Instance

In the preceding examples, we have assumed that the browser menu item labeled instance was selected. Now choose the item labeled class (Figure 9.7). All messages browsed will now be ones that are sent to the class itself. These are primarily instance creation messages. In many cases, these messages consist of documentation comments or examples of how to create instances of the class. A good way to learn about the Smalltalk-80 system is to explore the classes and see what examples are provided. The example methods typically include a comment that you can select and evaluate in order to invoke the example.

Choose the class category Graphics-Paths, and then choose the class name Spline (Figure 9.8). The browser menu item class should be selected. In the previous sequence of instructions, you had been directed to browse through the messages that can be sent to instances of a class. Now we can browse through the messages that can be sent to a class itself, in this case, to Spline.

Message categories that are typical for classes include class initialization (messages to create class variables), instance creation (messages to create new instances of the class), constants, queries, or examples. The description of class Spline consists of the message category examples. Choose it. In the message-selectors subview, choose the message selector

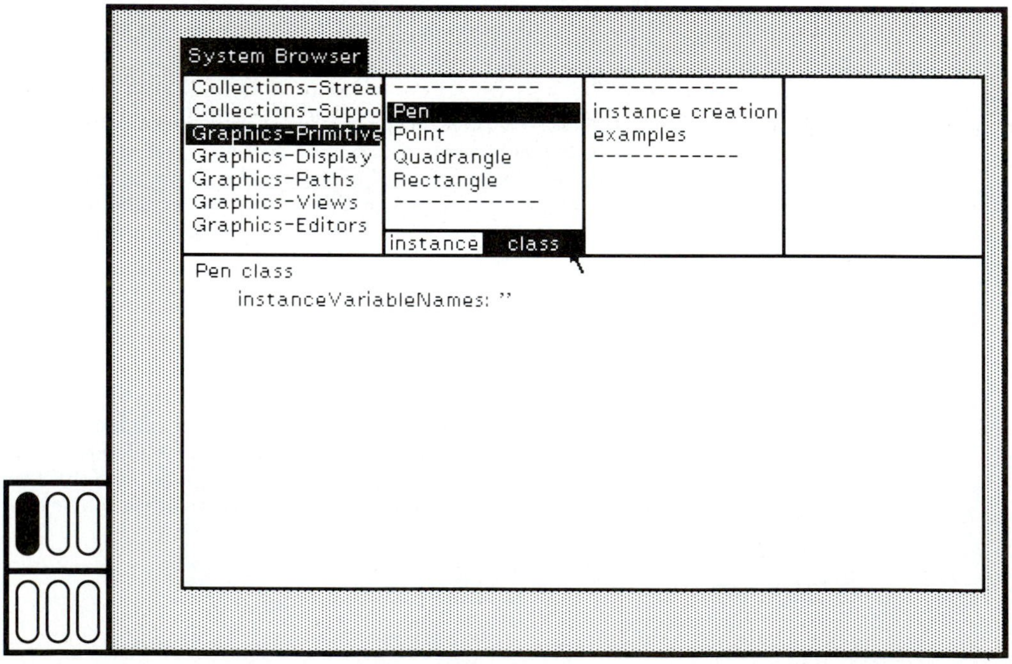

Figure 9.7

example. The selection of browser menu item class, category examples, and message selector example is shown in Figure 9.9a.

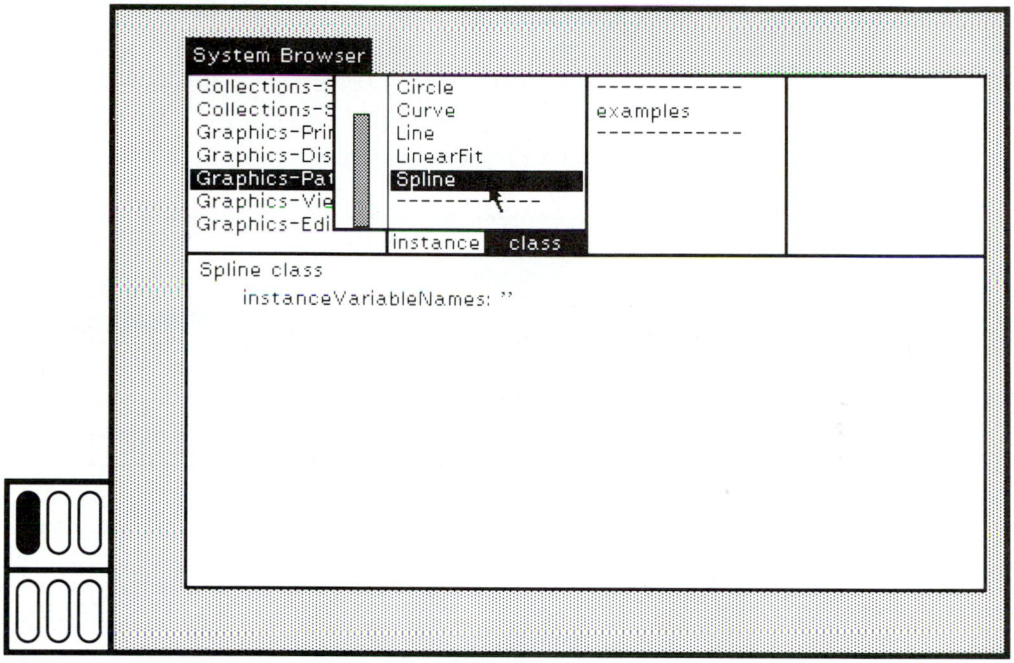

Figure 9.8

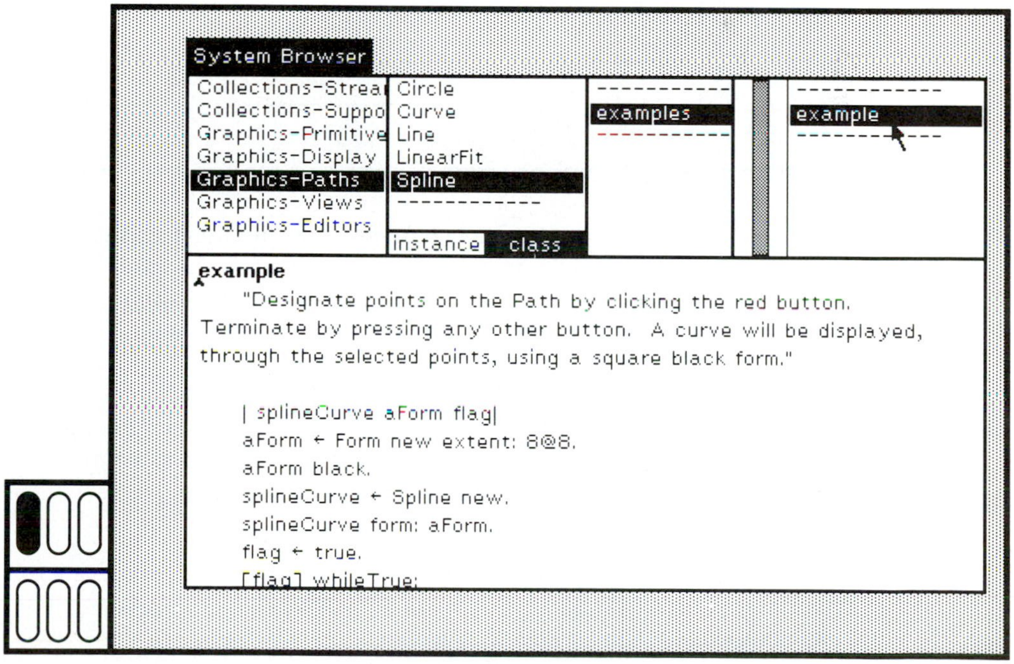

Figure 9.9a

The text subview now contains the definition of an example use of Splines. Read the comment to learn how to use the example. Now scroll to the end of the code and find text for the expression

Spline example

Select the expression and then choose the yellow button command do it so that you can try the example (Figure 9.9b).

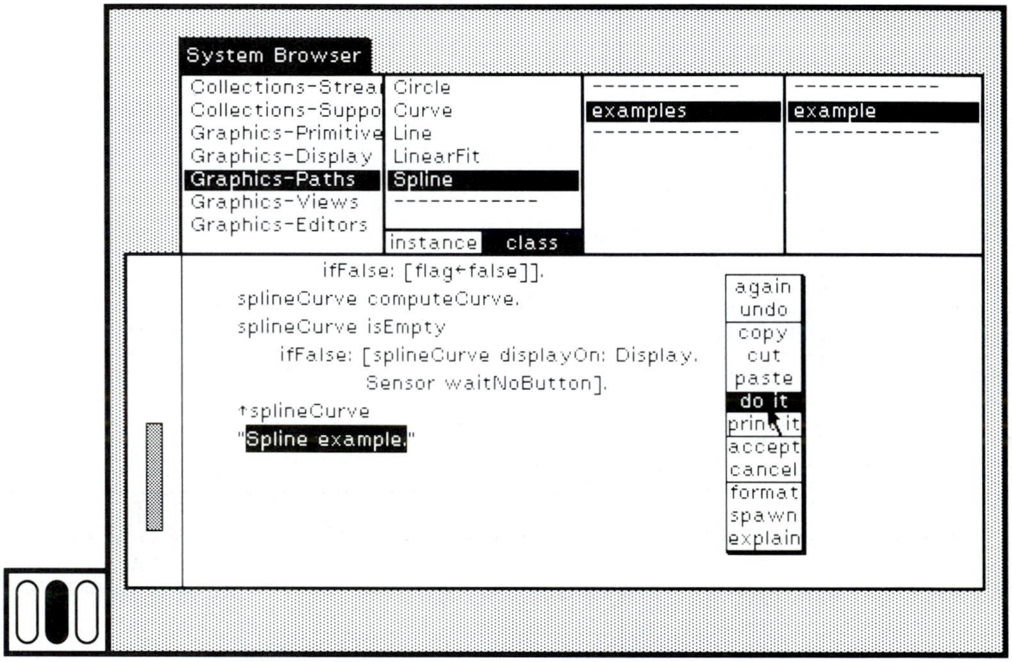

Figure 9.9b

According to the documentation included in the method, you point to several places on the screen by moving the cursor and clicking the red button (Figure 9.9c); you terminate by clicking either the yellow or blue button. The result is a curve computed using the algorithms of the spline (Figure 9.9d).

This example had the side effect of leaving marks about the screen. Choose the System Menu command restore display to clean things up. Explore other graphical objects and try the examples.

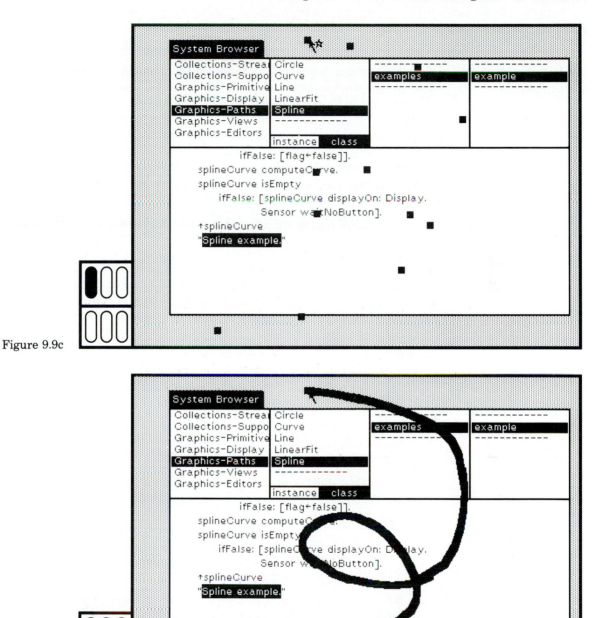

Figure 9.9c

Figure 9.9d

9.3

Browser Menu Commands

A yellow button menu can be accessed in each subview of the browser. The menus were illustrated in Figure 9.2. The use of each command is summarized in this and in the following sections.

There are three commands common to the four subviews containing list menus. These are commands for creating a file containing a version of the selected descriptions readable by the Smalltalk-80 interpreter (file out); for creating a file containing a human readable, well-formatted version of the selected descriptions (print out); and for creating a browser for a subpart of the system (spawn).

> In the Xerox systems, the command print out also creates a hardcopy version of the file.

file out	Creates a file whose name depends on the current menu selection. The file contains a Smalltalk-80 readable version of the descriptions of the selected item (classes in a category, single class, methods in a class protocol, or single method).
print out	Creates a file whose name depends on the current menu selection. The file contains a human readable ("pretty-printed") version of the descriptions of the selected item. (In a non-Xerox version of the system, this command may be identical to file out.)
spawn	Creates a browser in which only the classes included in the selected category can be accessed.

Class-Category Menu Commands

There are five additional commands in the menu of the class-category subview that pertain specifically to modifying the class categories.

file out	Creates a file whose name is the selected class category, followed by a period and the characters st. The file contains a Smalltalk-80 readable version of the descriptions of the classes in the selected category.
print out	Creates a file whose name is the selected class category. (In the Xerox system, the name is followed by a period and the characters press.) The file contains a human readable ("pretty-printed") version of the descriptions of the classes in the selected category.
spawn	Creates a browser in which only the classes included in the selected category can be accessed.

add category	Adds a new item to the class-category menu. When you choose this command, a prompter appears in which you type the category name. Choose the yellow button command accept, or type the "carriage return" key, to indicate that you are finished typing. The new category name is inserted before the current selection, and then becomes the current selection. If no item is selected when this command is chosen, then the new category is added at the end of the menu.
rename	Changes the name of the currently selected category. A prompter appears in which you edit the category name. Choose the yellow button command accept, or type the "carriage return" key, to indicate that you are finished typing.
remove	Removes the currently selected category of classes from the system. If there are any classes classified under the selected category, a confirmer appears to make certain that you wish to remove all the classes from the system. Choose yes if you do, no if you do not.
edit all	Displays the category names and message selectors in each category in the text view of the browser. The categories into which the classes are sorted can be changed using the text editor (see Section 12.6).
update	Makes certain that the classes viewed by the browser contain the latest information about these classes. This command is needed if new class descriptions are created outside this browser, for example, they are created by reading an external file, or by evaluating an expression, or by using a different browser. Such classes are categorized in a category not currently displayed in the browser.

When no class category is selected, the yellow button menu only contains the items add category, update, and edit all.

Class-Name Menu Commands

Commands in the yellow button menu for the class-name subview add queries you can make about the class—its position in the class hierarchy, a comment about the class, its definition, and its message categories. If no class name is selected, then the browser subview flashes to indicate that no yellow button menu items are appropriate.

file out	Creates a file whose name is the selected class, followed by a period and the characters st. The file contains a Smalltalk-80 readable version of the description of the class.

print out	Creates a file whose name is the selected class. (In the Xerox system, the name is followed by a period and the characters press.) The file contains a human readable version of the description of the class.
spawn	Creates a browser in which only the description of the selected class can be accessed.
spawn hierarchy	Creates a browser for the superclasses of the selected class, the selected class itself, and its subclasses, in hierarchical order.
hierarchy	Displays the names of the superclasses and subclasses of the selected class in the text view of the browser. The names are indented. A subclass name appears indented from the name of its superclass. Instance variable names declared in a class appear in parentheses after the class name.
definition	Displays the definition of the selected class in the text view of the browser. This definition can be edited. If you choose the yellow button command accept, the modified definition will be evaluated. In doing so, you can change the definition of the selected class; the system will recompile each method in the class and report any errors if previously declared variables are now undeclared. You can change the category of the class by editing the category name in the definition. The class-name menu will change appropriately. If you edit and change the class name of the definition, you can create a new class or modify one other than the selected class.
comment	Displays the current comment about the selected class in the text view of the browser. There is a default comment, namely This class has no comment, that appears when a more appropriate comment has not been provided. Edit the comment and choose the yellow button command accept to restore it.
protocols	The message categories or protocols into which the messages of a class are sorted can be changed. When you first create a class, no message categories are defined. You must add a category before you can define a method. Modifying message protocol is described in Chapter 11.
inst var refs	Displays a menu of the instance variables of instances of the selected class. Since instance variables are inherited, the menu shows the variables declared in each superclass, in alphabetical order; a line separates variables declared in each class. If you choose one of the items in the menu, a

message-set browser, as described in Chapter 10, is created for all methods that refer to the selected instance variable.

class var refs   Displays a menu of the class variables of instances of the selected class. Since class variables are inherited, the menu shows the variables declared in each superclass, in alphabetical order; a line separates variables declared in each class. If you choose one of the items in the menu, a message-set browser, as described in Chapter 10, is created for all methods that refer to the selected class variable.

class refs   Creates a message-set browser, as described in Chapter 10, for all methods that refer to the selected class.

rename   Changes the name of the selected class. A prompter appears in which you type the new class name. Choose the yellow button command accept, or type the "carriage return" key, to indicate that you are done typing. Creates a message-set browser on all methods that refer to the class.

remove   Removes the selected class from the system. When you choose this command, a confirmer will appear so that you can verify that you really want to carry out this destructive command. There is no "undo" command for retrieving removed classes.

Illustrations of some of the commands summarized above are given in the next sequence of figures. Figure 9.10a shows that class Pen is select-

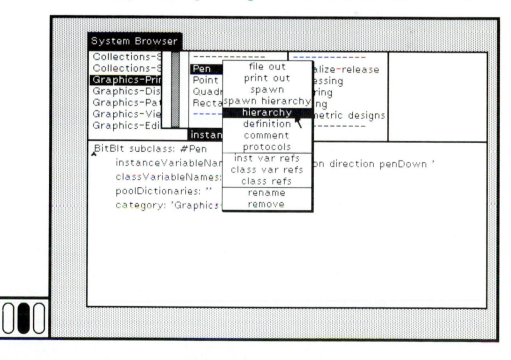

Figure 9.10a

ed and that its hierarchy is to be displayed; Figure 9.10b shows the hierarchy. Figures 9.10c and 9.10d show a comment about class Pen.

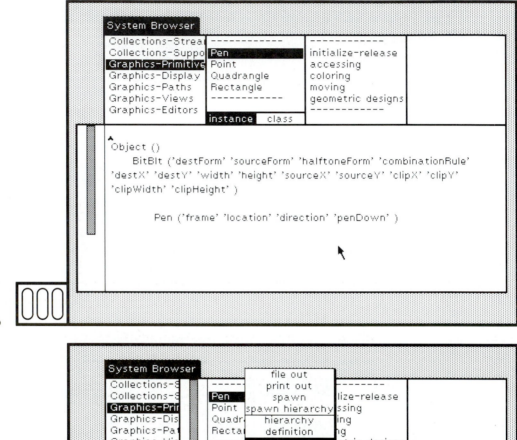

Figure 9.10b

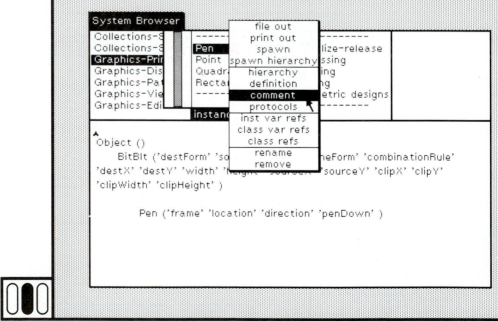

Figure 9.10c

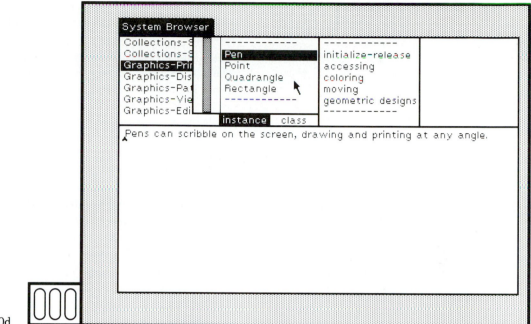

Figure 9.10d

Section 9.4 illustrates the spawn commands. Examples for commands inst var refs, class var refs, and class refs are given in Chapter 10 in which message-set browsers are explained. And the command rename is examined in Section 12.2.

Message-Category Menu Commands

The three common file and print commands appear in the yellow button menu of the message-category subview of the browser. In addition, commands that modify the message categories or protocols are provided. They are further explained in Chapters 11 and 12.

file out   Creates a file whose name is a concatenation of the selected class and message category, followed by a period and the characters st; spaces are replaced by hyphens. The file contains a Smalltalk-80 readable version of the description of the methods in the selected message category of the selected class.

print out   Creates a file whose name is a concatenation of the selected class and message category. (In the Xerox system, the name is followed by a period and the characters press; spaces are replaced by hyphens.) The file contains a human readable version of the descriptions of the methods in the selected message category of the selected class.

spawn	Creates a browser in which only the description of the selected category of messages for the selected class can be accessed.
add protocol	Adds another message category to the message-categories menu. A prompter appears in which you type the new name. The name is inserted before the currently selected category and then becomes the current selection. If no item is selected in the menu when this command is chosen, the new category is added at the end of the menu. If you type a name that already exists, it is moved to a new location (either before the current selection or at the end of the menu).
rename	Changes the name of the currently selected message category. A prompter appears in which you type the new name. If you type the name of a category that is already in the menu, no change happens.
remove	Removes the selected message category from the menu. If any messages are classified under this category, a confirmer appears to verify that you want to remove the messages from the system.

If no item is selected in the message-categories subview, then only the command add protocol is in the yellow button menu.

Message-Selector Menu Commands

Commands in the yellow button menu for the message-selector subview add queries you can make about methods and messages.

file out	Creates a file whose name is a concatenation of the selected class and message selector, followed by a period and the characters st; spaces and colons are replaced by hyphens. The file contains a Smalltalk-80 readable version of the description of the method for the selected message selector.
print out	Creates a file whose name is a concatenation of the selected class and message selector. (In the Xerox system, the name is followed by a period and the characters press; spaces and colons are replaced by hyphens.) The file contains a human readable version of the description of the method for the selected message selector.
spawn	Creates a browser in which only the description of the selected message for the selected class can be accessed.
senders	Creates a message-set browser for all methods in the system in which the selected message is sent.

implementors	Creates a message-set browser for all methods in the entire system which implement the selected message.
messages	Creates a menu of the message selectors for each message sent in the currently selected method. If you then choose one of these selectors, you create a message-set browser on all of its implementors.
move	Moves the selected message to another message category. A prompter appears in which you type the name of the designation message category. If it already exists, the message is reclassified. If the designation message category is new, it is added to the message-categories menu, at the end. The current message category remains the current selection. You can also type the name of a class and a protocol in order to copy the selected message to a different class. The syntax is className > protocolName. (If you type the class name of the currently selected class, the result is the same as though you did not mention the class name.)
remove	Removes the selected message from the selected class. A confirmer appears so that you can verify that you really want to carry out this destructive command. There is no "undo" command for retrieving removed messages.

The commands senders, implementors, and messages are explained in more detail in Chapter 10. Examples of modifying the protocols of a class are given in Chapter 11.

Text Subview Menu Commands

The yellow button menu for the text subview of the browser contains the text editing commands presented in Chapter 3 (again, undo, copy, cut, paste) and the expression evaluation commands of Chapter 6 (do it, print it). There are five additional commands.

format	The system has some notion of how to format a method so that the indenting and line breaks increase the human readability of the code. Choosing this command when the text view contains a method (that you have retrieved but have not modified as yet), creates a "pretty-printed" version of the code. You can then modify it to suit your own style.
accept	In the context of a method, this means "compile" the code. If there are any syntax errors, display them; if not, the compiled method is stored into the system. In the context of a class definition or comment, the text is an expression that is evaluated. In the context of categories, the syntax is checked and the new categories stored.

cancel

Text that appears in the subview has presumably been modified but you do not want to retain the modification. The text is replaced by the version prior to any modification. The commands accept and cancel work as pairs— cancel returns the text to the version last stored using accept.

spawn

Creates a browser for the currently selected message and the current version of the method (which possibly has been modified but not stored). The text in the original browser will be restored as though you had chosen the cancel command. The text in the new browser is not yet accepted as the compiled method.

explain

The text in a method consists of a sequence of tokens, for example, syntactic entities such as ↑ and], and variable names. Select one. The result of choosing the command explain is to determine a comment that explains the use of the selected token. The comment is inserted into the text, after the token. It becomes the selected text.

☐ *Spawning a Message Browser* As noted in the summary of commands, a way to create a browser on a single message is to choose the command spawn from the yellow button menu of the text subview of a browser. Suppose you have been editing a method, you have not yet saved the method by choosing the command accept, and then you decide that you want to put aside your work for awhile in order to explore the previous version of the method or to search in the browser for other information. Choose the spawn command. You are asked to designate a rectangular area for a browser for the currently selected message, with the edited text as the method. The text in the original browser will be restored as though you had chosen the cancel command. The text in the new browser is not yet accepted as the compiled method.

You might also use spawn to copy a view of a method onto the screen while you use the full browser to find other information. Any browser view of a method in which the editor is available can be used to change the method and then to recompile and re-store it. Changes made to a method in any view are shared by the whole system (although you might have to specifically request an update to see shared changes).

In the next figure, the text in the Pen method hilbert:side: has been edited from the original (Figure 9.11a). Spawning causes the original method to show in the system browser and the edited version shows in a newly created message browser (Figure 9.11b). Note that the difference is in the formatting of the visible conditional statement.

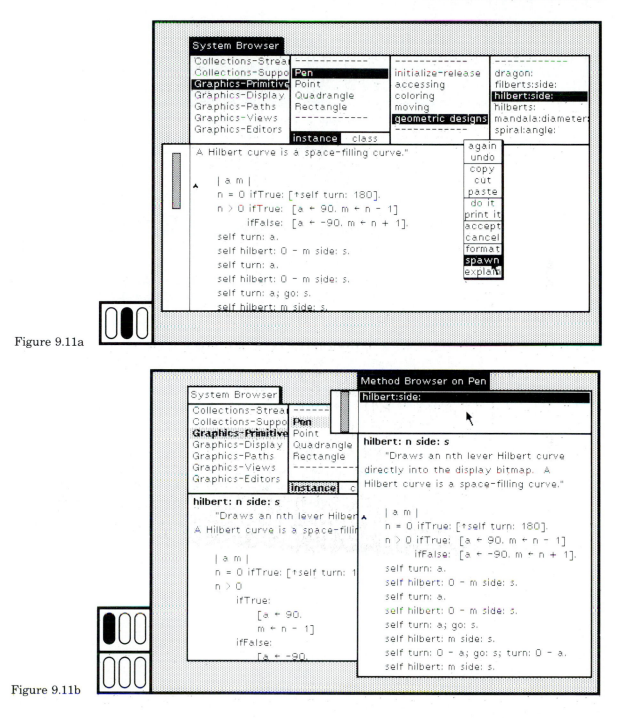

Figure 9.11a

Figure 9.11b

☐ *Explanations* There are several views in the system in which methods are retrieved and displayed, including the system browsers and the debugger. The yellow button menu in the text part of these views includes the command explain. You can choose this command to receive an explanation about a syntactic or semantic part of the method.

The command explain works by examining the current text selection and determining what role the text plays in the method. The text selection must be a single token (such as a period, message keyword, or variable name) or a syntactic construct (that is, a single-quoted, or double-quoted sequence of characters, or characters delimited by square brackets). In Figures 9.12a and 9.12b, an explanation is requested and received for the left-arrow (←). The explanation is inserted after the current text selection and then becomes the text selection.

The most significant explanation is for a single token that is a variable name or a message selector. The explanation will identify where the variable is declared, i.e., global, instance, class, or pool, and in which classes the message is defined, respectively. In Figures 9.13a and 9.13b, an explanation for the global variable Sensor is requested and received; it is an instance of class InputSensor.

In Figures 9.14a and 9.14b, an explanation for the class name Form is obtained. Typically the explanation is a comment, but, in some useful cases, it is an expression that can be evaluated in order to obtain further information. For example, if the token selected is a class name, then the explanation is a comment and an expression that can be evaluated in order to create a browser for just that class. The result of choosing do it when the explanation is selected (Figure 9.14c) is to create a browser for class Form (Figure 9.14d).

The best way to learn about explain is to try it. Once you learn how to use a browser and can retrieve a method, simply make selections of parts of the method and select the yellow button command explain. If no explanation is possible, it will say so.

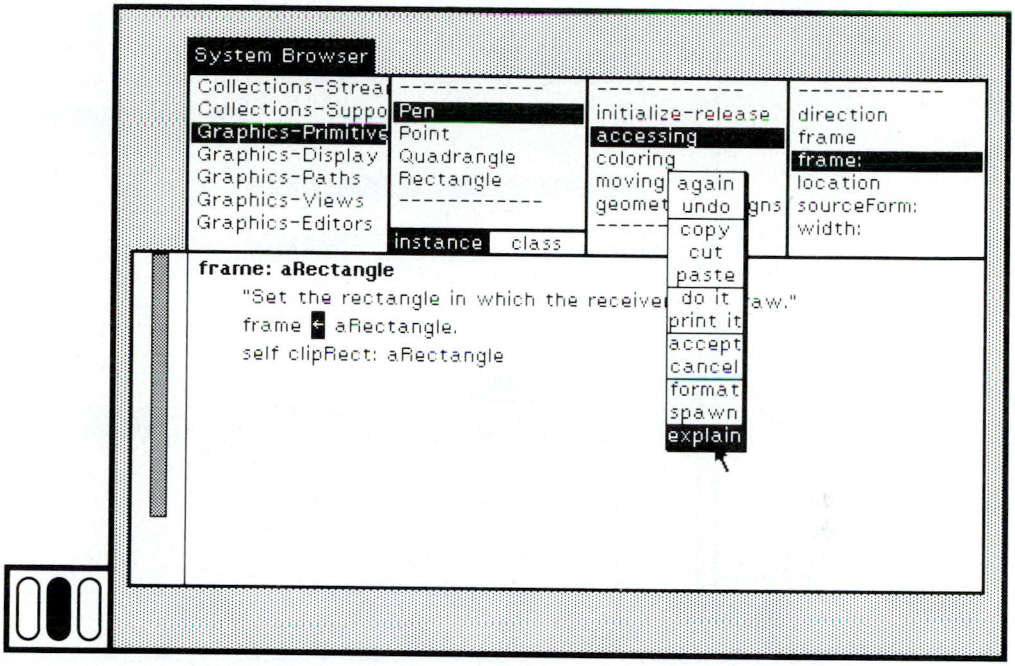

Figure 9.12a

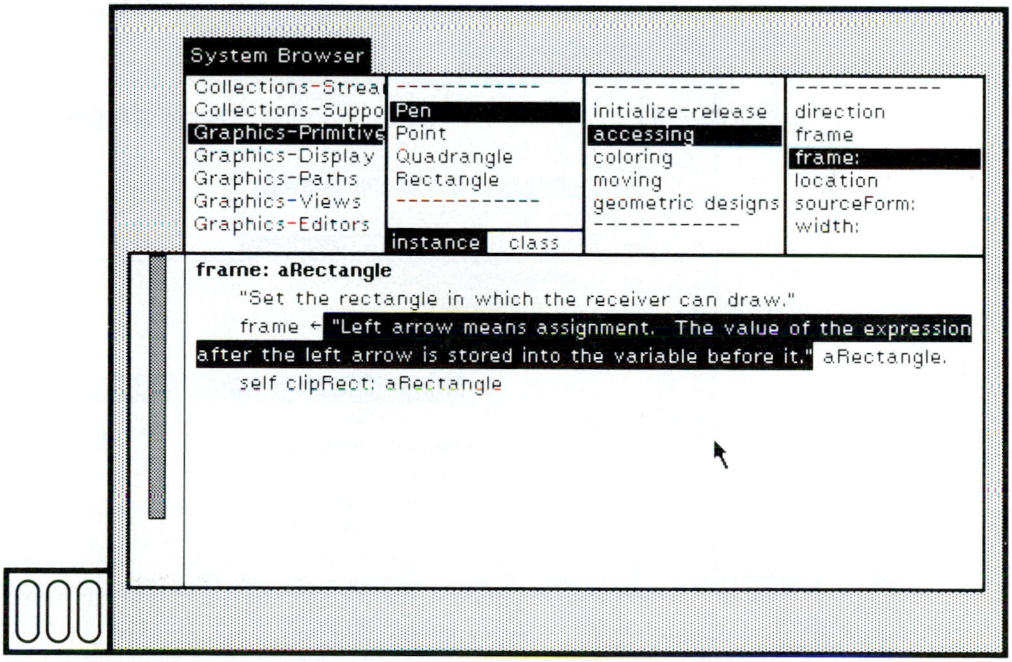

Figure 9.12b

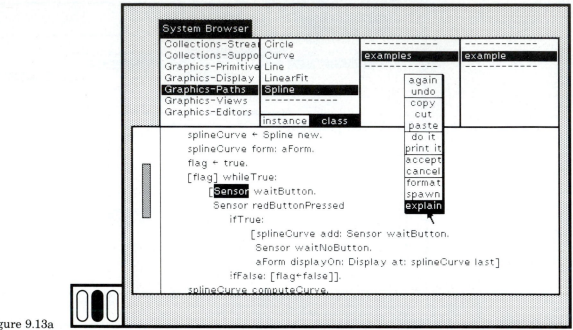

Figure 9.13a

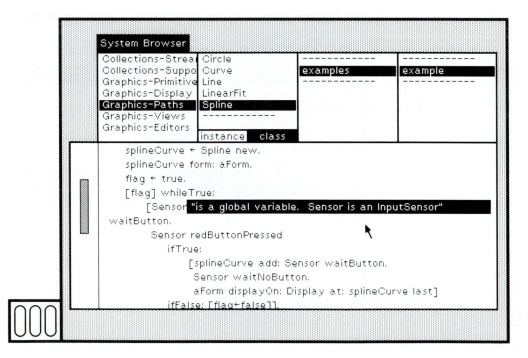

Figure 9.13b

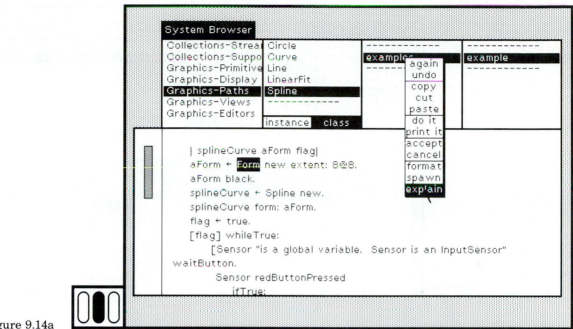

Figure 9.14a

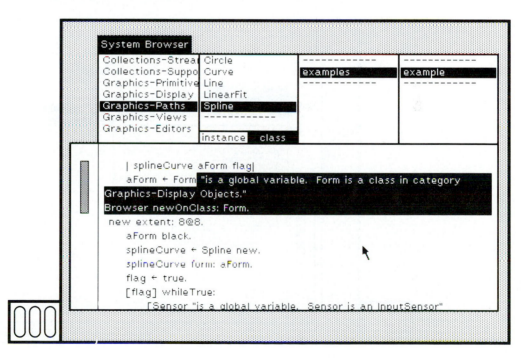

Figure 9.14b

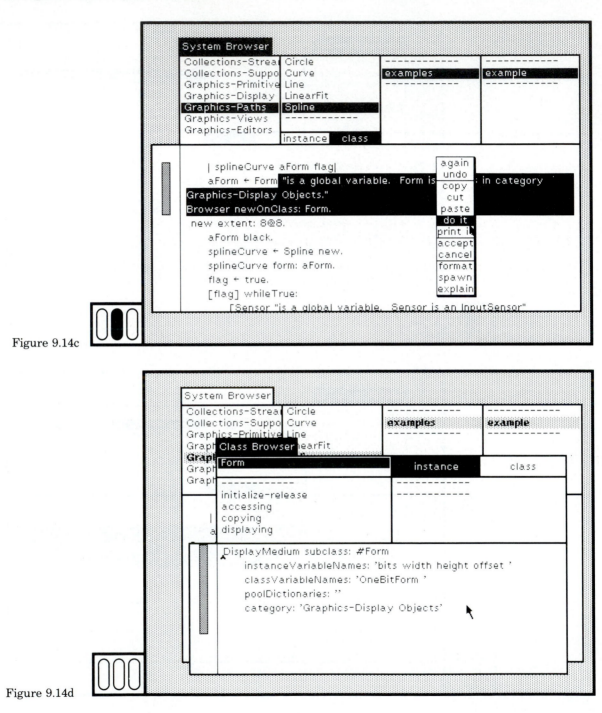

Figure 9.14c

Figure 9.14d

9.4

Browsing a Subset of the System

As noted in the previous sections, in each of the browser subviews containing list menus, the yellow button menu includes the command spawn. Choosing this command creates a browser for accessing a subset of the information available from the system browser. In particular, you can create a *System Category Browser* by choosing the command spawn in the yellow button menu of the class-categories subview (Figures 9.15a and 9.15b). This browser gives you access to all the classes within the currently selected class category only.

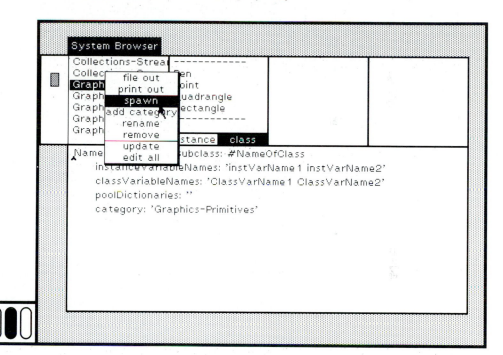

Figure 9.15a

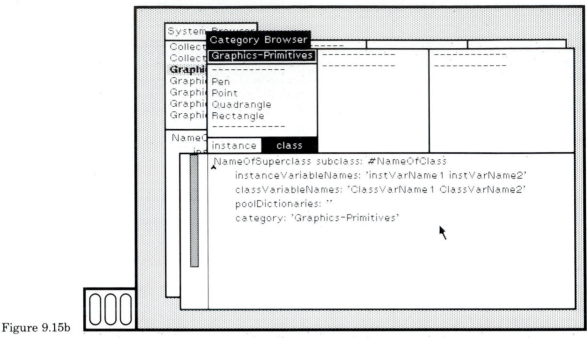

Figure 9.15b

You can create a *Class Browser* by choosing the command spawn in the yellow button menu of the class-names subview (Figures 9.16a and 9.16b). This browser gives you access only to the description of the currently selected class.

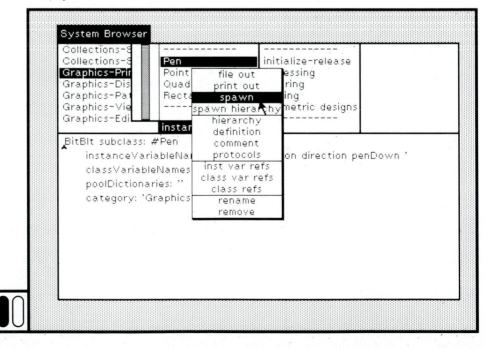

Figure 9.16a

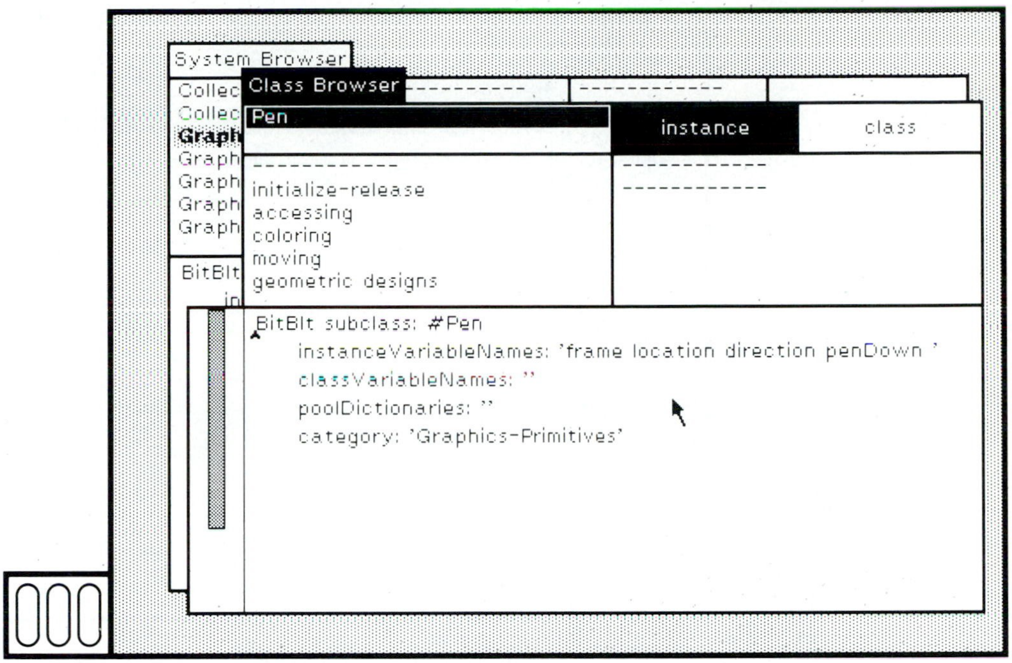

Figure 9.16b

You can create a *Message Category Browser* (or "protocol browser") by selecting the command **spawn** in the yellow button menu of the message-categories subview (Figures 9.17a and 9.17b). This browser gives

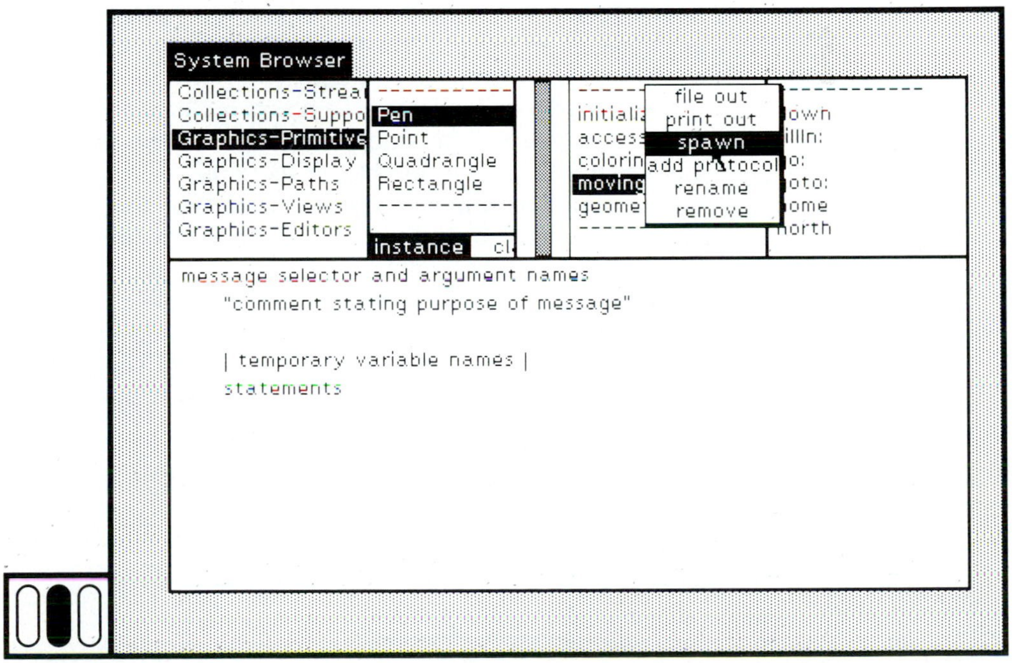

Figure 9.17a

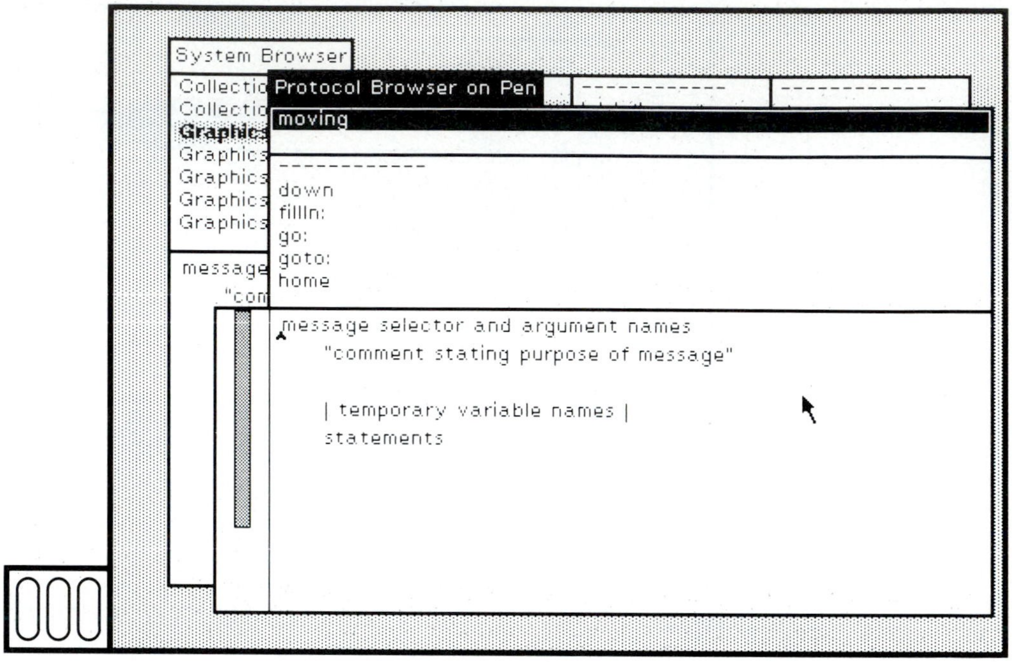

Figure 9.17b

you access only to the methods of the currently selected category of messages.

And you can create a *Message Browser* by selecting the command **spawn** in the yellow button menu of the message-selectors subview (Figures 9.18a and 9.18b). This browser gives you access only to the method of the currently selected message.

The purpose in providing so many optional views of the system classes is to support your ability to constrain the information with which you are working. You might, for example, be developing an application class and prefer to have a browser that only accesses this one class. You might be copying code from classes in one category into your new class, and thus you might find it convenient to focus your attention by having a class-category browser for this category. More signficantly, you might create an applications/programming environment in which you want your user to have access to a subset only of the system, to protect the user from dealing with too much extraneous information, or to protect the system from the user.

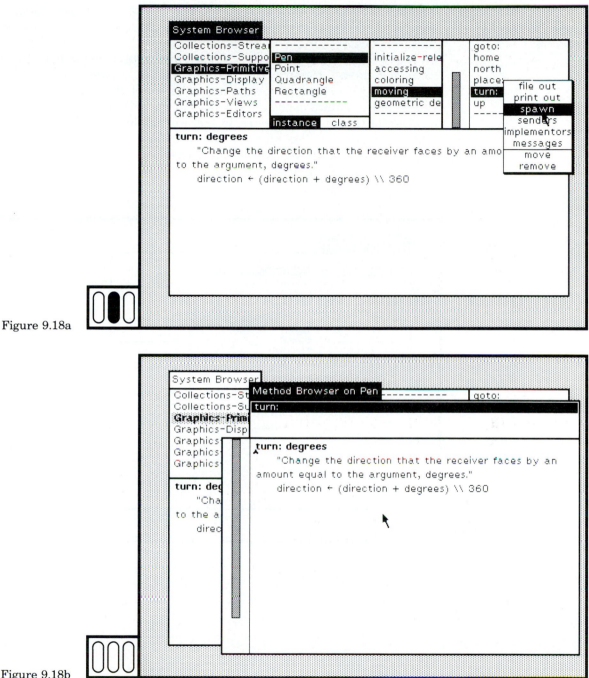

Figure 9.18a

Figure 9.18b

Another interesting browser that you can spawn is a *Class Hierarchy
Browser*. This browser gives you access to a class, its superclasses, and
its subclasses.

You create a class hierarchy browser by choosing the yellow button
command spawn hierarchy in the class-names subview of a system
browser (Figure 9.19a). The class-names menu of the new browser will
consist of the names of the superclasses of the selected class, the selected class itself, and its subclasses, in hierarchical order.

An example of a class hierarchy browser for Boolean, which is a subclass of Object and has two subclasses, True and False, is shown in Figure 9.19b. An example of a class hierarchy browser for Collection is
shown in Figure 9.19c.

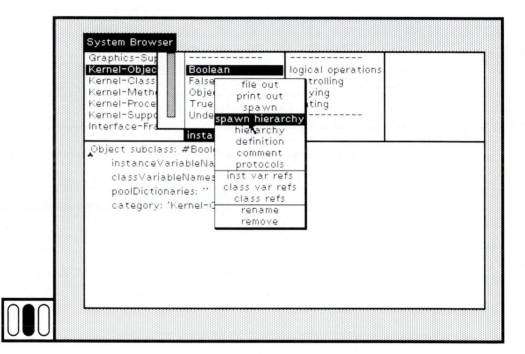

Figure 9.19a

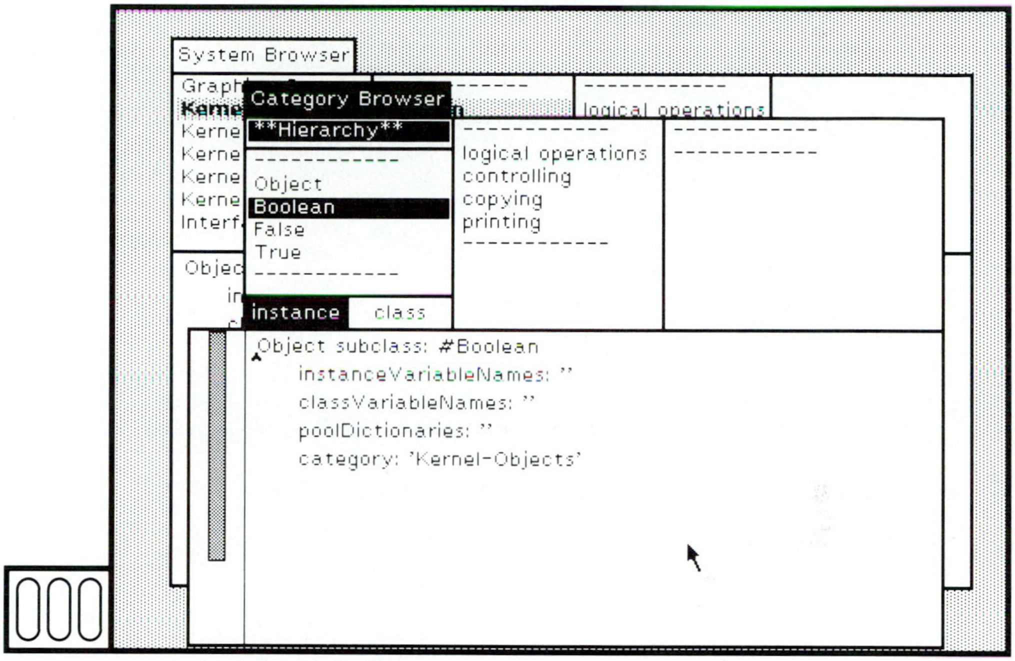

Figure 9.19b

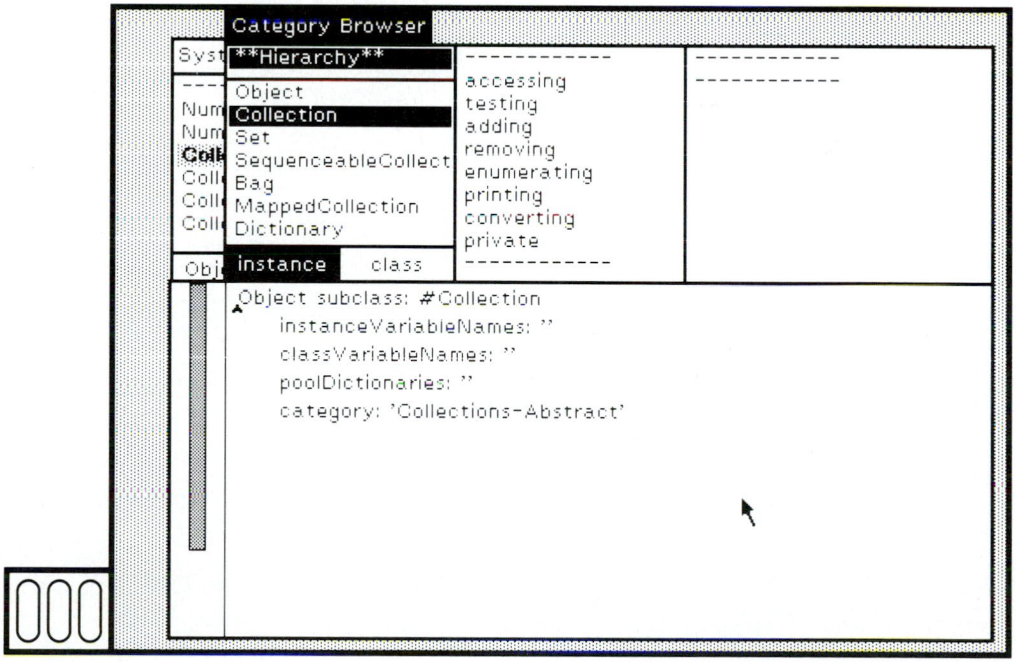

Figure 9.19c

10

Finding Out About Messages and Methods

Message-set Browsers provide a way of collecting and exploring a group of related messages. The name reflects the idea that the response to the query is a set of methods. Since a method is specified by a class and a message selector, these sets are viewed as a set of class/message pairs. This kind of browser makes it possible for you to inspect and modify the methods associated with each pair.

A message-set browser consists of two subviews. The top subview is a fixed list menu that indicates the names of the class/message pairs. When you choose one of the pairs, the associated method is displayed in the bottom subview. This bottom subview is a text subview in which you can edit the method and then choose the command accept to compile and store the changes.

Message-set browsers are created in order to answer one of three kinds of queries about messages:

- Which methods send a particular message?

- Which classes implement a particular message?

- Which messages are sent in a particular method?

These queries can be made in a system browser by choosing the yellow button commands senders, implementors, or messages, respectively, in the message-selector subview. These are useful browsers to employ when you are tracking down erroneous behavior in your programs, or when you are interested in trying to find out how a message is used or implemented in the system. For example, the combination of examining the hierarchy of a class and of browsing all implementors of a message defined in that class, helps identify where the method for that message is actually found by the interpreter during execution (in the class or in one of its subclasses or superclasses).

10.1

Which Methods Send a Particular Message?

Choosing the command senders creates a message-set browser for all methods in the entire system in which the selected message is sent. If no such methods exist, then the word Nobody appears in the System Transcript (if the transcript is a scheduled view and is not collapsed).

Suppose that you wish to understand how a particular message is used in the system. You can select the message in a class browser and read the comment. This will tell you the intended use of the message. You can then see examples of how to use the message by creating a message-set browser on all senders of the message. The next sequence of figures illustrates the steps: selecting a message in a class browser (Figure 10.1a), then choosing the command senders (Figure 10.1b).

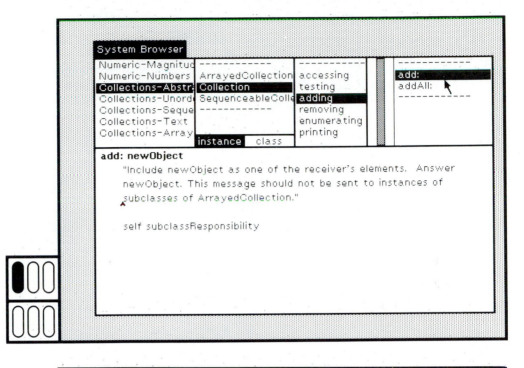

Figure 10.1a

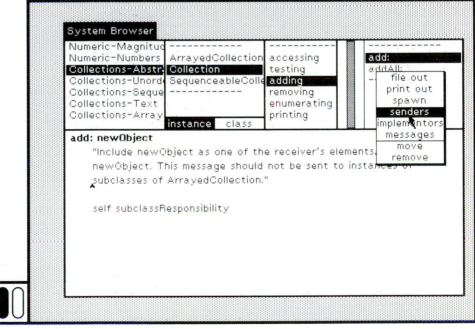

Figure 10.1b

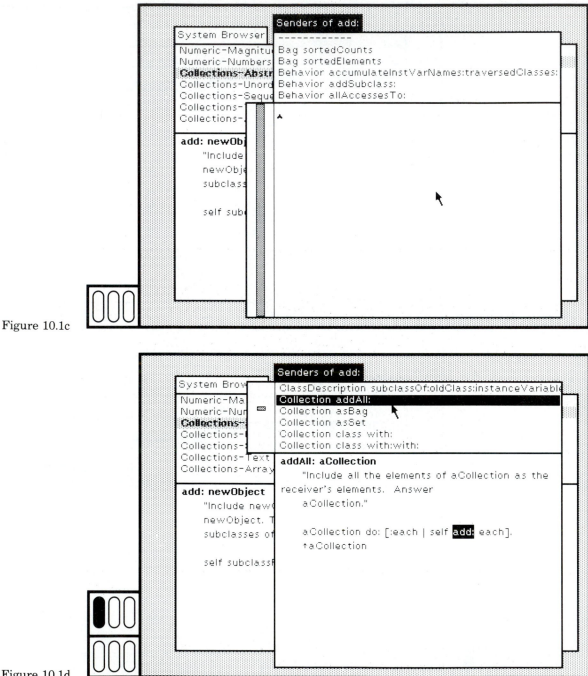

Figure 10.1c

Figure 10.1d

This gets the message-set browser (Figure 10.1c). Then choose one of the class/message pairs to see a method in which the message is used (Figure 10.1d).

10.2

Which Classes Implement a Particular Message?

Choosing the command implementors creates a message-set browser for all methods in the entire system which implement the selected message. If no such methods exist, then the word Nobody appears in the System Transcript (if it is scheduled and displayed on the screen). An example of finding all the implementors for the message selector add: is shown in Figures 10.2a and 10.2b.

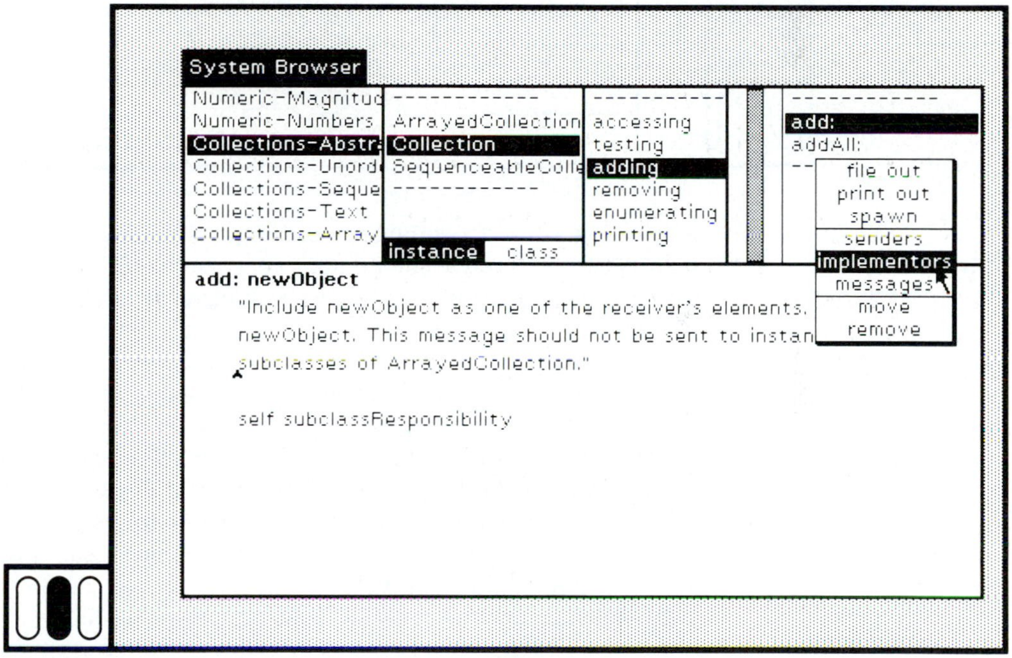

Figure 10.2a

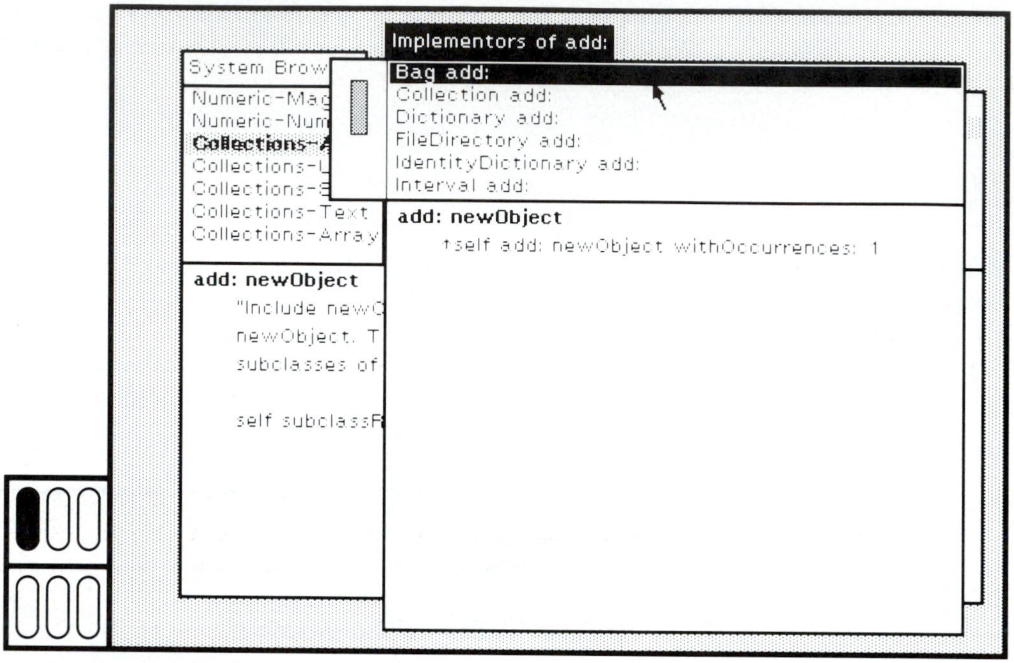

Figure 10.2b

Renaming a Message Selector

When you want to rename a message selector, you will find the commands senders and implementors very useful. Before renaming the message, you first find out if any subclasses exist that override the
implementation of the message. You do this by choosing the yellow button command implementors in the message-selectors subview. This will
give you a message-set browser that indicates which classes implement
the message. Then you choose the yellow button command hierarchy in
a class-names subview of a class browser. This will display the portion
of the class hierarchy in which the selected class (the one that contains
the message selector whose name you want to change) resides. If any of
the subclasses of the selected class implement the message, you will
have to rename them as well.

In order to do the rename, first edit the original method in order to
replace the message selector. Then choose the yellow button command
accept. Now both the old and the new messages exist. Do the same for
each subclass—you can do the editing in the message-set browser of the
implementors. Second, select the message selector to be removed and
then choose the yellow button command senders in the class browser
message-selectors subview. This will give you a message-set browser on
all methods that send messages with the old selector, unless none exist.
Edit each method in which you wish to use the new message selector
name. Close the message-set browser. Now choose the implementors
command again, just to make certain that you found all the references

that have to be changed. If all are correctly changed, you can remove the old message in the class and in each subclass using the command remove from the yellow button menu of the message-selectors subview.

10.3

Which Messages are Sent in a Particular Method?

Choosing the command messages creates a menu of the selectors for each message sent in the currently selected method (Figures 10.3a and 10.3b). You can then select one of these in order to create a message-set browser on all of its implementors (Figures 10.3c and 10.3d). Notice that this menu is a list menu; it remains on the screen until you click a button. If you press the red button inside the menu area, you can select one of the menu items; when you release the button, the item is chosen. Like a pop-up menu, releasing the button outside the menu chooses no item. After clicking a button, the menu is removed from the screen.

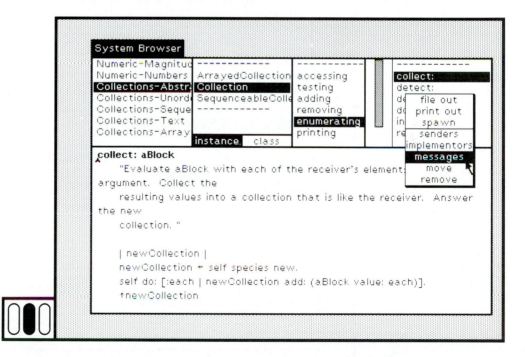

Figure 10.3a

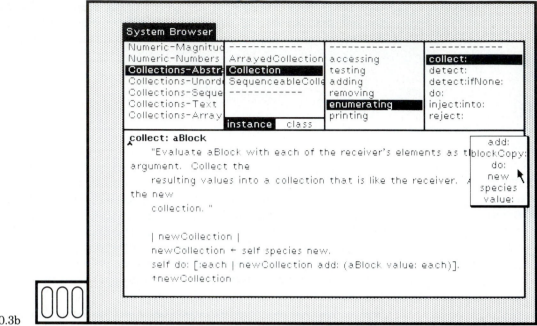

Figure 10.3b

Figure 10.3c

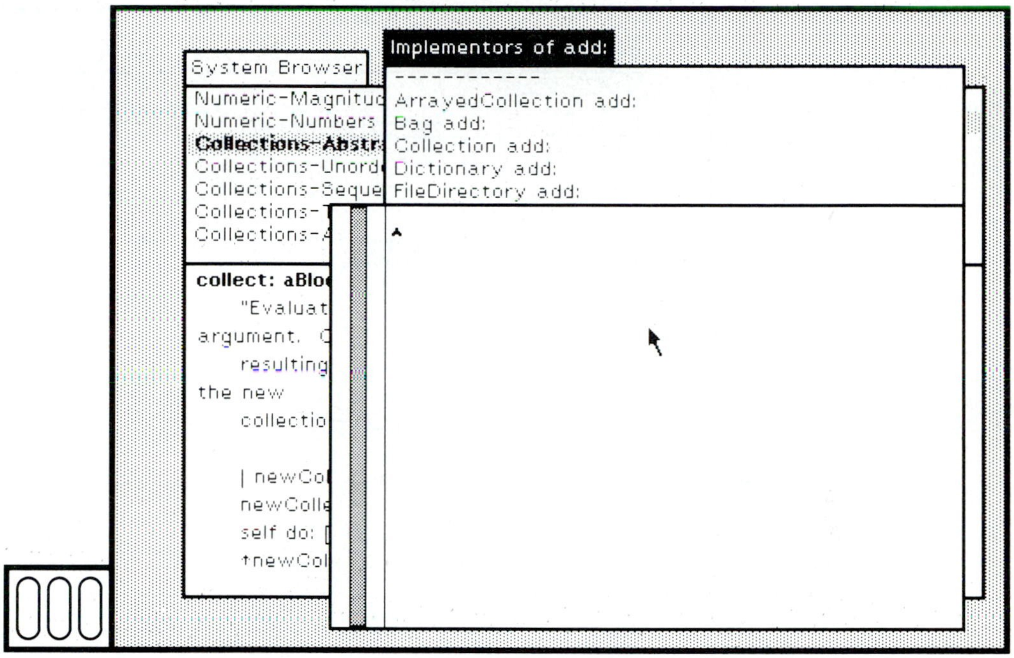

Figure 10.3d

The messages command is useful in trying to understand how a method actually works. It supports your ability to track down comments about the methods for each of the messages sent.

Note that in the examples, the message blockCopy: appears as one of the messages in the selected method. This message is inserted by the compiler whenever a block is used in a method.

☐ *Practice Investigating Messages* Using the system browser, choose class category Collections-Abstract (class-categories subview), choose class Collection (class-names subview), and, in the class-names subview, choose the yellow button command hierarchy. The selections and hierarchy are shown in Figure 10.4. Collection is the top of a large hierarchy of data structures for the system. It is an abstract class, meaning no instances of it should be created. It serves the purpose of defining a common protocol for several similar classes, such as Set and OrderedCollection.

Choose message category adding and then message selector add:. The method is defined as self subclassResponsibility. This means that subclasses of Collection for which instances can be created must reimplement the method in order to complete the description of the class.

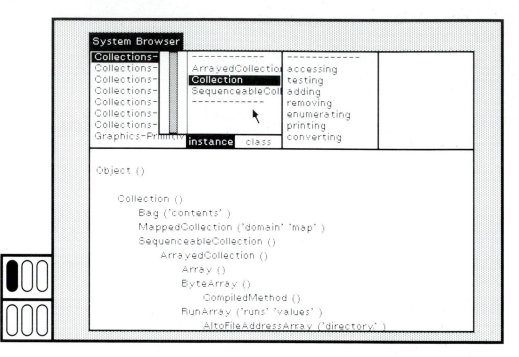

Figure 10.4

Suppose you implemented the collection data structures and you want to find out whether all the subclasses of Collection are complete with respect to the message add:. One way to make this determination is to find all the classes that implement the message add: and see if all the subclasses of Collection are in the list. Some will not be, for example, class SequenceableCollection. This subclass is itself abstract. You can find where add: is implemented by choosing in the message-selectors subview the yellow button command implementors. The browser thus created is a message-set browser giving you a list of the classes in which the message add: is implemented. If you choose an item from this list, you can see the actual implementation. By selecting Collection in the browser and choosing the command hierarchy, you can determine all the subclasses of Collection to be compared to those referred to in the message-set browser.

Find the message addAllFirst: in class OrderedCollection. The class is categorized under Collections-Sequenceable; the message is categorized under adding. In the message-selectors subview, choose the yellow button command senders (Figure 10.5a). Watch the System Transcript; the word Nobody will appear (Figure 10.5b). This indicates that no objects in the system send the message; it was included for protocol completeness. (Recall that if no System Transcript appears on your screen, so that you can not try this example, you can create one by choosing the System Menu command system transcript.)

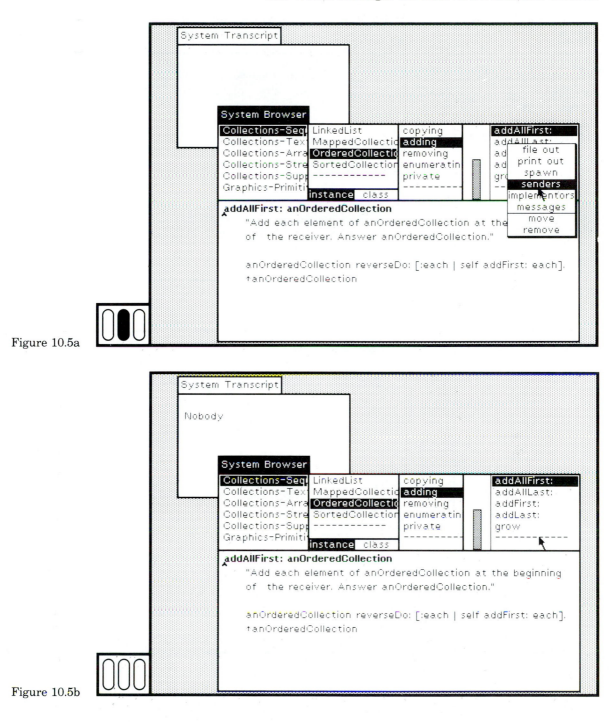

Figure 10.5a

Figure 10.5b

10.4

Which Methods Reference a Particular Variable or Literal?

A message-set browser can also be obtained by sending one of several available messages to the object Smalltalk, an instance of SystemDictionary. All of the expressions listed in this section are present as templates in the System Workspace, so you can find them, edit the arguments, and evaluate the expressions.

Smalltalk browseAllCallsOn: #keywordSymbol

(where the keywordSymbol is a single keyword such as at:, put:, +, or up) will create a message-set browser for all messages whose methods send a message with keyword keywordSymbol. The result of evaluating

Smalltalk browseAllCallsOn: #add:

is shown in Figure 10.6.

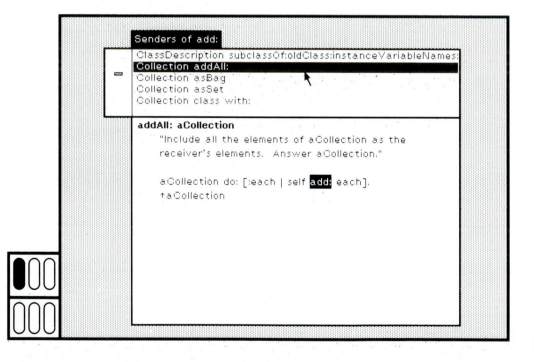

Figure 10.6

207

10.4 Which Methods Reference a Particular Variable or Literal?

The expression

Smalltalk
    browseAllCallsOn: #firstKeywordSymbol
    and: #secondKeywordSymbol

creates a message-set browser for all messages in the system whose methods send a message with both keywords firstKeywordSymbol and secondKeywordSymbol. For example, the result of evaluating

Smalltalk browseAllCallsOn: #at: and: #at:put:

is shown in Figure 10.7. The messages browseAllCallsOn: and browseAllCallsOn:and: can be sent to individual classes to obtain a message-set browser for methods in the class and its subclasses.

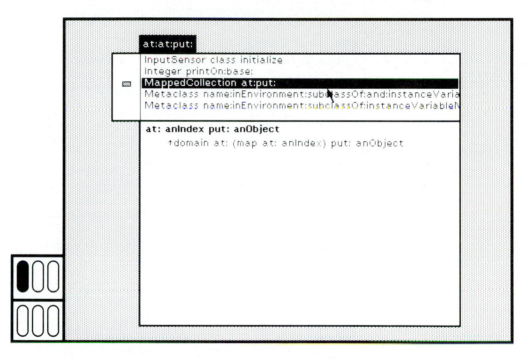

Figure 10.7

In order to obtain a message-set browser that provides access to all methods in the system that reference a particular literal, aSymbol, (see Chapter 5 for the definitions of syntactic parts), evaluate an expression of the form

Smalltalk browseAllCallsOn:
    (aSystemDictionary associationAt: #aSymbol)

For example, the result of evaluating

Smalltalk browseAllCallsOn: (Smalltalk associationAt: #Transcript)

is shown in Figure 10.8, and the result of evaluating

Smalltalk browseAllCallsOn: (TextConstants associationAt: #Centered)

is shown in Figure 10.9.

An additional way to obtain all the implementors of a message is to evaluate an expression of the form

Smalltalk browseAllImplementorsOf: #messageSelector

For example, the result of evaluating

Smalltalk browseAllImplementorsOf: #at:put:

is shown in Figure 10.10.

An expression of the form

Smalltalk browseAllSelect: aBlockWithOneArgument

creates a message-set browser on all methods such that when the block is evaluated with the method as its argument, the result is true. As an example, you can try

Smalltalk browseAllSelect: [:meth | meth numLiterals > 40]

creates a message-set browser showing methods that have more than 40 literals (Figure 10.11).

Please note that the Smalltalk-80 system restricts methods to have no more than 64 literals.

209

10.4 Which Methods Reference a Particular Variable or Literal?

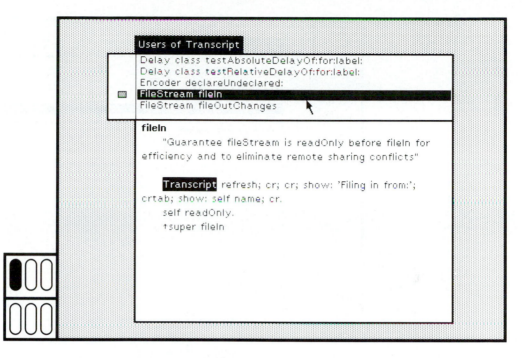

Figure 10.8

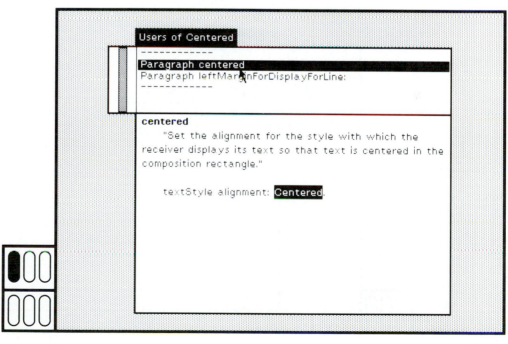

Figure 10.9

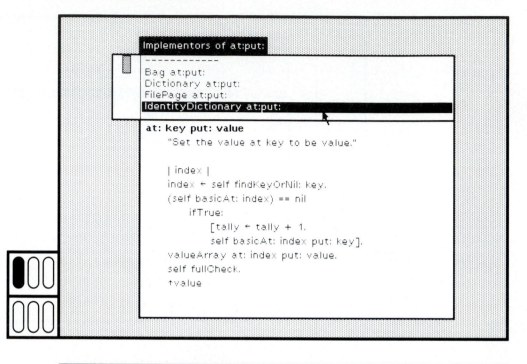

Figure 10.10

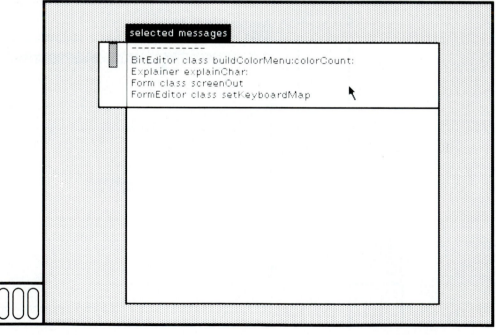

Figure 10.11

211

10.4 Which Methods Reference a Particular Variable or Literal?

The yellow button menu items in the class-names subview of a system browser also support making inquiries about variable references. If you choose either inst var refs or class var refs (Figure 10.12a), a menu of the instance or class variables of the class is displayed (Figure 10.12b). If you choose one of the variables, a message-set browser is created for each method in the class or its subclasses that references the variable (Figure 10.12c).

If you choose the class-names subview yellow button command class refs (Figure 10.13a), a message-set browser for all methods in the system that reference the class is created (Figure 10.13b).

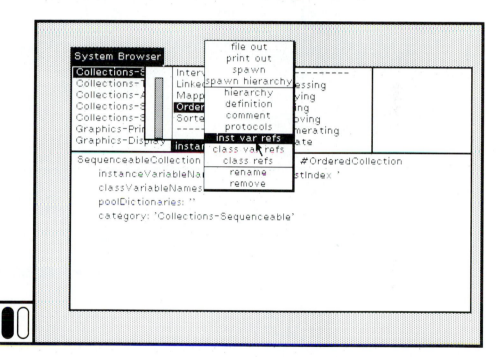

Figure 10.12a

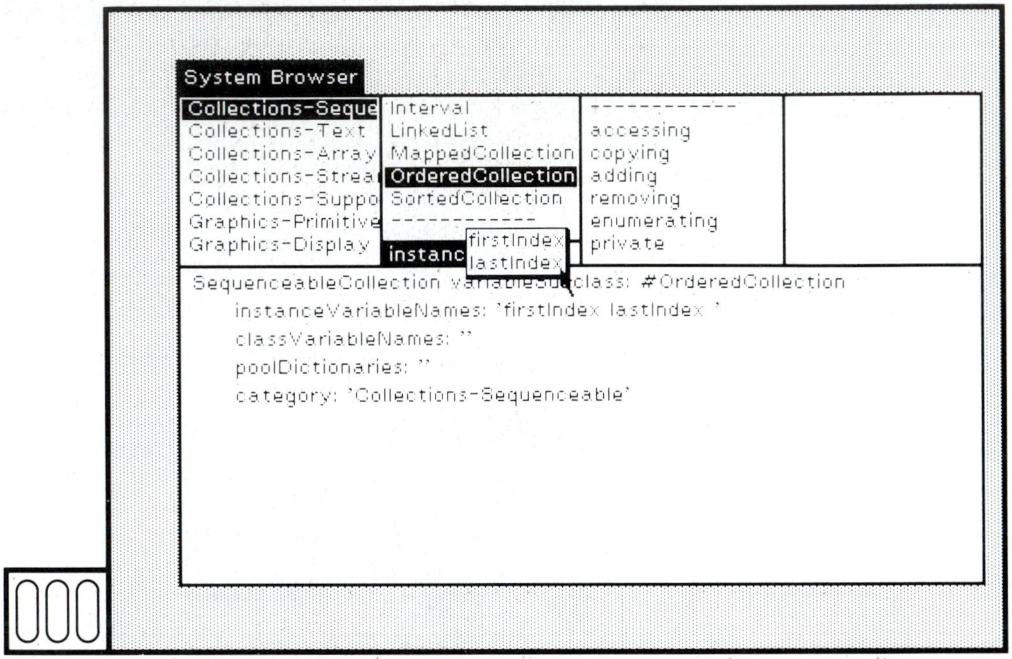

```
System Browser
Collections-Seque  Interval        ------------
Collections-Text   LinkedList      accessing
Collections-Array  MappedCollection copying
Collections-Strea  OrderedCollection adding
Collections-Suppo  SortedCollection removing
Graphics-Primitive ------------    enumerating
Graphics-Display   instanc firstIndex  private
                           lastIndex
SequenceableCollection variableSubclass: #OrderedCollection
    instanceVariableNames: 'firstIndex lastIndex '
    classVariableNames: ''
    poolDictionaries: ''
    category: 'Collections-Sequenceable'
```

Figure 10.12b

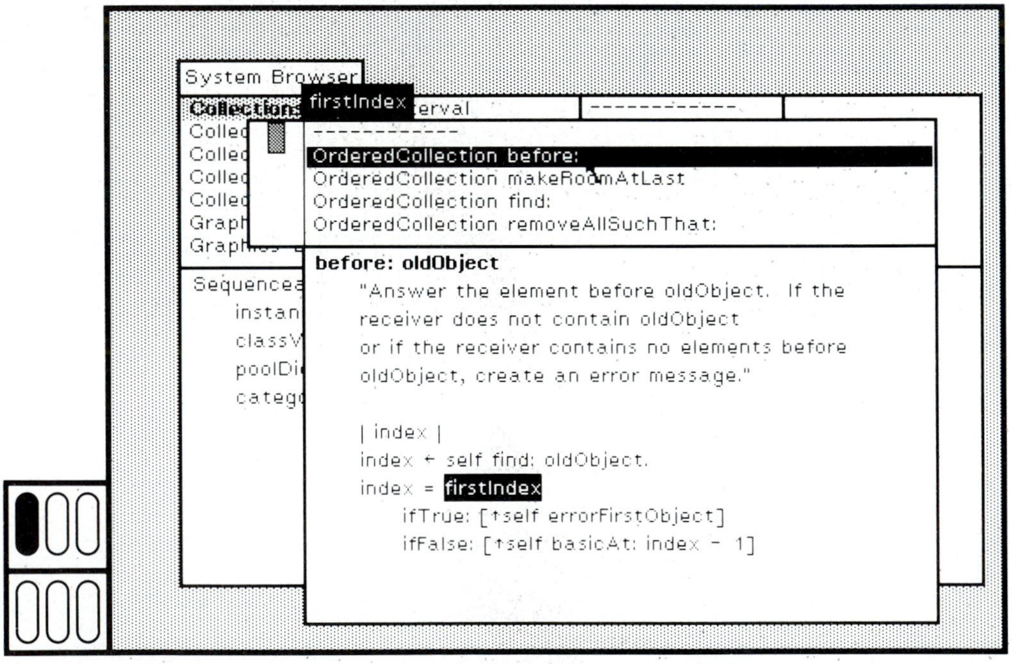

```
System Browser
Collections  firstIndex  erval      ------------
Colle                   ------------
Colle          OrderedCollection before:
Colle          OrderedCollection makeRoomAtLast
Colle          OrderedCollection find:
Graph          OrderedCollection removeAllSuchThat:
Graph
             before: oldObject
Sequencea       "Answer the element before oldObject.  If the
   instan        receiver does not contain oldObject
   classV        or if the receiver contains no elements before
   poolDi        oldObject, create an error message."
   categc
                | index |
                index ← self find: oldObject.
                index = firstIndex
                    ifTrue: [↑self errorFirstObject]
                    ifFalse: [↑self basicAt: index - 1]
```

Figure 10.12c

213

10.4 Which Methods Reference a Particular Variable or Literal?

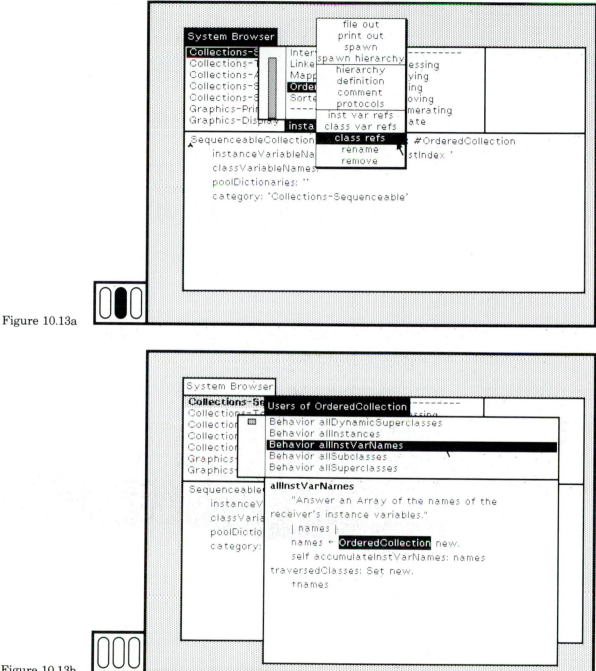

Figure 10.13a

Figure 10.13b

PART THREE

How to Modify Existing Classes and Create New Classes

In Part Two, you were introduced to four standard system views: inspectors, browsers, notifiers, and debuggers. These views are used to find out about the objects that exist in the Smalltalk-80 programming environment. You can program by creating instances of existing classes and sending messages to these instances. If the capabilities of the existing classes are insufficient for accomplishing your programming tasks, you will have to modify one or more of the existing classes, or you will have to create new classes.

The purpose of Part Three is to show you how to use the system browser for modifying existing classes and for creating new classes. The examples given demonstrate how inspectors can support you in testing the new classes that you add to the system. The organization of classes (class categories) and messages (message protocols) act as a form of documentation. Thus it is important to understand the system class organizations and how to create organizations for your applications classes.

As in Part Two, we assume that the system sources are accessible to you. Without them, you will be able to access the methods. But you will not be able to access the class or method comments, nor the actual method argument names.

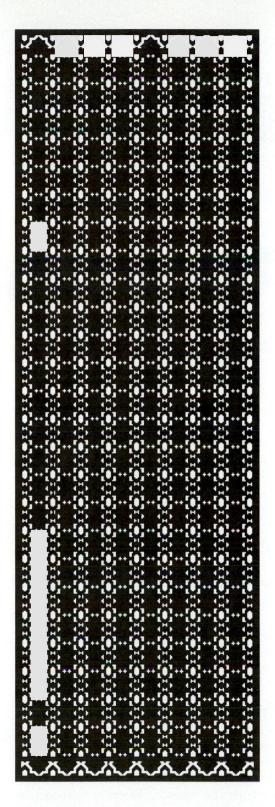

11

Modifying Existing Class Descriptions

Start by making certain that you have a system browser open on the display screen. If one does not already exist, choose the System Menu command browser. If one does exist, make it the active view. A newly created browser is shown in Figure 11.1.

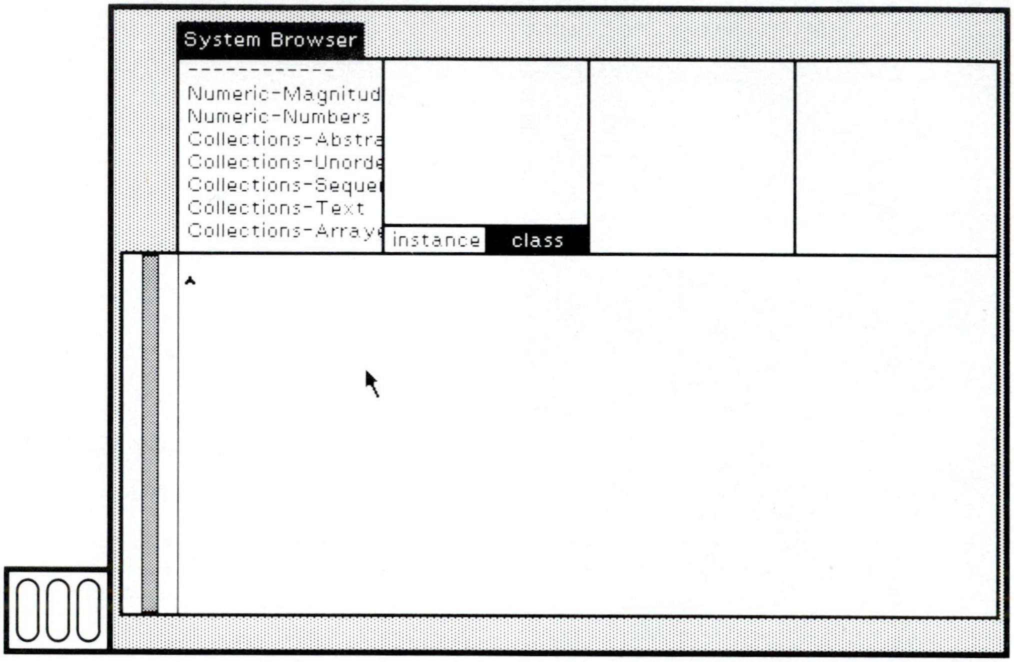

Figure 11.1

In order to learn how to make a change to the system, you will be asked to follow several examples in which you change existing methods and add new methods to existing classes. The three examples provided here

- use and modify the example of creating a geometric design with class Pen,

- add the ability to class Array to create a bar chart, a graphical display of an array of elements, and

- add the ability to class SequenceableCollection to compute all possible combinations of the elements of a collection.

11.1

Modifying Existing Methods

Exercise 1: Use class Pen to create geometric designs.

For the first example, you have to find the existing method that you will modify. Choose class category Graphics-Primitives, class Pen, browser menu item class, message category examples, and message selector example. The method associated with the message example is shown in the text subview of the browser. The result of these selections is shown in Figure 11.2a.

Notice that at the end of the method is a comment (text enclosed in double quotes). To try this example use of class Pen, select the comment

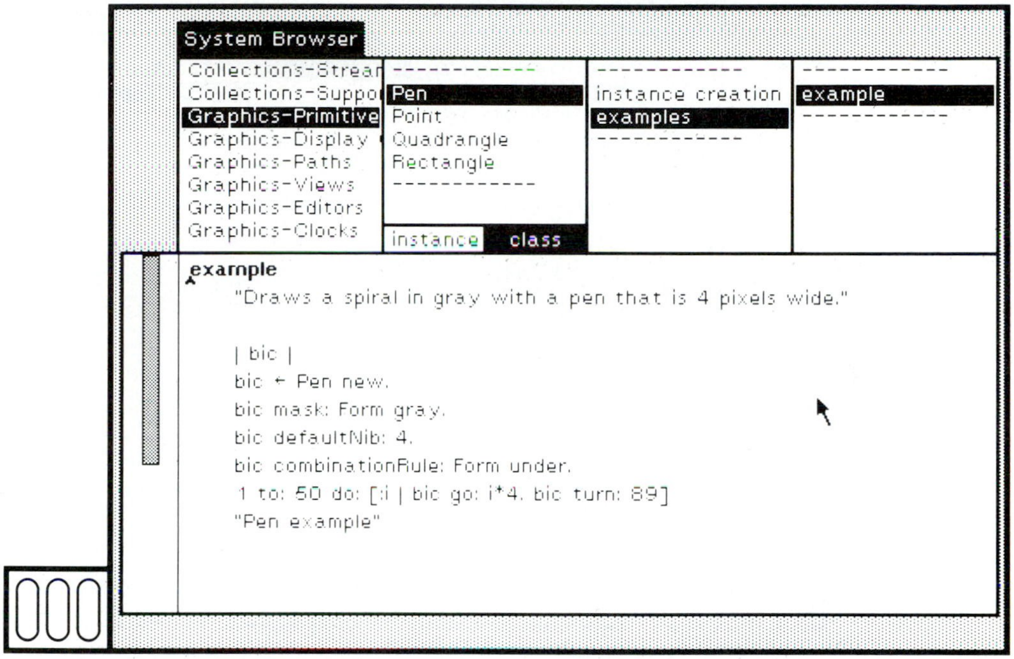

Figure 11.2a

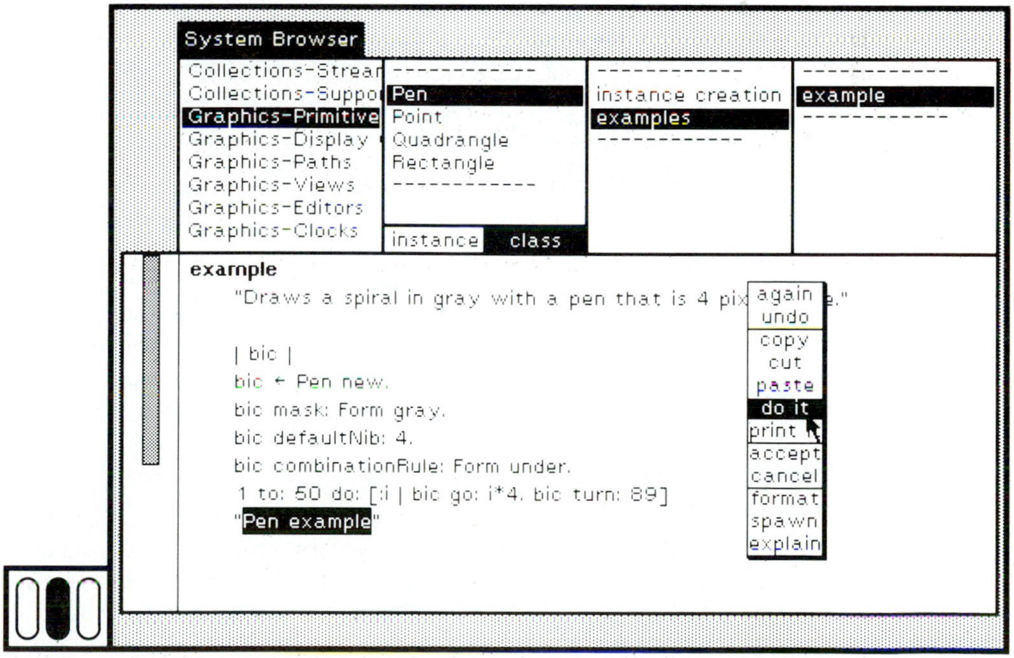

Figure 11.2b

text (do not select the double quotes), and then choose the yellow button command do it (Figure 11.2b). A geometric design appears on the screen (Figure 11.2c).

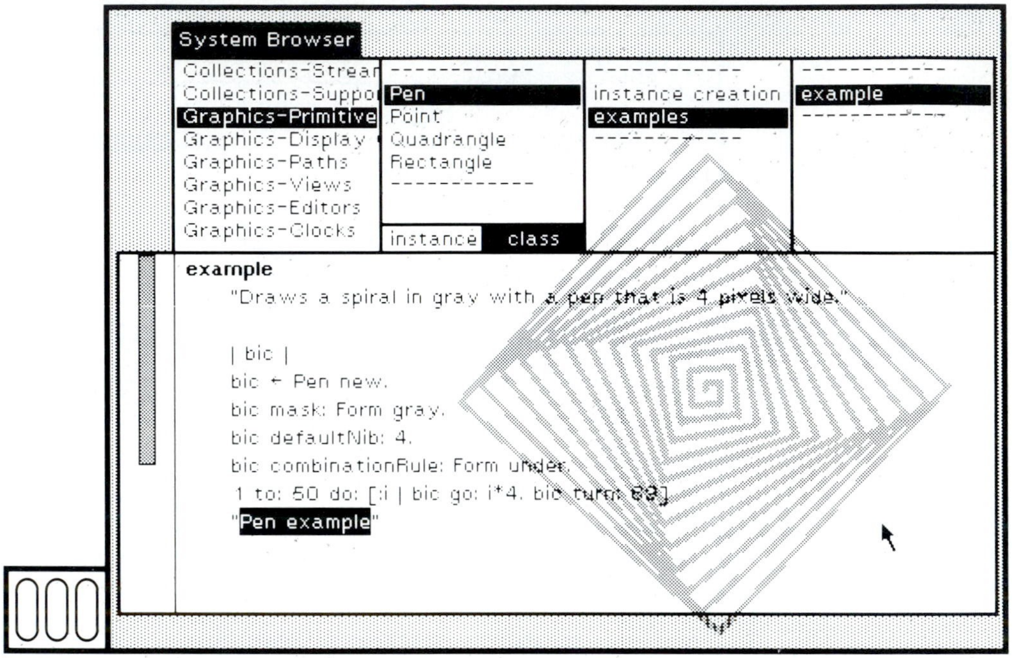

Figure 11.2c

To create this design, you sent the class Pen the message example. The method associated with example was found in the class protocol for Pen. The first statement of the method creates an instance of Pen, and assigns it to the temporary variable bic. Instances of class Pen respond to messages to change their line drawing characteristics. In particular,

mask: Form gray	The halftone mask that determines "color" of the drawing ink. Other masks include Form darkGray, Form lightGray, and Form black.
defaultNib: 4	The shape of the source form or "brush" is a 4 x 4 square. Squares of different sizes can be used by specifying different integers as the message argument.
combinationRule: Form under	The mode for mixing the bits of the source and destination Forms can be varied, either Form under, Form over, Form reverse, or Form erase, can be used as the message argument.

The second, third, and fourth statements of the example method send these messages in order to set the characteristics of bic. The fifth message is an iteration in which the Pen travels some distance (go: i * 4) and changes orientation (turn: 89); as the Pen travels, it paints a line using its current brush, mask, and combination rule.

You can now experiment with variations of the example design. First, erase the geometric design that was the side effect of the previous example by choosing the System Menu command restore display.

In the Pen method example, change the mask. Select the message gray sent to the Form (the second statement in the method) as shown in Figure 11.3a; then type the new message darkGray. The typing change is shown in Figure 11.3b. Change the size of the square brush. Select the message argument, 4, as shown in Figure 11.3c. Type the new argument, 2; the result is shown in Figure 11.3d.

Now choose the yellow button command accept (Figure 11.3d). The message accept in this context means "compile the code." Compilation means translate the Smalltalk-80 statements into machine executable form (i.e., create an instance of CompiledMethod). The changed method is automatically loaded into the running system, ready for you to try.

Select the expression Pen example (as you did earlier), and then choose the yellow button command do it. The modified geometric design shows on the screen (Figure 11.4).

You can keep experimenting in this way. Instead of using the message defaultNib: to specify the brush shape, try the message sourceForm:. The message argument is an instance of class Form. (You can try using one of the cursors that exist, such as Cursor normal or Cursor crossHair). Also, try changing the mode of mixing bits to Form reverse when you use different source Forms, otherwise the results will be mostly black.

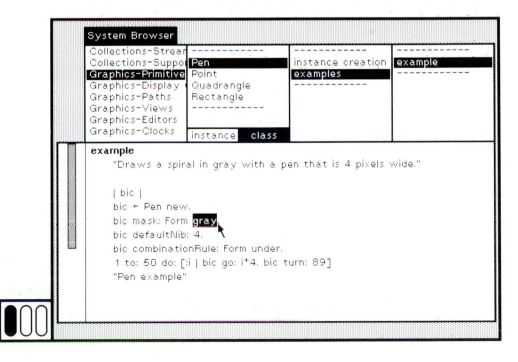

Figure 11.3a

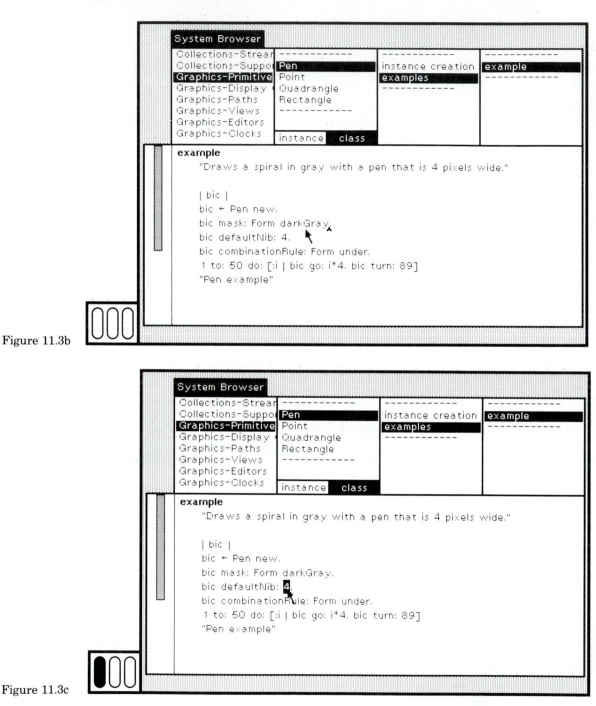

Figure 11.3b

Figure 11.3c

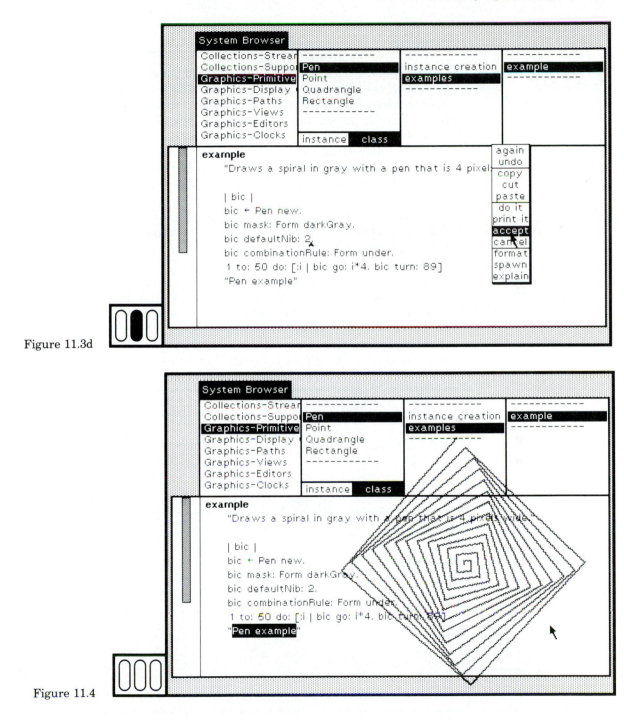

Figure 11.3d

Figure 11.4

11.2

Modifying Protocols

Exercise 2: Modify class Array to display bar charts.

The next example demonstrates a way in which you can get another graphical effect on the screen. It was chosen primarily to introduce the mechanisms for adding a new method to an existing class, not to be a typical example of how to handle graphical presentation. There are a number of interesting ways to handle graphical presentation of information, such as views and menus. The approach taken in creating the Smalltalk-80 system user interface is introduced in Chapter 15.

In this example, you will add one method to class Array. The result of the method is to create a bar-chart representation of the elements of an Array whose elements are numeric. As an argument to the message to Array, you specify the labels that will appear along the horizontal axis of the bar chart, one label for each element.

To add a method to an existing class, you can use a system browser. Choose the class category Collections-Arrayed. Choose the class name Array. Make certain the menu item instance is selected. Your browser should resemble the one shown in Figure 11.5.

Now you need to choose a message category. Let's assume the appropriate message category does not exist. You must create a new category.

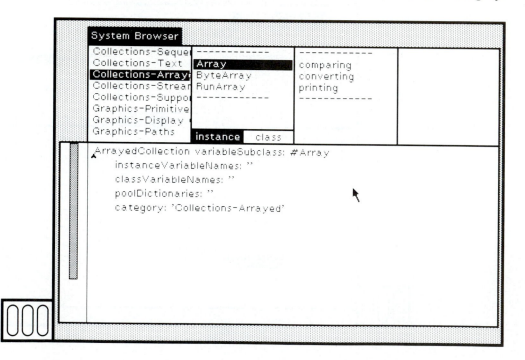

Figure 11.5

There are two ways to modify the message protocol of a class:

1. Use the commands in the yellow button menu of the message-category subview.

2. Choose the yellow button command protocols in the class-names subview.

The first approach is the preferred one; the second, which involves direct editing of a textual presentation of all the categories, is available in case you have to do a large reorganization. An explanation of each follows.

With the cursor in the message-category subview, but no category selected, press the yellow button. The menu has one item, add protocol (Figure 11.6a). Choose it. A prompter appears (Figure 11.6b) in which you type the new protocol name. After typing the name (graphical views is used in Figure 11.6c, although misspelled), choose the yellow button command accept or type the "carriage return" key on the keyboard. The new name is added to the message-category subview menu (Figure 11.6d).

When you choose add protocol, the new protocol name is appended to the end of the message-category subview menu, and is selected. If a category was already selected when you invoked the add protocol command, then the new category is inserted before this selected one.

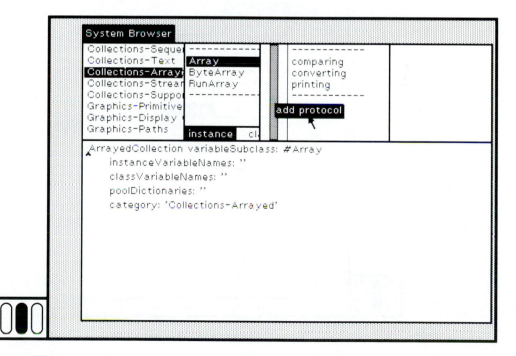

Figure 11.6a

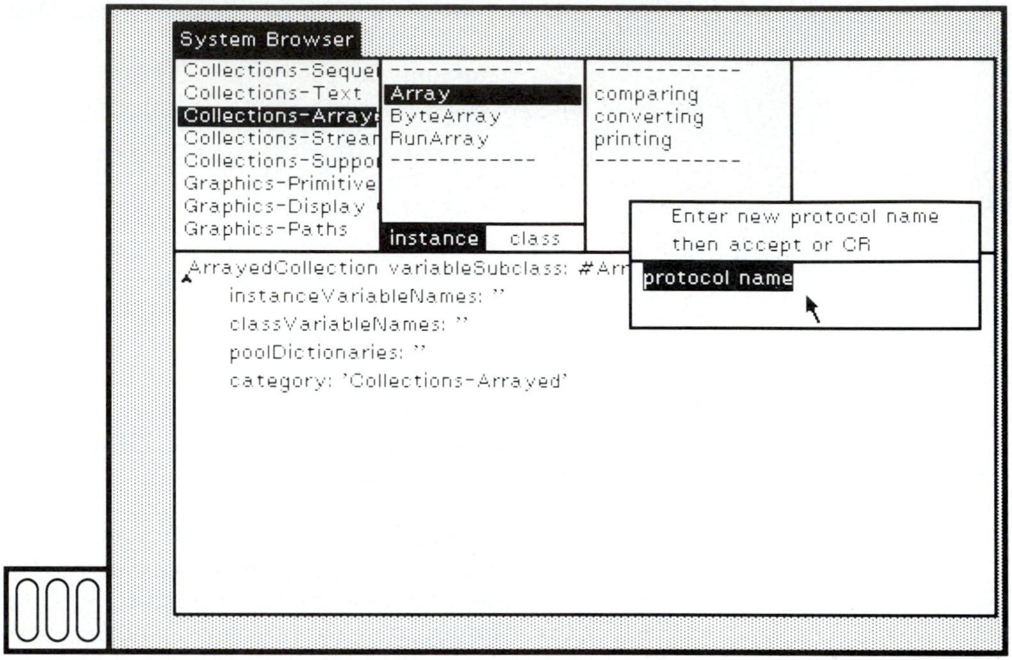

Figure 11.6b

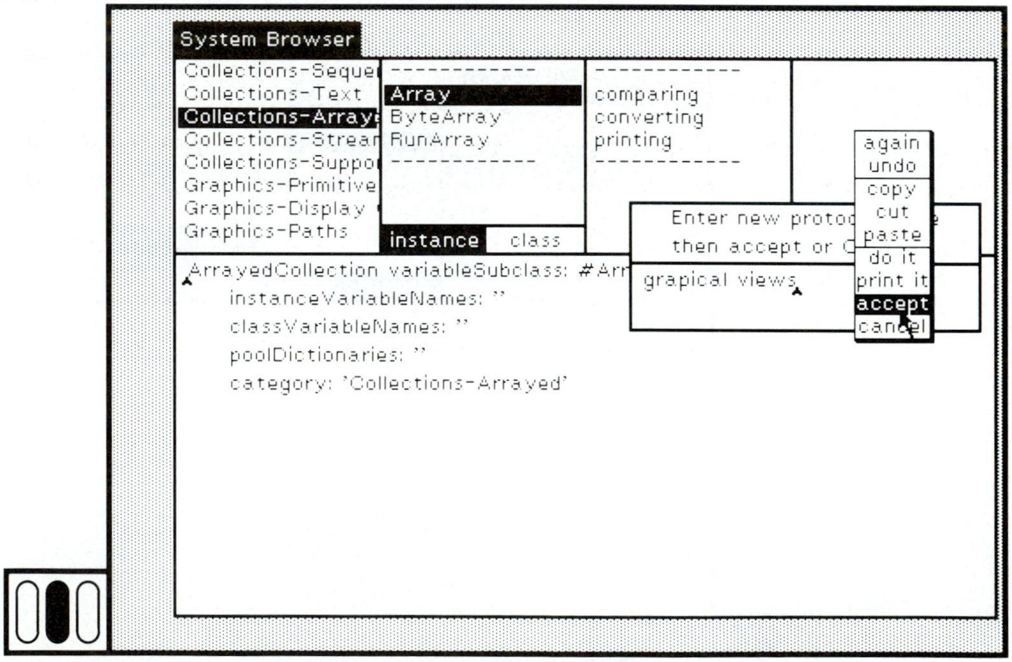

Figure 11.6c

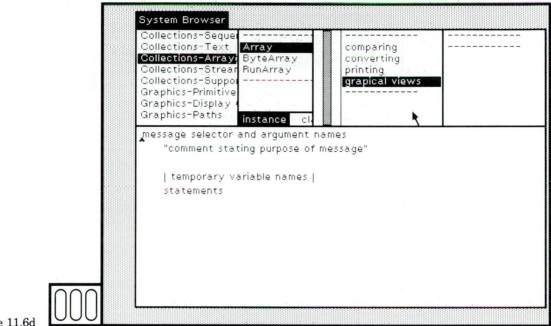

Figure 11.6d

When a category is selected, the yellow button menu includes commands rename and remove, as well as add protocol. If you choose the command rename, a prompter appears that contains the selected name. Edit it, then choose the prompter yellow button command accept or type the "carriage return" key. For example, notice that we mistyped the name graphical views in Figure 11.6c. With the misspelled name selected, choose the command rename (Figure 11.7a). The prompter appears, showing the current name (Figure 11.7b). Edit the text and choose the yellow button command accept (Figure 11.7c). The name in the message-category menu changes (Figure 11.7d).

If you choose the command rename, and the name you provide is the same as an already existing protocol name, then nothing changes.

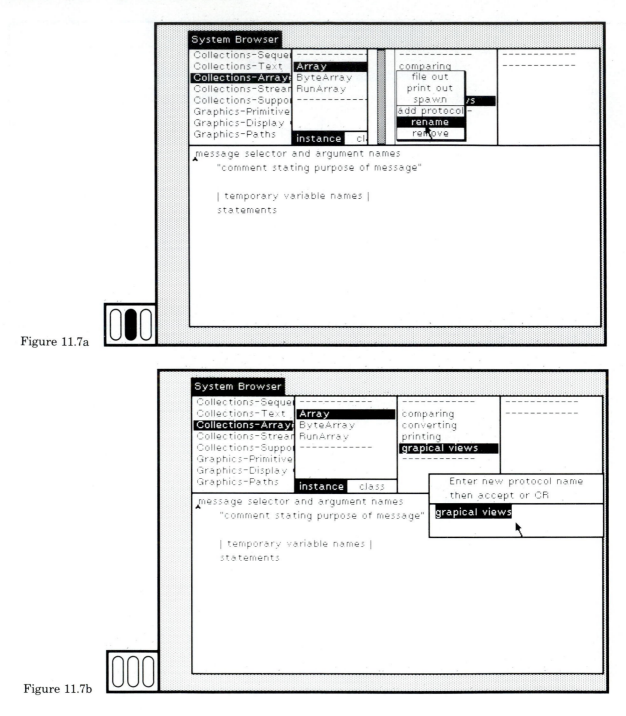

Figure 11.7a

Figure 11.7b

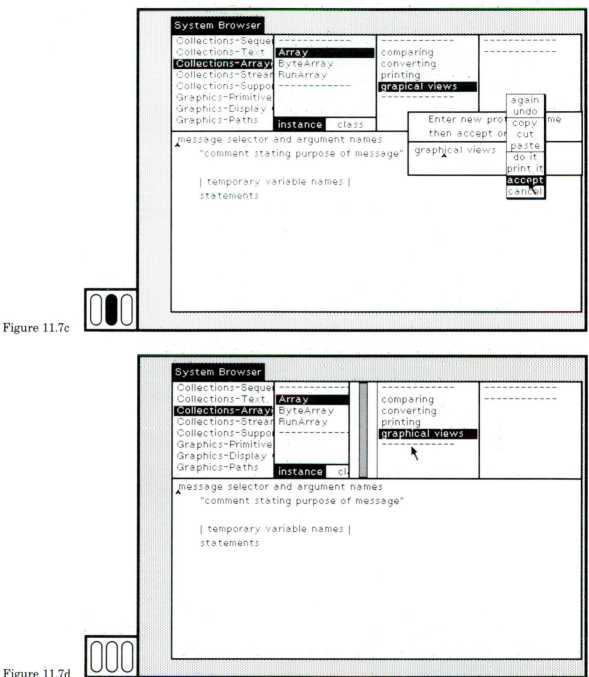

Figure 11.7c

Figure 11.7d

If you choose the command remove, and there are no message selectors in the selected category, the category is immediately deleted. If there are messages in the selected category, a confirmer appears because the deletion means that all messages in the category are deleted (Figure 11.8).

The second way of modifying the protocol for a class is to choose the yellow button command protocols in the class-names subview of the browser (Figure 11.9a). A list of message categories and message selectors within each category appears in the text subview of the browser (Figure 11.9b). The syntax for each category/selectors combination is of the form

('category name' selector1 selector2 selector3)

To add a protocol, insert a new name, delimited by single quotes and embedded in parentheses.

('new name')

An example is shown in Figure 11.9c in which the new category name graphical views is appended at the end. Choose the yellow button com-

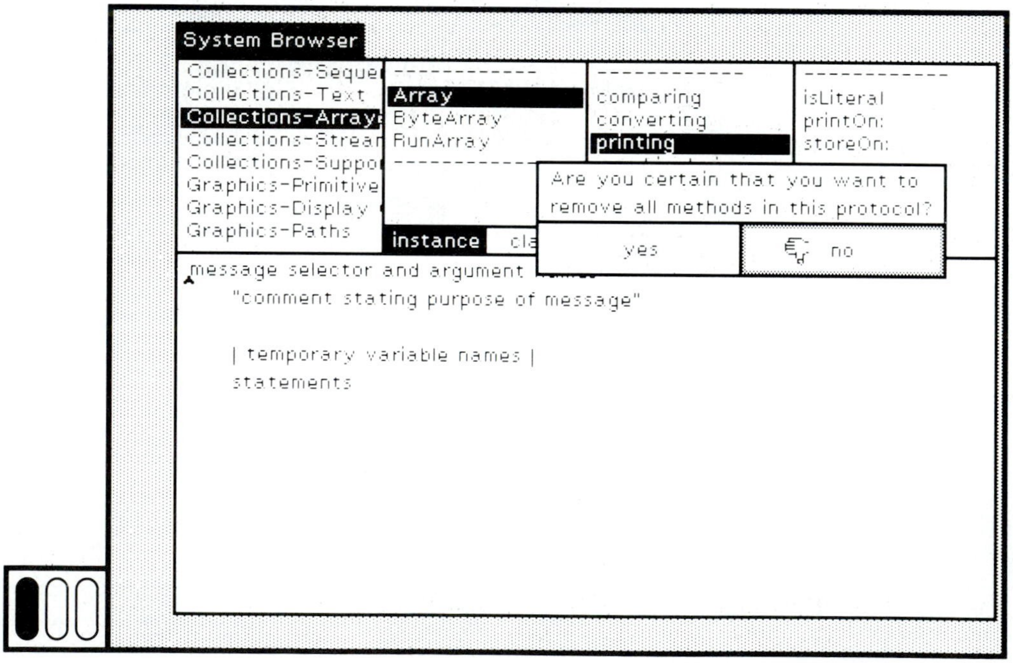

Figure 11.8

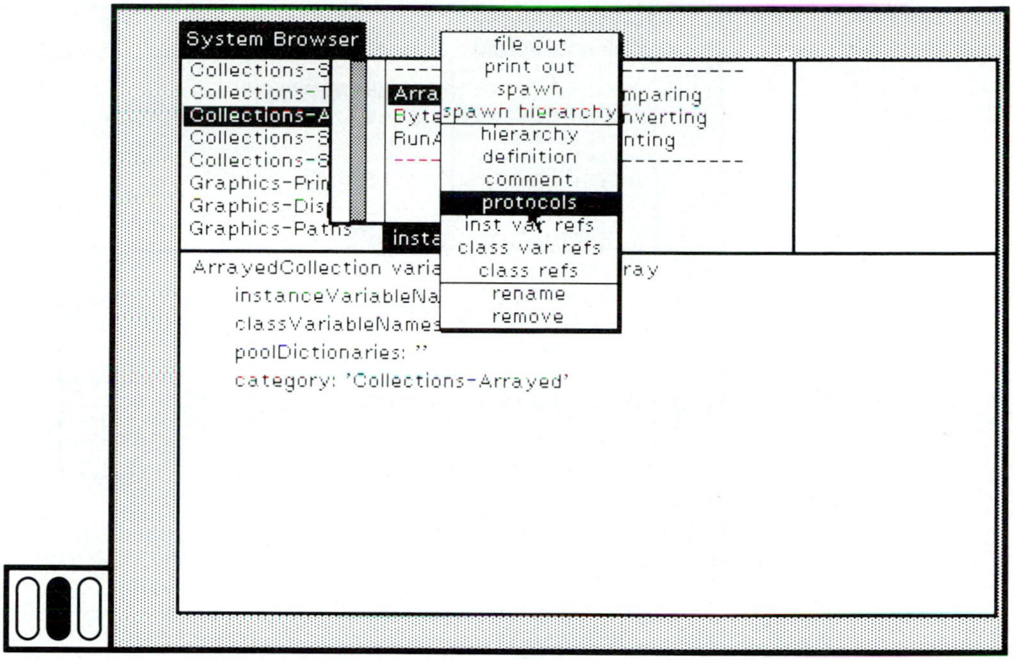

Figure 11.9a

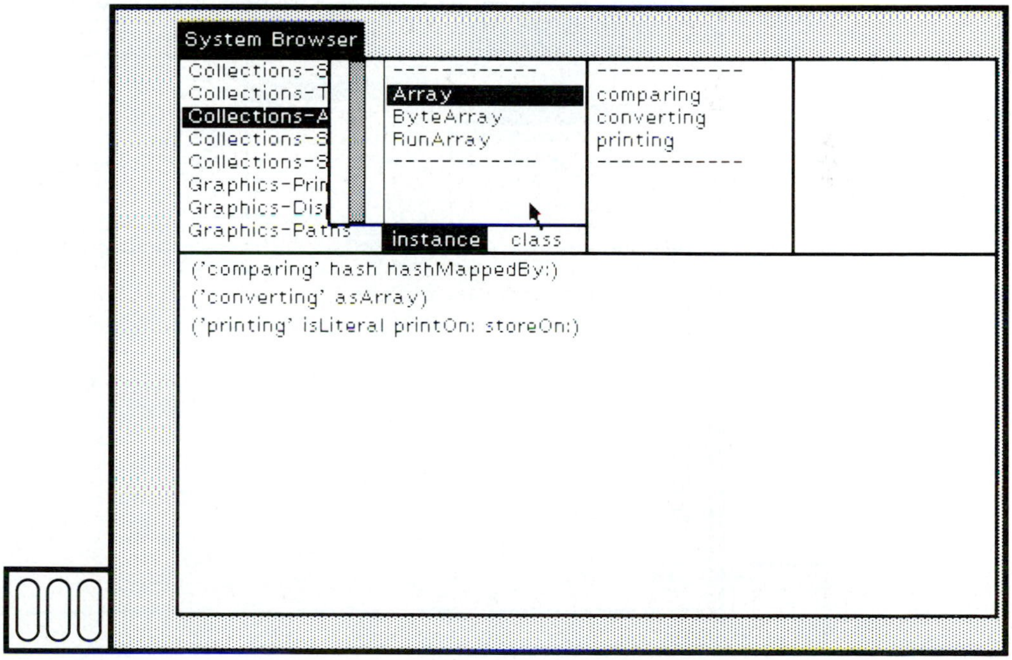

Figure 11.9b

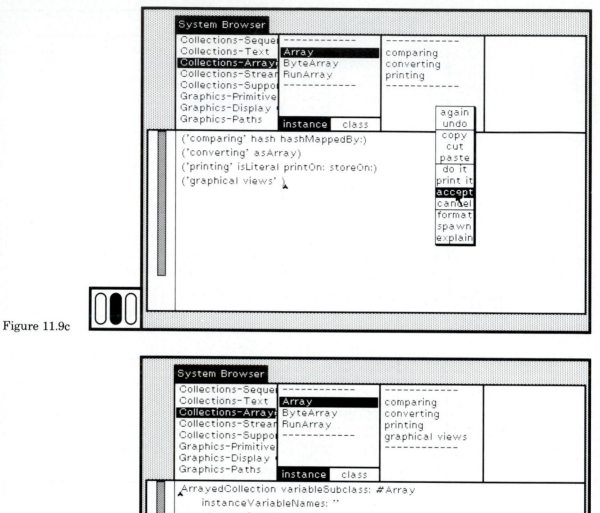

Figure 11.9c

Figure 11.9d

mand accept in the text subview to have the system check the syntax of the category specifications, and to add the category to the menu in the browser. The result is shown in Figure 11.9d.

11.3

Adding New Methods

Choose the new category graphical views. A template for defining a new method appears in the text subview of the browser, as shown in Figure 11.10a. You edit this template with the desired message pattern, comment, and statements. In Figure 11.10b, the message selector and argument names part of the template is selected; typing the actual pattern replaces the selected text (Figure 11.10c). The example message pattern is displayBarChartWithLabels: anArray.

> The name of the message argument has no semantic meaning in the Smalltalk-80 programming language. However, as a matter of style and documentation, the message argument name is made up from the name of the class or superclass of the instance that can be an argument to the message. In this example, the argument name indicates that the argument should be an instance of Array or of a subclass of Array.

Now select the comment part of the template (Figure 11.10d) and type an appropriate comment. The comment shown in Figure 11.10e includes an expression that is an example use of the method. Users of this method can browse to read the comment, and then see an example use of it by executing the expression.

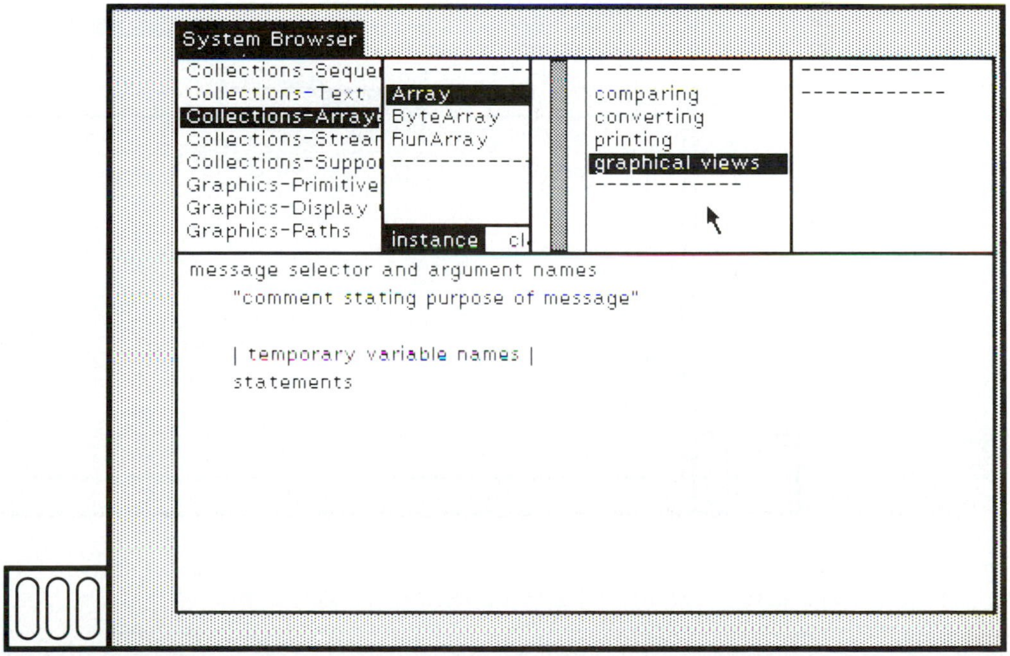

Figure 11.10a

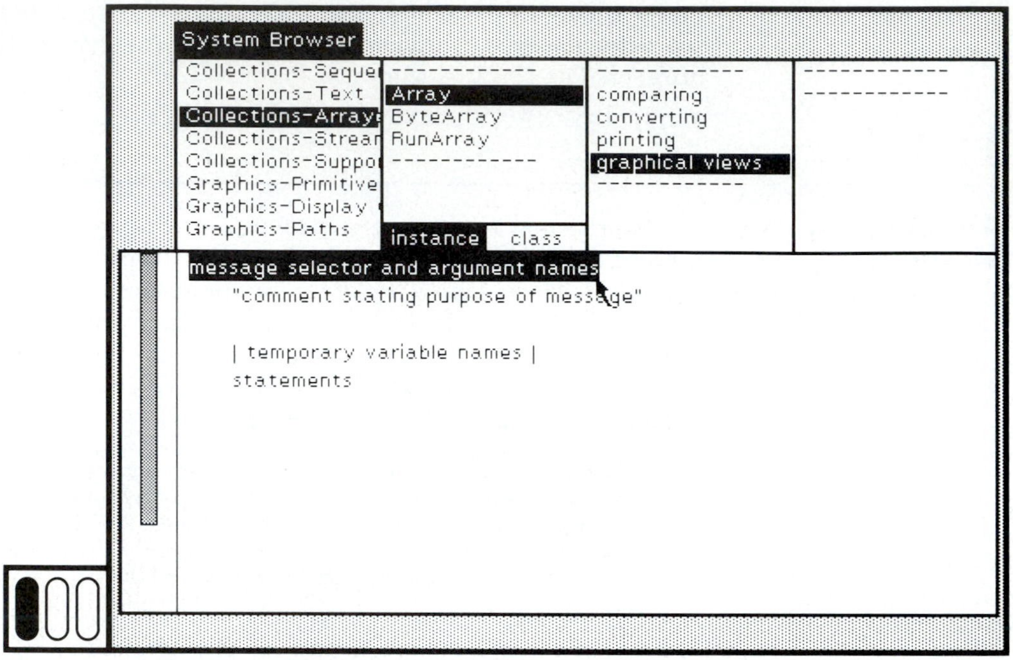

Figure 11.10b

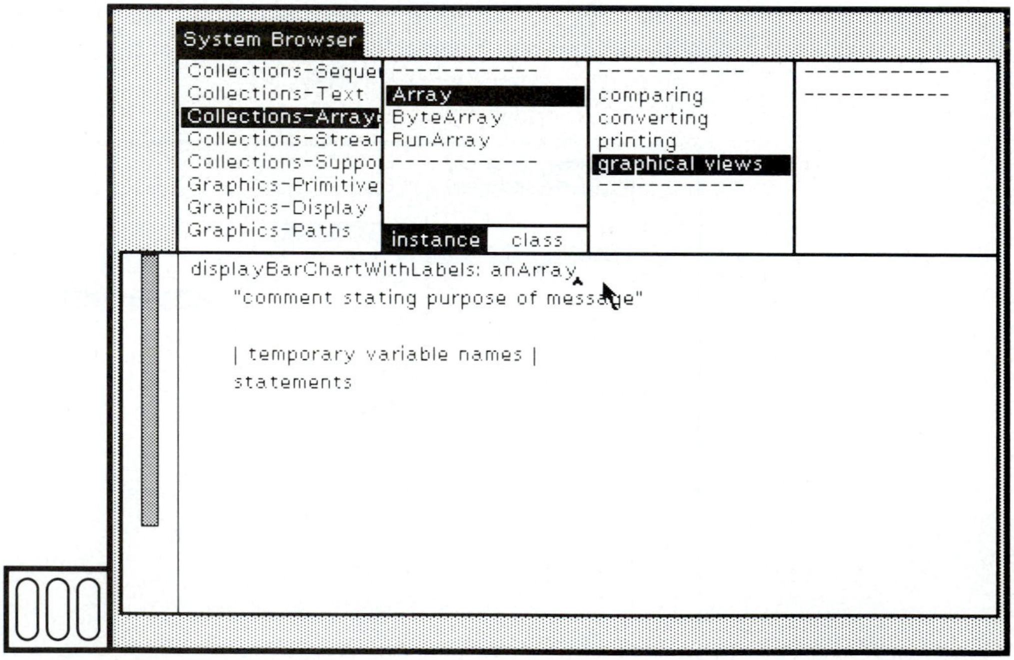

Figure 11.10c

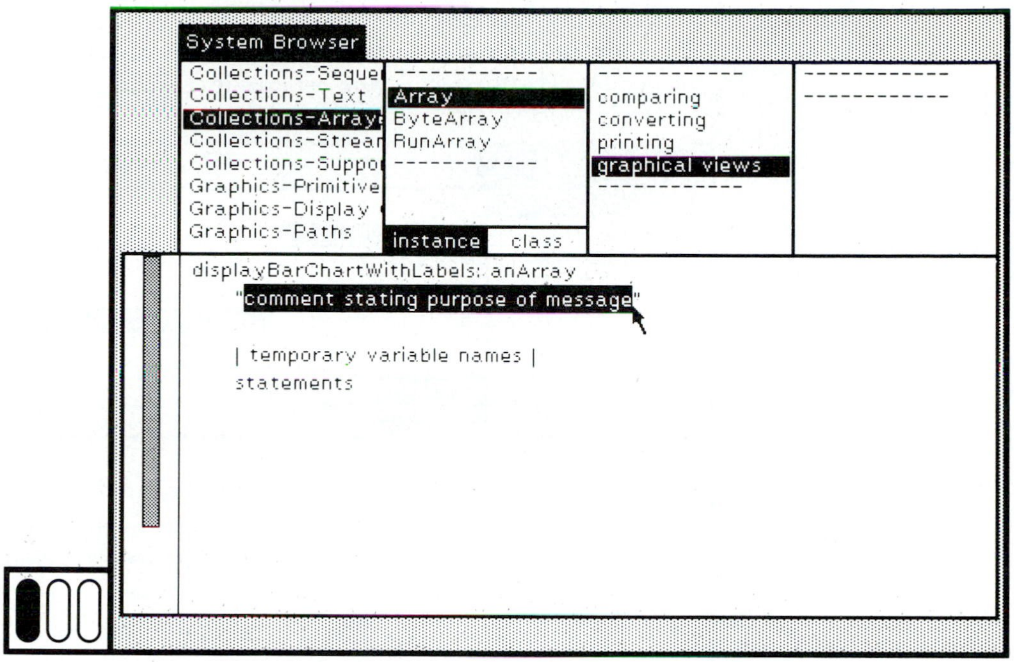

System Browser

Collections-Seque
Collections-Text
Collections-Array
Collections-Strea
Collections-Suppo
Graphics-Primitive
Graphics-Display
Graphics-Paths

```
-----------      -----------      -----------
Array            comparing
ByteArray        converting
RunArray         printing
-----------      graphical views
                 -----------
instance   class
```

displayBarChartWithLabels: anArray
    "comment stating purpose of message"

    | temporary variable names |
    statements

Figure 11.10d

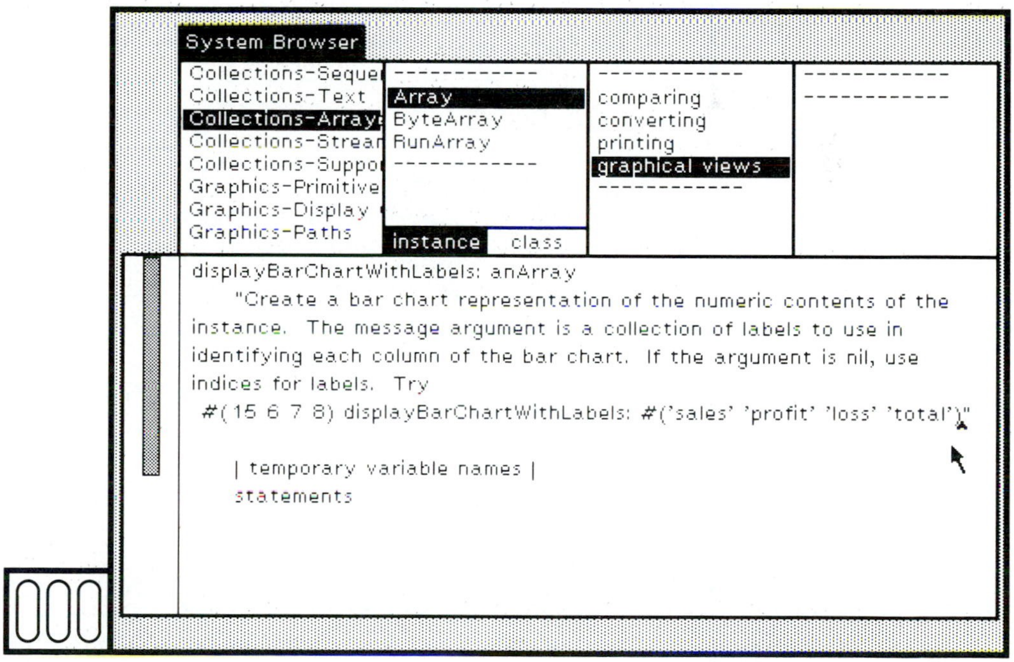

System Browser

Collections-Seque
Collections-Text
Collections-Array
Collections-Strea
Collections-Suppo
Graphics-Primitive
Graphics-Display
Graphics-Paths

```
-----------      -----------      -----------
Array            comparing
ByteArray        converting
RunArray         printing
-----------      graphical views
                 -----------
instance   class
```

displayBarChartWithLabels: anArray
    "Create a bar chart representation of the numeric contents of the
instance. The message argument is a collection of labels to use in
identifying each column of the bar chart. If the argument is nil, use
indices for labels. Try
    #(15 6 7 8) displayBarChartWithLabels: #('sales' 'profit' 'loss' 'total')"

    | temporary variable names |
    statements

Figure 11.10e

Now select the temporary variable names part of the template and replace it with rect spacing maxHeight factor labeling top dispRect. Then select the statements part and replace it (Figure 11.10f).

```
System Browser

Collections-Arr ------------      ------------      ------------
Collections-Str Array             comparing         ------------
Collections-Sup ByteArray         converting
Graphics-Primit RunArray          printing
Graphics-Displa ------------      graphical views
Graphics-Paths                    ------------
Graphics-Views
Graphics-Edito instance  class

displayBarChartWithLabels: anArray
    "Create a bar chart representation of the numeric
contents of the instance.  The message argument is a
collection of labels to use in identifying each column of the
bar chart.  If the argument is nil, use indices for labels.  Try
#(15 6 7 8) displayBarChartWithLabels: #('sales' 'profit'
'loss' 'total')"


| rect spacing maxHeight factor labeling top dispRect |
rect ← Rectangle fromUser.
spacing ← rect width + self size // self size.
maxHeight ← 0.
1 to: self size do: [ :i |
    maxHeight ← maxHeight max: (self at: 1)].
factor ← (rect height - 30) / maxHeight.
labeling ← (anArray == nil or: [anArray size < self size]) not.
Display fill: rect mask: Form white.
1 to: self size do: [ :i |
 (labeling ifTrue: [anArray at: i] ifFalse: [i printString])
  displayAt: rect bottomLeft -(0@30)+(((spacing*(i-1))+1)@0).
((self at: i) isKindOf: Number)
        ifFalse: [self error: 'element is not numeric'].
top ← rect top+rect height-30-((self at: i)*factor) asInteger.
dispRect ←
    (rect left+ 1+(spacing*(i-1)))@top
        corner: (rect left+(spacing*i)-1)@(rect bottom-30).
Display fill: dispRect mask: Form black.
Display fill: (dispRect insetBy: 2@2) mask: Form gray]
```

Figure 11.10f

Note that since the template is simply unstructured text, you can select all of it and replace it with the desired method. The example did the selection and replacement in parts to emphasize the parts of a method that can be specified. The system will not force you to provide comments, nor will it enforce naming conventions.

There are eight statements in the method that are commented here.

rect ← Rectangle fromUser.

Create a new Rectangle. The user of the method will have to designate the origin and corner of the Rectangle. Be careful to provide sufficient space for the Rectangle.

spacing ← rect width + self size // self size.

Compute the amount of space that can be used for the width of each column. The pseudo-variable self refers to the Array.

maxHeight ← 0.

Determine the largest element of the Array.

1 to: self size do: [:i |
    maxHeight ← maxHeight max: (self at: i)].

factor ← (rect height - 30) / maxHeight.

Compute the scaling factor to get the bar chart columns to fill the available space. The height of each column is the Array element times this scaling factor. 30 is the space left for the labels.

labeling ← (anArray = =nil or: [anArray size < self size]) not.

Compute a Boolean (true or false) that indicates whether the bar chart will be specially labeled. There are no special labels if the message argument anArray is nil, or if the message argument does not contain a label for each element. When there is no special label, the element index will be displayed.

Display fill: rect mask: Form white.

Display is an instance of DisplayScreen. The message fill:mask: is used to paint a rectangular area of the screen with some "color." Here the rectangle is the space to display the bar chart; the color, all white, is the background for the bar chart.

The eighth statement is an iteration in which each column is printed. For each element of the Array, that is, for the index i starting at 1 and ending at the size of the Array, determine the label (it is either anArray at: i, or it is the index converted to a string, i printString) and display the label within and at the bottom of the rectangle (displayAt:). Make certain that the Array element is numeric; if not, report an error. Otherwise, compute the top (top) of the next column, then compute the column's rectangle (dispRect). Now modify the display screen to show the column; the column has a 2 x 2 black border, so first display the column all in black (Display fill: dispRect mask: Form black) and then display the gray area inset from the edge (Display fill: (dispRect insetBy: 2@2) mask: Form gray).

```
1 to: self size do:
   [ :i |
   (labeling ifTrue: [anArray at: i] ifFalse: [i printString])
       displayAt: rect bottomLeft - (0@30) + (((spacing * (i - 1)) + 1)@0).
   ((self at: i) isKindOf: Number) ifFalse: [self error: 'element is not numeric'].
   top ← rect top + rect height - 30 - ((self at: i) * factor) asInteger.
   dispRect ← (rect left + 1 + (spacing * (i - 1))) @ top
                    corner: (rect left + (spacing * i) - 1) @ (rect bottom-30).
   Display fill: dispRect mask: Form black.
   Display fill: (dispRect insetBy: 2@2) mask: Form gray]
```

After you have typed these eight statements, choose the yellow button command accept. The method is compiled and loaded into the system; the message selector appears selected in the message-selector subview of the browser.

Check that you typed correctly. If not, edit the method and choose the command accept again. If you choose accept but have mistyped something, a syntax error message may be inserted into your code just before the point of the error. If this happens, cut out the error message and correct the (probably misspelled) token. Then choose the command accept again. Alternatively, a menu may appear that indicates an undeclared variable or message selector. One of the commands in the menu is abort. Choose it, then edit the method to correct the error, and choose the command accept again.

Try the new method by selecting the expression in the comment and choosing the yellow button command do it (Figure 11.11a). First you are asked to designate the rectangle in which the bar chart will appear in the same way you designate a standard system view. A possible result is shown in Figure 11.11b. (Note that the image is not in a system view and cannot be selected for reframing, moving, closing, and so on. To erase the bar chart, choose the System Menu command restore display.)

If you did not copy the method correctly, but what you typed was successfully compiled, two things could have happened.

1. You successfully obtained a result, but it does not look right. Recheck your method to find the difference between code presented here and what you typed. Edit the method, choose the command accept again, and then try the example again.

2. You did not get a bar chart, but instead a view called a notifier appears to tell you something is wrong. This notifier indicates a runtime error. It is like the one described at the end of Section 8.5. In the notifier, choose blue button command close, and then

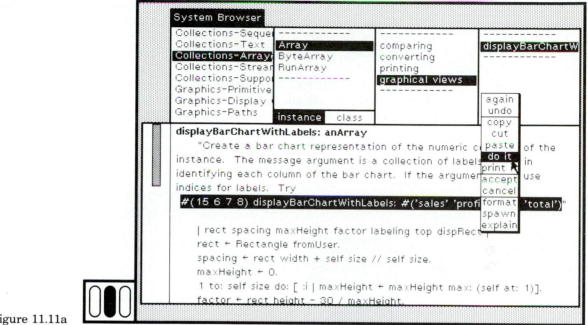

Figure 11.11a

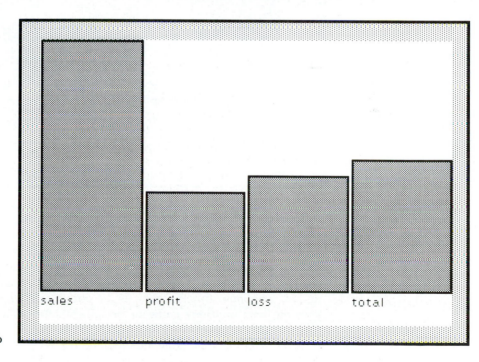

Figure 11.11b

proceed as suggested for case 1. The most common runtime error is that an object does not understand a message sent to it. Often this is because a period or parentheses was forgotten, or you misspelled the message keywords.

There are a number of ways in which you can modify the method to produce different effects. Try to change the background to light gray, rather than white (Display fill: rect mask: Form lightGray), and the column tone to dark gray instead of gray (Display fill: (dispRect insetBy: 2@2) mask: Form darkGray). A new bar chart created with these changes is shown in Figure 11.11c.

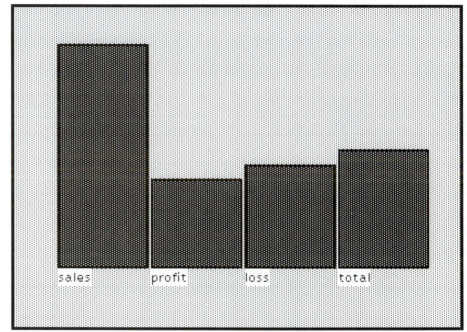

Figure 11.11c

Exercise 3: Modify SequenceableCollections to do combinations of the elements of the collection.

This exercise is similar to Exercise 2 in that it demonstrates how to modify an existing class description in order to add new functionality to a class. It differs in that several methods, rather than just one, must be added. The new functionality is to obtain an OrderedCollection of all possible combinations (subsets or subcollections) of the elements of a SequenceableCollection. For example, the result of sending the Array #(a b c) the message combinations should be

OrderedCollection ((a b c) (b c) (a c) (c) (a b) (b) (a) ())

The design of the algorithm is to recursively call on a method that computes subsets of all the combinations of elements, eliminating one element at a time, and collecting the result of each call into an OrderedCollection. The index of the element to be eliminated is called the order of the elimination; it is an index into the SequenceableCollection. The top-level call to this method (combinations:) uses the message argument 0; the top-level call is specified in the method associated with the message combinations. The two messages, combinations and combinations:, will be categorized in message category enumerating of class SequenceableCollection. An instance of any subclass of SequenceableCollection, such as Array or String, will be able to compute all of its combinations. The two methods are as follows.

combinations
  " Answer a collection containing all the combinations of the
  receiver's elements, e.g., #(a b c) combinations. "

  ↑self combinations: 0
combinations: order
  " Answer a collection containing a subset of all the combinations of the
  receiver's elements. "

  | combinations |
  combinations ← OrderedCollection with: self.
  1 to: self size - order do:
   [:i |
    combinations
     addAll: ((self copyWithoutIndex: i) combinations: self size - i)].
  ↑combinations

The method for combinations: includes the expression

self copyWithoutIndex: i

The message copyWithoutIndex: must be defined for SequenceableCollections. In the example, it is categorized in message category copying as shown on the next page.

copyWithoutIndex: omitIndex
" Answer a copy of the receiver, omitting the element at omitIndex, e.g.,
#(a b c) copyWithoutIndex: 2 = #(a c). "

```
| copy |
copy ← self species new: self size - 1.
copy replaceFrom: 1 to: omitIndex - 1 with: self startingAt: 1.
copy
    replaceFrom: omitIndex to: copy size
    with: self startingAt: omitIndex + 1.
↑copy
```

Now that we know what we want to do, let's see how to use the
Smalltalk-80 programming interface to add the methods. In a system
browser, choose class category Collections-Abstract, class name
SequenceableCollections, message category copying, and the browser
menu item instance, as shown in Figure 11.12a. In the text subview,
edit the text of the method template. Replace the message pattern, comment, and statements to specify the method for copyWithoutIndex:
omitIndex. Choose the yellow button command accept (Figure 11.12b).
The new method is added to the message-selector menu of the browser
(Figure 11.12c).

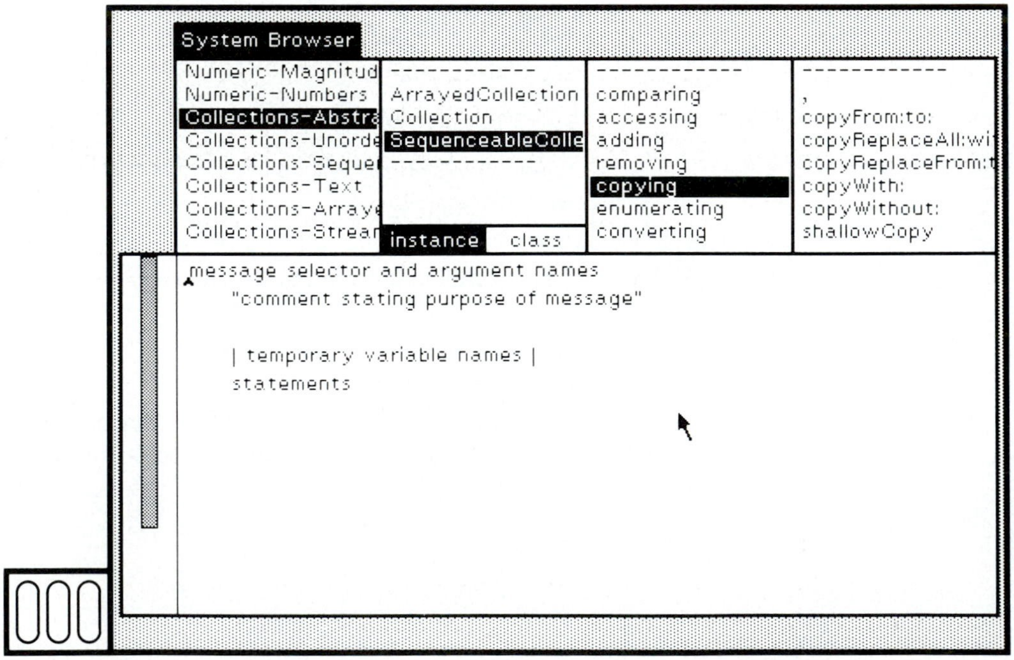

Figure 11.12a

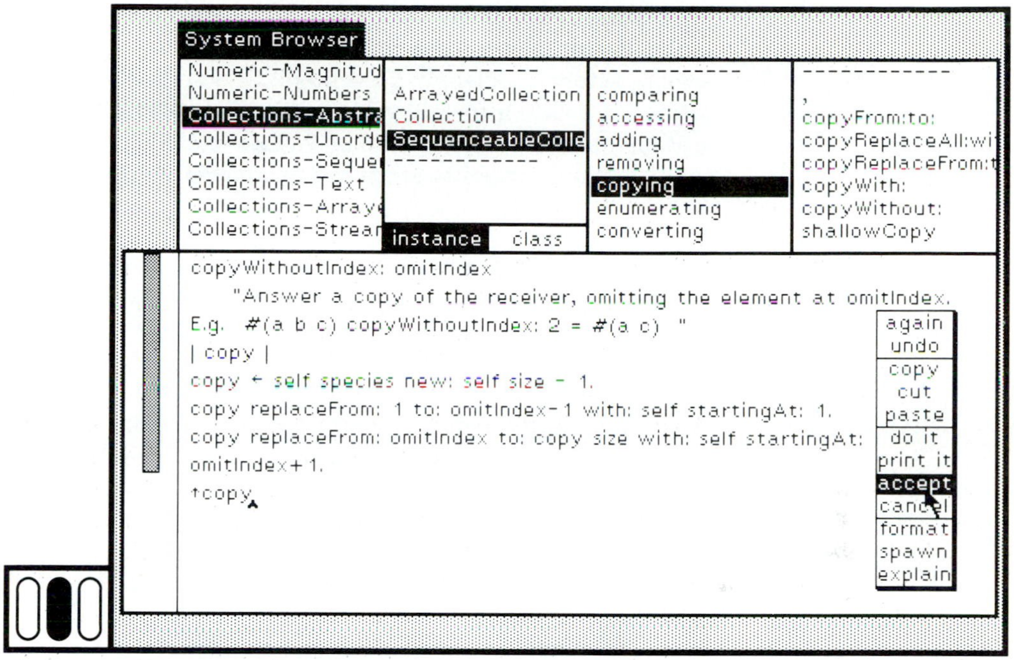

Figure 11.12b

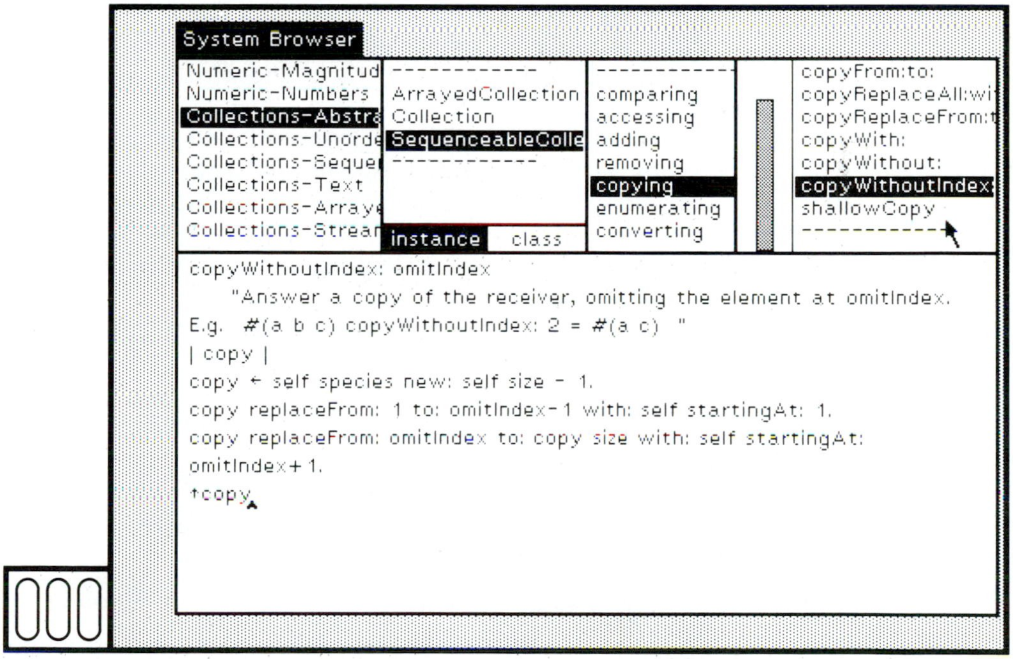

Figure 11.12c

☐ *Formatting*   When we typed the method, we were not careful to format the statements (use indentation and line change so that the message selectors are clearly presented). Choose the yellow button command format to create a formatted version (Figure 11.13a). Edit the formatted statements to change anything you do not like. Choose the yellow button command accept to store the formatted version (Figure 11.13b).

☐ *Testing*   Open a workspace in which you can try out the new method (choose the System Menu command workspace). Type the expression

#(a b c) copyWithoutIndex: 2

Select the expression and then choose the yellow button command print it (Figure 11.14a). Make sure that you get the result (a c).

Try other SequenceableCollections, such as a String.

'string' copyWithoutIndex: 3

The result should be a new String, 'sting'.

These tests are shown in Figure 11.14b. If your results are different, check to make certain that you copied the method correctly. Edit the method if necessary, and then choose the yellow button command accept.

Now choose the message category enumerating, as shown in Figure 11.15a. In the text subview, edit the text of the method template. Replace the message pattern, comment, and statements to specify the method for combinations:. Choose the yellow button command accept (Figure 11.15b). The new method is added to the message-selector menu of the browser.

By choosing combinations: in the message-selector menu, it is deselected, and the method template appears again. Edit the template to specify the method for combinations. Choose the yellow button command accept (Figure 11.15c). The new message selector is added to the menu.

In the workspace, try the new method. Type, select, and evaluate expressions such as those shown in the workspace in Figure 11.15d.

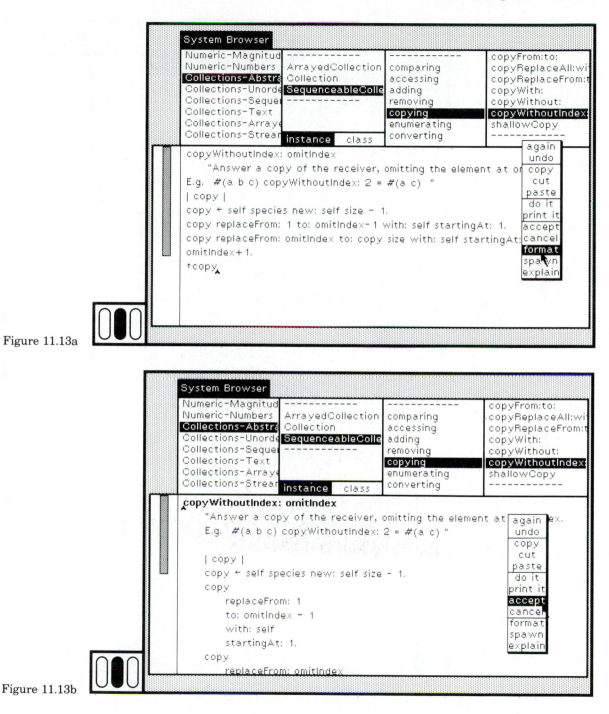

Figure 11.13a

Figure 11.13b

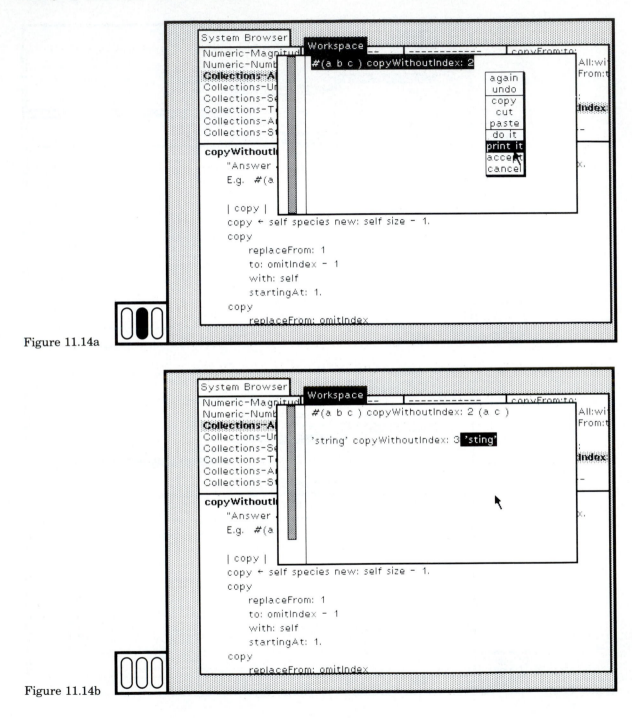

Figure 11.14a

Figure 11.14b

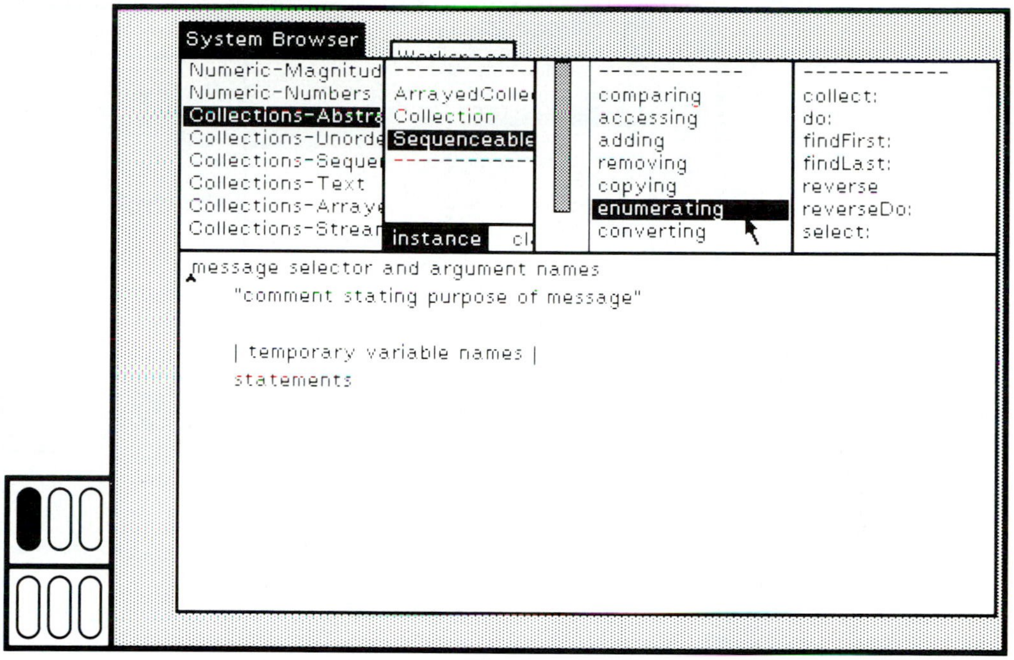

Figure 11.15a

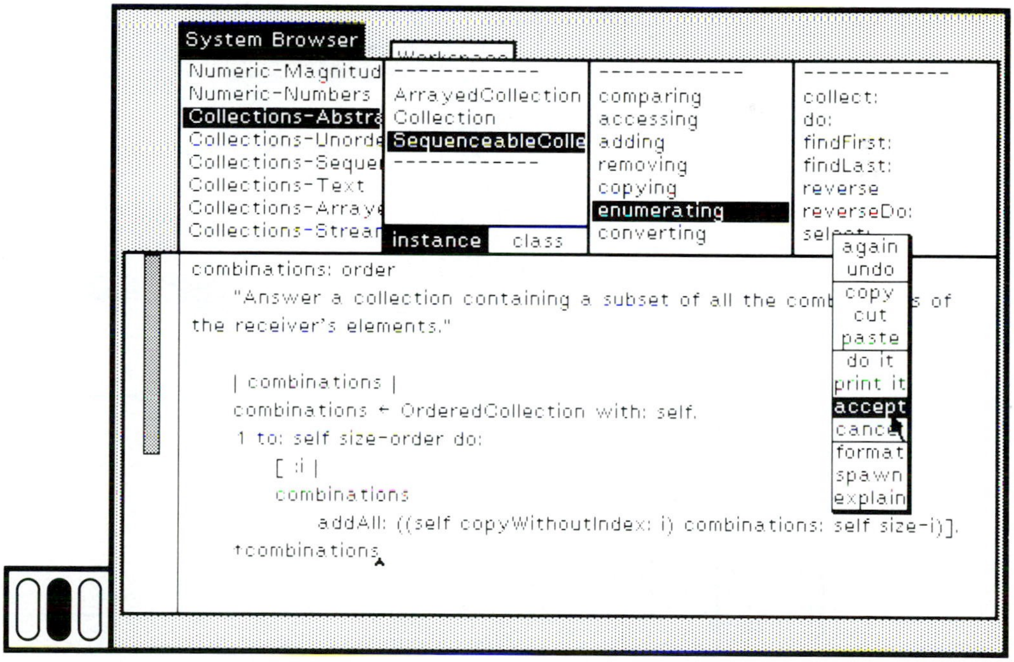

Figure 11.15b

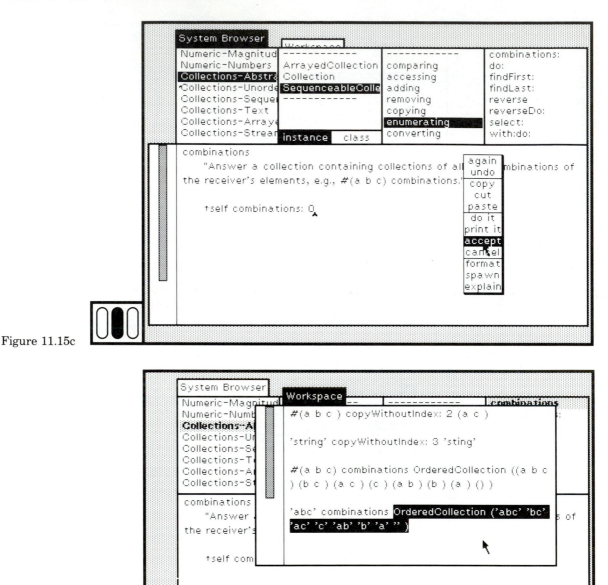

Figure 11.15c

Figure 11.15d

11.4

Modifying Class Comments

In the previous section, you saw how existing methods can be edited and recompiled, how protocol names are specified, and how new methods are added to a class description. A method can include a comment about its intended use; comments can be interspersed among the statements in order to explain the algorithm.

Comments can be provided for the class as a whole, to document its potential use in the system. In a system browser, choose class category Graphics-Primitives, and choose class name Rectangle. In the class-names subview, choose the yellow button command comment (Figure 11.16a). A comment about the selected class appears in the text subview (Figure 11.16b). You can edit this text. For example, you can insert more commentary. The changed comment is stored when you choose the yellow button command accept in the text subview (Figure 11.16c).

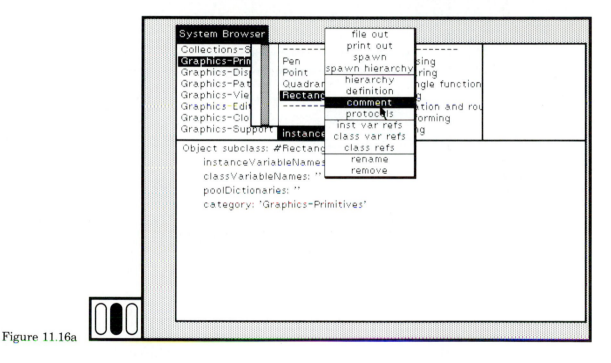

Figure 11.16a

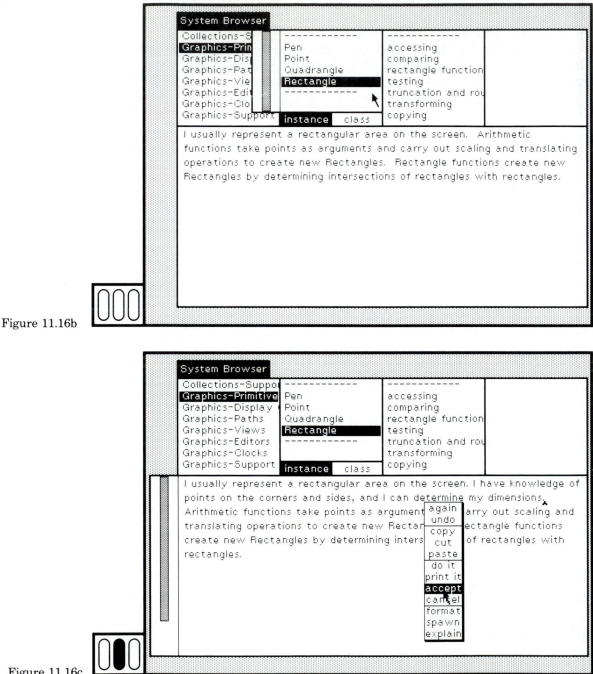

Figure 11.16b

Figure 11.16c

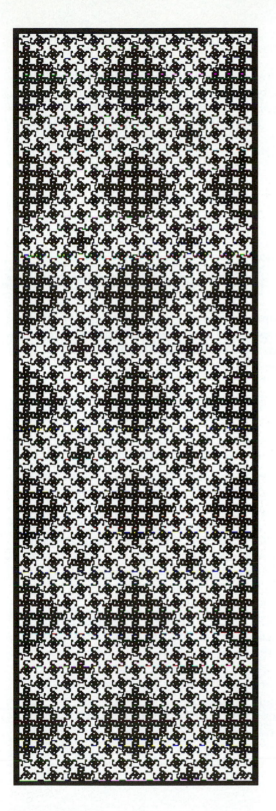

12

Modifying Existing Class Definitions

The class definition of an existing class is obtained by choosing the class name in a system browser, or by choosing the yellow button command definition in the class-names subview of a browser. The definition consists of six parts:

- name of superclass

- name of class

- instance variable declarations

- class variable declarations

- pooled dictionary declarations

- class category name

Each of these parts can be changed by editing the text of the definition that appears in the text subview of the browser, and then choosing the yellow button command accept. The consequences of these actions will be described in the following sections.

12.1

Name of Superclass

Changing the name of the superclass means that you are changing the (inherited) methods to which instances of the class can respond, and you are changing the (inherited) variables that describe each instance. In the browser shown in Figure 12.1a, class category Graphics-Paths and class name Arc are selected. The superclass name has been selected in the definition of Arc. Change the superclass name by replacing the text. In Figure 12.1b, the superclass for Arc has been changed from Path to Object. Choose the yellow button command accept to indicate that you are done editing and that the change should be made.

If the new name already exists or if the first letter is not capitalized, a notifier will appear on the screen. After you understand the problem, close the notifier and correct the definition. If the new name is acceptable, the system recompiles all the methods and will report if the change causes some methods to refer to undeclared variables. The report is displayed in the System Transcript view, as shown in Figure 12.1c. Both Arc and its subclass Circle have been recompiled. One of the methods of Circle refers to the variable form, which was declared in Path and is therefore no longer within the scope of the methods of class Circle.

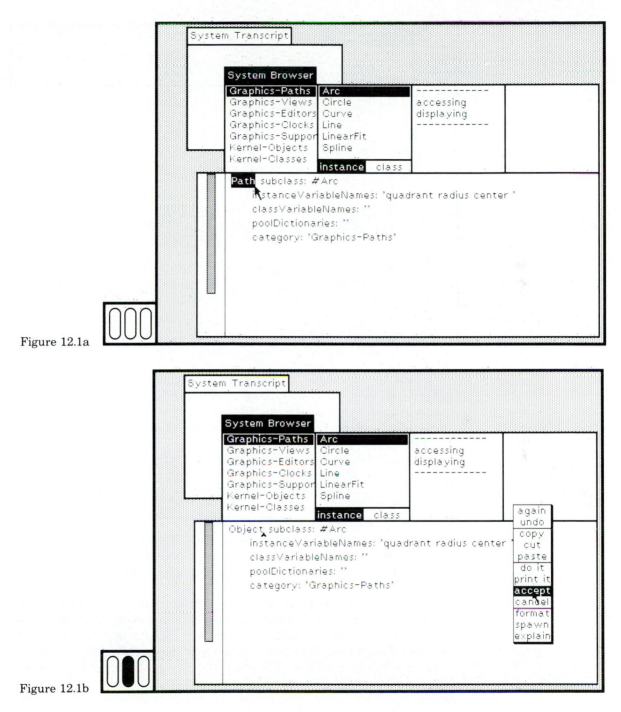

Figure 12.1a

Figure 12.1b

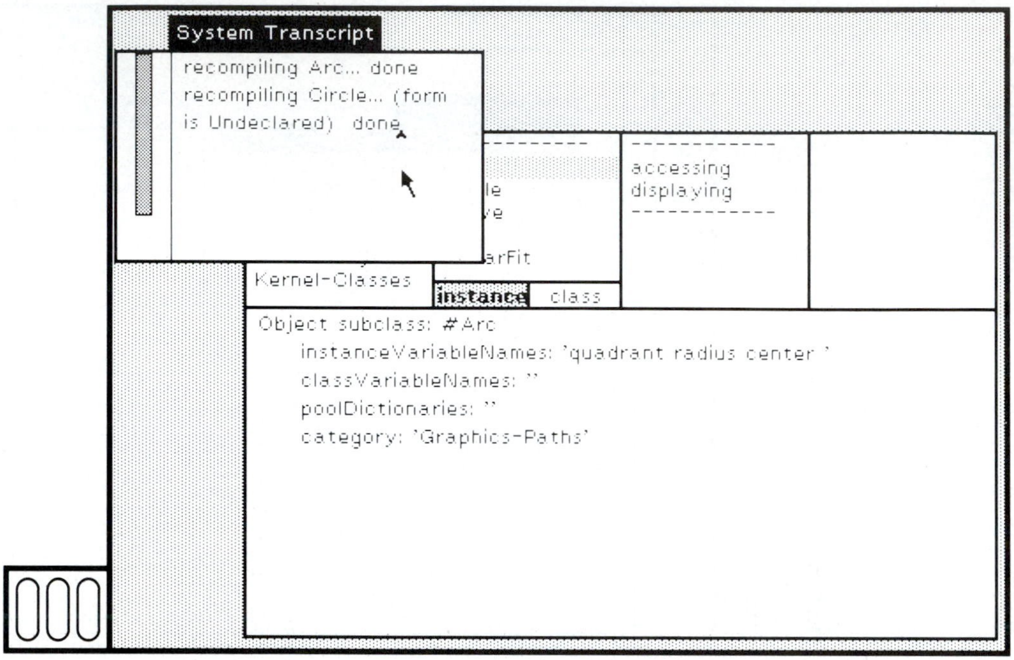

Figure 12.1c

As will be illustrated in the section on changing instance variable declarations (Section 12.3), adding or deleting instance variables means that any existing instances will automatically be updated. When appropriate, you must check to make certain that all existing instances properly initialize any new variables.

12.2

Name of Class

Editing the class name is a way to create a new class description with the same definition as the old. The new class will be categorized in the selected class category, unless the class category is changed in the definition text.

Editing the class name is not the way to rename a class. You rename a class by choosing the yellow button command rename in the class-names subview (Figure 12.2a). A prompter appears in which you type the new class name. Type Parc. When you are done typing the name, terminate by choosing the yellow button command accept or by pressing the "carriage return" key (Figure 12.2b). This prompter is unscheduled, so you must respond. If you change your mind, simply leave no characters in the prompter and terminate.

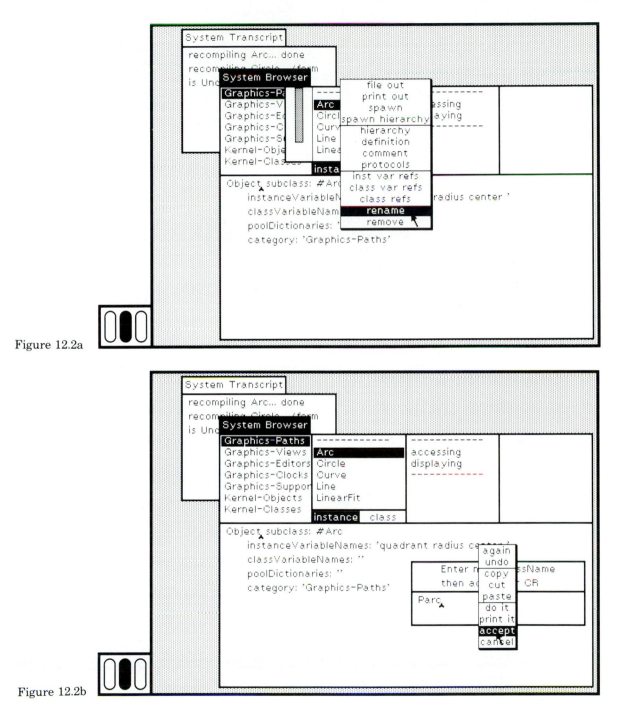

Figure 12.2a

Figure 12.2b

When you rename a class, the name in the browser menu is updated and is selected. All subclasses refer to the class by its new name. Compiled methods that refer to the class are also correct. However, since the system source code is just text stored on a local disk or stored on a remote file server, all the source code text does not have updated references to Parc. (This is potentially confusing. The system compiled-code references to Arc have effectively all been updated to Parc, but the source code text is handled independently.)

To remind you to find each method in which the class is referenced, the system searches for all references to the class (as indicated in the System Transcript). If any exist, a special browser is created (Figure 12.2c). This is a message-set browser, as defined in Chapter 10. You are asked to designate the rectangular area for the browser. The browser menu will contain references to class/messages whose associated methods contain references to Parc. However, the text will still show the word Arc (Figure 12.2d). Replace the word with Parc and choose the yellow button command accept (Figure 12.2e). If you do this for all the methods, when you later browse the system, you will have the correct source code text.

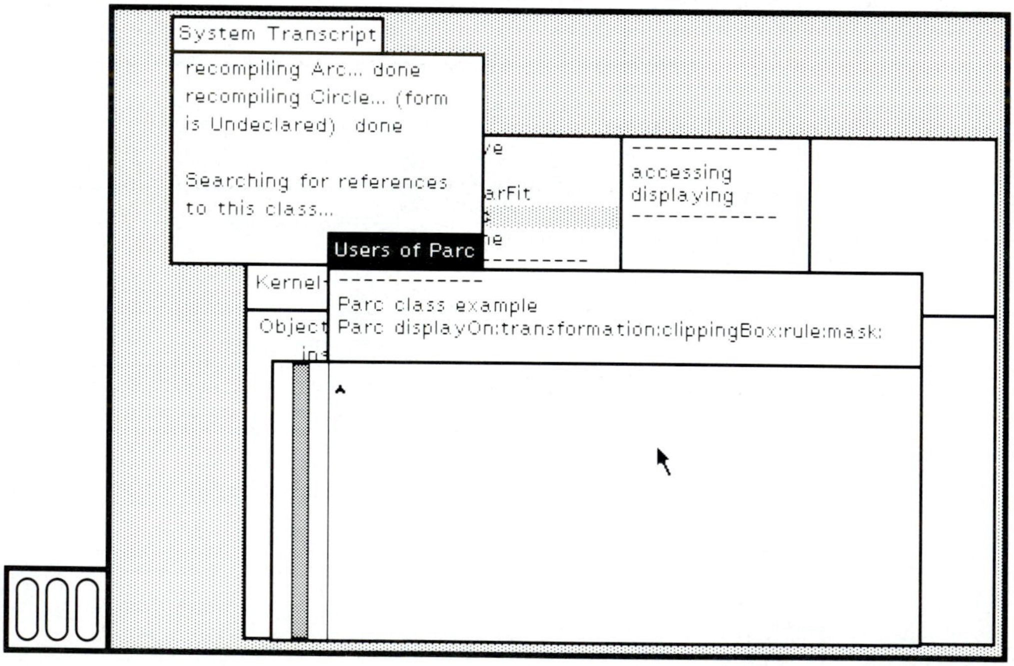

Figure 12.2c

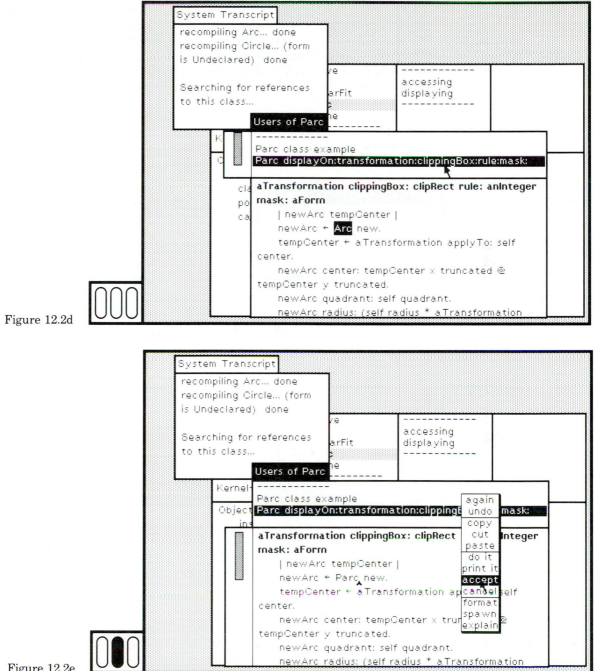

Figure 12.2d

Figure 12.2e

Alternatively, you can evaluate an expression to rename a class. The message rename: is understood by all class objects; the message argument is a String representing the new name for the class. For example, let's do the previous example again (the illustrations assume that you did not do it before) and change the name of class Arc to be Parc. As shown in Figure 12.3a, type and select the expression

    Arc rename: ′ Parc ′

and choose the yellow button command do it.

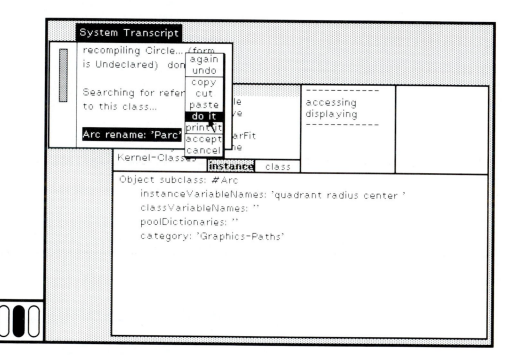

Figure 12.3a

The task is complete, although the view in the browser has not been updated (Figure 12.3b). Deselect the class category Graphics-Paths by pointing to it with the cursor and clicking the red button (i.e., choosing it again). Then choose the category again (Figure 12.3c). In this way, you request that the menu of class names be updated. Notice the item Parc is now at the end of the menu.

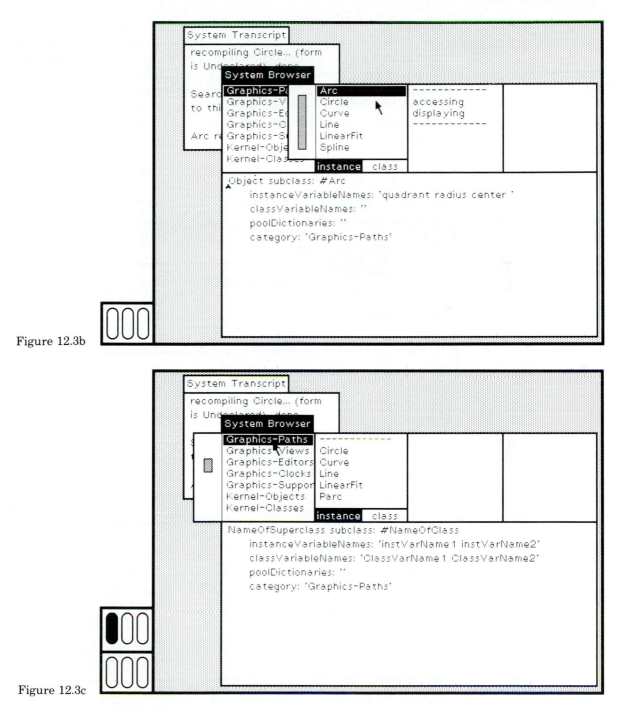

Figure 12.3b

Figure 12.3c

If you now select the definition of a subclass of Parc, Circle, in Figure 12.3d, its superclass properly refers to the new name. All of the compiled code works correctly. However, the source code has not been changed; it still shows the word Arc in the text. To update the source code, you will have to edit the text yourself. In the System Workspace, edit the template for browsing all calls on a particular object. Find an expression like the following and change the argument symbol to be #Parc.

Smalltalk browseAllCallsOn: (Smalltalk associationAt: #Parc)

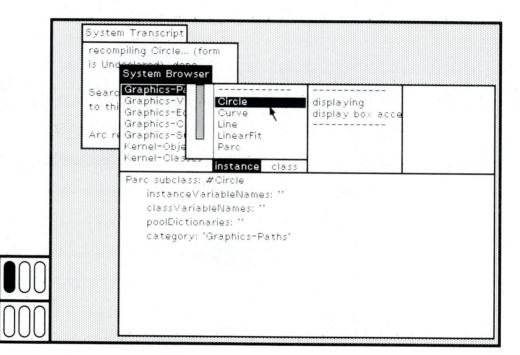

Figure 12.3d

Select the expression and choose the yellow button command do it. In this way you obtain the message-set browser that gives you access to all methods whose text references Arc rather than Parc, as previously shown in Figures 12.2c and 12.2d.

12.3

Instance Variable Declarations

To illustrate the effect of changing the instance variable declarations, an example of modifying Parc is given in this section (Parc was formerly Arc if you followed the previous example). Start by undoing the example of Figure 12.1b, so that Parc, once again, is a subclass of Path. Open a workspace and type the expressions shown in Figure 12.4a. Evaluating these expressions declares two temporary variables, aForm and anArc; creates a new instance of Form referred to by aForm; creates a new instance of Parc referred to by anArc; initializes the new Parc with radius 50.0, quadrant 4, and center wherever you point with the cursor and click any button (Sensor waitButton). (The cursor changes to an arrow with an asterisk—the execute cursor—until you click the button.) The Parc is then drawn on the display screen (Display). And, finally, an inspector for the Parc is created. The image of the Parc and the inspector for the instance are shown in Figure 12.4b.

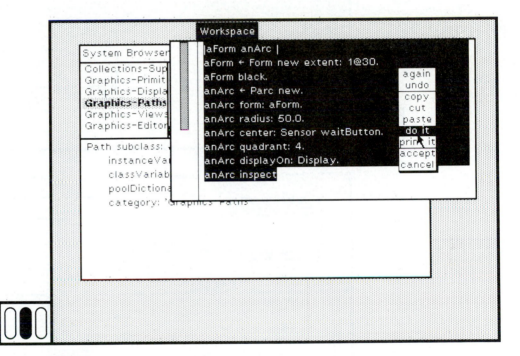

Figure 12.4a

Notice that the instance of Parc has five instance variables; their names appear in the menu of the inspector. Two of the variables are declared in the superclass Path, and three are declared in Parc. Now return to the browser and change the superclass of Parc to be DisplayObject (Figure 12.4c). The inspector is no longer correct. Close it by choosing the blue button command close (Figure 12.4d).

Return to the workspace and once again evaluate the expressions that create a Form. A notifier appears (Figure 12.4e). The message form: was implemented in class Path. By changing the superclass of class Parc, the message form: is no longer part of the protocol of Parc. The instance variable form and the message form: must be specified in class Parc.

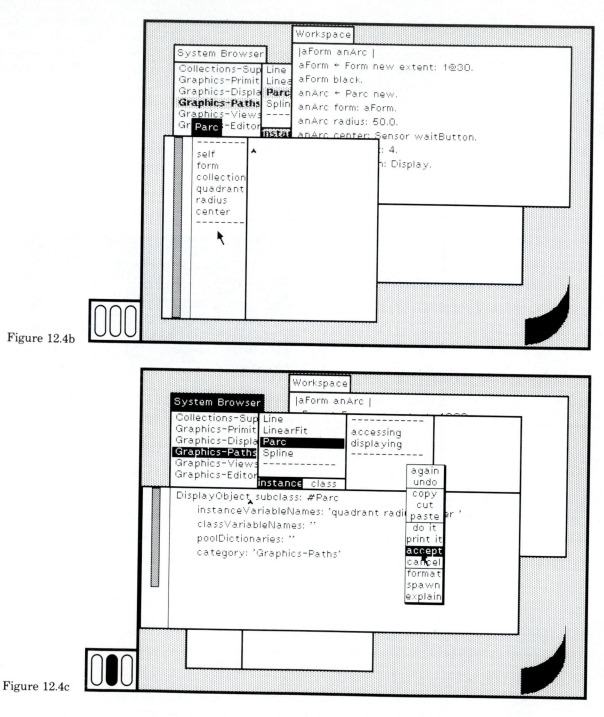

Figure 12.4b

Figure 12.4c

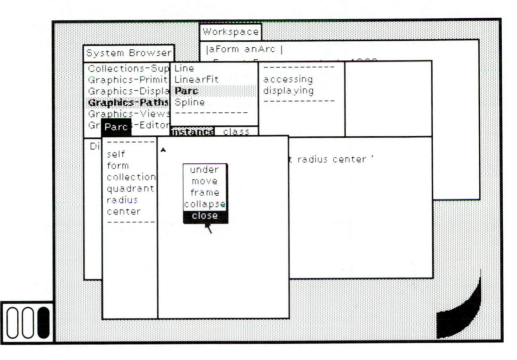

Figure 12.4d

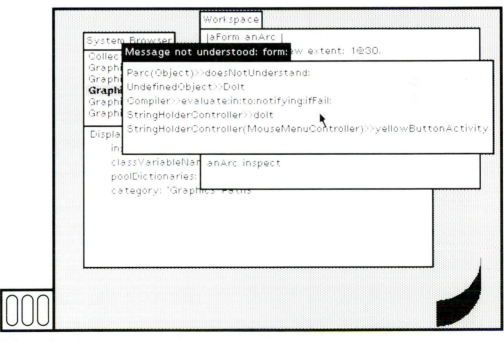

Figure 12.4e

First add the instance variable form to Parc. Edit the class definition and choose the yellow button command accept (Figure 12.4f). Now copy form: from Path to Parc. Choose the class category Graphics-Primitives, class Path, protocol accessing, and message selector form:. Choose the yellow button command move (Figure 12.4g).

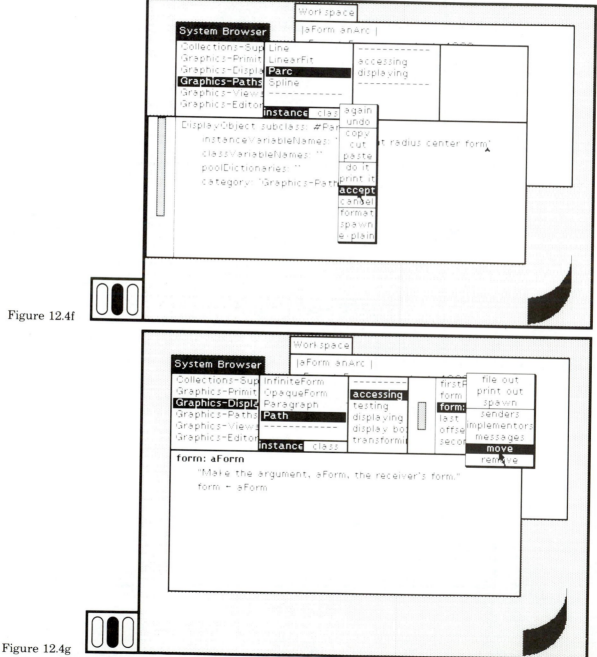

Figure 12.4f

Figure 12.4g

In the prompter that appears, type Parc > accessing and then choose the yellow button command accept (Figure 12.4h). This then copies the method to class Parc. Do the same copying sequence for the message form so that both methods are in Parc (Figure 12.4i).

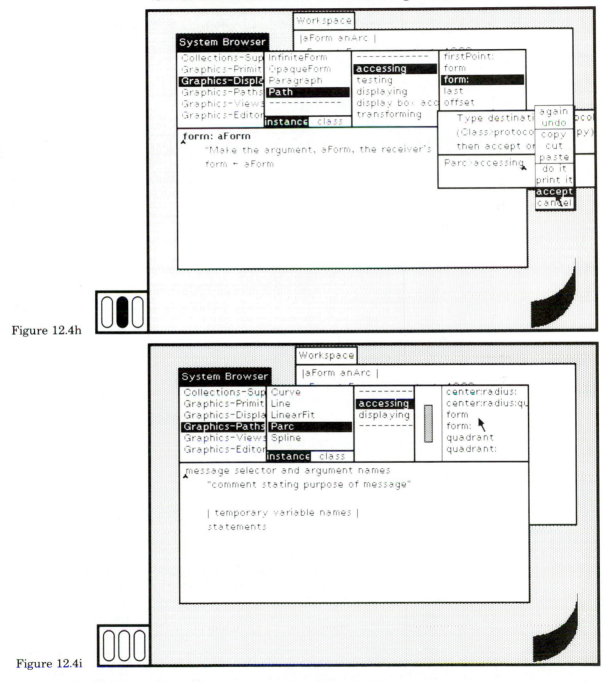

Figure 12.4h

Figure 12.4i

Return to the workspace and once again evaluate the expressions that create a Form, a Parc, and an inspector for the Parc. This time the inspector shows four instance variable names in the menu (Figure 12.4j).

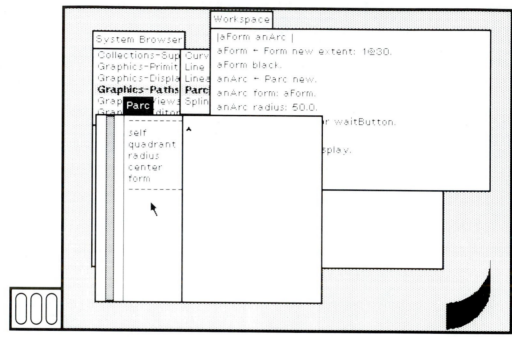

Figure 12.4j

The method for form: simply assigns a value to the instance variable form. If existing instances of Parc must have this variable initialized, evaluate an expression such as the following one.

Parc allInstancesDo: [:each | each form: (Form new extent: 1@30)]

12.4

Class Variable Declarations

Adding or deleting class variables is similar to adding or deleting instance variables in that the methods of the class and its subclasses are recompiled. If any method references a variable no longer in the scope of the method, the name of the variable is printed in the System Transcript. Typically, initialization of class variables is done in methods specified in the class protocol rather than in the instance protocol, although both are feasible. By convention, class protocol has a category class initialization and a message selector initialize whose method does the class variable initialization. An example from class Cursor is shown in Figure 12.5.

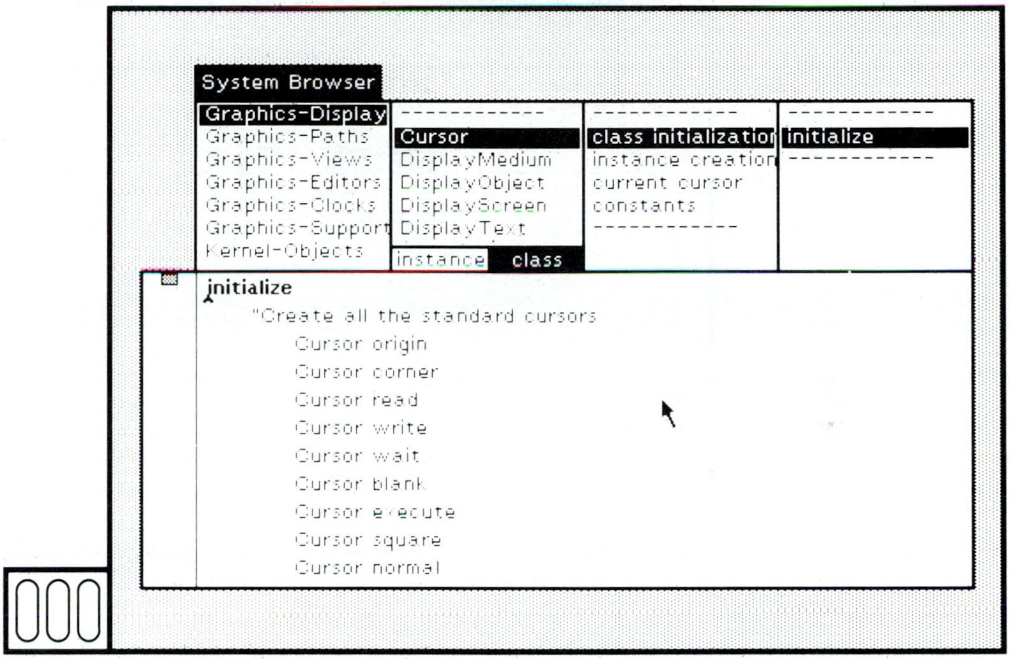

Figure 12.5

12.5

**Pooled
Dictionary
Declarations**

Adding a name of a pooled dictionary in the class definition means that any variable name declared as a key in that dictionary is now within the scope of the methods of the class and its subclasses. Deleting a pooled dictionary reference means that possibly several variables have been removed from the scope of the class methods. There is no special initialization needed if a pooled dictionary is added to a class definition. An example of class DisplayText in which a pooled dictionary, TextConstants, is declared as shown in Figure 12.6.

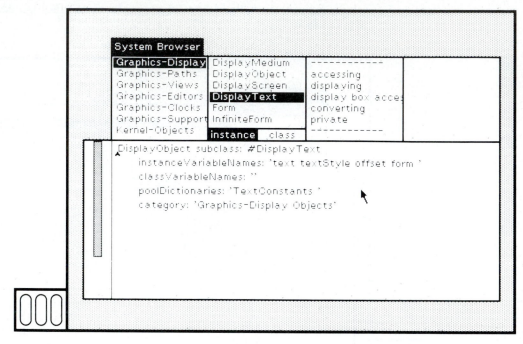

Figure 12.6

12.6

Class Category

To change the category of class, you can edit the category reference in the class definition. The class is moved to the new category and the browser is updated. There are two cases of things you can do—move the class to an existing category, or move the class to a new category.

In Figure 12.7a, the definition of class Path is shown in a browser. Part of the class category, originally Graphics-Display Objects, is selected. Replace the selected part by Primitives as shown in Figure 12.7b. Choose the yellow button command accept to indicate that Path should be moved to the existing category Graphics-Primitives.

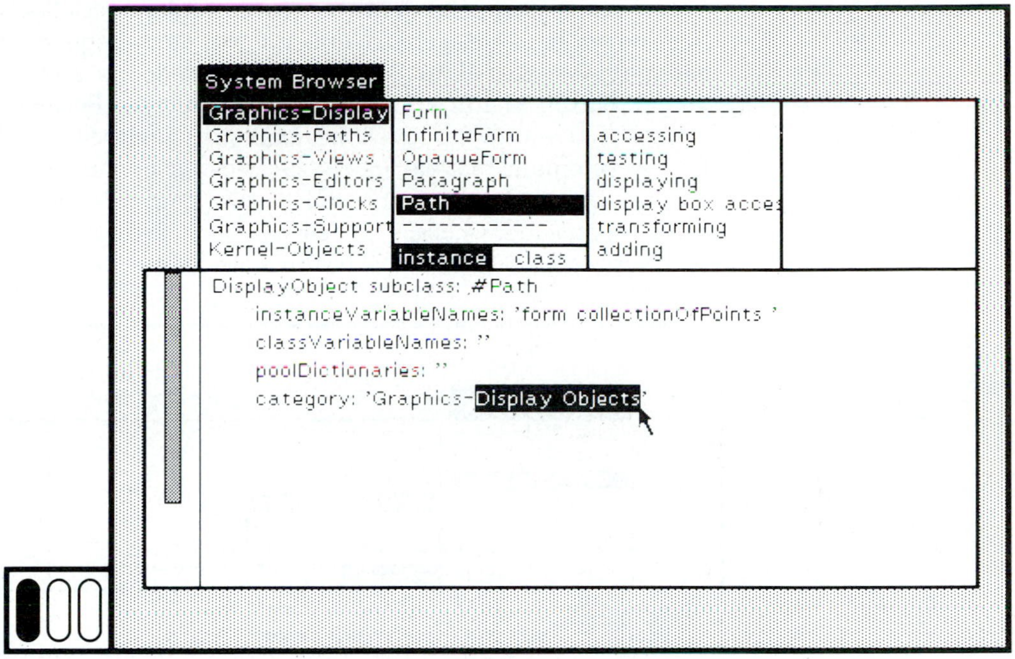

Figure 12.7a

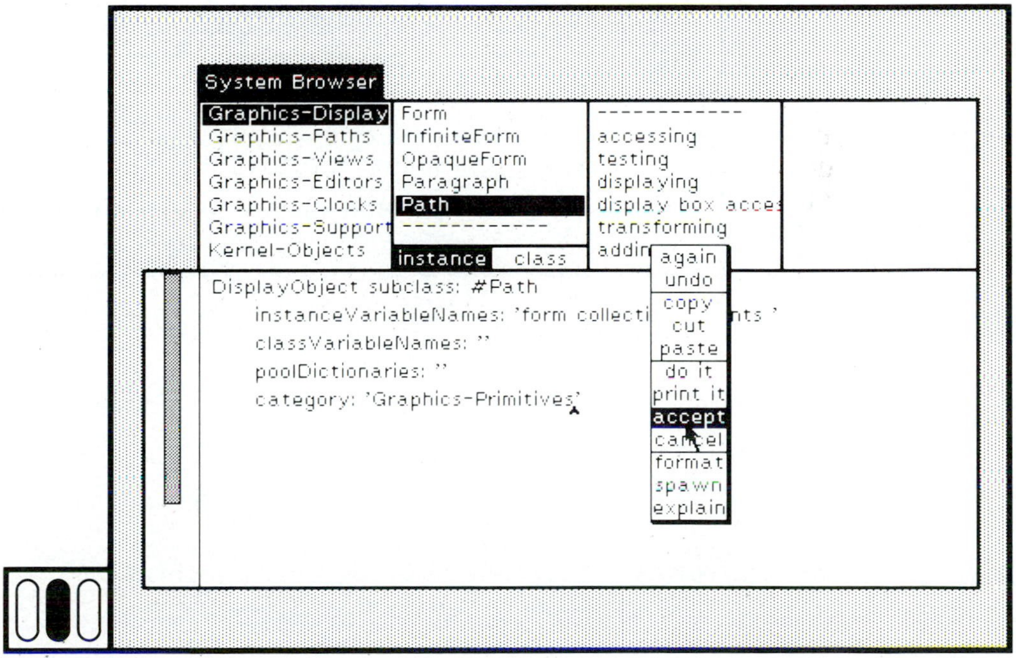

Figure 12.7b

In Figure 12.8a, the definition of class MappedCollection is shown in a browser. It is categorized under Collections-Sequenceable. The class category is changed to Collections-Miscellaneous after you choose the yellow button command accept (Figure 12.8b). Because this is a new category, the browser must be explicitly updated. Choose the yellow button command update in the class-category subview of the browser (Figure 12.8c). Scroll to the end of the class-category menu. The new category appears. Choose the new category, Collections-Miscellaneous, to see that MappedCollection is in the class-names menu (Figure 12.8d).

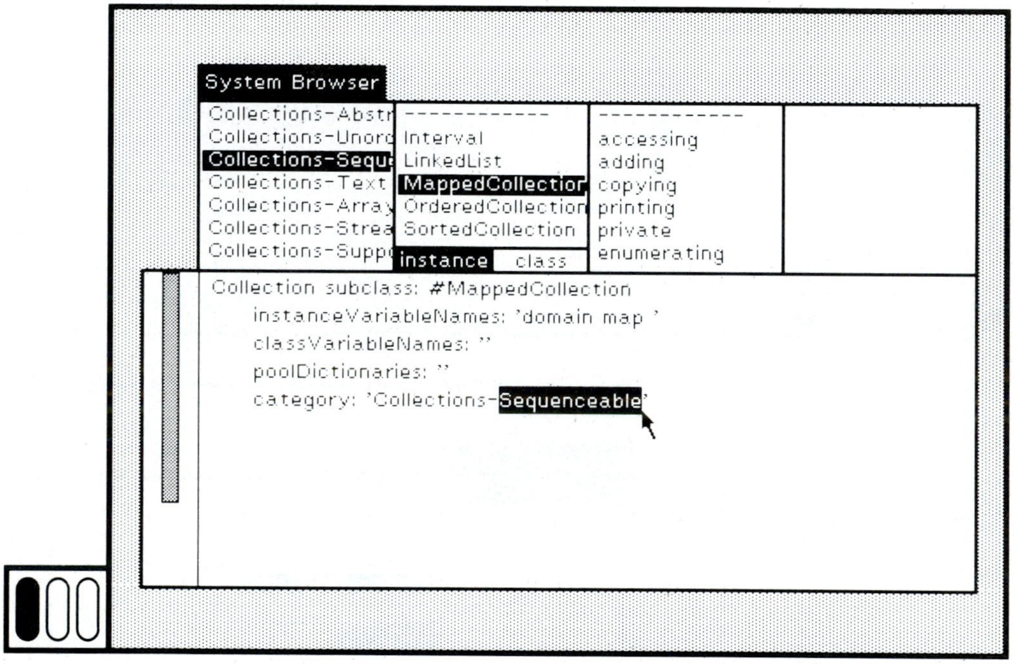

Figure 12.8a

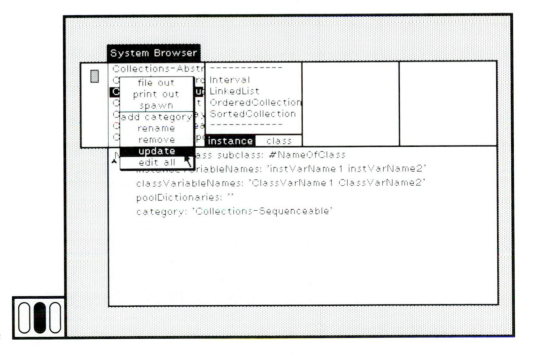

Figure 12.8b

Figure 12.8c

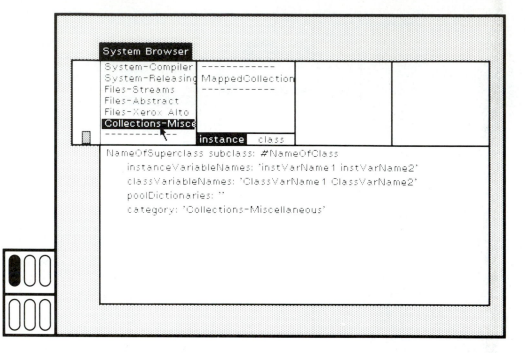

Figure 12.8d

The two examples just presented show how to move a class into a new category, either one that existed or one that is created anew. It is possible to create a new category by choosing the command add category from the yellow button menu of the class-category subview. Adding a class category works in a way that is analogous to adding a new message protocol (see Section 11.2). The yellow button menu also includes the commands rename and remove. These also work in a way analogous to the commands used for renaming and removing message protocols.

The command edit all is in the class-category subview yellow button menu. If you choose this command, the class categories and class names in each category appear in the text subview of the browser. The syntax for the categorization is like that for the organization of the message protocol/message selectors. You can modify the organization and then choose the text subview yellow button command accept. The syntax will be checked and, if correct, the class categorization will be updated. You should not attempt to remove access to a class by deleting it. You cannot specify more than one category for a class. And you cannot create a new class simply by inserting its name in a category.

13

Creating a New Class Description

Class Commander represents an object that controls several line-drawing Pens and coordinates their drawing a design. The class was presented as a graphics example in the book *Smalltalk-80: The Language and its Implementation*; it is presented here to illustrate the process of creating and testing a new class description. A Commander is an Array of Pens. Pens controlled by a Commander can be given directions by having the Commander enumerate each Pen and evaluate a block containing Pen commands. So, if a Commander's Pens should each go: 100, for example, then the Commander can be sent the message

do: [:each | each go: 100]

Alternatively, the Commander itself can be made to respond to the message go: 100, where the method associated with the message go: consists of the enumeration message.

A Commander also responds to messages to arrange its Pens so that interesting designs based on symmetries can be created. The message shown in the figures is fanOut. The purpose of fanOut is to arrange the Pens so that their angles are evenly distributed around 360 degrees.

13.1

Define a New Class

You have already reviewed all the parts of the browser that are used in creating class descriptions, with the exception of declaring a new class by editing the template for a class definition. When you want to add a new class description to the system, you first decide on the class category in which you want to access the class. Choose that category. A template for specifying the class appears in the text subview. (See Section 12.6 on how to add a new category.)

Class category Graphics-Display Objects is an appropriate category for class Commander. Choose this category (Figure 13.1a). The class definition template is in the form of a message to a class. The first word in the template represents the message receiver (NameOfSuperclass). It should be replaced by the name of the class that is to be the superclass of the new class. Select this word (Figure 13.1b). Type the superclass name; in this example, the superclass is Array (Figure 13.1c). The message pattern consists of keywords (those words with trailing colons) that should not be changed, and message arguments. None of the syntax for literals should be changed (that is, the hash mark # and the single quotes). The message argument for the keyword subclass: must be a symbol constant; the rest of the arguments must be string constants.

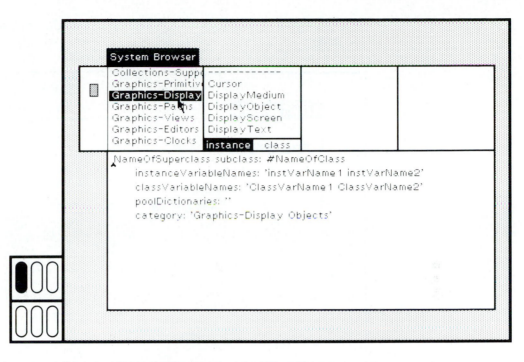

Figure 13.1a

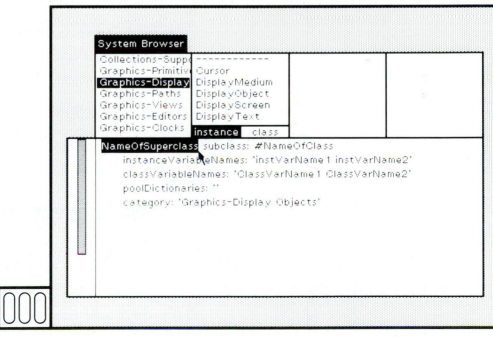

Figure 13.1b

The desired class name is Commander. Select the first message argument NameOfClass (Figure 13.1c) and replace it with Commander (Figure 13.1d). Select the "dummy" instance variable names instVarName1

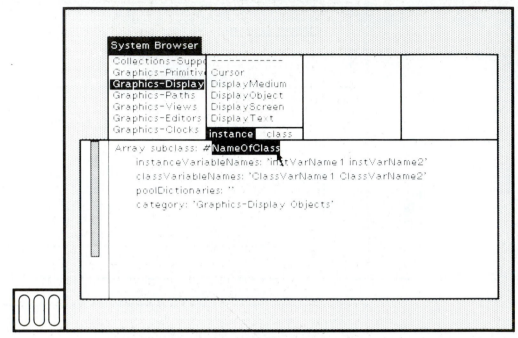

Figure 13.1c

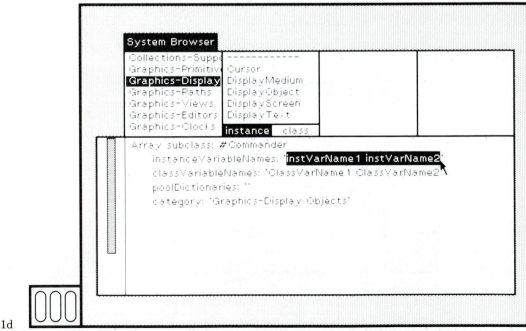

Figure 13.1d

and instVarName2, and remove them by choosing the yellow button command cut (Figure 13.1e). Similarly, remove the "dummy" class variable names ClassVarName1 and ClassVarName2 (Figure 13.1f). (Notice

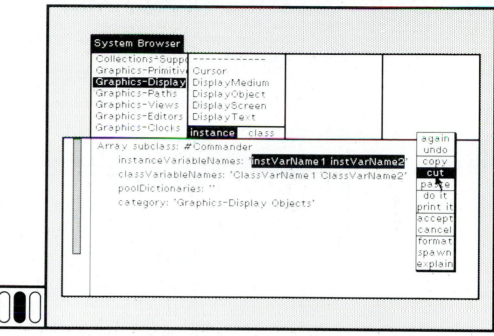

Figure 13.1e

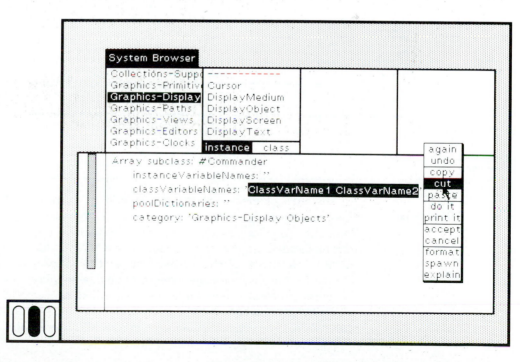

Figure 13.1f

that if you do add class variable names, the first letter of the name should be capitalized.) Now evaluate the message expression by choosing the yellow button command accept.

Class Commander is now defined in the system. Its name appears in the browser class-names menu (Figure 13.2). Because it is a subclass of Array, class Commander must be a "variable subclass," which means that its instances may have different numbers of indexable instance variables. The system automatically made this designation. All of the capabilities that support browsing, querying, and modifying system classes are available for this and any user-defined class.

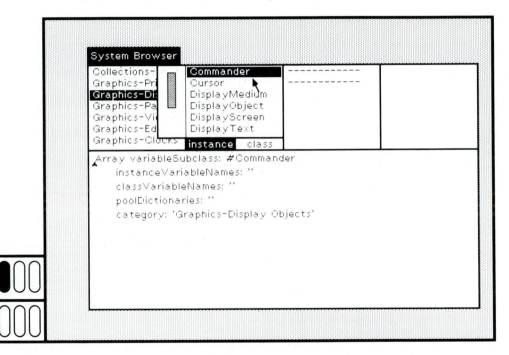

Figure 13.2

13.2

Define the Class Protocol

An instance of class Commander should be initialized by sending the class the message new: with an integer representing the number of Pens that the Commander must coordinate. The message new: must be reimplemented in the class protocol of Commander in order to create the Pen elements of the array. Choose the browser menu item class (Figure 13.3a). The message-category subview displays the categories for the class protocol; none have been specified as yet. Add the protocol name instance creation by choosing the yellow button command add protocol in the message-category subview (Figure 13.3b). The prompter

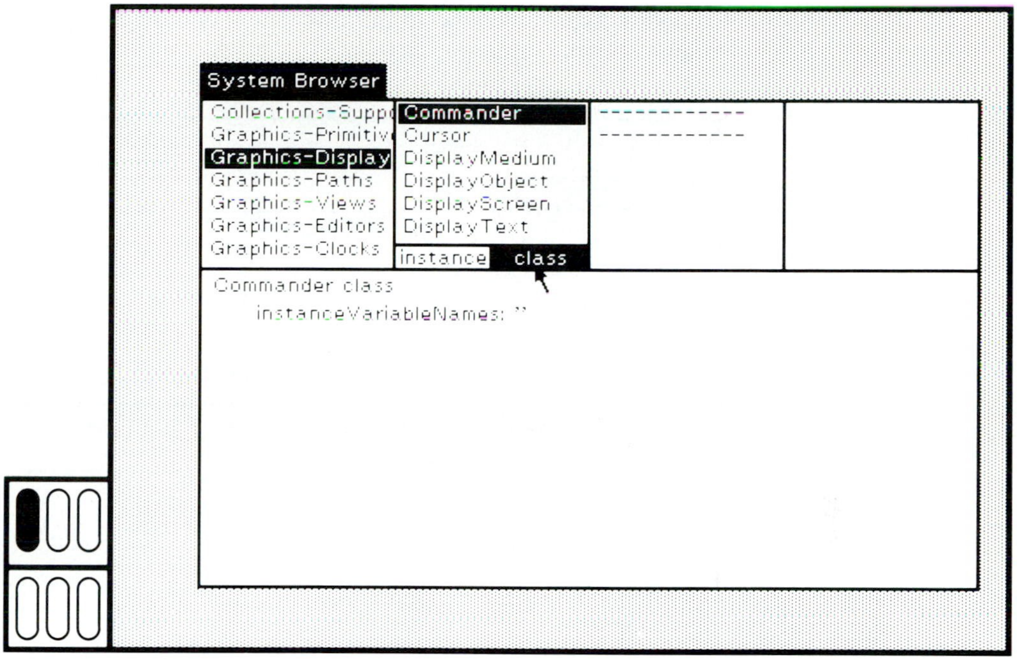

Figure 13.3a

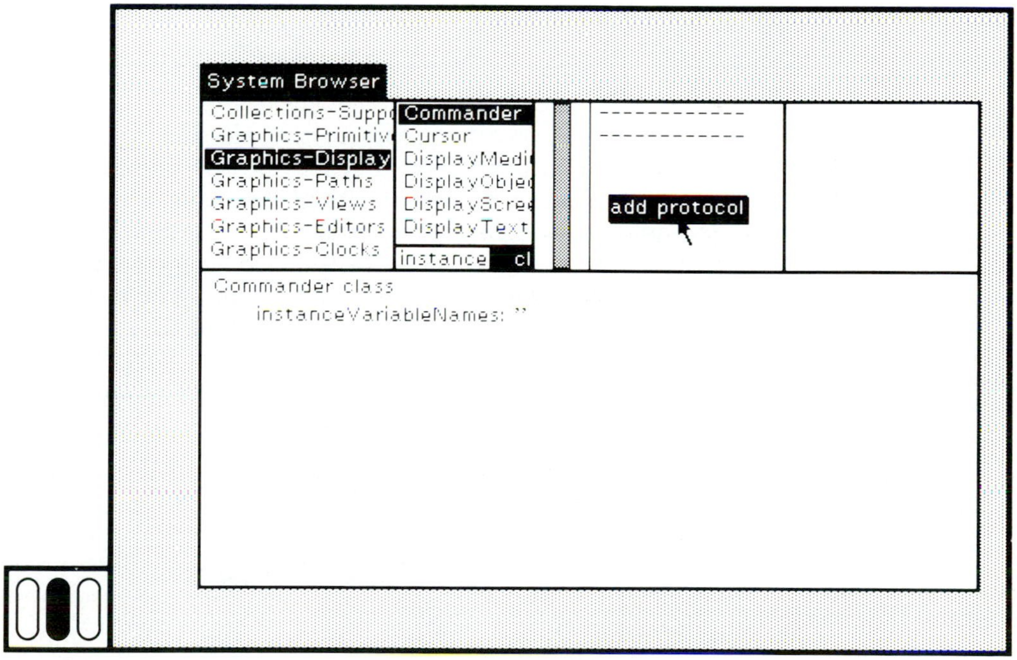

Figure 13.3b

appears; type the new name and then choose the yellow button command accept (Figure 13.3c).

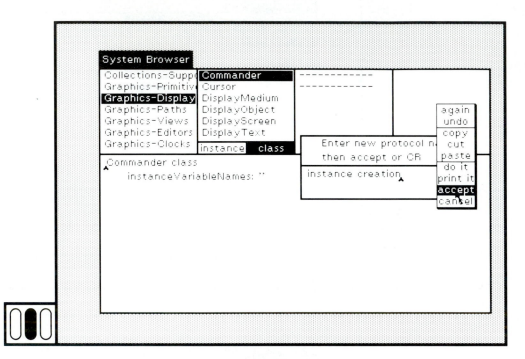

Figure 13.3c

The new protocol appears in the message-category subview (Figure 13.3d). It is automatically selected and the method template appears in the text subview. Edit the method template to specify the new method for new: (shown in Figure 13.3e). This method creates an instance of Commander and assigns it to the temporary variable newCommander. For each element of the Commander array, a new Pen is created and stored. The new instance is returned as the result of the method. Choose the yellow button command accept in the text subview to compile the method and add it to the class description.

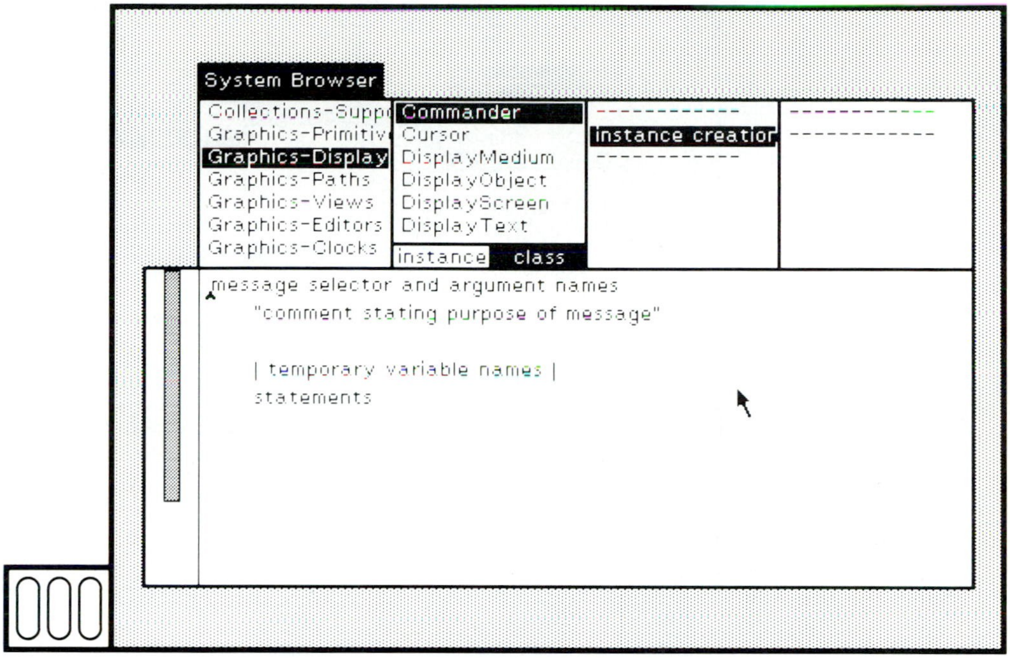

Figure 13.3d

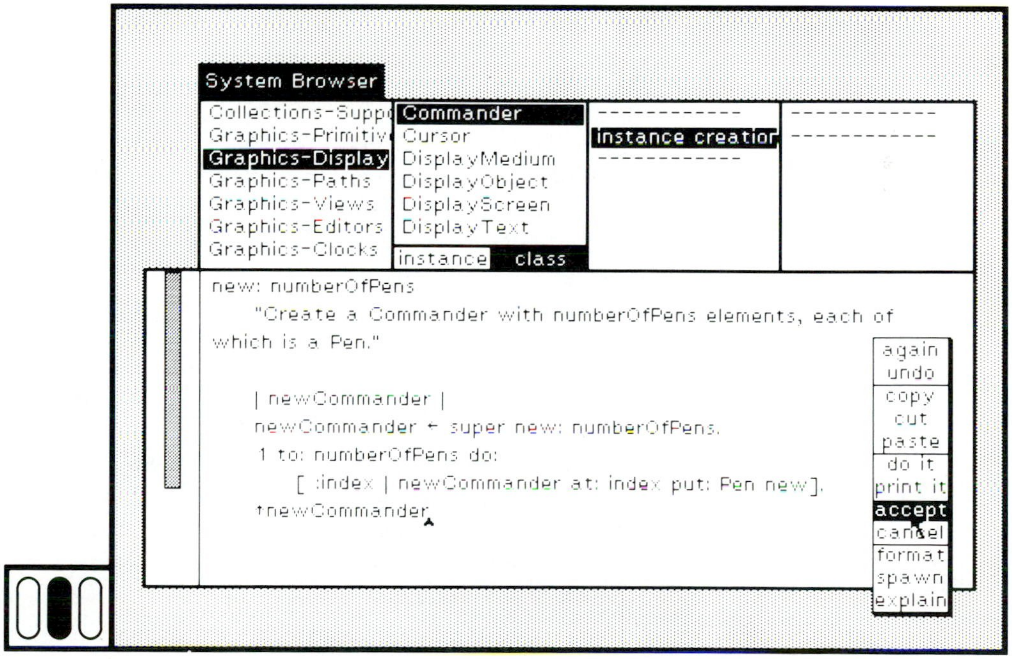

Figure 13.3e

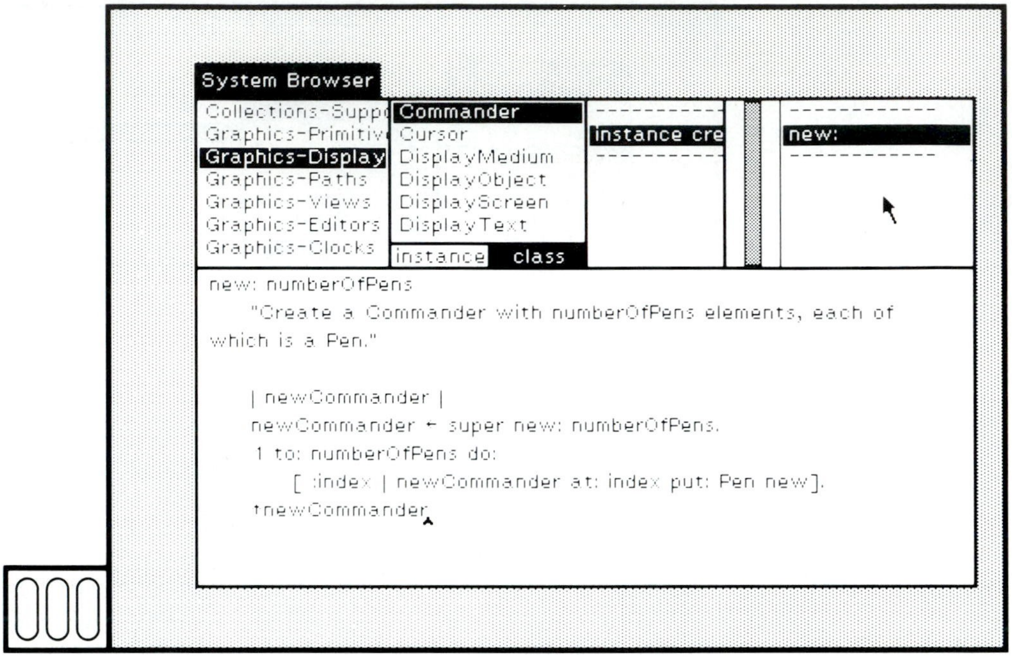

Figure 13.3f

```
System Browser
Collections-Supp┊Commander    ┊----------┊  ┊----------┊
Graphics-Primitiv┊Cursor       ┊instance cre┊  ┊new:      ┊
Graphics-Display ┊DisplayMedium┊----------┊  ┊----------┊
Graphics-Paths   ┊DisplayObject┊          ┊  ┊          ┊
Graphics-Views   ┊DisplayScreen┊          ┊  ┊          ┊
Graphics-Editors ┊DisplayText  ┊          ┊  ┊          ┊
Graphics-Clocks  ┊instance  class┊        ┊  ┊          ┊

new: numberOfPens
    "Create a Commander with numberOfPens elements, each of
which is a Pen."


    | newCommander |
    newCommander ← super new: numberOfPens.
    1 to: numberOfPens do:
        [ :index | newCommander at: index put: Pen new].
    ↑newCommander
```

The message selector new: appears in the message-selector menu (Figure 13.3f). Find out whether this method works. In the text subview, type the creation message Commander new: 4. (Note that we typically opened up a separate workspace in which to type and evaluate expressions. However, any text view in which the text editor and the do it command are available can be used.) Send the new instance of Commander the message inspect. The expression is shown in Figure 13.4. Select it and choose the yellow button command do it.

You designate a rectangular area in which the inspector will appear. In the inspector, choose the pseudo-variable self. The value that prints shows that the array has four elements, each a Pen (Figure 13.5). Do not close the inspector because we will use it again.

Now let's go back to the browser to add line-drawing messages to Commander. Before you will be able to make new selections in the browser, you have to indicate that the text you typed in the text subview was temporary and not to be saved. Do so by choosing the yellow button command cancel (Figure 13.6).

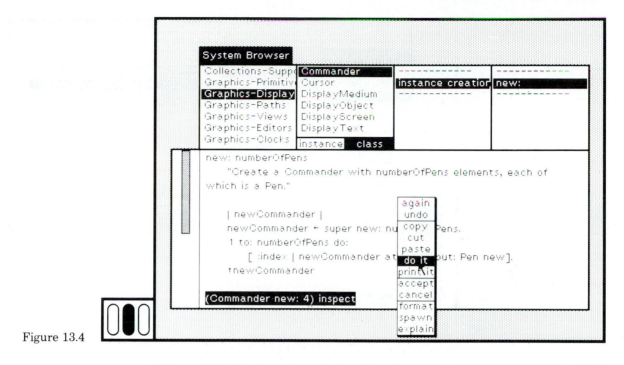

Figure 13.4

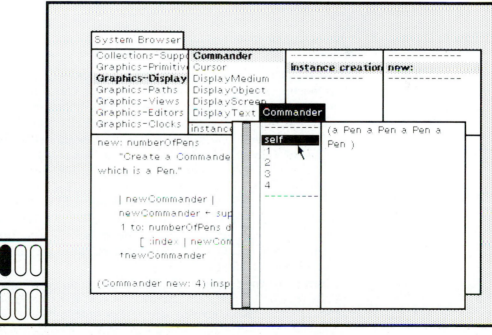

Figure 13.5

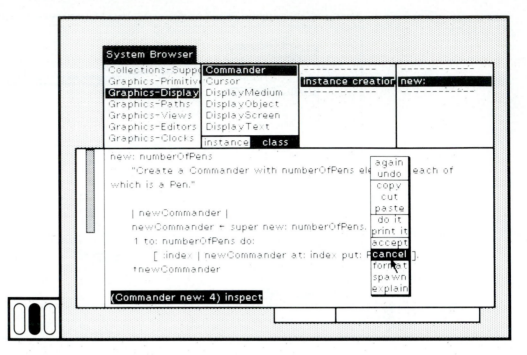

Figure 13.6

13.3

Define the Instance Protocol

Now select the browser menu item instance and specify three protocols, distributing, moving, and geometric designs. You can use the add protocol command. A faster way to add more than one protocol is to choose the yellow button command protocols in the class-names subview (Figure 13.7a), and then edit the text subview as explained in Section 11.2 (Figure 13.7b). Choose yellow button command accept.

Choose the category distributing and edit the method template to specify the method for fanOut (Figure 13.8a). This method consists of one enumeration statement in which each element of the Commander is retrieved (self at: index) and sent the message turn:. Each element is (360/ self size) degrees away from its neighbor. Choose the yellow button command accept. The message selector is added to the menu in the browser (Figure 13.8b).

Return to the inspector for the instance of Commander created earlier. Inspect one of its elements by choosing the element (for example, element 2), and then choosing the yellow button command inspect (Figure 13.9a). An inspector for the Pen is created. Choose its instance variable direction and note that the value is 270.0 (degrees) (Figure 13.9b). This value is the default for all Pens.

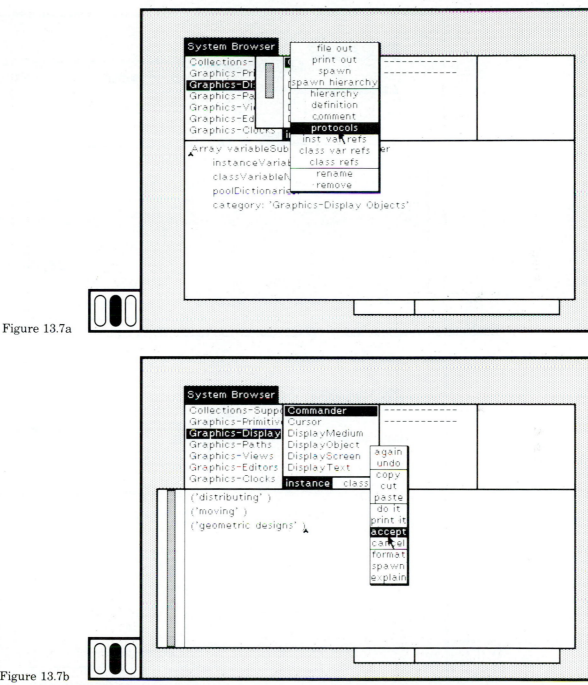

Figure 13.7a

Figure 13.7b

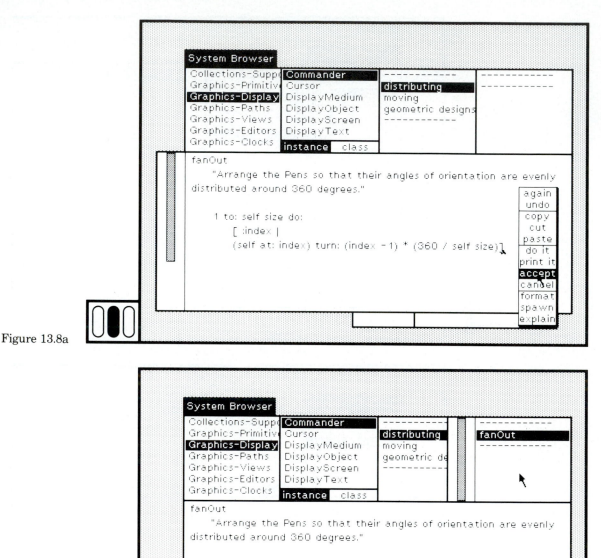

Figure 13.8a

Figure 13.8b

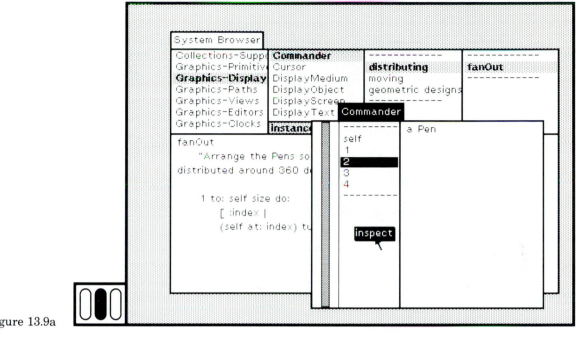

Figure 13.9a

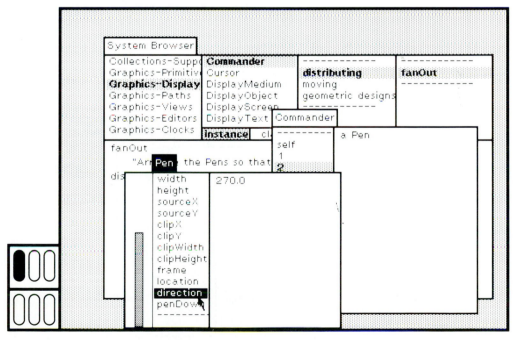

Figure 13.9b

Direct each of the Commander's Pens to "fan out" around 360 degrees by evaluating the expression self fanOut within the text subview of the inspector for the Commander. Type and select the expression, and then choose the yellow button command do it (Figure 13.10). Now check the value of the variable direction of the Pen whose inspector was created (Figure 13.11). This is the second of four Pens; each Pen orientation should differ by 360/4=90 degrees. The first Pen should remain at 270 degrees, the second should be at 270+90=360=0, as indicated.

Continue to test the new Commander. In the inspector for the Commander, type the expression

self do: [:each | each defaultNib: 4. each go: 100]

which directs each of the Pens to draw, with a 4 x 4 square brush, a straight line 100 pixels long. Type and select the expression, and choose the yellow button command do it (Figure 13.12a). The result is a "plus" sign as shown in Figure 13.12b.

Add more messages to the class description for Commander. Add the messages turn: (Figure 13.13) and go: (Figure 13.14) to the category moving. Add the message spiral:angle: (Figure 13.15) to the category geometric designs.

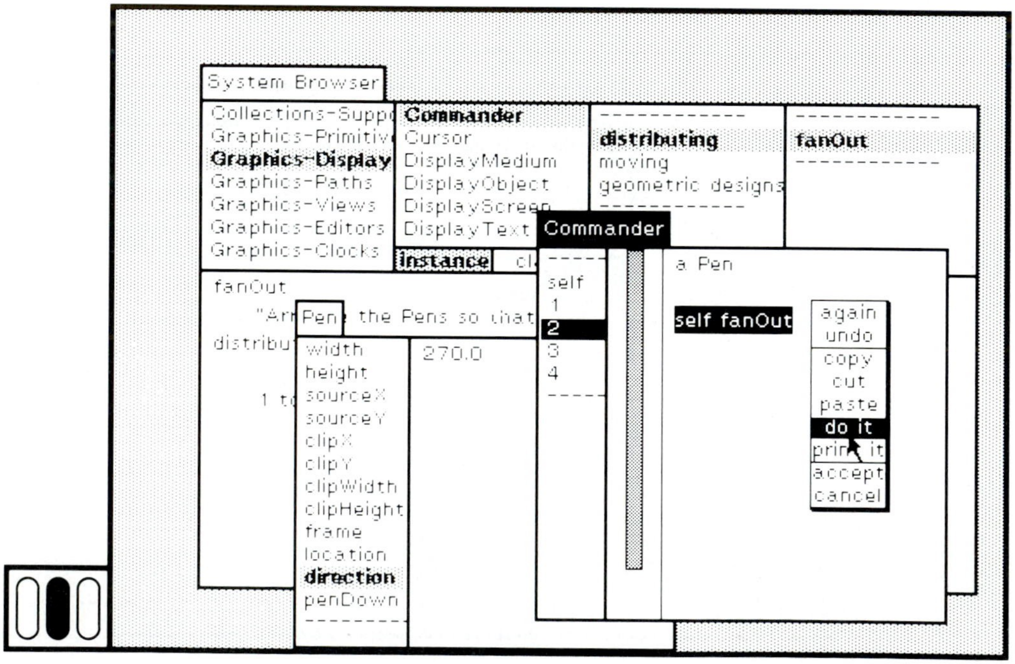

Figure 13.10

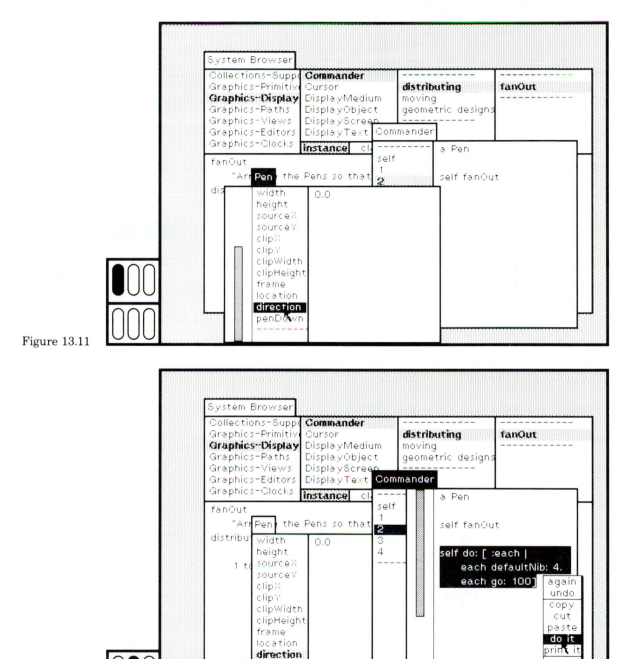

Figure 13.11

Figure 13.12a

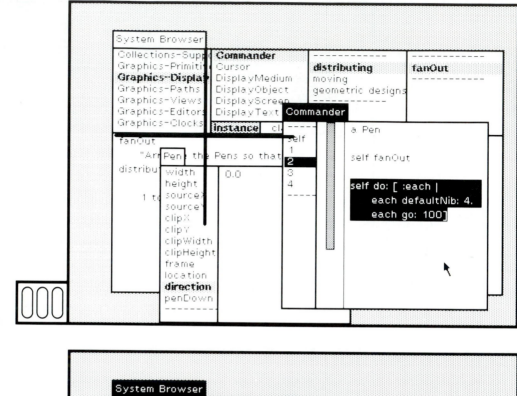

Figure 13.12b

Figure 13.13

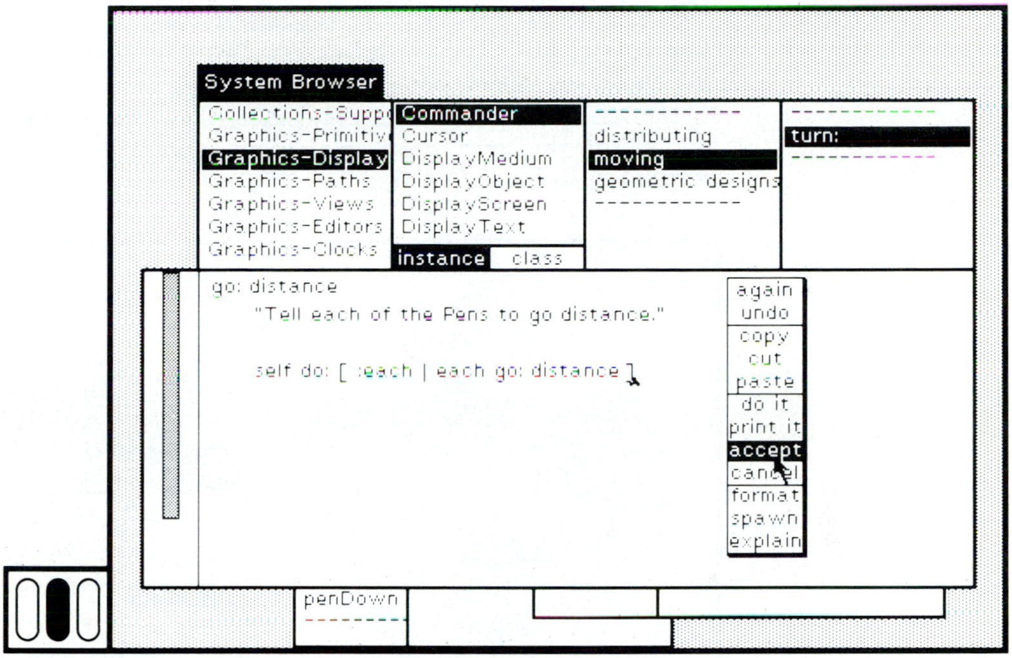

Figure 13.14

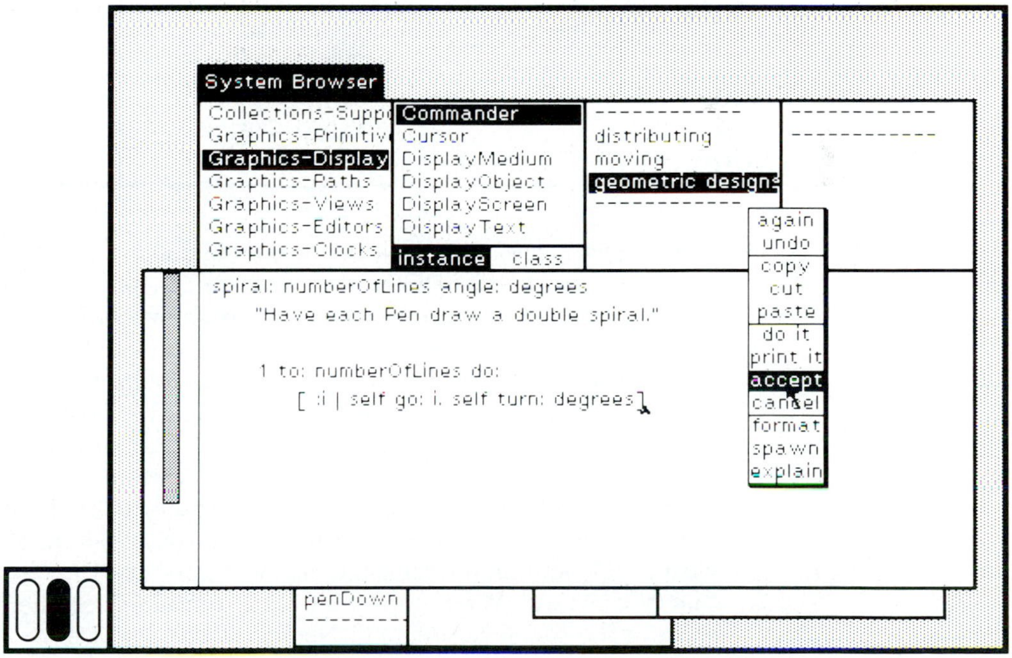

```
System Browser
Collections-Supp  Commander     ------------   turn:
Graphics-Primitiv Cursor         distributing   ------------
Graphics-Display  DisplayMedium  moving
Graphics-Paths    DisplayObject  geometric designs
Graphics-Views    DisplayScreen  ------------
Graphics-Editors  DisplayText
Graphics-Clocks   instance  class
```

```
go: distance
    "Tell each of the Pens to go distance."

    self do: [ :each | each go: distance ]
```

```
again
undo
copy
cut
paste
do it
print it
accept
cancel
format
spawn
explain
```

```
penDown
--------
```

Figure 13.15

```
System Browser
Collections-Supp  Commander     ------------   ------------
Graphics-Primitiv Cursor         distributing   ------------
Graphics-Display  DisplayMedium  moving
Graphics-Paths    DisplayObject  geometric designs
Graphics-Views    DisplayScreen  ------------
Graphics-Editors  DisplayText
Graphics-Clocks   instance  class
```

```
spiral: numberOfLines angle: degrees
    "Have each Pen draw a double spiral."

    1 to: numberOfLines do:
        [ :i | self go: i. self turn: degrees]
```

```
again
undo
copy
cut
paste
do it
print it
accept
cancel
format
spawn
explain
```

```
penDown
--------
```

Now let's test these new messages. Create a workspace or use any text view to evaluate the test expressions. For example, in the inspector for the Commander, set the brush of each of its Pens to be a 1 x 1 square, send each Pen home, and then direct the Commander to go: 50 and create the spiral geometric design. The expressions and the result are shown in Figure 13.16.

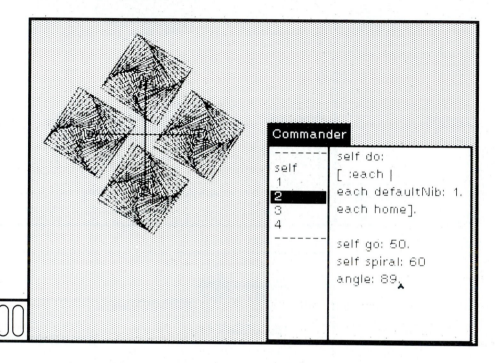

Figure 13.16

In a workspace, create a new Commander for six Pens, each with a 1 x 1 square brush. Direct the Pens to fan out, go a distance of 50 pixels, and then make a spiral design, as shown in Figure 13.17.

You have now created and (incrementally) tested a new class description. To save your work, choose the yellow button command file out in the class-names or class-category subviews. This creates a file in which the class description is written in a format that can be read by another Smalltalk-80 system. The file name is the class name or class category name followed by a period and the characters st (meaning "Smalltalk" file). The class description is still part of your system. But if you start with a new system (or someone else wants to use your work), then note that the System Workspace includes a template for the expression for reading the file ((FileStream fileNamed: 'fileName') fileIn).

Suppose you choose file out in the class-names subview, with Commander selected. Then the file created is named Commander.st. To

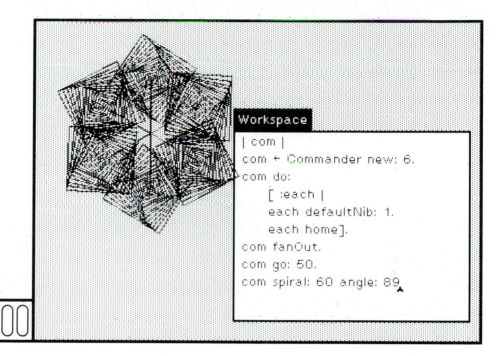

Figure 13.17

read the file and thereby bring the definition of Commander into a new system, evaluate the following expression in that system

(FileStream FileNamed: ' Commander.st ') file In

More information about saving your work and about external files is given in Part Five.

> As additional exercises, you might add the messages defaultNib: and home to class Commander. In each case, the Commander would distribute the message to its Pens.
>
> An interesting exercise to try is to modify the system browser so that you can retain reference to a full query—class category, class, protocol, and selector. The idea is to add a list menu subview to the browser that is initially empty. Add a browser yellow button command save query. When you choose this command, the current menu selections of the browser are saved as a menu item of the new list menu. If you choose such a menu item, the browser selections are all changed appropriately.

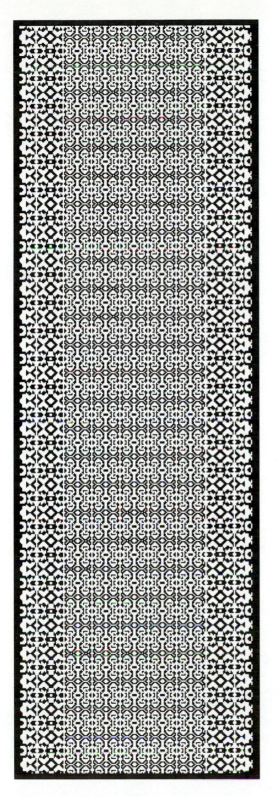

14

Improving Performance

We have seen that you can determine whether your methods work correctly by inspecting the state of the objects involved in the interactions. Another question you might ask is what percentage of the total time in evaluating the expression is spent carrying out various messages? You can answer this question by using the Smalltalk-80 *spy*.

The purpose of the spy is to carry out an analysis of a block of code. The analysis consists of the (nested) sequence of message-sends and the total percentage of time taken up evaluating the original message. The spy creates a workspace labeled Spy Results in which this hierarchy is printed.

The best way to understand the spy is to follow an example of its use. Suppose you are interested in analyzing the evaluation of the expression

Smalltalk keys asSortedCollection

This expression takes all the entries in the SystemDictionary, Smalltalk, and sorts their keys in alphabetical order. To spy on the execution of this sort request, evaluate the expression

MessageTally spyOn: [Smalltalk keys asSortedCollection]

In other words, the spy is run by sending the message spyOn: to the class MessageTally. The analysis is carried out on the argument.

When the analysis is completed, you are asked to designate a workspace in which three levels of information are printed. First, it indicates the number of tallies, that is, the number of times the execution of the expression was interrupted to determine which message currently is being sent. Then it provides a description of the tree, and itemizes the "leaves" of the tree (the messages at the lowest level of nesting).

In sorting the keys of the SystemDictionary, Smalltalk, the tallies are

54 tallies

Note that if you try this example, you might get slightly different results because of differences in the statistical sampling (in the number of interrupts).

The second level of information is the description of the tree itself. You can follow the sequence of message calls: 53.7% of the time was spent evaluating SortedCollection class new:; 22.2% in Collection asSortedCollection; and 24.1% in Dictionary keys. (By SortedCollection class new:, is meant send the message new: to the class SortedCollection.) Of the 53.7% in SortedCollection class new:, most of the time was spent in String < =, which in turn spent most of its time in primitives. The message asSortedCollection is primarily a call on addAll:, which calls reSort, which calls sort:to: recursively.

Corresponding to each leaf of the tree is a number representing the relative amount of time spent executing the method. Thus, in sorting the keys of the SystemDictionary, Smalltalk, 37.0% of the time was spent executing the message compare: for a String, 7.4% was spent in the method for SortedCollection sort:to:, and so on. The purpose of the third level of information, **Leaves**, is to gather in one place many occurrences of some message that, if listed separately, appears insignificant.

```
**Tree**
53.7 SortedCollection class new:
| 51.9 String < =
|   50.0 String compare:
|     37.0 primitives
|     11.1 Character asUppercase
24.1 Dictionary keys
| 24.1 Set add:
|   14.8 Set findElementOrNil:
|   |  13.0 primitives
|   7.4 Set atNewIndex:put:
|   7.4 Set fullCheck
|     5.6 Set grow
|       5.6 Set noCheckAdd:
|         5.6 Set findElementOrNil:
22.2 Collection asSortedCollection
22.2 SortedCollection addAll:
18.5 SortedCollection reSort
| 18.5 SortedCollection sort:to:
|   18.5 SortedCollection sort:to:
|     16.7 SortedCollection sort:to:
|       14.8 SortedCollection sort:to:
|         11.1 SortedCollection sort:to:
|           5.6 SortedCollection swap:with:
|           3.7 SortedCollection sort:to:
3.7 Set do:
**Leaves**
37.0 String compare:
18.5 Set findElementOrNil:
11.1 Character asUppercase
9.3 SortedCollection swap:with:
7.4 SortedCollection sort:to:
3.7 Set do:
```

When you know where the execution is spending its time, you can try to improve that method to run faster, thus impacting overall execution of the activity.

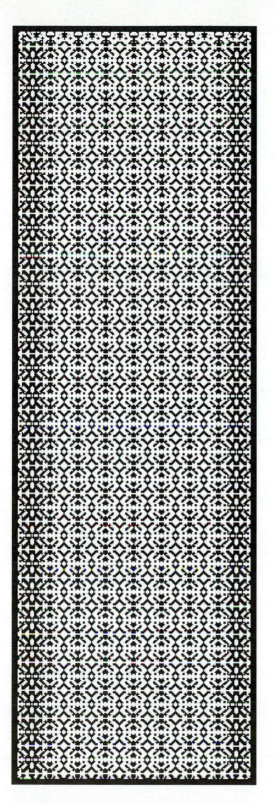

15

Examples of Creating or Changing Browsers

One of the typical kinds of things that programmers do in the Smalltalk-80 system is create special purpose browsers, either as additional software development tools or as applications. Example browsers for applications might be:

calendar   browsing personal or group schedules for visitors, talks, trips out of town, meetings

electronic mail   browsing mail sent to you, your responses, and any notes about the mail

book index   browsing the information in a book (An example is given in a doctoral dissertation by Steve Weyer [*Searching for Information in a Dynamic Book*, Xerox PARC Technical Report SCG-82-1, February, 1982].)

budget   browsing a database of financial plans, income, and expenditures

Example browsers that count as software development tools might be a protocol browser or a project browser. A protocol browser is one that lets you access the complete protocol of a class; by "complete," we mean the messages implemented in the superclasses as well as in the class. A project browser gives you direct access to all existing projects, regardless of how they were created. Implementations for each of these two browsers are given in this chapter as models to follow as you try to figure out how to use the system components for creating views and controllers. Detailed tutorials on the implementation of the user interface and on creating graphical interfaces to applications are provided in the forthcoming book *Smalltalk-80: Creating a User Interface and Graphical Applications.*

In trying these examples, you should be careful not to make mistakes while typing the text. If you find that you are making many mistakes and are confused by the error handling mechanisms of the system, you might put off reading this chapter until after you review Part Four "How to Find and Correct Errors."

15.1

A Protocol Browser

The first example browser is one in which you can examine the message interface of a particular class. This protocol browser should have the following characteristics:

- The browser should have two subviews, one containing a list menu and the other editable text.

- The list menu subview is a list of the messages implemented by a class and its superclasses.

- The text subview is an area in which to edit the selected method, as you would in a message-set browser.

- The message selectors should display in the list menu in alphabetical order.

- The name of the class in which each message selector is defined should be indicated in the list menu.

- Selecting a message selector should cause its method to display in the text subview.

- The method should be editable and recompilable.

- The standard queries about the message should be accessible, namely senders, implementors, and messages.

We call this browser a *Protocol Browser*. This section contains step-by-step instructions for creating the browser. From this example, you can obtain a glimpse into some of the components that are available in the Smalltalk-80 system for creating graphical user interfaces, namely StandardSystemViews, CodeViews, SelectionInListViews, and ActionMenus.

In a system browser, create a new class category named Interface-Protocol (Figures 15.1a and 15.1b). The new category is automatically selected and a template for defining the new class is displayed in the text subview. Edit the template to define ProtocolBrowser as a subclass of Object (Figure 15.2). It should have four instance variables, as follows:

list	An OrderedCollection whose elements are Strings, each of which represents a message selector and the class in which the message is defined. This is the information that will be displayed in the list menu of the browser.
classDictionary	A Dictionary whose keys are message selectors and whose values are the classes in which the message is defined. This is used for looking up methods when an item in the list menu is chosen.
selectedClass	Either nil, if no list menu item is selected, or the class defining the selected message selector.
selectedSelector	Either nil, if no list menu item is selected, or the selected message selector.

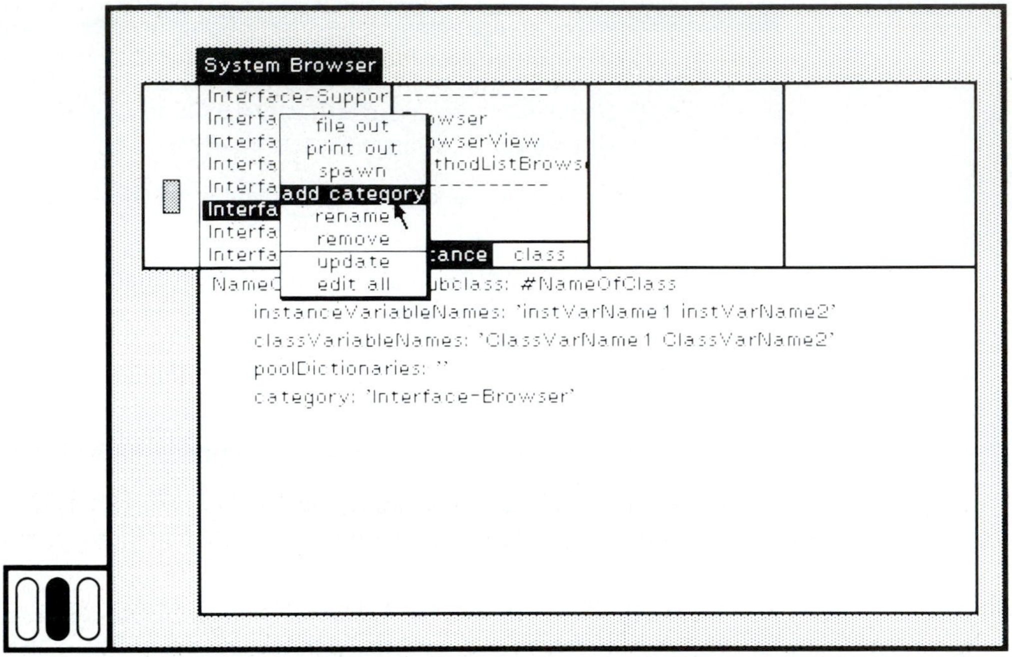

System Browser

Interface-Suppor
Interfa ------------
Interfa   file out   owser
Interfa   print out   wserView
Interfa   spawn   thodListBrows
Interfa add category ----------
Interfa   rename
Interfa   remove
Interfa   update   ance   class
NameC   edit all   bclass: #NameOfClass
        instanceVariableNames: 'instVarName1 instVarName2'
        classVariableNames: 'ClassVarName1 ClassVarName2'
        poolDictionaries: ''
        category: 'Interface-Browser'

Figure 15.1a

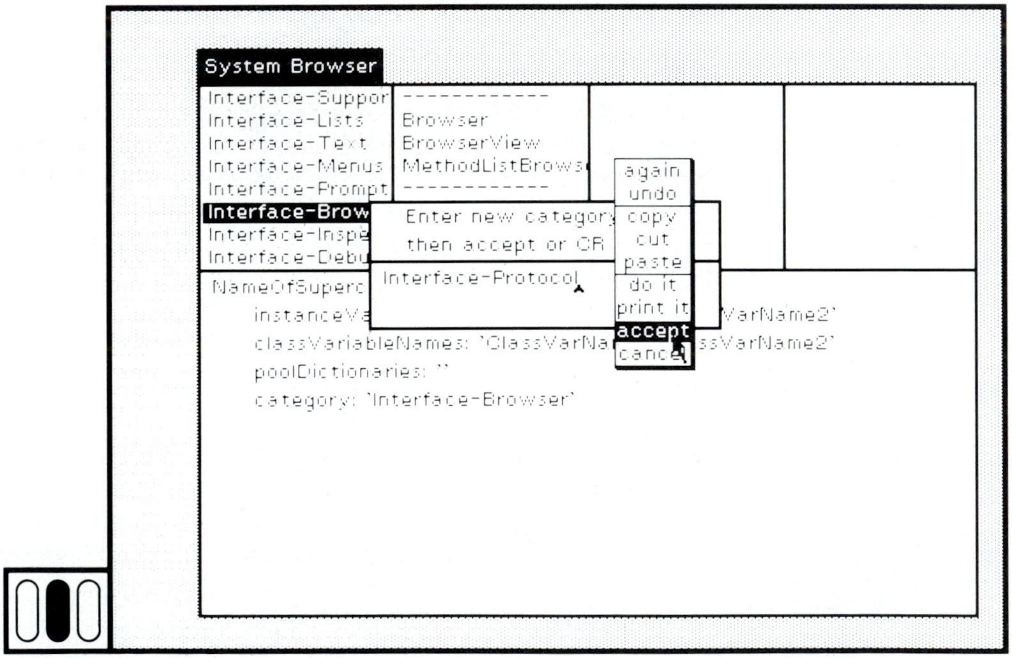

System Browser

Interface-Suppor ------------
Interface-Lists   Browser
Interface-Text   BrowserView
Interface-Menus   MethodListBrows
Interface-Prompt   ------------
Interface-Brow
Interface-Inspe   Enter new categor
Interface-Debu   then accept or CR
NameOfSuperc
        instanceV   Interface-Protocol
        classVariableNames: 'ClassVarNa
        poolDictionaries: ''
        category: 'Interface-Browser'

again
undo
copy
cut
paste
do it
print it
accept
cancel

Figure 15.1b

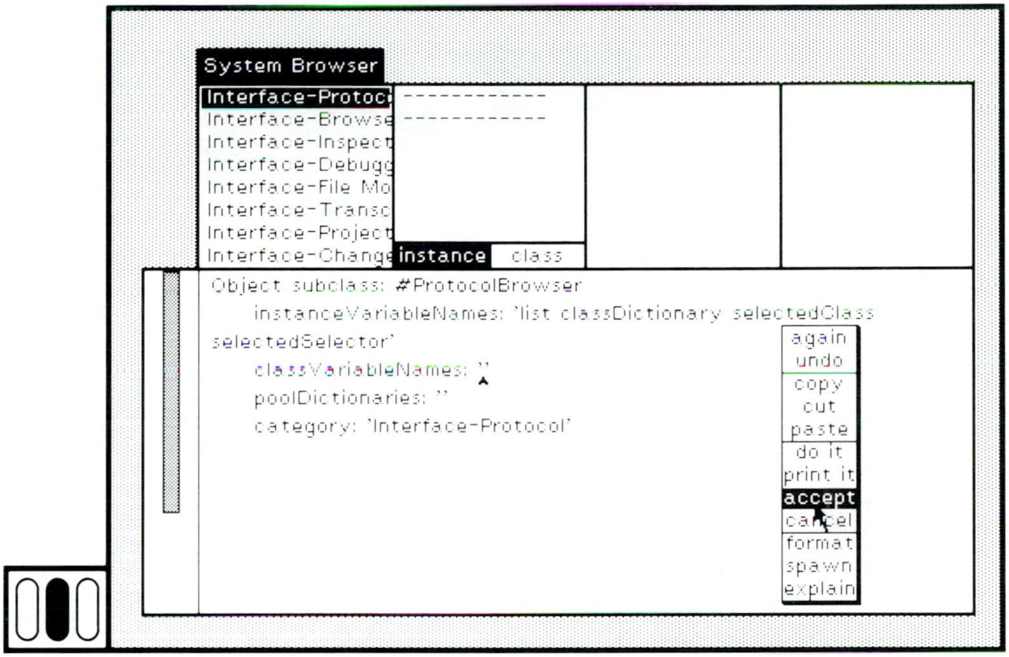

Figure 15.2

The ProtocolBrowser should have no class variables. Remember to cut out the "dummy" class variable names from the method template.

After you have typed the class definition, choose the yellow button command accept. The new class is added to the class-names menu and is selected. In the class-names subview, choose the yellow button command comment (Figure 15.3a). The words This class has no comment appear in the text subview. Edit it to provide a comment on the role of the class (Figure 15.3b). Within the comment, you can also provide a template for creating an instance of the class, such as

ProtocolBrowser openForClass: className

Choose the yellow button command accept to save the comment.

> The protocol name private has no special meaning to the system. By convention, we use this name to categorize messages that are sent by the object to itself, rather than by other objects to it.

The next step is to define the instance creation message openForClass:. Choose the browser menu item class so that you can define class protocol.

> Note that when you choose class, the system attempts to guess what other selections you might also wish to see. Since you were examining the comment for class ProtocolBrowser, the system guessed you might want to see the comment about ProtocolBrowser's class (i.e., its metaclass). Currently this class has no comment.

Add the protocol name instance creation (Figures 15.4a and 15.4b).

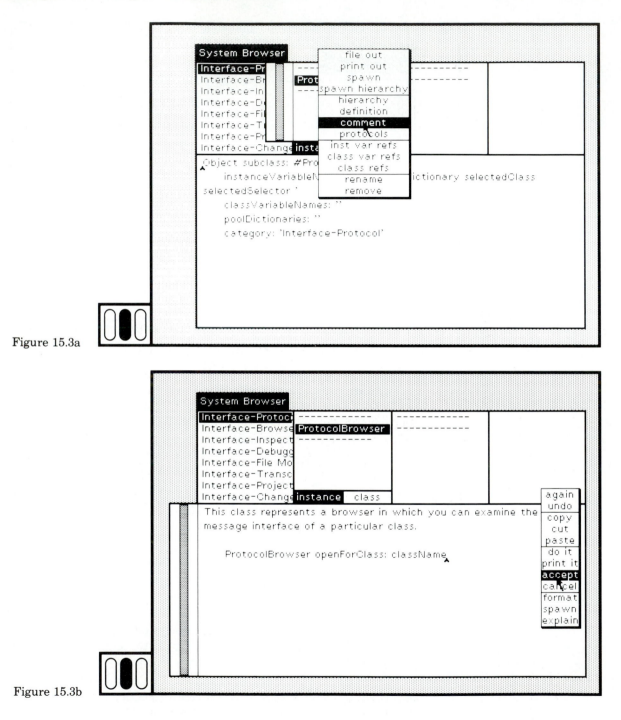

Figure 15.3a

Figure 15.3b

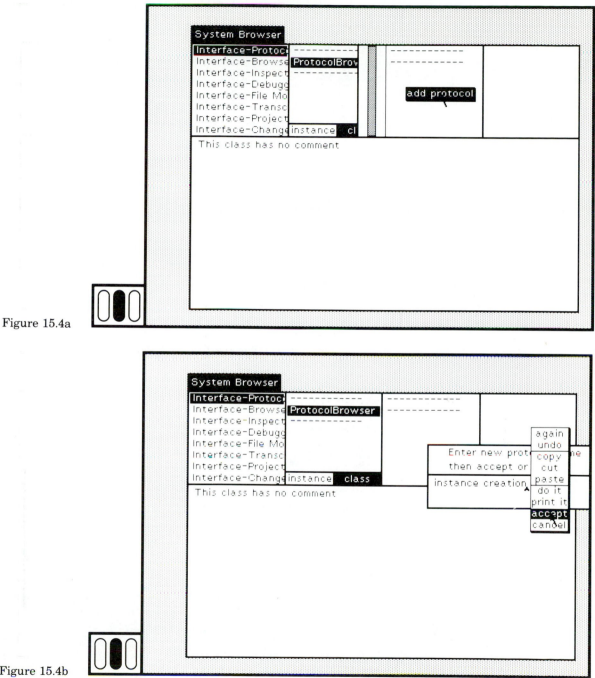

Figure 15.4a

Figure 15.4b

Examples of Creating or Changing Browsers

openForClass: aClass
" Create and schedule a browser for the entire protocol
of the class. "

| topView aPBrowser label |
aPBrowser ← super new on: aClass.
label ← 'Entire protocol of: ', aClass name.
topView ←
    StandardSystemView
        model: aPBrowser
        label: label
        minimumSize: 200 @ 200.
topView
    addSubView:
        (SelectionInListView
            on: aPBrowser
            aspect: #selector
            change: #selector:
            list: #selectorList
            menu: #selectorListMenu
            initialSelection: nil)
    in: (0@0.0 extent: 1@0.3)
    borderWidth: 1.
topView
    addSubView:
        (CodeView
            on: aPBrowser
            aspect: #text
            change: #acceptText:from:
            menu: #textMenu
            initialSelection: nil)
    in: (0@0.3 extent: 1@0.7)
    borderWidth: 1.
topView controller open

In this method, the temporary variable aPBrowser is created as an instance of class ProtocolBrowser and is initialized by sending it the message on:. The label of the browser is then defined to be

Entire protocol of < class name >

where < class name > denotes the place in which the actual name of the class appears.

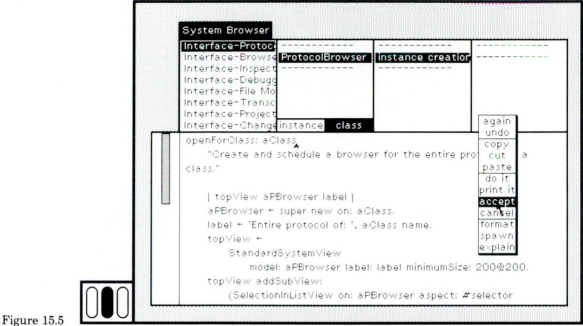

Figure 15.5

The rest of the method consists of four main steps.

1. Create an instance of StandardSystemView.

2. Create an instance of SelectionInListView and make it a subview of the StandardSystemView.

3. Create an instance of CodeView and make it a subview of the StandardSystemView.

4. Send a message to the StandardSystemView to obtain its controller, that is, the class that provides the user interaction scheduling (StandardSystemController), and then send a message to the controller to open a rectangular area for itself on the display screen and to make its view the active view. The user will be asked to designate the rectangular area.

Each of StandardSystemView, CodeView, and SelectionInListView, are subclasses of View. View provides protocol for managing a hierarchical nesting of subviews, and for managing the windowing transformations needed so that the user can move and reframe the view and so that all the subviews will maintain their relative positions and sizes. The subview insertion message used in this example is addSubView:in:borderWidth. The first argument indicates the subview that is to be inserted, the second indicates the relative position and size of the subview, and the third the width of the frame around the subview.

Once your example protocol browser works, you can play with these numbers to see the affect of any changes.

When the StandardSystemView is created, it is informed of the object to be viewed on the display screen, its label, and its minimum size.

A SelectionInListView is one of the kinds of menus in the system. Its instance creation message requires six arguments.

on:	The object, one aspect of which is viewed by the list menu.
aspect:	A Symbol identifying the menu to other parts of the view.
change:	A Symbol denoting the message selector for changing the information that shows in the list menu.
list:	A Symbol denoting the message selector for retrieving the list of strings that show in the list menu.
menu:	A Symbol denoting the message selector for obtaining the yellow button menu; nil if there is no menu.
initialSelection:	A String representing the initial current selection; nil if no initial selection.

A CodeView represents a view of text that is editable and in which the command accept means to compile. Its instance creation message requires six arguments.

on:	The object, one aspect of which is text.
aspect:	A Symbol denoting the message selector for retrieving the text that is displayed.
change:	A Symbol denoting the message selector for changing the text that is displayed.
menu:	A Symbol denoting the message selector for obtaining the yellow button menu; nil if there is no menu.
initialSelection:	A String representing the initial current selection (subpart of the text displayed highlighted); nil if no initial selection.

Once you have defined the instance creation message openForClass:, then choose the browser menu item instance so that you can specify the instance protocol. In the message-category subview, choose the yellow button command add protocol so that you can add the protocol private (Figure 15.6a and 15.6b). Do the same for protocol names list access and text access.

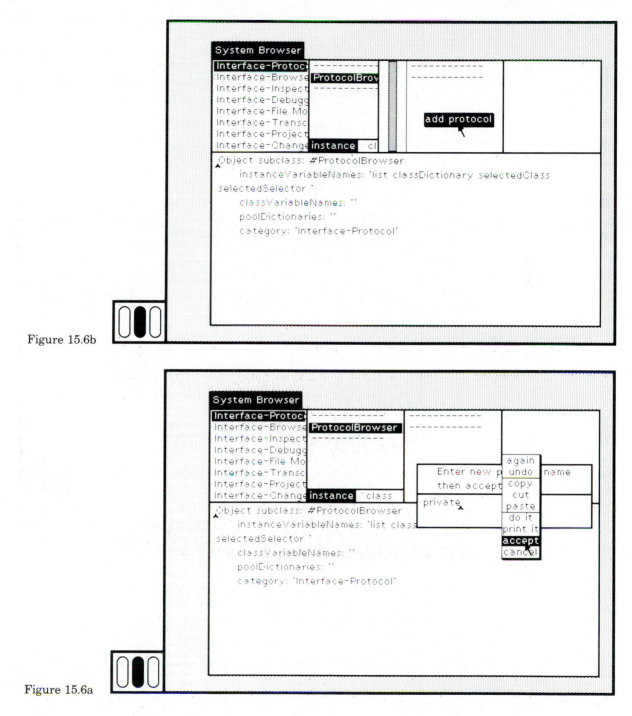

Figure 15.6b

Figure 15.6a

Choose the protocol name private and edit the method template to specify the method for on:.

on: aClass
    " Create the protocol browser for the class, a Class. "

```
| defClass |
list ← OrderedCollection new.
classDictionary ← Dictionary new.
aClass allSelectors asSortedCollection do:
    [ :selector |
    defClass ← aClass whichClassIncludesSelector: selector.
    list add: selector printString, ' (' , defClass name , ')'.
    classDictionary add: (Association key: selector value: defClass)]
```

Only two of the instance variables are initialized, list and classDictionary. For each selector specified in the class (aClass allSelectors), the class in which the selector is defined is determined (whichClassIncludesSelector:) and then the selector, followed by a tab, left parenthesis, defining class name, and a right parenthesis, is added to list. The selector and the defining class are then stored as an entry in classDictionary.

> Remember to type carefully to specify a tab before the left parenthesis. The tab will be used in another method for distinguishing the selector from the class name.

Choose the yellow button command accept (Figure 15.7).

> The protocol name private has no special meaning to the system. By convention, we use this name to categorize messages that are sent by the object to itself, rather than by other objects to it.

You now have to define the messages that access the information for the SelectionInListView and the CodeView. There are two list-accessing messages, selectorList and selector:; there are two text-accessing messages, text and acceptText:from:. The methods are shown in Figures 15.8, 15.9, 15.10, and 15.11. Note that in the implementaiton of selector:, the list menu item is a String that must be parsed to determine the selected selector and class. Instances of String respond to messages such as copyUpTo: that support the parsing. The message changed: is specified in class Object as broadcasting the fact that an object changed so that any dependents, such as a model, its view, or controller, can choose to update itself.

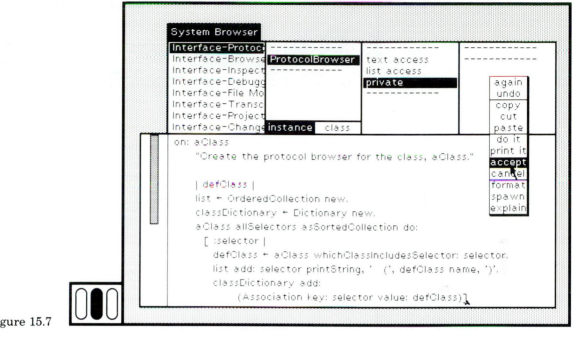

Figure 15.7

Figure 15.8

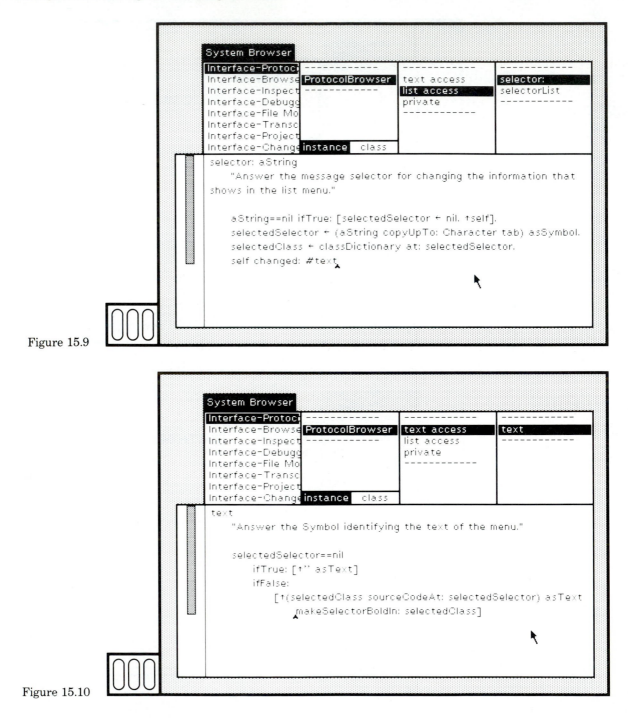

Figure 15.9

Figure 15.10

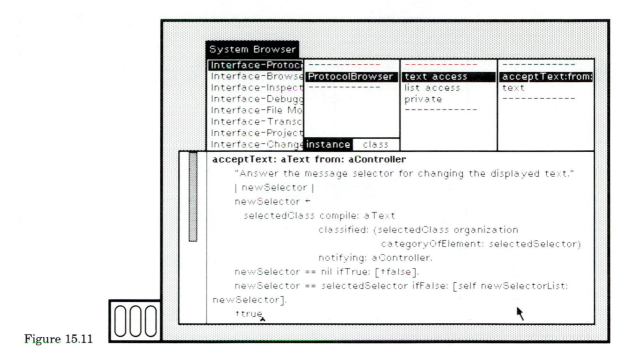

Figure 15.11

Although we have not as yet specified the yellow button menus, you can now try out the protocol browser. Evaluate an expression of the form

ProtocolBrowser openForClass: < className >

In the workspace in Figure 15.12a, we substituted True for < className > to open a ProtocolBrowser on the class True, a subclass of Boolean (Figure 15.12b). If you select a menu item, the method shows in the text subview. Scrolling works. So does the blue button menu for framing, moving, and so on. Much of the programming work has already been done for you!

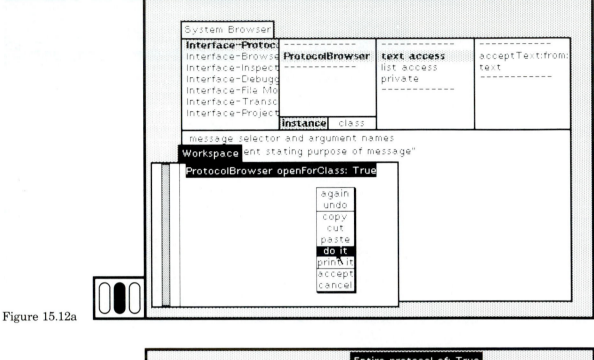

Figure 15.12a

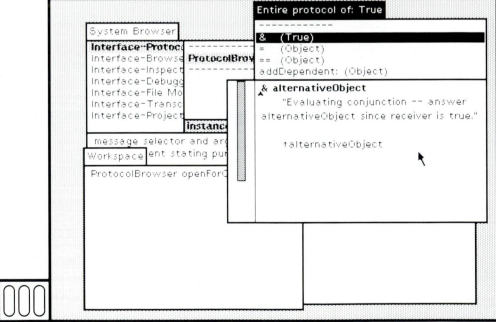

Figure 15.12b

If you try to use the yellow button menu, you will receive an error notification. Leave the ProtocolBrowser on the screen.

Let's define two messages, textMenu and selectorListMenu. Each of these creates an instance of class ActionMenu, an object that represents a pop-up menu that can have lines between its items. An ActionMenu is created with the message labels:lines:selectors:. Here are the three arguments

labels: A String of the menu items, each item separated by a carriage return. The withCrs message to instances of String returns a String that substitutes a carriage return character in place of any \ characters. Thus you can use the \ to indicate the line change.

lines: An Array of numbers indicating after which item to draw a line.

selectors: An Array of message selectors that will be invoked if the corresponding menu item is chosen.

The convention is that the object being viewed will be sent the message, although in several notable cases, such as editing text, the controller (paragraph editor) receives the messages.

The yellow button menu for the CodeView is for text editing, as in a browser text subview. Edit the method template to specify the message textMenu (Figure 15.13a).

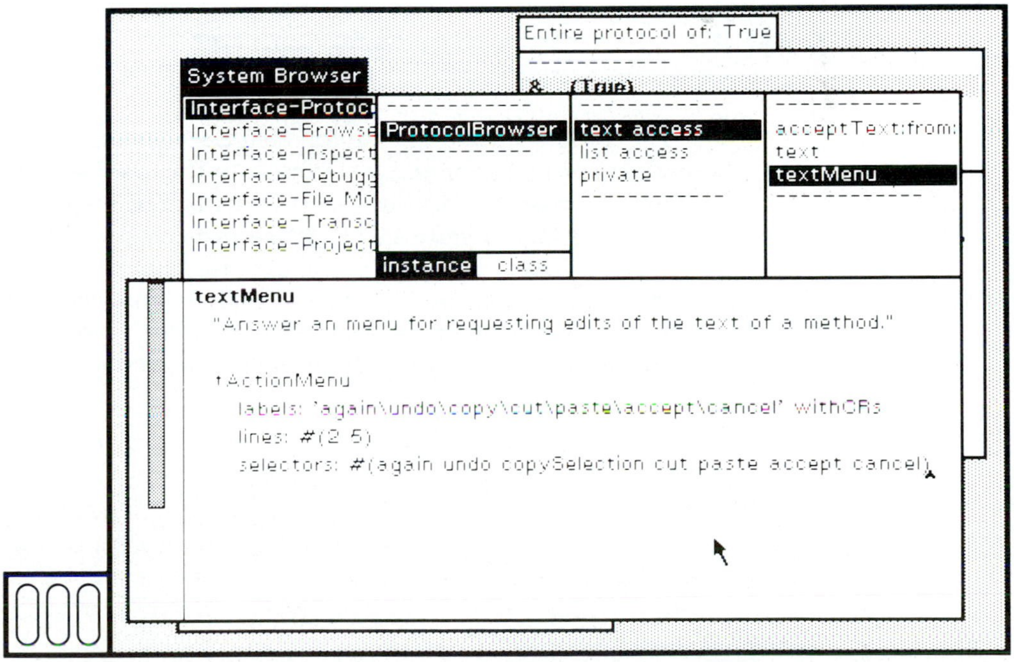

Figure 15.13a

Since the messages are the standard ones used in all views in which paragraphs are edited (TextViews as well as CodeViews), you do not need to do anything further in order to use the yellow button menu. Return to the protocol browser you made earlier, and try using the menu (Figure 15.13b).

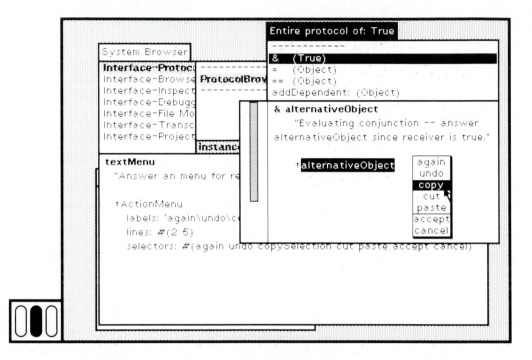

Figure 15.13b

The yellow button menu for the SelectionInListView is for asking questions about the messages, similar to the queries available in the list menu of a message-set browser. It is defined in response to the message selectorListMenu (Figure 15.14). If the response to selectorListMenu is nil, then the subview will flash to indicate that no menu is appropriate.

The three messages, browseSenders, browseImplementors, and browseMessages, will be sent to the ProtocolBrowser. Figures 15.15, 15.16, and 15.17 show their definitions, categorized under list functions.

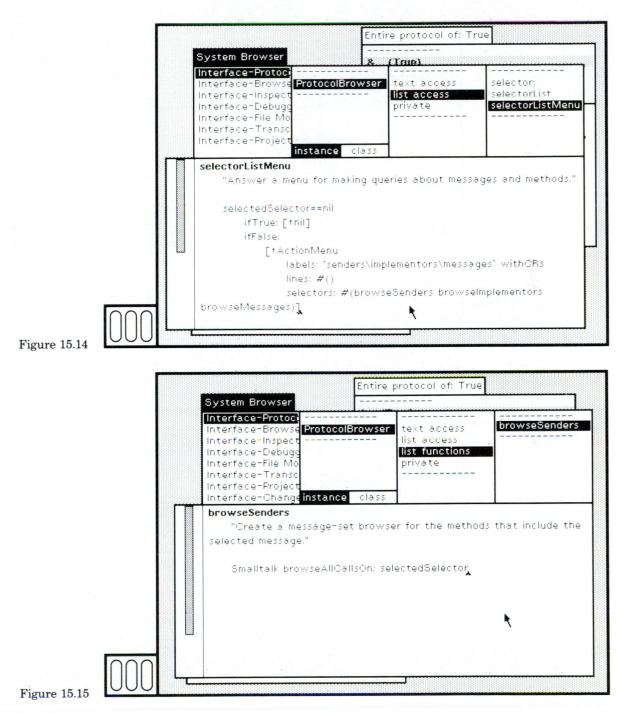

Figure 15.14

Figure 15.15

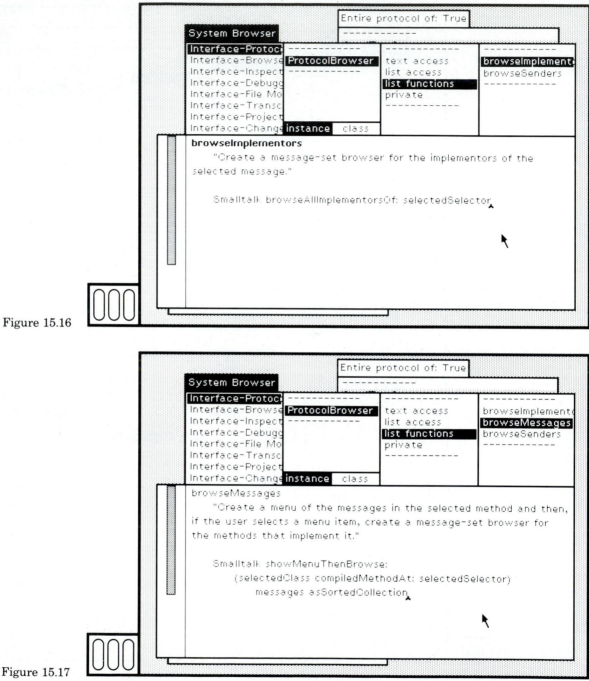

Figure 15.16

Figure 15.17

Now return to the protocol browser you created (or open a new one), and try out the menus for the top view (Figure 15.18). Close the browser when you are done experimenting.

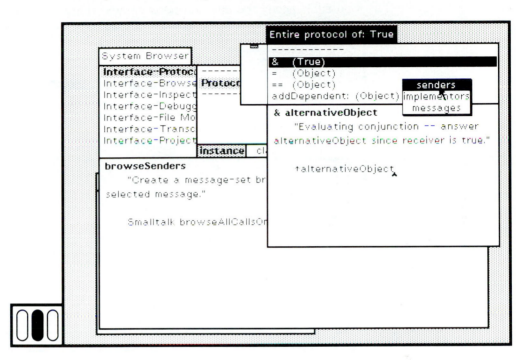

Figure 15.18

Notice that the yellow button menus for the ProtocolBrowser seem to work differently than the ones you have been using in the system in that they do not remember the last item you chose. This is because the menu is recreated each time you press the yellow button, rather than remembered as a class variable. The use of class variables to store the menu is described in the next section.

An interesting modification of this example is to be able to specify that protocol from one or more superclasses should not be included in the protocol browser. In particular, a user will probably not want to see the protocol of class Object included.

Suppose we wish to create a protocol browser for only some of the protocol of a class.

ProtocolBrowser openForClass: aClass without: aCollection

The second argument would be an Array of classes whose protocol should be excluded. Add the message openForClass:without: to the class protocol of class ProtocolBrowser (Figure 15.19). The only difference between this method and that of openForClass: is the ProtocolBrowser creation message (on:without:) which must be implemented, and the label, which says Some of the protocol... rather than Entire protocol.... When you add this new method and choose the yellow button command accept, another menu will probably appear stating that the message on:without: is new. Choose the command proceed as is, since your intention is to specify the missing message next (Figure 15.20).

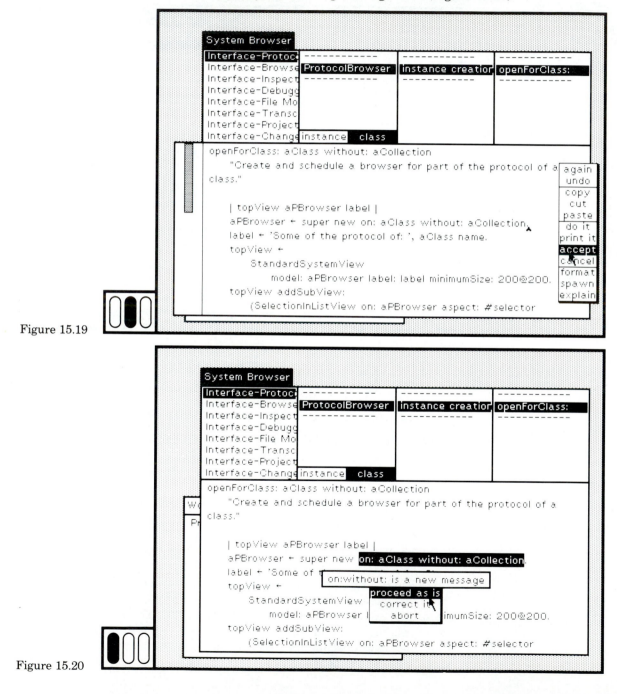

Figure 15.19

Figure 15.20

You can create the new method openForClass:without: by copying the method for openForClass: and editing it, changing the first few lines. Similarly, you can create the new method on:without: by copying and editing the method for on:.

Now choose the browser menu item instance and the message category private, and then specify the method for on:without: (Figure 15.21). It differs from the method for on: only in checking the argument aCollection; if the defining class is in the collection, then the message is not added to the instance variable list.

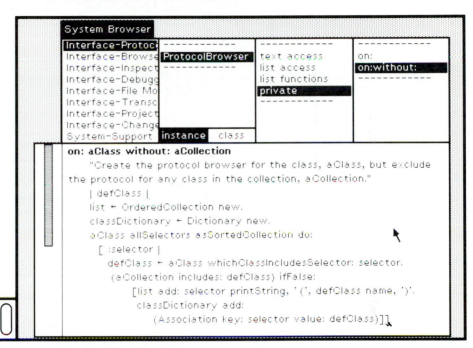

Figure 15.21

Figure 15.22 shows an example for class True when class Object is omitted. It was obtained by evaluating the expression

ProtocolBrowser openForClass: True without: (Array with: Object)

Only messages implemented in Boolean and True are accessible from this protocol browser.

Another kind of protocol browser that you might try is to be able to switch between the messages to an instance of the class and the messages to the class itself, as is done in the system class browser. You can examine the implementation of class Browser for examples of how to create such a protocol browser.

The implementation of file list provides another good example of how to create a simple browser. Examine the code for classes FileListView and FileListController.

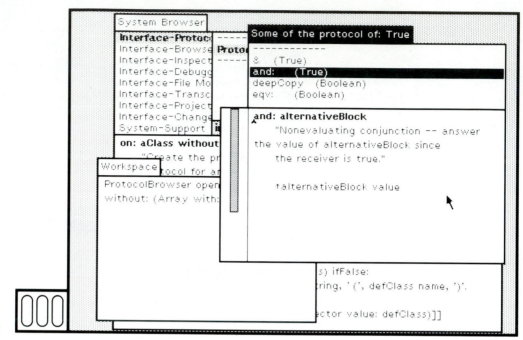

Figure 15.22

15.2

A Project Browser

The next example is a browser for creating and accessing projects. It could be used in place of the hierarchical access to projects available in the standard Smalltalk-80 system. We call this a *Project Browser*. It should have the following characteristics:

- The browser should have two subviews, one containing a list menu and the other editable text.

- The list menu should contain the titles of projects.

- The text should be a description of the project; the user should be able to edit the text and to cancel any changes.

- Selecting a project title should display the description in the text subview.

- The yellow button menu in the list menu should support adding new projects, removing existing projects, and entering a project. Adding a new project should prompt the user to specify a project title. Removing a project should require a confirmation if the project has open views or unsaved changes.

- Whenever a new project browser is created, it should provide access to every project in the system, regardless of the project in which each was created.

A project browser can be created in a manner very similar to the protocol browser of the previous section. The list menu subview will be an instance of SelectionInListView and the text subview will be a CodeView. However, the command accept in the CodeView will not mean compile; it will mean store the text as the description of the selected project. As in the ProtocolBrowser, commands do it and print it will not be supported in the example project browser.

In a system browser, select the existing class category named Interface-Projects and then edit the template in the text subview to define ProjectBrowser as a subclass of Object (Figure 15.23). It should have two instance variables as follows.

projects   A Set of all the instances of class Project that exist in the system.

currentProject   Either nil, if no list menu item is selected, or the currently selected Project.

The class ProjectBrowser has no class variables.

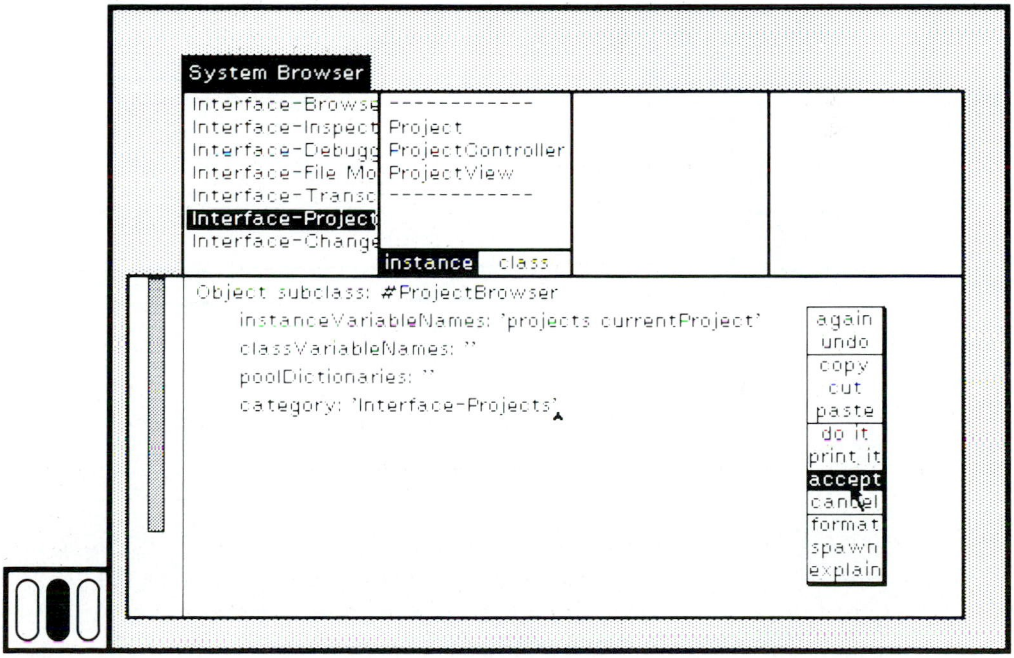

Figure 15.23

After you have typed the class definition, choose the yellow button command accept. The new class is added to the class-names menu and is selected. In the class-names subview, choose the yellow button command comment and provide a comment on the role of the class (Figure 15.24). You can also provide an expression for creating an instance of the class. ProjectBrowser open.

Choose the yellow button command accept to store the comment. The next step is to define the instance creation message open. Choose the browser menu item class so that you can define class protocol. Add the protocol name instance creation and then edit the method template to define the message open.

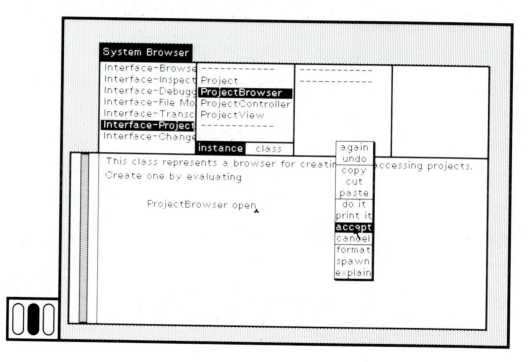

Figure 15.24

open
     " Create and schedule a browser for all the projects in the system "

```
| topView aBrowser |
aBrowser ← super new initialize.
topView ←
    StandardSystemView
        model: aBrowser
        label: 'Project Browser'
        minimumSize: 200 @ 200.
topView
    addSubView:
        (SelectionInListView
            on: aBrowser
            printItems: true
            oneItem: false
            aspect: #currentProject
            change: #currentProject:
            list: #projectList
            menu: #projectMenu
            initialSelection: nil)
        in: (0@0.0 extent: 1@0.4)
        borderWidth: 1.
topView
    addSubView:
        (CodeView
            on: aBrowser
            aspect: #text
            change: #acceptText:from:
            menu: #textMenu
            initialSelection: nil)
        in: (0@0.4 extent: 1@0.6)
        borderWidth: 1.
    topView controller open
```

This method is the same as the one used in creating a ProtocolBrowser, with the exception of the proportions used for the subviews, and the message sent to SelectionInListView to create an instance. The message used here contains two additional arguments associated with the keywords printItems: and oneItem:.

printItems: A Boolean, either true or false. The argument of the keyword list: is a message to the browser. It returns an OrderedCollection, either of strings that can be printed in the list menu, or of objects that must be sent the message printString in order to obtain the entry in the list menu. If the argument to printItems: is false, the response will be strings; if the argument is true, then the message printString should be sent. We plan to keep a list of Projects rather than string representations of Projects, so the argument must be true.

oneItem: If it is known that a list menu contains only one item, then it will be automatically selected if the argument to this keyword is true. There may be more than one Project, so the argument is false.

Once you have defined the instance creation message open, then choose the browser menu item instance so that you can specify the instance protocol. In the message-category subview, add the protocol names initialize-release, list access, list functions, and text access (Figure 15.25).

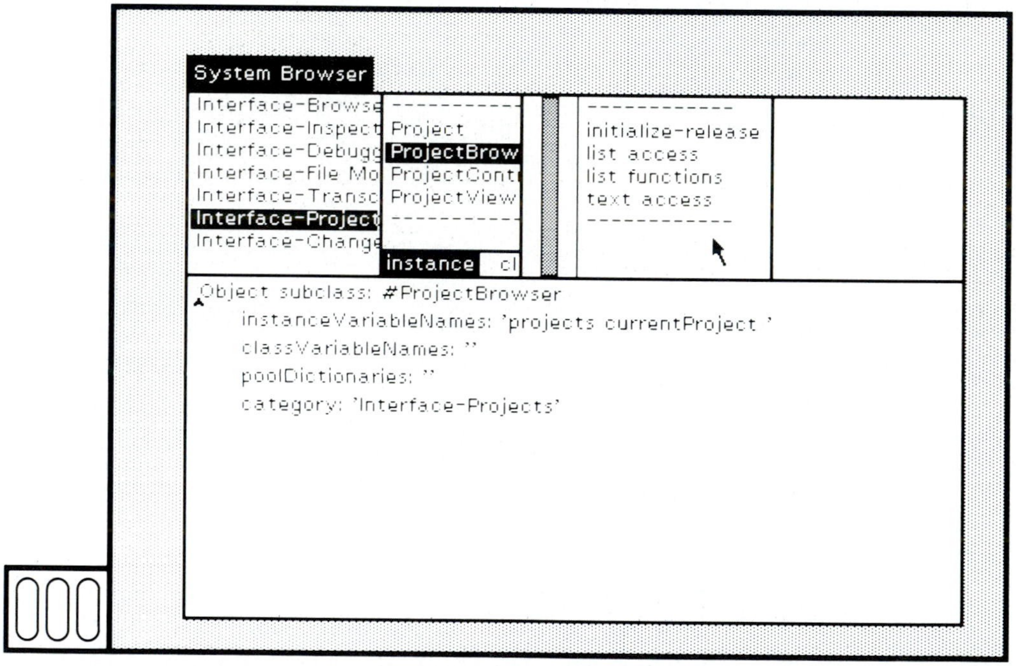

Figure 15.25

The message initialize is sent from the instance creation message open to initialize the instance variables. Only the instance variable projects is initialized; it is assigned an OrderedCollection of all the instances of class Project currently in the system (Figure 15.26).

Under the category list access, define the method for projectList (Figure 15.27). This is the message sent to obtain the list of items for the list menu.

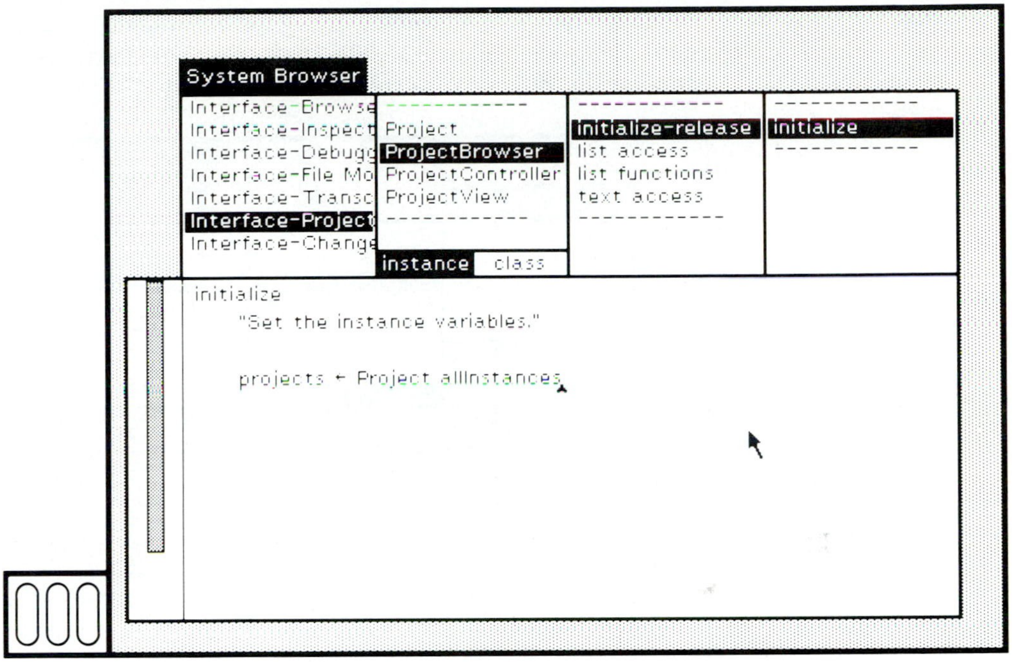

Figure 15.26

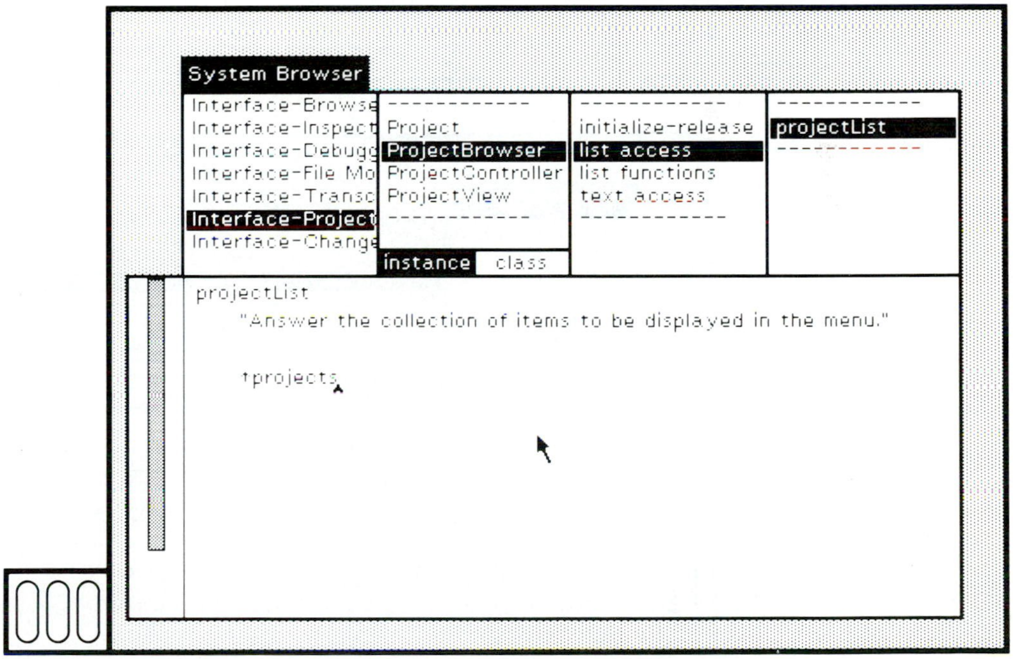

Figure 15.27

Also define methods for currentProject (Figure 15.28) and currentProject: (Figure 15.29); these are the messages used to set and change the reference to the currently selected project.

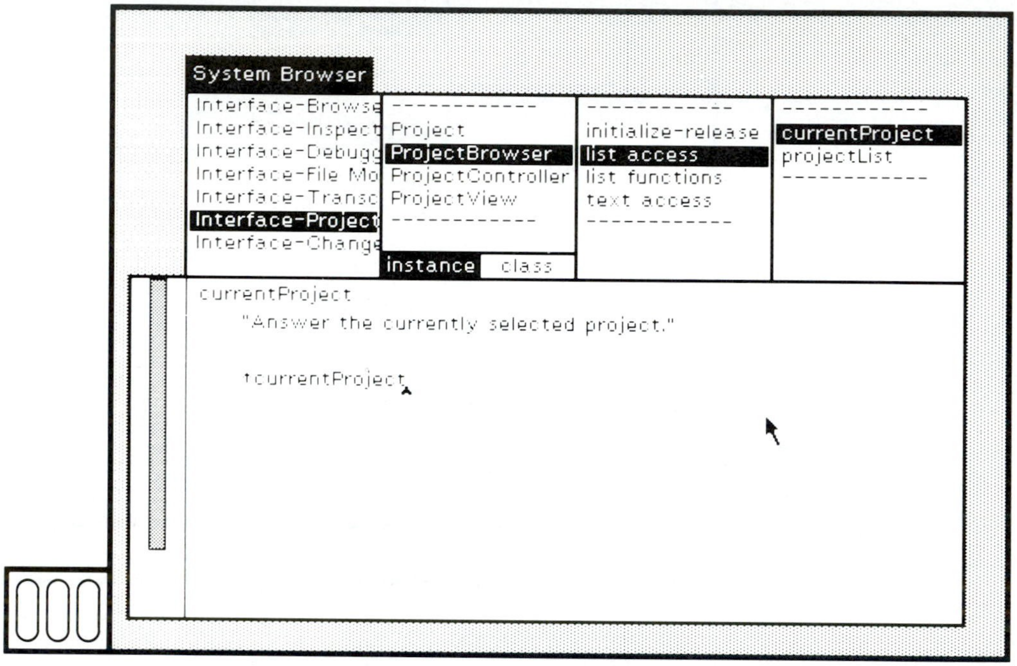

Figure 15.28

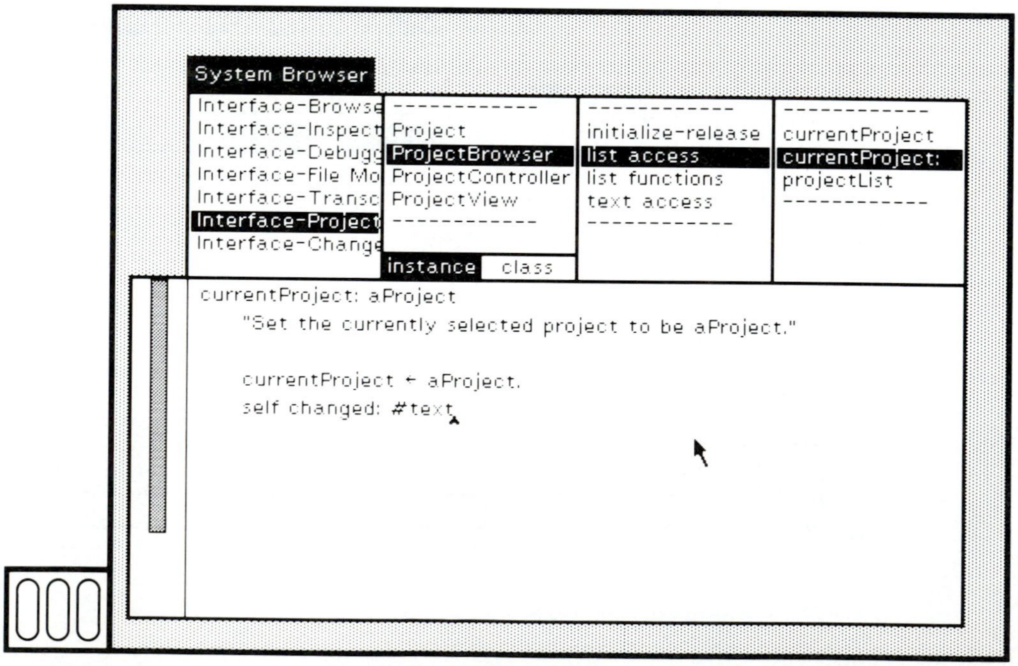

Figure 15.29

The second statement of the method for currentProject: is self changed: #text. The purpose of this message is to broadcast the fact that the list menu selection has changed and that, therefore, any objects dependent on the selection may wish to change. Subviews are dependent on one another and are notified when one another announces a change. The subview CodeView must change the text it displays whenever the menu selection changes.

According to the arguments of the creation message for the CodeView, you must define methods for text (Figure 15.30) and acceptText:from: (Figure 15.31). The response from text is the current project's description, converted from a String to an instance of Text. The purpose of acceptText:from: is to store the String representation of the text that appears in the CodeView in order to update the description of the current project. These methods are defined under the category text access.

Although we have not as yet specified the yellow button menus, you can now try out the project browser. First use the System Menu command project to create two projects other than the one in which you are working (Figure 15.32). In each of them, type some text and choose the

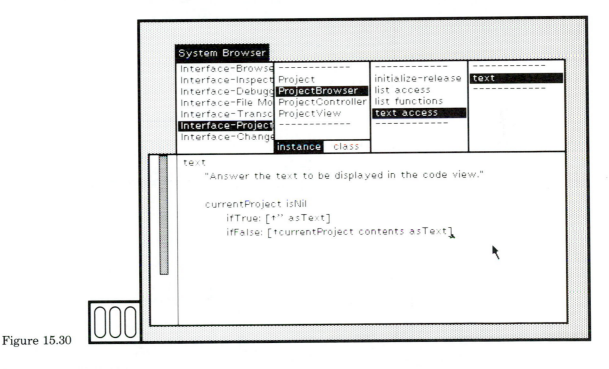

Figure 15.30

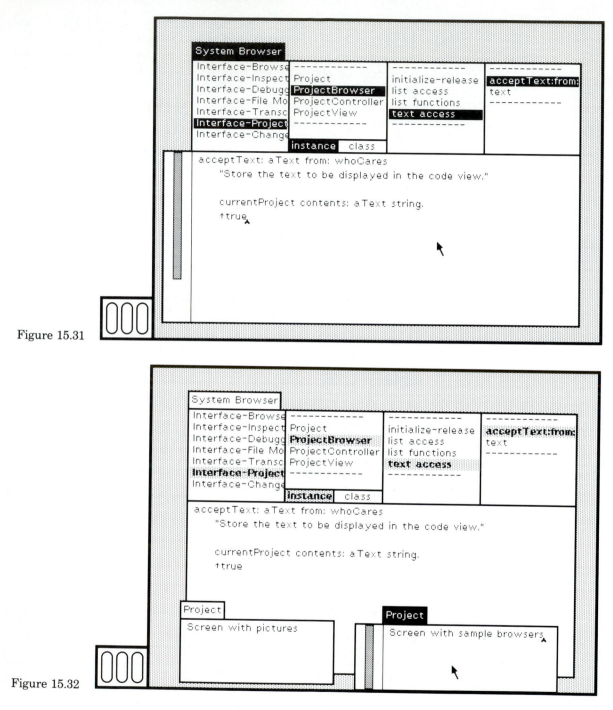

Figure 15.31

Figure 15.32

yellow button command accept. This stores a description for each project so that you will be able to distinguish them in the browser. Evaluate the expression (Figure 15.33)

ProjectBrowser open

(Recall that this expression was included in the comment for the class ProjectBrowser.)

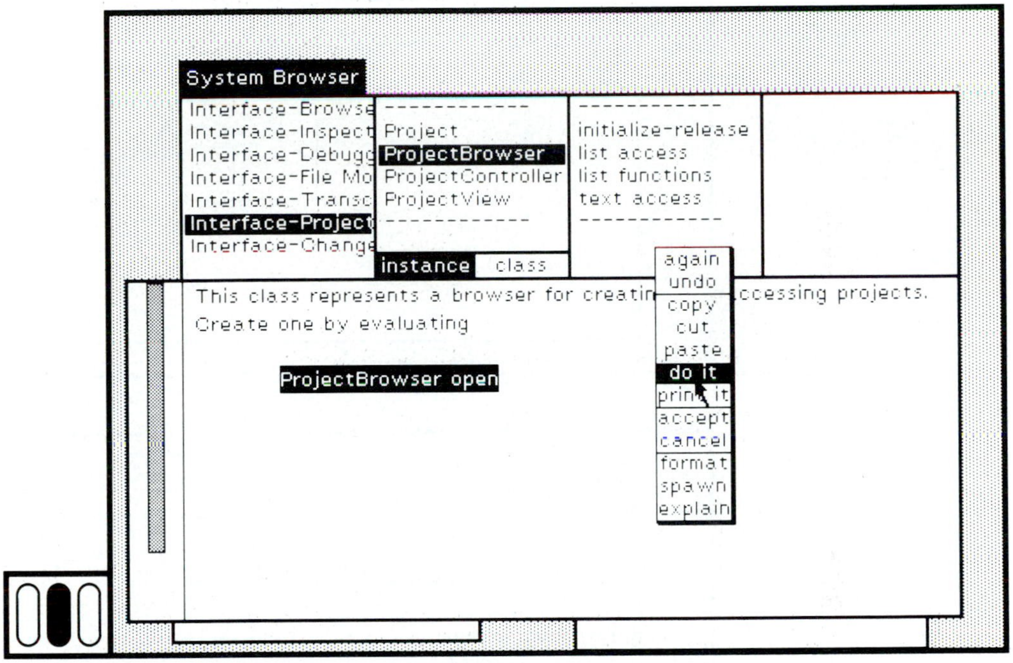

Figure 15.33

You are asked to designate a rectangular area in which the browser appears (Figure 15.34). In this new browser, you can select projects and the descriptions will be displayed. Since the project browser is constructed using a StandardSystemView, the blue button menu is immediately available. Notice, however, that each item in the projects menu simply refers to the words a Project, rather than to some unique label or title. Instances of class Project have no titles. To improve the projects menu, you will have to modify class Project to declare an instance variable for the title and to access the title. We will make this change to class Project in Section 15.3.

We must now specify the yellow button menus. In this example, we will declare two class variables in which to maintain a reference to each menu so that they do not have to be recreated each time the yellow button is pressed (as was done in the protocol browser example), and so that the last selection is remembered.

Examples of Creating or Changing Browsers

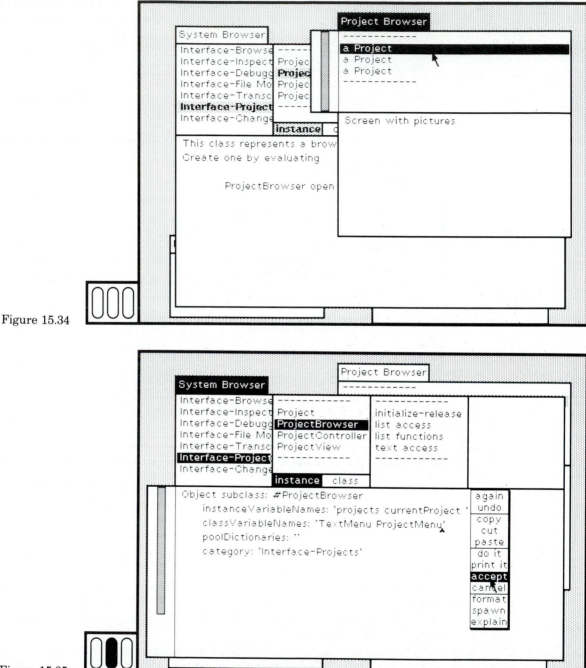

Figure 15.34

Figure 15.35

In the class-names subview of the system browser, choose the yellow button command definition. Edit the definition of the ProjectBrowser to add class variables TextMenu and ProjectMenu. Choose the yellow button command accept (Figure 15.35). The class ProjectBrowser is recompiled. (Note that this change can be made even though a ProjectBrowser may be open.)

Under the instance protocol name text access, specify the method for textMenu (Figure 15.36).

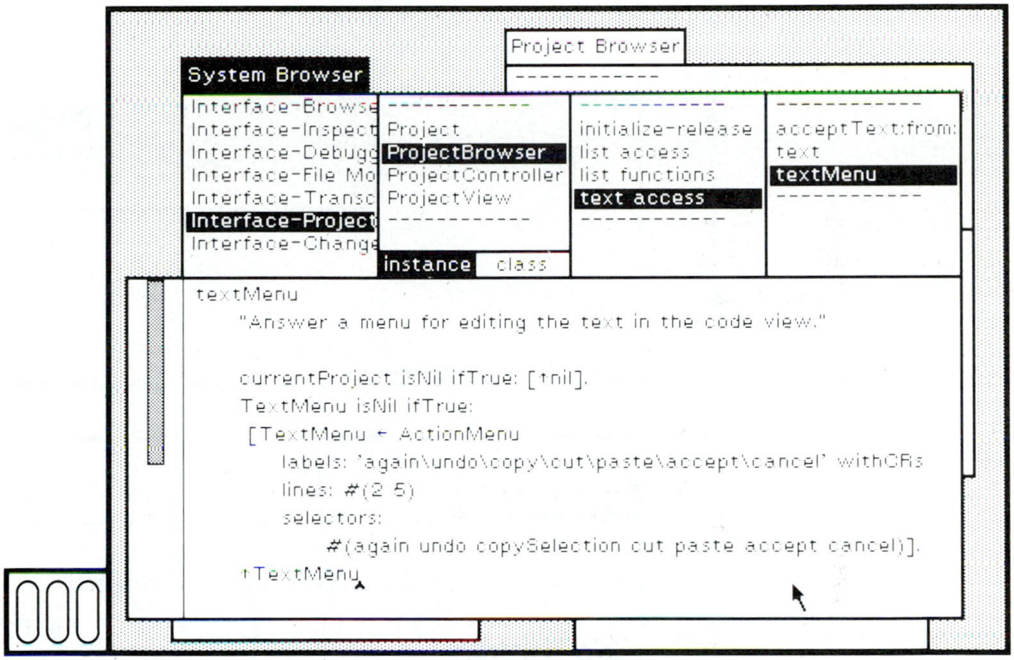

Figure 15.36

The menu is an instance of ActionMenu that is only created if the class variable TextMenu is nil; otherwise the menu is accessible as the class variable TextMenu. If there is no selection, then no text editor for a project description is needed. The method returns the value nil to indicate this. According to the implementation of ActionMenu, you try to obtain the menu when no project is selected, the subview will flash. If you now return to the project browser, you will notice that you can press the yellow button and obtain the menu. Modify one of the project descriptions to try the editor (Figure 15.37). (Notice that the commands do it and print it were not included in the menu.) Under the instance protocol name list access, specify the method for projectMenu (Figure 15.38).

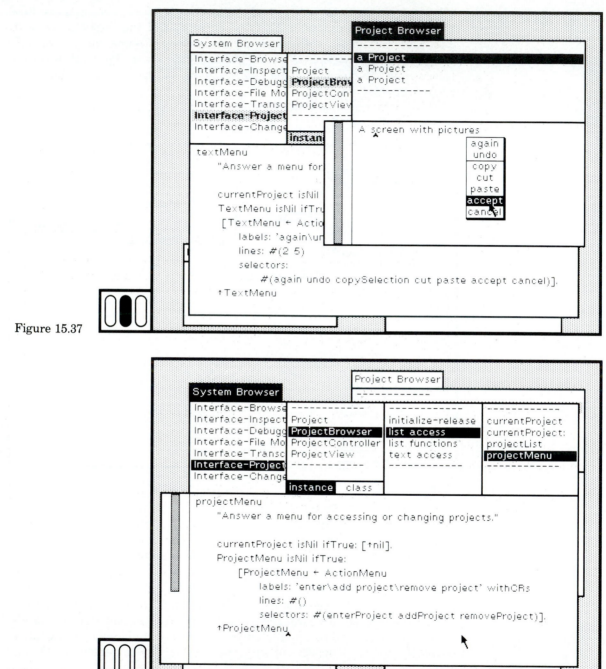

Figure 15.37

Figure 15.38

The menu has three commands.

enter	Enter the selected project.
add project	Add a new project to the menu. Prompt the user for a project title. Initially the new project has no description.
remove project	Remove the selected project, unless it is the one in which the user is currently running.

The messages associated with each item must be specified in the instance protocol of class ProjectBrowser. Figures 15.39, 15.40, and 15.41, show the methods for enterProject, addProject, and removeProject; they are each categorized under the protocol for list functions,

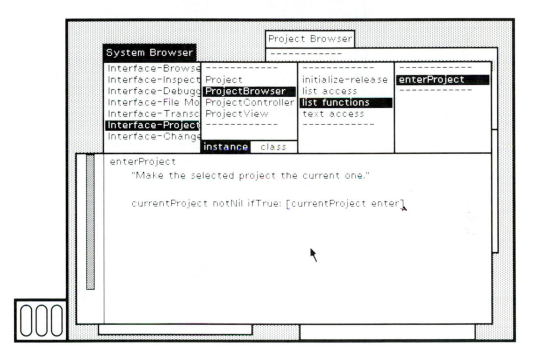

Figure 15.39

The method for removeProject has several interesting aspects. First, if no project is selected, the command means nothing. Second, if the project selected is the project in which you are currently running, deleting that project is very dangerous. The message error: will cause an error notification (notifier view) to appear, warning you that you are trying to do something that should not be done. If you try to remove the project in which you are running and get the notifier, simply choose the blue button command close to erase the notifier from the screen.

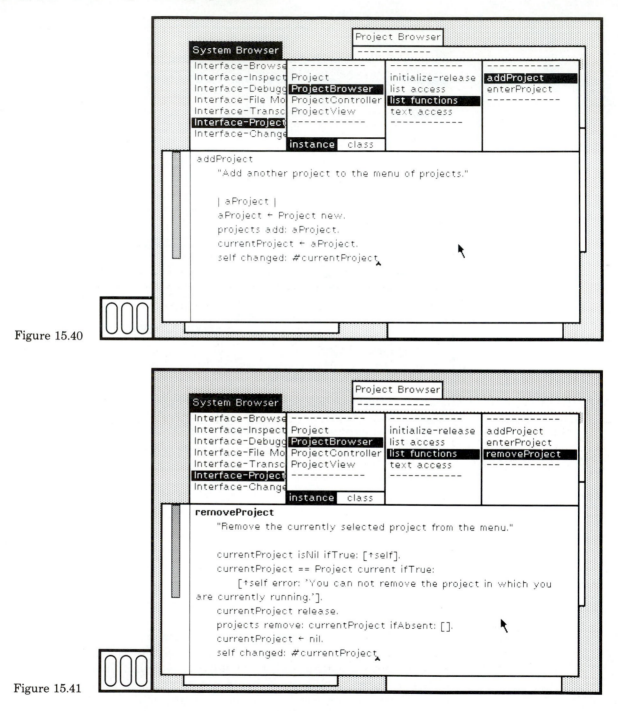

Figure 15.40

Figure 15.41

The third statement is currentProject release. The message release is sent to a Project so that it can remove from the system any views that it knows about. The style of using the viewing and controlling components of the system includes sending the message release to a view whenever it is erased from the screen and should no longer be accessible.

> You can improve on this method. For example, you might check to see if the project to be removed has any views or unsaved changes and, if so, you can inform the user and ask for confirmation. The system class Confirmer can be used for this purpose.

The last statement of the method broadcasts the fact that the menu changed again. Note that this time the argument is the Symbol #currentProject, whereas in the earlier example the argument was #text; these arguments help the CodeView decide what messages to send to the model to obtain updated information.

Try the yellow button commands. Enter a project (Figure 15.42). Create some views in the new project, including a project browser (recall that to create a project browser you evaluate the expression ProjectBrowser open). Use the project browser to return to the original project. Try to remove a project, and to add a new one.

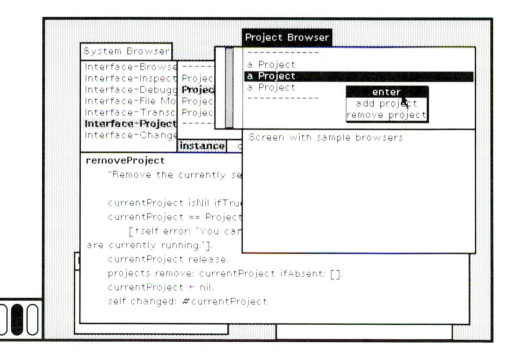

Figure 15.42

Notice that if no item is selected and you try to obtain the yellow button menu in the list menu subview of the project browser, the subview flashes. However, when no item is selected in the subview, it is appropriate to be able to invoke the command to add a new project. The method for projectMenu in class ProjectBrowser can be changed. One such change is shown in Figure 15.43. When the currentProject is nil, the menu is an ActionMenu of one item, add project; when currentProject is not nil, the menu is an ActionMenu of three items. (In fact, the class variable ProjectMenu is no longer used.) Figure 15.44 shows the yellow button menu that appears when no item is selected in the subview.

We have fulfilled all but one specification for the ProjectBrowser. We still have to provide a prompter for the title of a new project. To do so, we must first modify class Project.

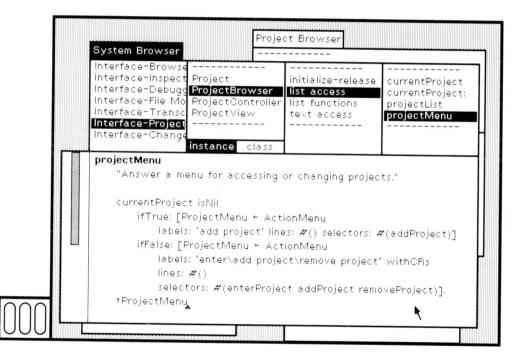

Figure 15.43

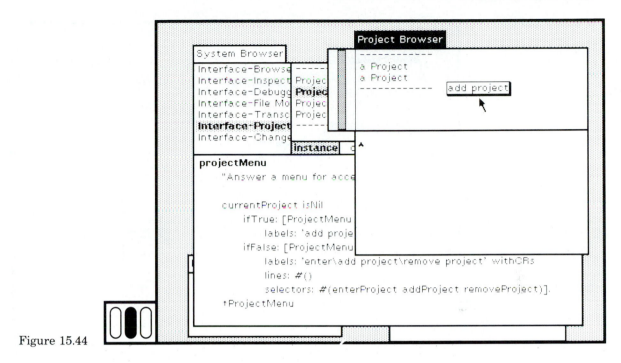

Figure 15.44

15.3

**Modify Class
Project**

Close any example project browsers and project views that you might have created by choosing the blue button command close in each view.

In the system browser, choose the class name Project. The definition for Project displays in the text subview of the browser. Change the definition by adding the instance variable title (Figure 15.45). Choose the yellow button command accept. The class is recompiled. All existing instances of Project are updated to have one additional instance variable; in each case, the initial value of the variable is nil.

Each of the existing projects must be given a title before you can change the way in which Projects print a description of themselves. One way to solve this problem is to create an inspector for all existing projects by evaluating the expression Project allInstances inspect (Figure 15.46a). There is at least one Project, the one in which you are currently running.

Choose each project, one at a time, and open an inspector on it (Figure 15.46b). Choose the instance variable name title. In the text subview of the inspector, type a literal String that is the title for this project (Figure 15.46c). Choose the yellow button command accept to store the title. Do this for each existing Project. Close each inspector.

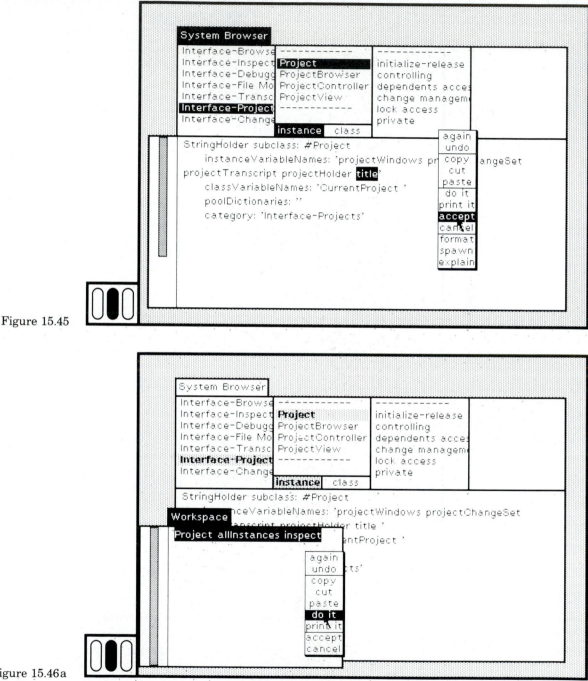

Figure 15.45

Figure 15.46a

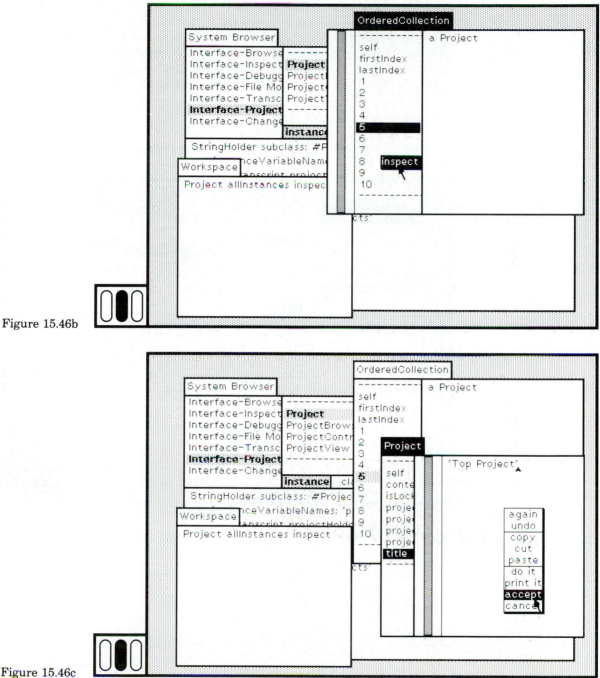

Figure 15.46b

Figure 15.46c

Currently, when a Project prints a description of itself, it uses the default description, a Project, specified in the method for printOn: as defined in class Object. We want a Project to print its title instead. Create the protocol printing for class Project, and specify a new method for printOn: (Figure 15.47). You must also provide a message for setting the value of title that can be used in creating a new Project. The value should be an instance of String. Add the message title: to the category initialize-release (Figure 15.48).

Now open a new project browser. You can see that each existing project now displays its title in the list menu (Figure 15.49).

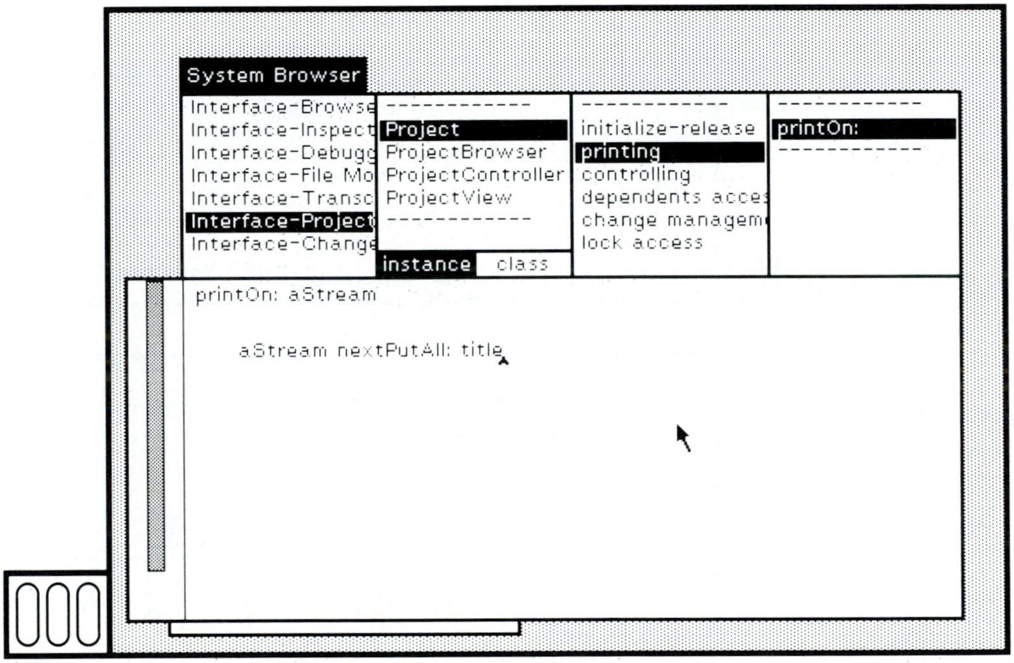

Figure 15.47

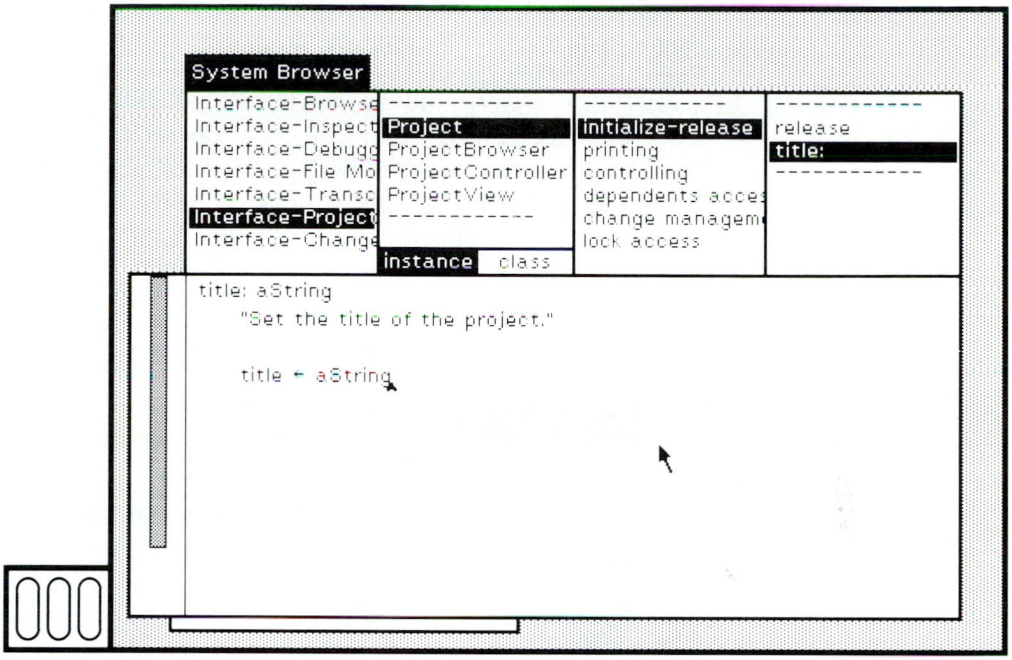

Figure 15.48

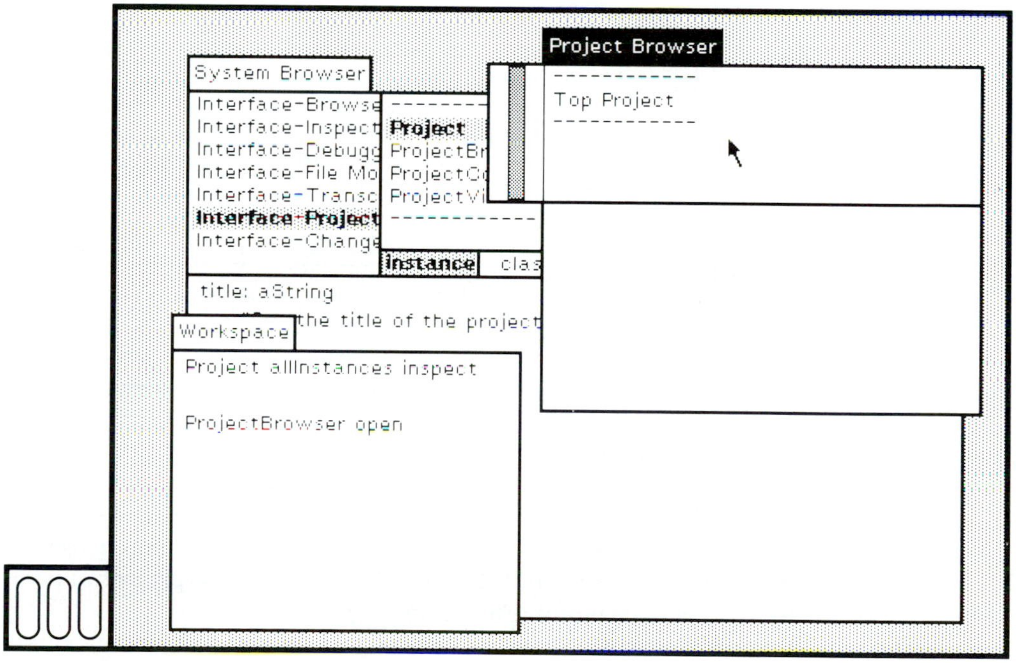

Figure 15.49

The next step is to change the method associated with addProject in class ProjectBrowser to prompt for a title. The new method is shown in Figure 15.50. It uses an instance of the system class FillInTheBlank to request a title, then sends the newly created project the message title: in order to store the response. The two arguments in the creation of the FillInTheBlank instance specify the noneditable text that appears in the upper subview, stating what kind of information is expected, and the editable text that appears in the lower subview. In this case, the "default" title, a Project, will appear in the lower subview; it can then be edited by the user.

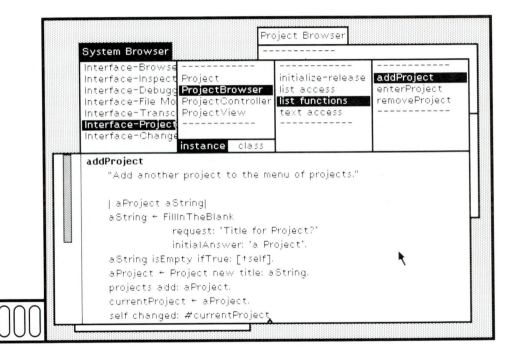

Figure 15.50

The user of this kind of prompter can abort the action of adding a project by typing nothing in the lower subview. The second statement in the method for addProject tests to see if the response is nothing (isEmpty) and, if so, terminates (↑self).

Try it. Choose the yellow button command add project (as shown earlier). A prompter appears. The initial response is the default title a Project (Figure 15.51a). Edit the response and then choose the yellow button command accept (Figure 15.51b). The new project appears in the project browser menu (Figure 15.51c).

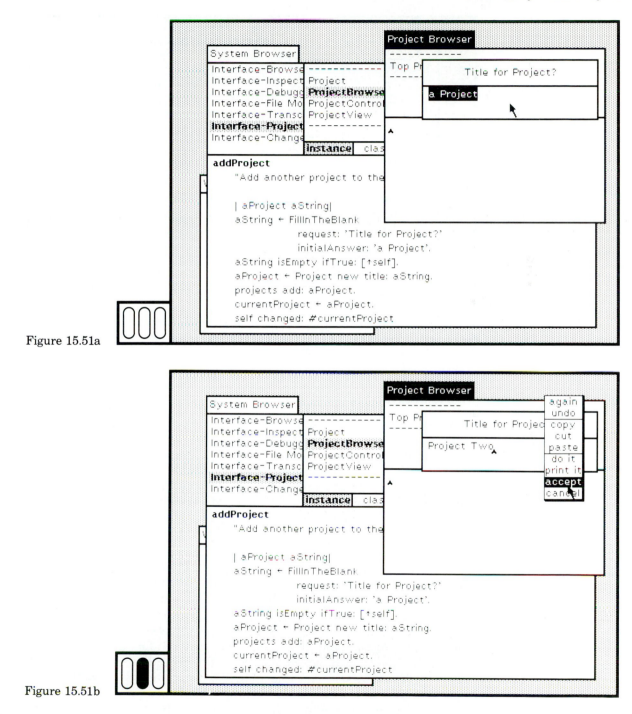

Figure 15.51a

Figure 15.51b

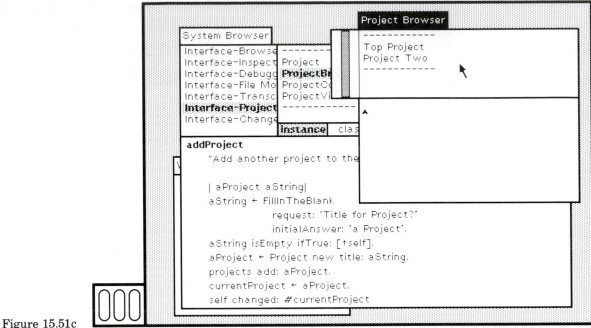

Figure 15.51c

15.4

**Change the
System Menu**

It would be more convenient to be able to create a project browser with
the same ease that we can create a system browser, that is, by choosing
an item from the System Menu.

The creation of the System Menu is specified in the system class
ScreenController. In the system browser, choose the class category Inter-
face-Support and then choose the class name ScreenController. Choose
the browser menu item class. The only message selector in the category
class initialization is initialize. Choose it (Figure 15.52). The System Menu
is a PopUpMenu. PopUpMenu is an alternative way to create menus
that know about item labels and lines, similar to ActionMenu. A
PopUpMenu does not store the messages associated with the menu
items. Class ScreenController has two class variables in which the
PopUpMenu and the corresponding array of messages are stored
(ScreenYellowButtonMenu and ScreenYellowButtonMessages). To modify
the System Menu, you must edit the method for ScreenController
initialize. Delete the exit project and project items in the menu labels and
insert project browser. The line numbers must change as well as the
messages. Delete the messages exitProject and openProject, and insert
the new message openProjectBrowser. Choose the yellow button command accept to recompile the method (Figure 15.53).

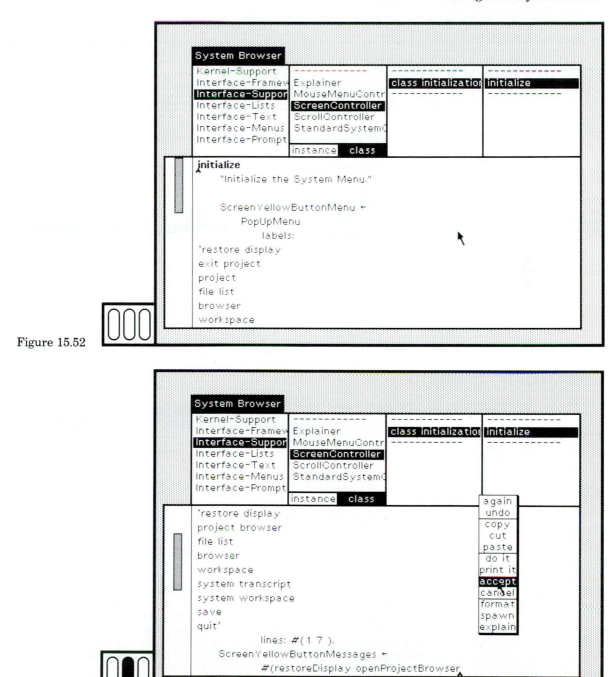

Figure 15.52

Figure 15.53

You need to update the class variables and to inform existing instances of ScreenController that the menu has changed. This is done by evaluating the expressions

ScreenController initialize.
ScreenController allInstancesDo: [:sc | sc initializeYellowButtonMenu]

that appear at the end of the method initialize, as shown in Figure 15.54.

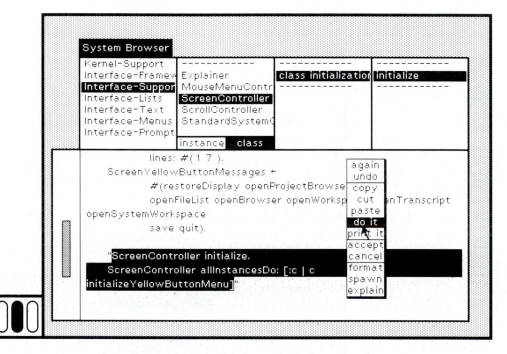

Figure 15.54

The ScreenController must be able to response to the message openProjectBrowser. The method is shoiwn in Figure 15.55. Add this method to ScreenController. The System Menu is now changed so that you can try it out (Figure 15.56).

Now that you can create project browsers using the System Menu, you will find that adding projects and removing projects must be broadcast in some way to all existing project browsers. Moreover, unless you are careful, broadcasting a message to change a browser will cause it to redisplay. If project browsers from different projects redisplay on the single display screen, this will look very peculiar. Thus you might prefer to add a menu item to the yellow button menu of the project browser list menu subview, update projects. You can broadcast the addition and removal information without updating the display of the browser, and then select the new menu item update projects to obtain the proper display. This is the technique adopted by the system browser. Perhaps you can think of an improved approach. Also note that if you do change the menu for the project browser, you must reset all the class variables referring to the menu.

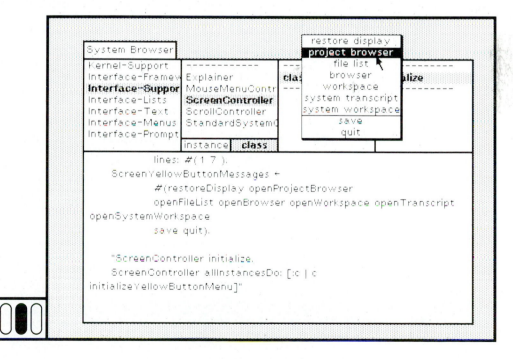

Figure 15.55

Figure 15.56

PART FOUR

How to Find and Correct Errors

In the previous book parts, you were introduced to the views and menus that provide support in finding out information about existing system functionality and in creating new functionality. In examples presented, we attempted to minimize the errors you would encounter. The purpose of Part Four is to explain how to find and correct errors, in particular, syntax errors and runtime execution errors. The examples will ask you to create errors so that you can learn how to correct them. The error-handling support takes the form of error correction aides, error notification (either in-line error messages or use of the notifier view), and the debugger view. The debugger is used to find an error that occurs during execution of an activity, and it is used to find out how an activity is implemented.

16

Spelling Correction

A major area of research in the development of programming environments has been to provide on-line assistance to the programmer. Some of the earliest work in this area was done in the context of the development of the Interlisp programming environment under the research title of "programmer's assistant." [W. Teitelman, "Automated Programmering—The Programmer's Assistant," *Proceedings of the Fall Joint Computer Conference*, Dec. 1972; W. Teitelman and L. Masinter, "The Interlisp Programming Environment," IEEE *Computer* Magazine, April 1981, pp. 25-33]. One of the results of this research was the introduction of the DWIM, or "do-what-I-mean" spelling correction, approach to interaction and error handling.

Adapted from this research on spelling correction, the Smalltalk-80 system includes the ability to assist the programmer by correcting misspellings of variable names and message selectors. Spelling correction is done within the context in which you are working, that is, within the scope of the variables and message selectors of a class definition or of an interrupted context. This chapter describes the spelling correction mechanisms as you might encounter them when evaluating expressions in a workspace. Chapter 17 explores the way in which the Smalltalk-80 parser reports syntax errors in method definitions, and the way the system uses the spelling corrector to help you correct these errors. And Chapter 18 illustrates how you are notified of runtime errors that are associated with unrecognized message selectors, and how the spelling corrector can help you determine the correct message selectors.

Figure 16.1a shows a workspace in which the text consists of a temporary variable declaration for bic, and an expression to assign an instance of class Pen to the variable spelled bik. This could either be an undeclared variable name, or a misspelling. If you select this text and then choose the yellow button command do it, the system guesses that bik is an undeclared variable. This variable is selected and a menu of optional next actions is displayed (Figure 16.1b). Four of these actions involve declaring the variable; one tries to fix its spelling.

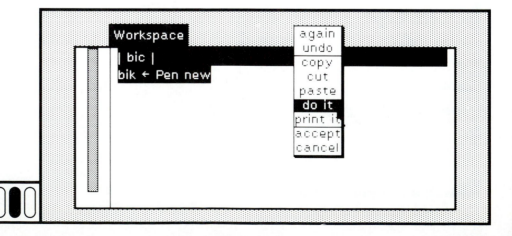

Figure 16.1a

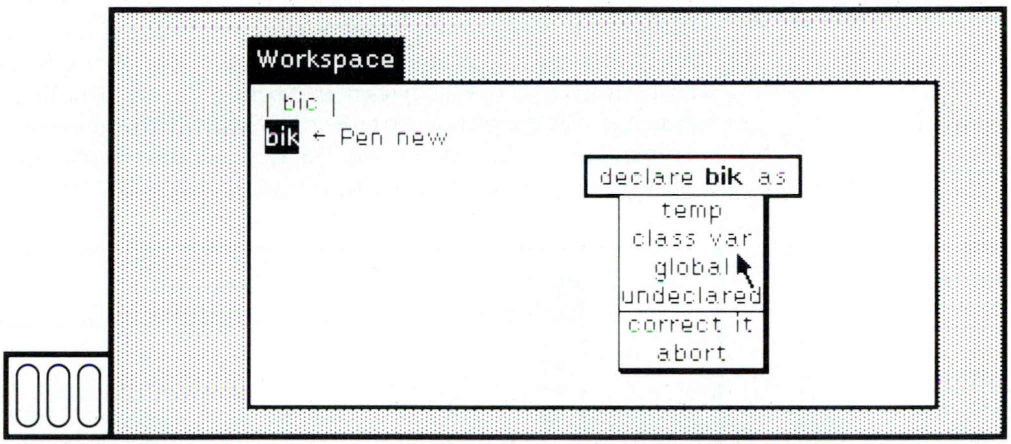

Figure 16.1b

temp	Declares the variable to be a temporary. The variable name will be inserted into the text, delimited by the vertical bars. If the vertical bars do not already exist in the text view, they are added. (See Figures 16.4a, 16.4b, and 16.4c in which this declaration is illustrated.)
class var	Declares this variable to be a class variable of the class of the method in which the error was found. If the error is found in the text subview of the inspector, then this declaration will make the variable a class variable of the inspector. At the level of a workspace, the class is assumed to be UndefinedObject, the class of the object nil. (All class variable names must start with a capital letter.)
global	Declares this variable to be a global variable, which means that the variable is included in the system dictionary, Smalltalk. (All global variable names must start with a capital letter.)
undeclared	Leaves this variable undeclared, which means it is included in the system dictionary, Undeclared. A message that states that the variable is undeclared prints in the System Transcript, if it appears on the screen.
correct it	Tries to determine the most likely correction. (This is done by searching the known symbols in the system for the closest match.)
abort	Forgets the attempted evaluation.

Choose the command correct it (Figure 16.1c). The system determines that the most likely correction for bik is bic. A confirmer is displayed indicating that the proposed correction is bic. Confirm the choice by choosing the command yes (Figure 16.1d). The correction replaces the erroneous variable in the text of the workspace (Figure 16.1e) and the expressions are successfully evaluated.

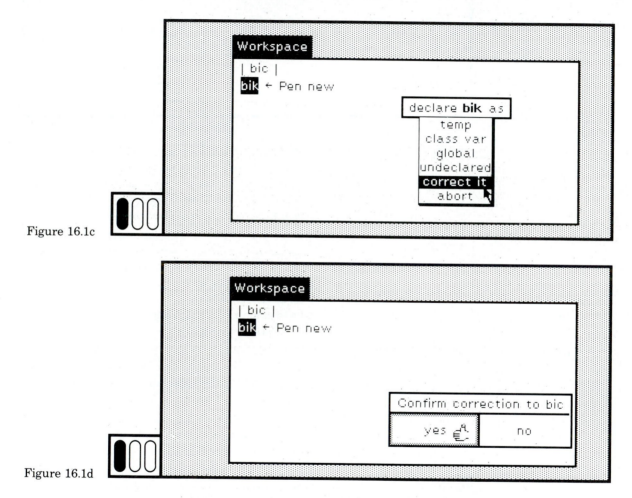

Figure 16.1c

Figure 16.1d

In Figure 16.2a, a statement has been added to the text in the workspace, but the trailing colon for the keyword go was omitted. The attempt to evaluate the expressions fails. The erroneous message selector is selected, and a menu appears indicating that the problem is that the message go might be a new message (Figure 16.2b).

Figure 16.1e

Figure 16.2a

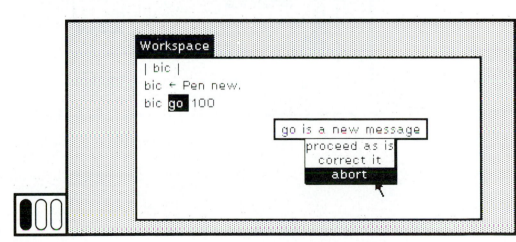

Figure 16.2b

The menu indicates three optional actions.

proceed as is	Proceeds on the assumption that this message will eventually be implemented. This is a likely occurrence if you take a top-down approach to programming. This option really only has meaning in the context of compiling a new method, not in the context of evaluating an expression in a workspace.
correct it	Tries to determine the most likely correction.
abort	Forgets the attempted evaluation.

Choose the command abort.

As shown in Figure 16.2c, the keyword go was corrected to be go:, and then a third statement was added. The attempt to evaluate these expressions fails (Figure 16.2d). A menu appears indicating that the problem is that the message trn: might be a new message. Choose the action correct it. The system guesses that turn: was intended (Figure 16.2e). Confirm that this is the correct message by choosing the confirmer menu item yes. The correction is made in the text of the workspace. The evaluation is restarted, and the new Pen draws a line on the display screen (Figure 16.2f).

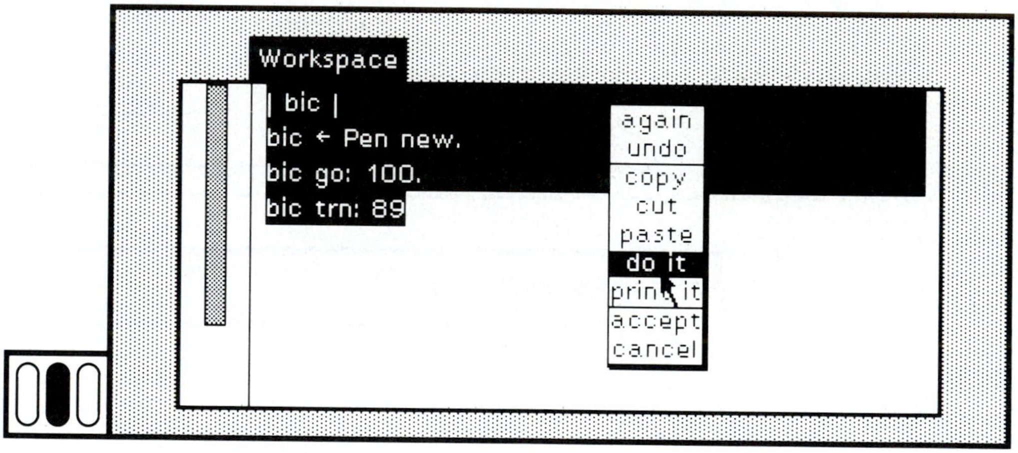

Figure 16.2c

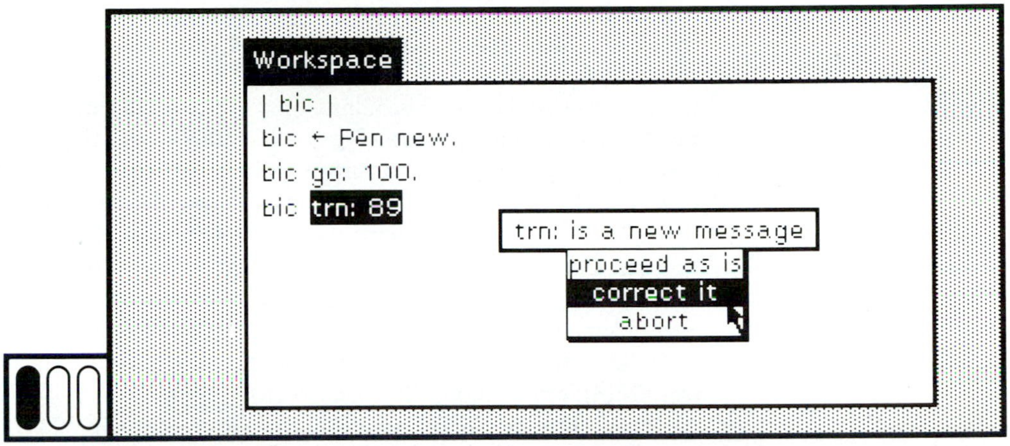

Figure 16.2d

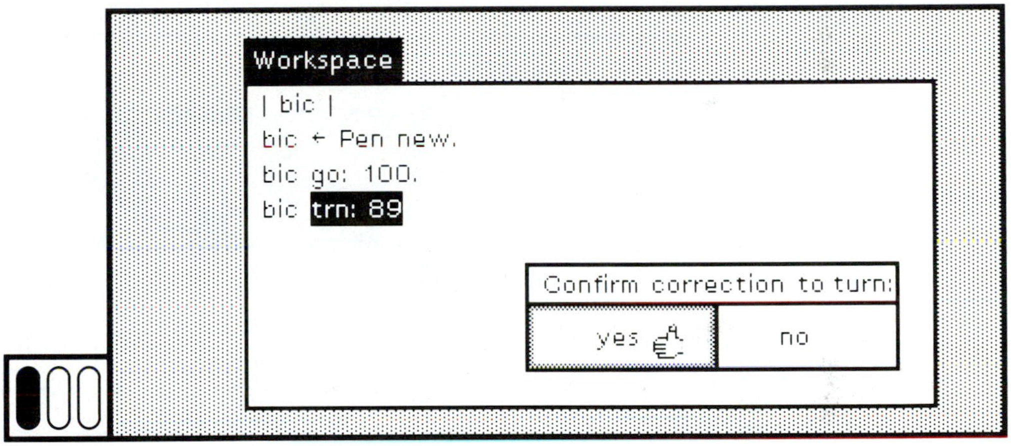

Figure 16.2e

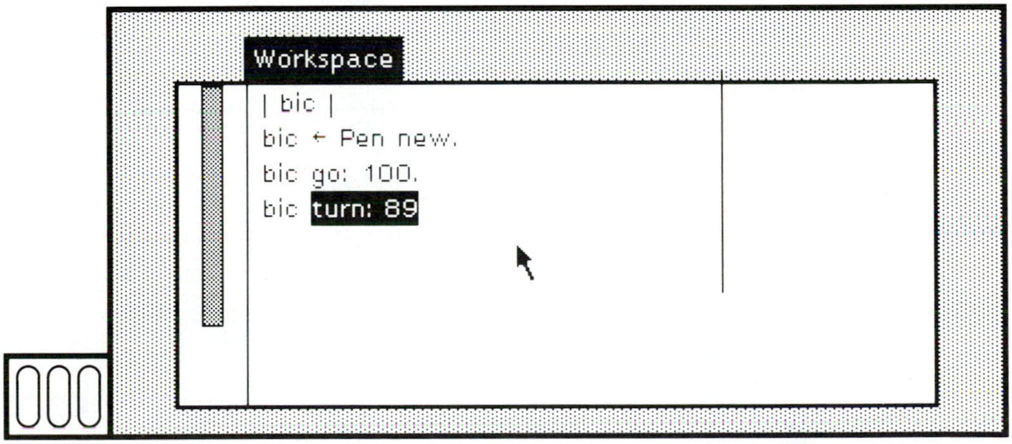

Figure 16.2f

For the next example, edit the statements in the workspace so that there are four expressions; the second (and new one) changes the form source (the "brush") of the Pen to be a new Form. Evaluate the statements (Figure 16.3a). The class name Form was misspelled as indicated by the menu that appears (Figure 16.3b). Choose the command correct it. The system guesses that an appropriate correction for Fom is Form (Figure 16.3c). Confirm by choosing the menu item yes. Evaluation is restarted, but another error is found (Figure 16.3d); a message is not known. Choose the abort command. Parentheses are needed. Notice also that the argument to extent: should be an instance of Point. Make both corrections (Figure 16.3e).

Delete the declaration of bic as a temporary variable; evaluate the remaining expressions (Figure 16.4a). The system notices that bic is not declared (Figure 16.4b). Choose the item temp in the correction menu that appears. The declaration is inserted into the text (Figure 16.4c).

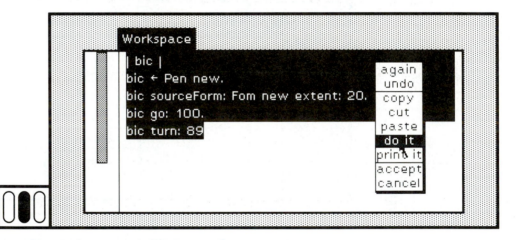

Figure 16.3a

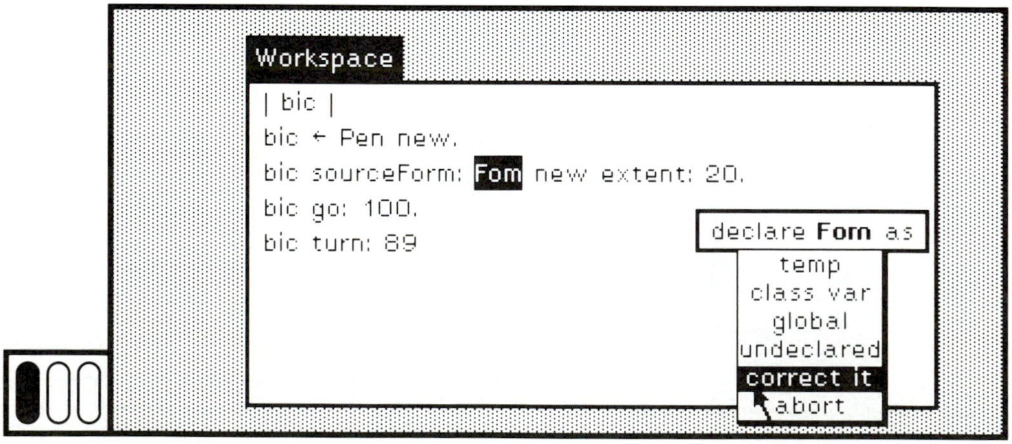

Figure 16.3b

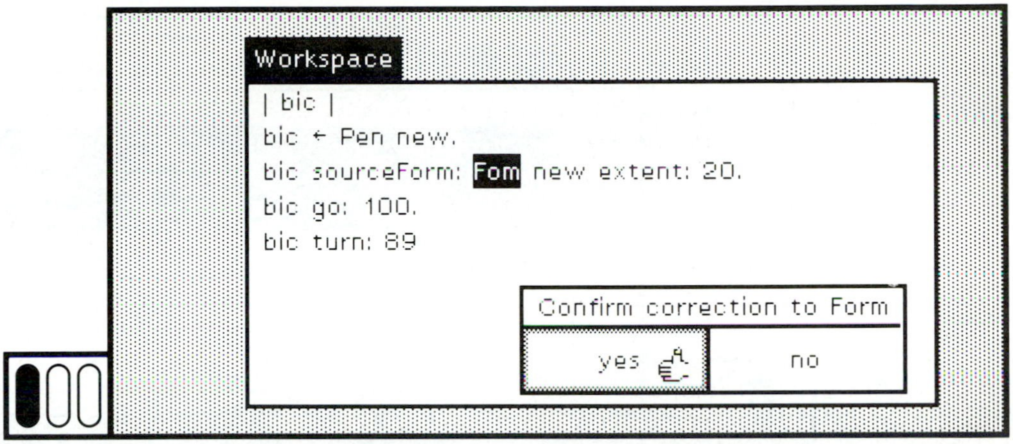

Figure 16.3c

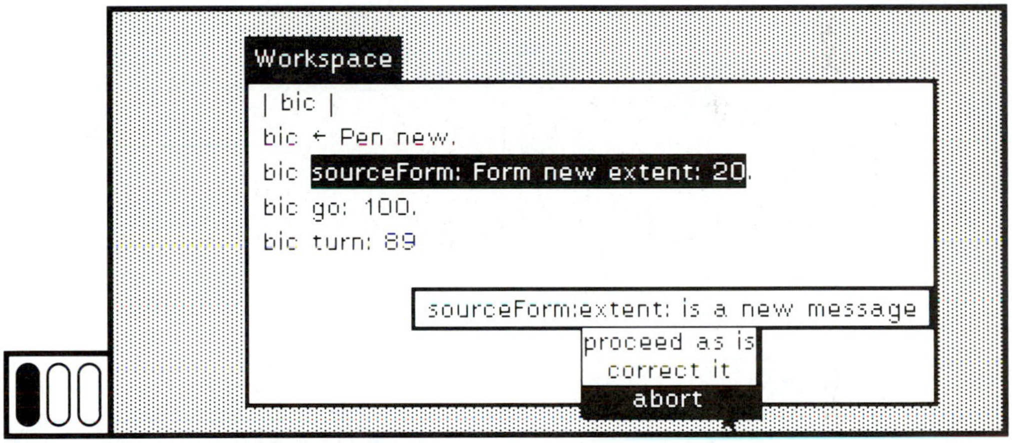

Figure 16.3d

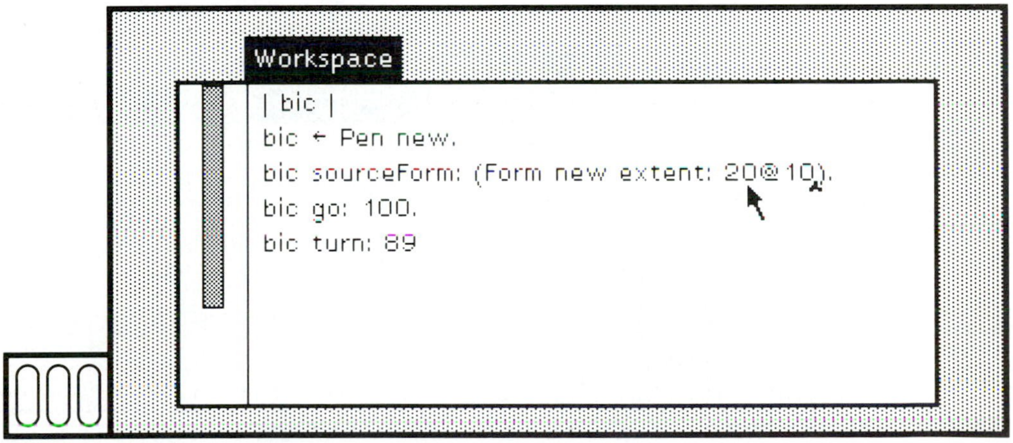

Figure 16.3e

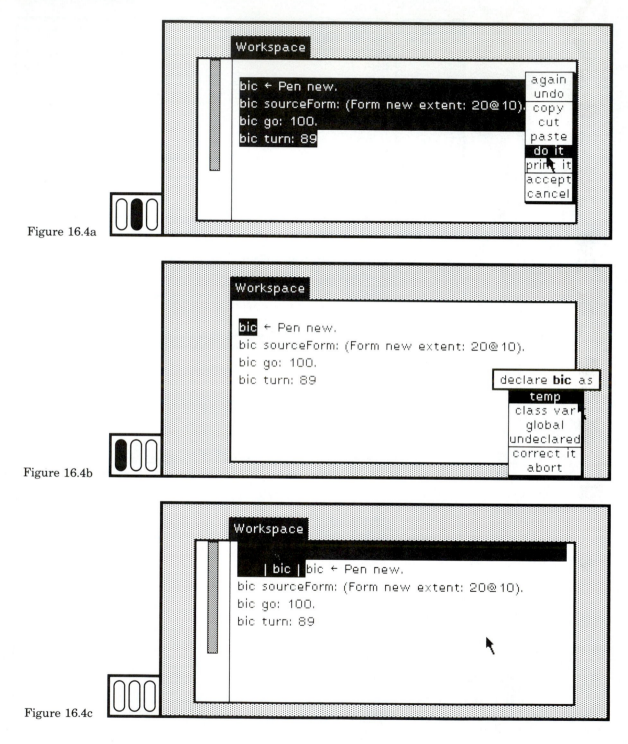

Figure 16.4a

Figure 16.4b

Figure 16.4c

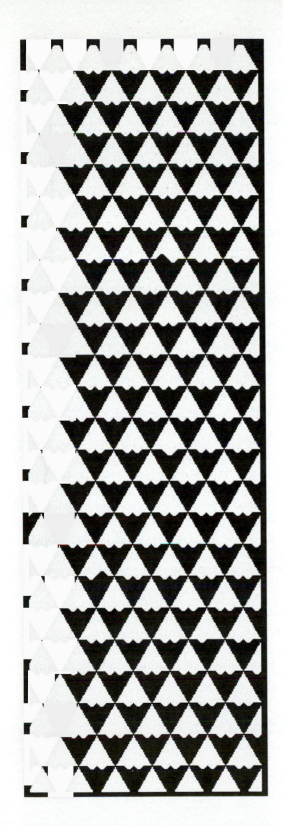

17

Syntax Errors

A compiler is used in three places in the Smalltalk-80 system:

1. when you add a method to a class description by choosing the command accept in a system browser,

2. when you evaluate an expression by choosing either the command do it or print it, and

3. when you file in a class description from an external file.

This chapter illustrates the kinds of syntax errors you can encounter in the first two cases; Section 22.2 describes the third case.

17.1

Variable Name or Message Selector Errors

The spelling corrector is a part of the syntax analysis available when you compile class methods. To illustrate the kind of syntax errors that you can encounter, follow an example implementation of the class FinancialHistory. We will continue to work on this FinancialHistory example for several consecutive chapters, so try to save your work between sessions.

Add the class category Financial Tools and define the class FinancialHistory. The class definition is shown in Figure 17.1. (If you have forgotten how to add class categories and classes, review Chapter 9.) Choose the browser menu item class so that you can define a message understood by the class FinancialHistory. This message is an instance creation message. Add the class protocol instance creation.

In protocol instance creation, type the method for initialBalance: shown in Figure 17.2a. Choose the yellow button command accept. The method for initialBalance: consists of sending the new instance of FinancialHistory the message setInitialBalance: so that the instance variables can be initialized. This message is not implemented as yet, so a correction menu, like the ones introduced in Chapter 16, appears. The menu states that setInitialBalance: is a new message (Figure 17.2b). The next thing you will do is define this message, so choose the action proceed as is to complete the compilation of the method initialBalance: (Figure 17.2c).

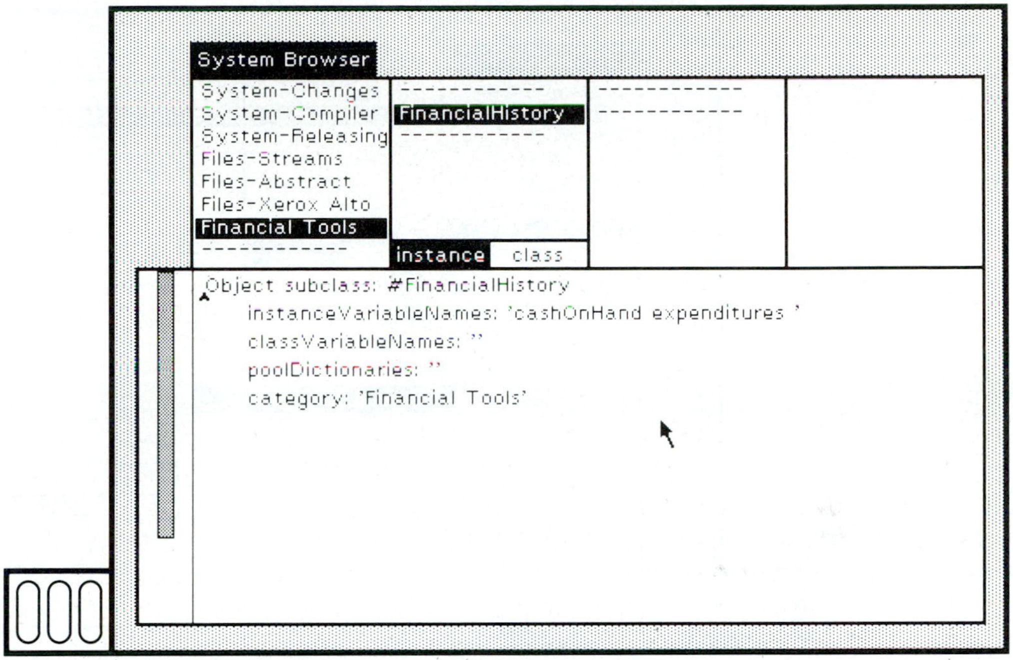

Figure 17.1

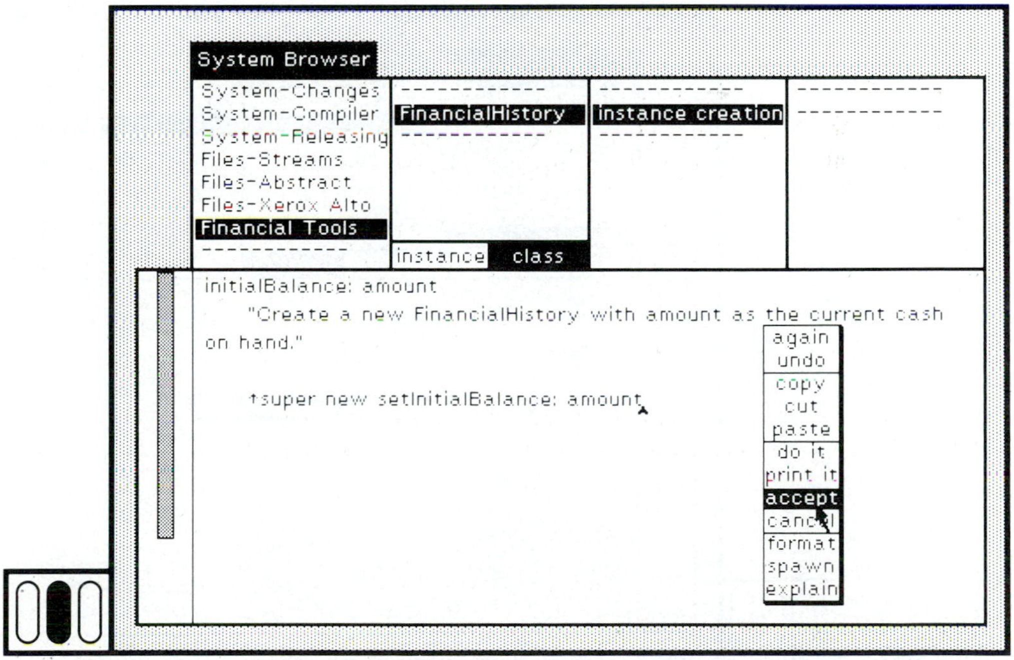

Figure 17.2a

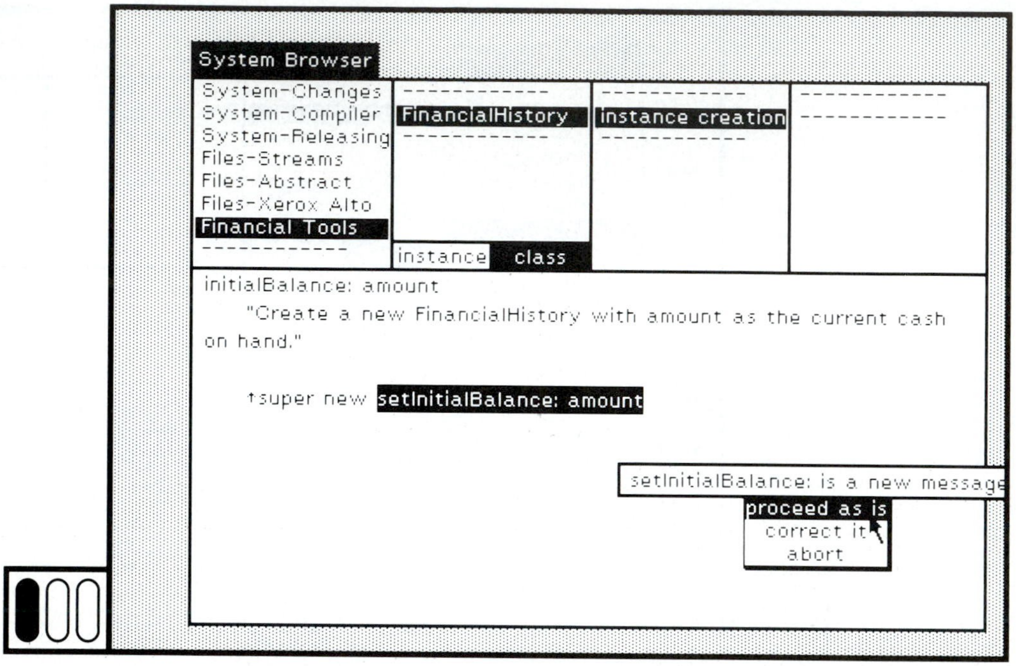

Figure 17.2b

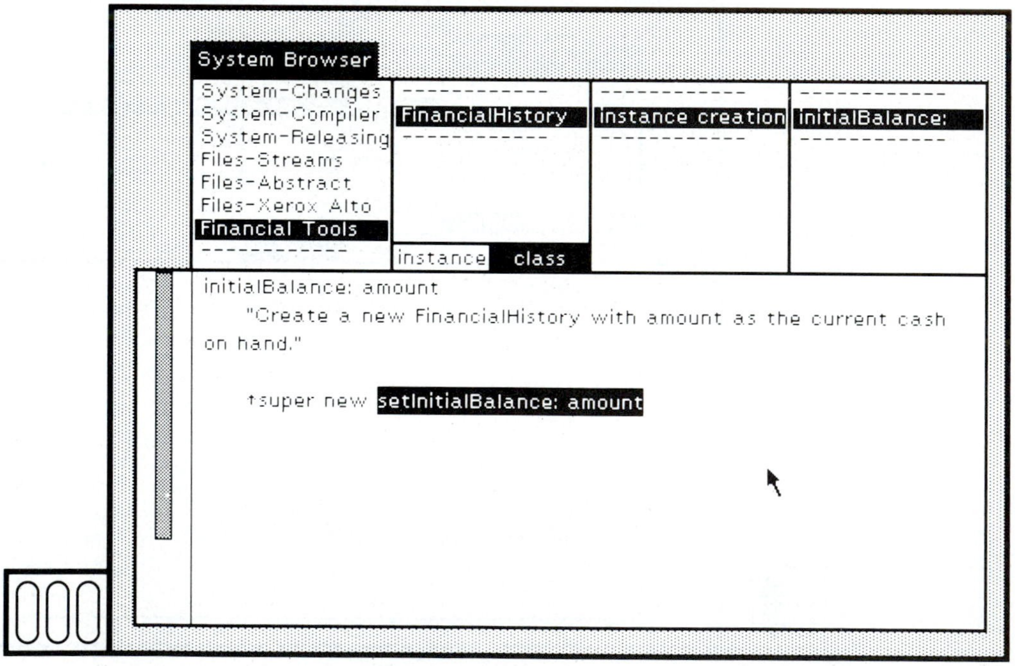

Figure 17.2c

Now choose the browser menu item instance and add instance protocols transactions, inquiries, and private. Under private, we will categorize
all messages that should only be sent by an instance of FinancialHistory
to itself (self). Define setInitialBalance: under the protocol private (Figure
17.3a). Notice that for the example, you are to mistype the instance
variable cashOnHand—the o should not be capitalized. A correction
menu appears indicating that cashonHand is not declared (Figure
17.3b). Choose the command correct it.

A confirmer appears indicating that the probable correction is
cashOnHand. Confirm by choosing the menu item yes (Figure 17.3c). As
a result of your choosing yes, the corrected variable name is inserted
into the method, the method is successfully compiled, and the message
selector is added to the browser menu (Figure 17.3d).

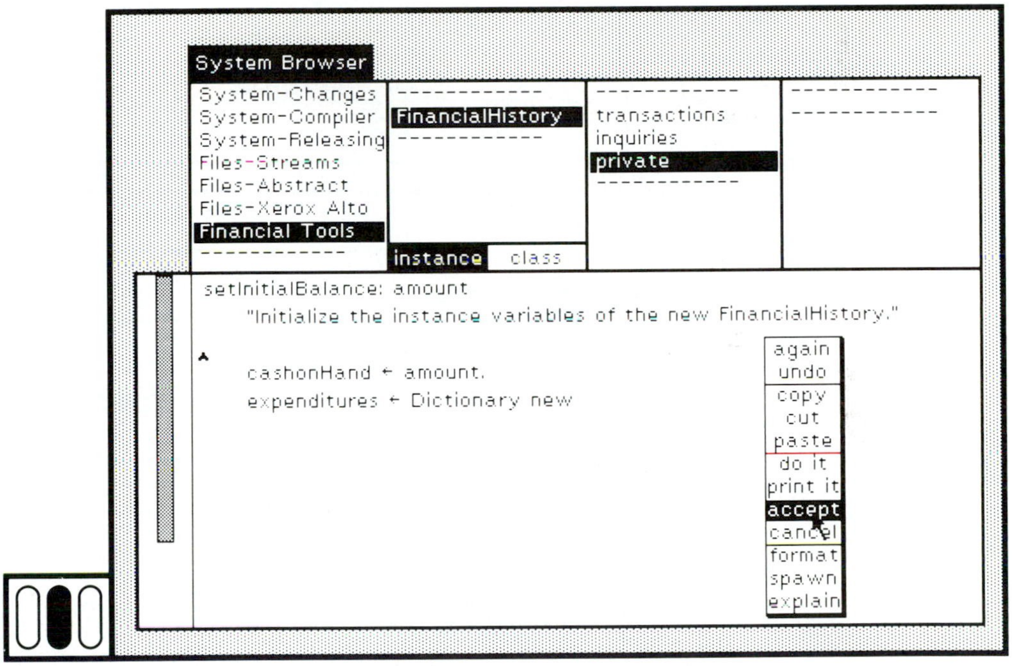

Figure 17.3a

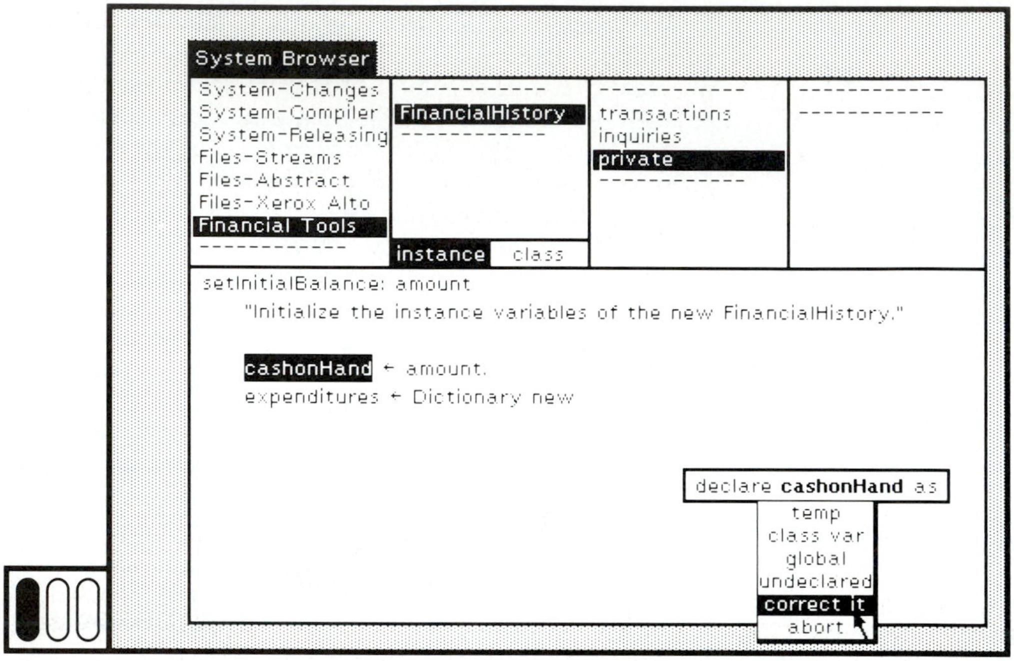

Figure 17.3b

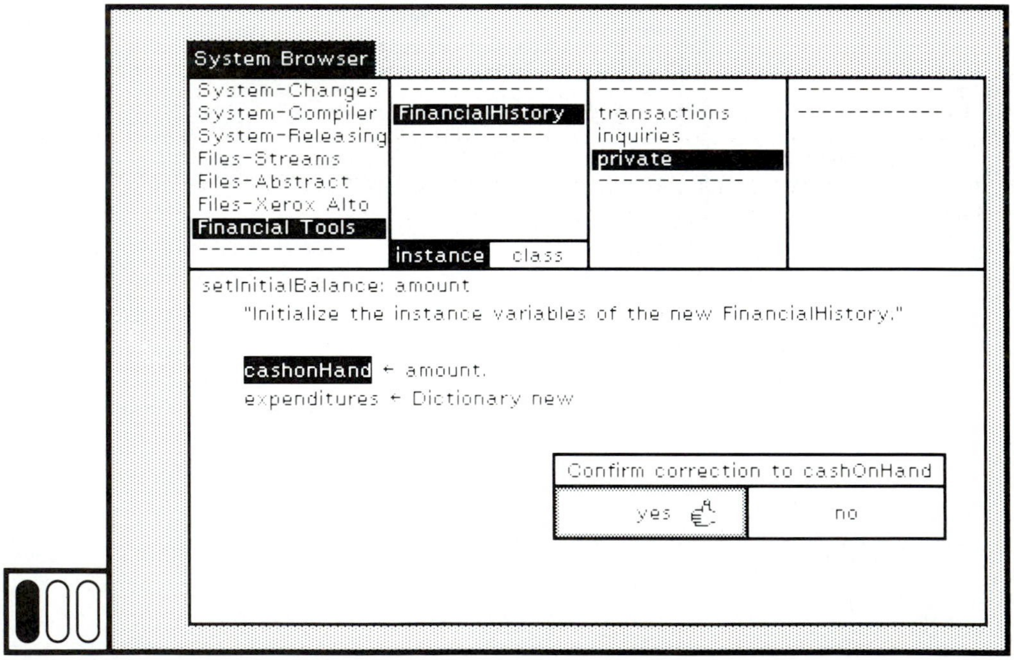

Figure 17.3c

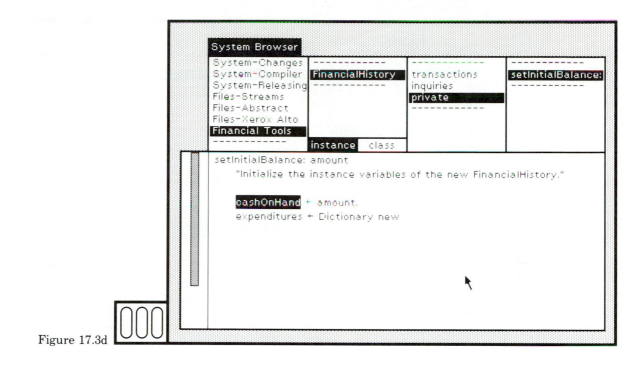

Figure 17.3d

17.2

Poorly-Formed Statements or Methods

Choose the protocol transactions and specify the method for spend: amount for: reason (Figure 17.4a). Notice that you are to omit an argument. When you choose the yellow button command accept, a syntactic error is found (Figure 17.4b). The error message, Argument expected->, is inserted into the text, preceding the point of the error, so that an arrow points to the location of the error or to the location at which the error can be corrected. Type the correction so that the error message is replaced by the argument name reason, and choose the yellow button command accept again (Figure 17.4c).

This time the new message totalSpentOn: is noticed (Figure 17.4d). We will define this message later so choose the action proceed as is. The method is compiled successfully and added to the class (Figure 17.4e).

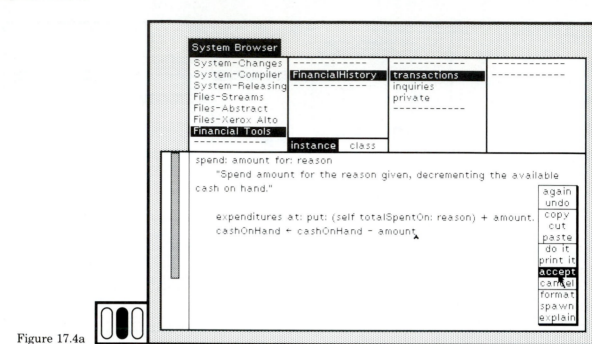

Figure 17.4a

Figure 17.4b

```
System Browser
System-Changes    ------------    ------------    ------------
System-Compiler   FinancialHistory  transactions   ------------
System-Releasing  ------------    inquiries
Files-Streams                     private
Files-Abstract                    ------------
Files-Xerox Alto
Financial Tools
------------      instance   class
```

```
spend: amount for: reason                              again
    "Spend amount for the reason given, decrementing   undo    ilable
cash on hand."                                         copy
                                                       cut
                                                       paste
    expenditures at: reason put: (self totalSpentOn: re do it   amount.
    cashOnHand ← cashOnHand - amount                   print it
                                                       accept
                                                       cancel
                                                       format
                                                       spawn
                                                       explain
```

Figure 17.4c

```
System Browser
System-Changes    ------------    ------------    ------------
System-Compiler   FinancialHistory  transactions   ------------
System-Releasing  ------------    inquiries
Files-Streams                     private
Files-Abstract                    ------------
Files-Xerox Alto
Financial Tools
------------      instance   class
```

```
spend: amount for: reason
    "Spend amount for the reason given, decrementing the available
cash on hand."

    expenditures at: reason put: (self totalSpentOn: reason) + amount.
    cashOnHand ← cashOnHand - amount  totalSpentOn: is a new message
                                      proceed as is
                                        correct it
                                         abort
```

Figure 17.4d

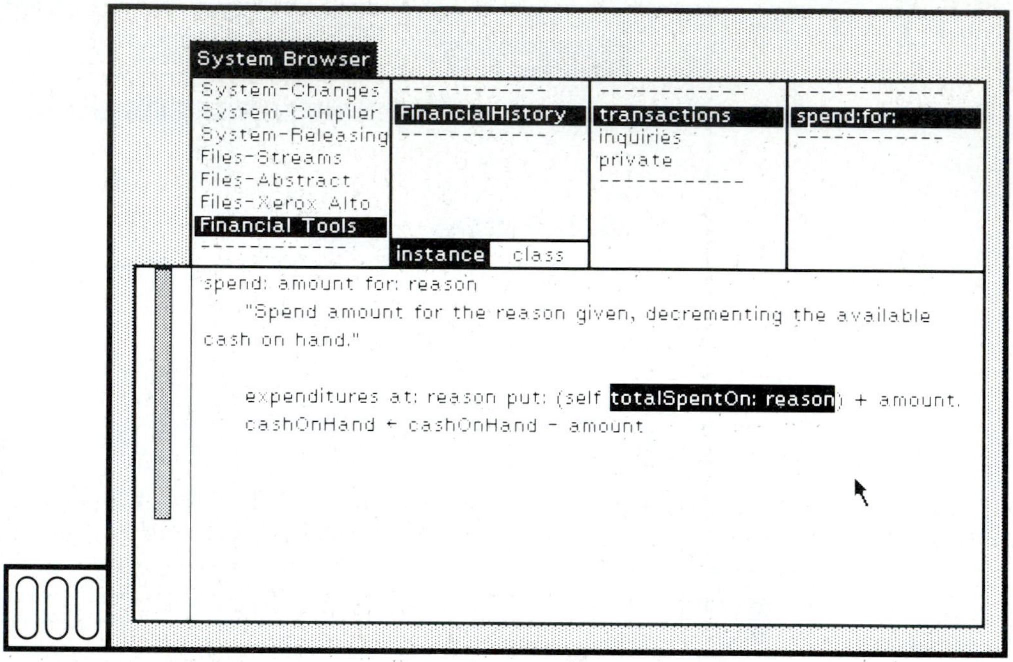

Figure 17.4e

The syntax errors you might make when you try to evaluate an expresson or compile a class method fall into three categories:

1. something expected was missing

2. there was a bracketing error

3. you tried to do something you can not do

Expected parts of a method that can be missing are the argument name, as illustrated by the previous example in Figure 17.2a; an expression after an assignment symbol ($\leftarrow$) or after a return symbol ($\uparrow$); a vertical bar; and a period or right bracket at the end of the method. Also nothing more might be expected if the compiler thinks the method has ended, although something more exists.

Bracketing errors may exist for parentheses, comment quotes ("), square brackets, and string quotes ('). Another common mistake is omitting the period at the end of a statement (other than after the last statement of a method).

Three things you can not do that will be noticed as syntactic errors are to store into a pseudo-variable (self, super, true, false, or an argument), to cascade to a constant or to super, and to cascade certain control messages (ifTrue:ifFalse:, ifFalse:ifTrue:, whileTrue:, and whileFalse:).

To illustrate another syntactic error, add the method totalSpentFor: to class FinancialHistory; categorize it under inquiries as shown in Figure 17.5a. (For now, please ignore the fact that the message used in the method for spend:for: was totalSpentOn:, not totalSpentFor:. You are making this error so that we can illustrate another kind of error in Chapter 18.) Choose the yellow button command accept. A syntax error message is inserted into the text at the end of the method (Figure 17.5b) because, when you typed the method, you forgot the closing right bracket. Replace the error message with the right bracket and choose the command accept again. The method is added to the class (Figure 17.5c).

Remember to save your work, either by making

1. a snapshot (see Sections 1.4 and 23.1) or

2. a file that describes the class.

In the system browser, choose FinancialHistory and then choose yellow button command file out. The file name will be FinancialHistory.st.

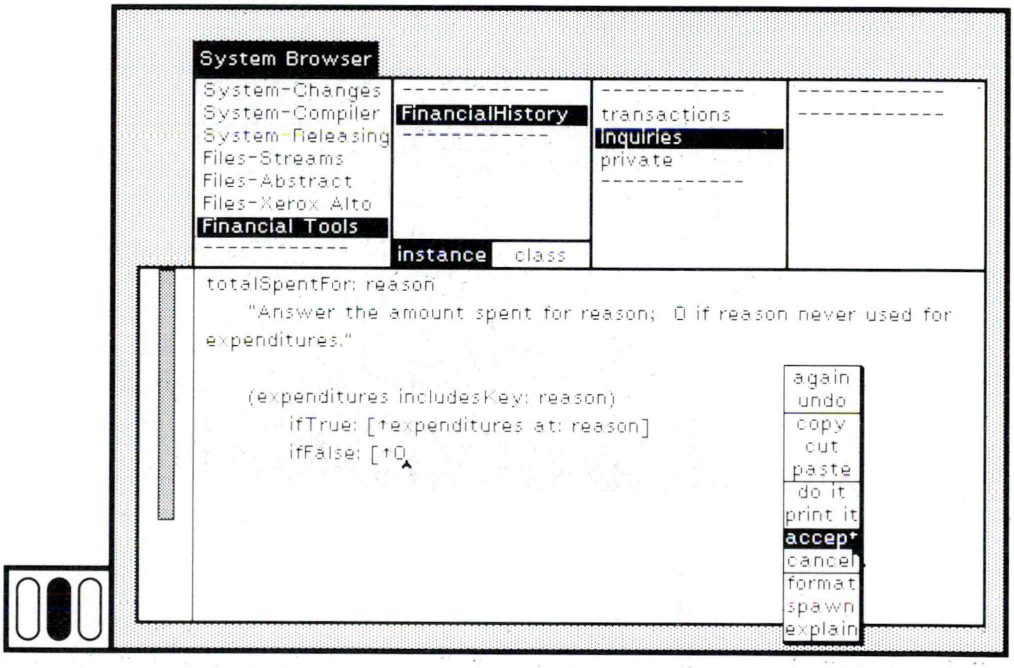

Figure 17.5a

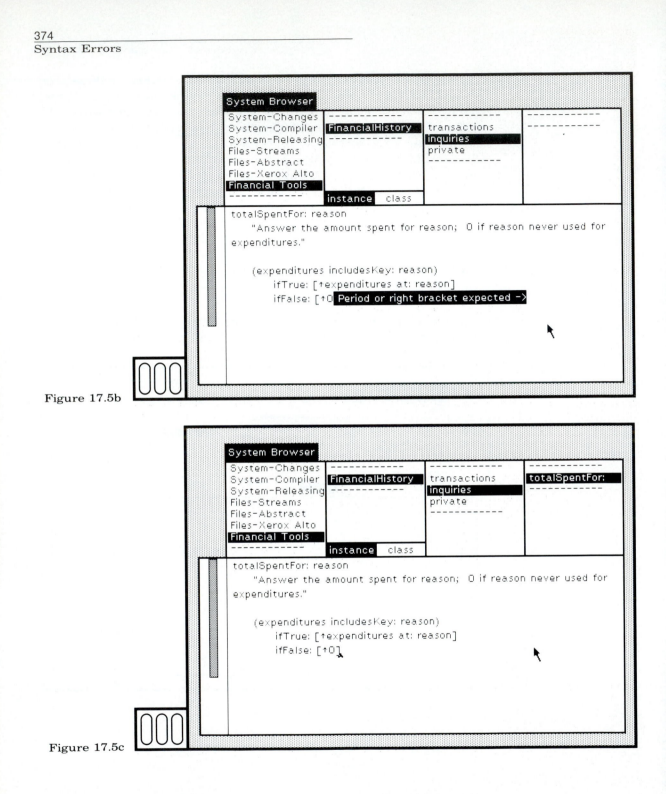

Figure 17.5b

Figure 17.5c

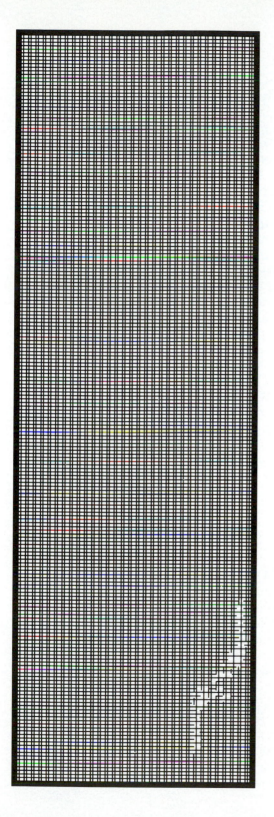

18

Notification of an Execution Interrupt

A *message-send* is the activity of sending a message to an object. A *notifier* is a view that is displayed on an interruption of a message-send. Since responding to a message involves sending a message, a notifier is basically a view on a sequence of message-sends. Each of the messages displayed in the view has been sent, but has not yet received replies.

There are a number of ways to interrupt a message-send, four of which are described in Chapter 20: the programmer sets a breakpoint, the user types the "control" and "c" keys at the same time, the system runs out of space, and recursion occurs in the system error handler.

This chapter explores interrupts that occur whenever a runtime error is encountered. Most runtime errors occur because a message was sent to an object that does not understand the message, that is, the message selector was not specified in the class of the object or in any of its superclasses. The error could be that the message selector was incorrect, or that the receiver of the message was the wrong kind of object. The other kinds of interrupts are discussed in Chapter 20.

18.1

Incorrect Message Selector

The FinancialHistory example in Chapter 17 will be used to illustrate the way a notifier is used to locate a runtime error. If the class is not already in your system, we assume you created a file containing the class description, as discussed at the end of Chapter 17. Evaluate the expression, (FileStream oldFileNamed: 'FinancialHistory.st') fileIn to retrieve the class.

Open a workspace and type the instance creation message

FinancialHistory initialBalance: 450

This creates a new instance of FinancialHistory with 450 as the cash on hand. Inspect this new instance by sending it the message inspect. (Remember that the instance creation expression must be parenthesized as shown in Figure 18.1a, otherwise the precedence rules cause the message inspect to be sent to the number 450.) Create the inspector and examine the values of its variables (Figure 18.1b). In the text subview of the inspector, type an expression to spend some of that cash.

self spend: 100 for: 'rent'

Evaluate the expression by choosing the yellow button command print it (Figure 18.1c). A notifier appears (Figure 18.1d). It consists of two parts: a title that states the reason for the execution interrupt, and a list of the last few interrupted message-sends.

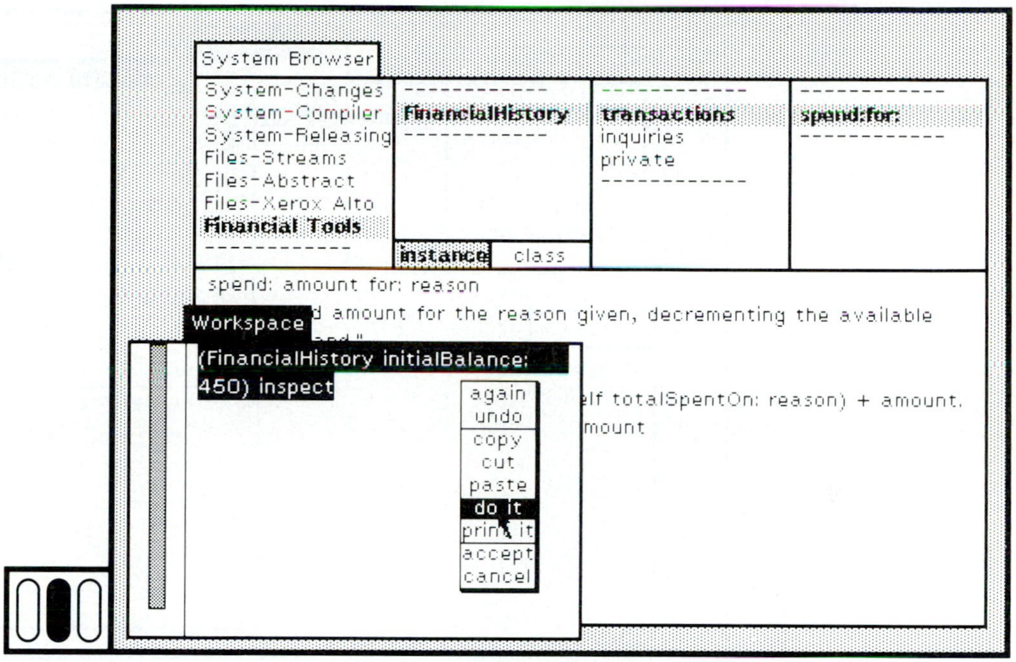

Figure 18.1a

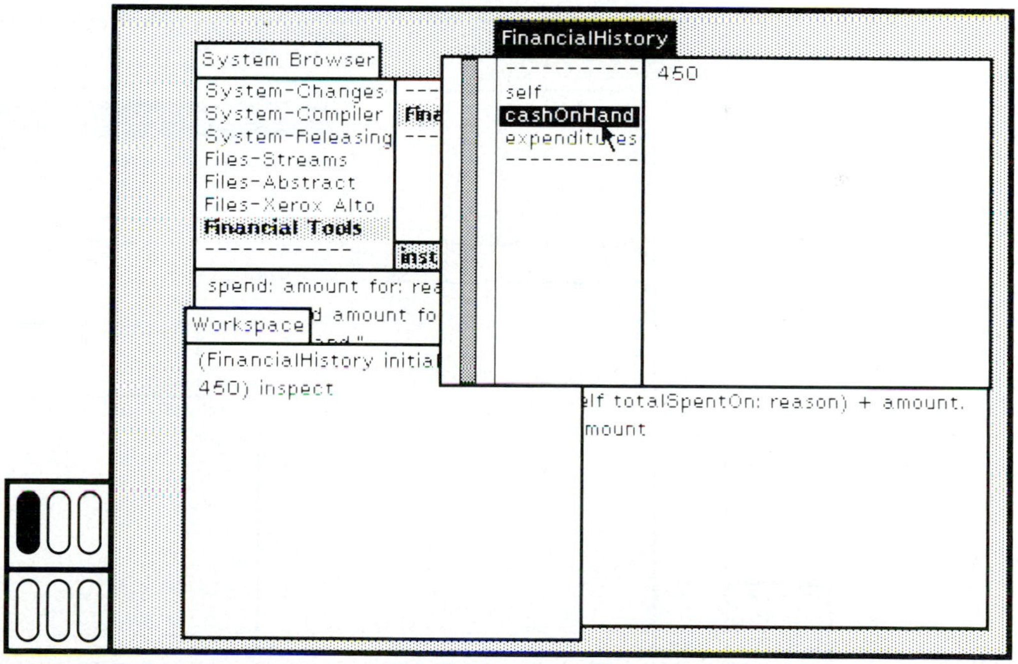

Figure 18.1b

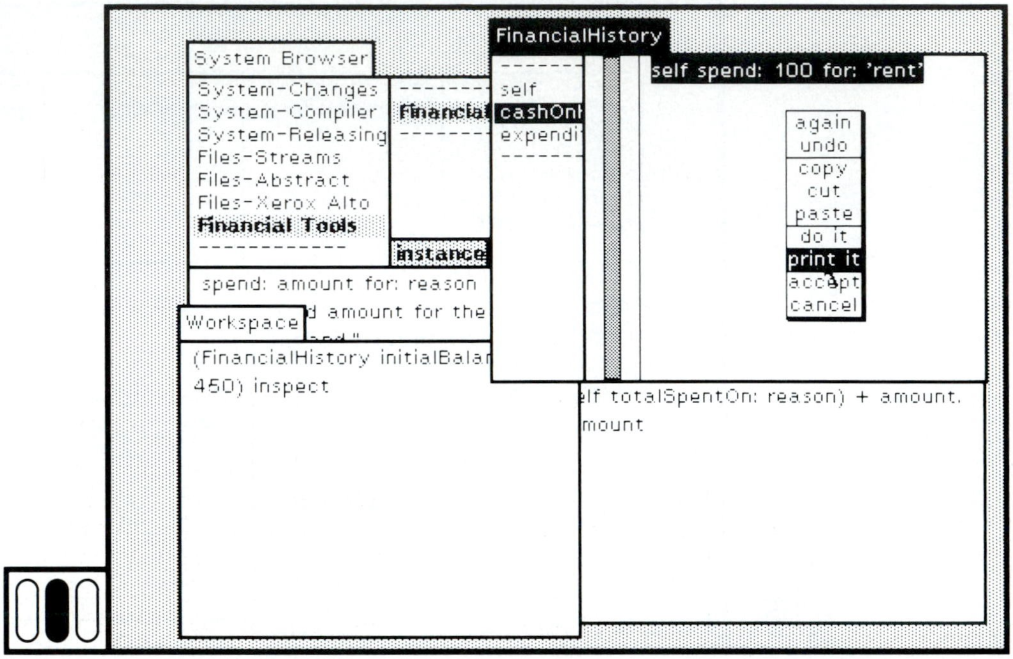

Figure 18.1c

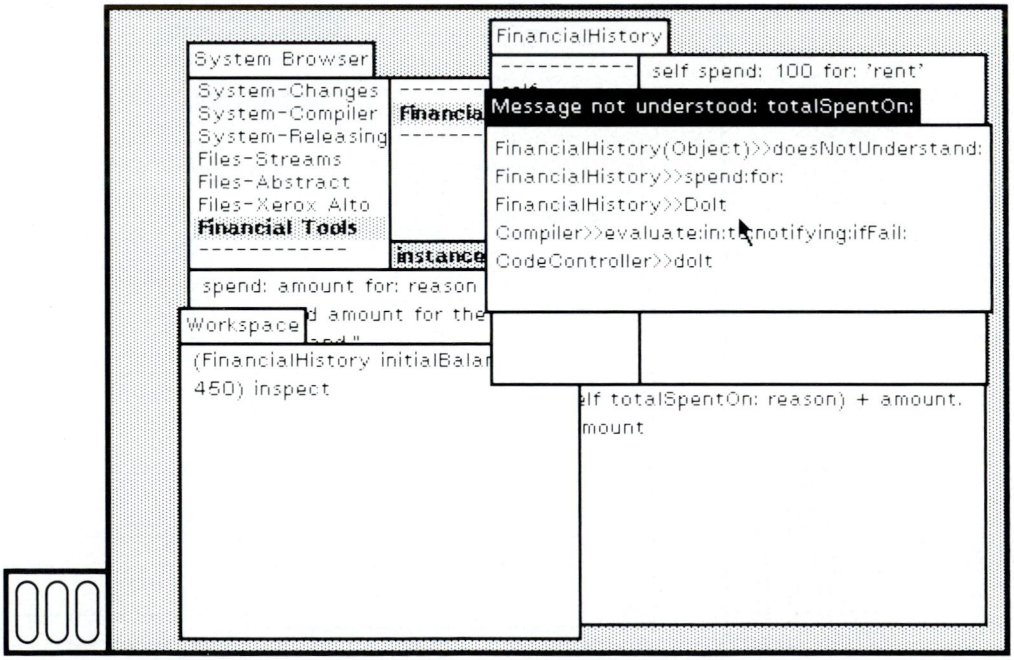

Figure 18.1d

You might decide from this information that you have seen enough information, that everything is satisfactory, and that you want to proceed with the evaluation. You can do so by choosing the yellow button command proceed. Or you might want to stop the evaluation and do something else. You can do this by selecting the blue button command close. Of course, the view is non-preemptive; you can just leave it on the screen and do something else, returning to deal with the interrupted situation at a later time.

The message shown in the Figure 18.1d says that the message totalSpentOn: was not understood. Of course, this happened because you specified the method for totalSpentFor:, not totalSpentOn:, when following the example in Chapter 17. The yellow button menu of the notifier includes the command correct. Choose it (Figure 18.1e). The system determines that the message should probably have been totalSpentFor: (Figure 18.1f). Choose the menu item yes in the confirmer to indicate your agreement. Evaluation proceeds, using the corrected message selector, so that the $100 is spent on rent. The method associated with spend:for: returns the FinancialHistory as its value (Figure 18.1g).

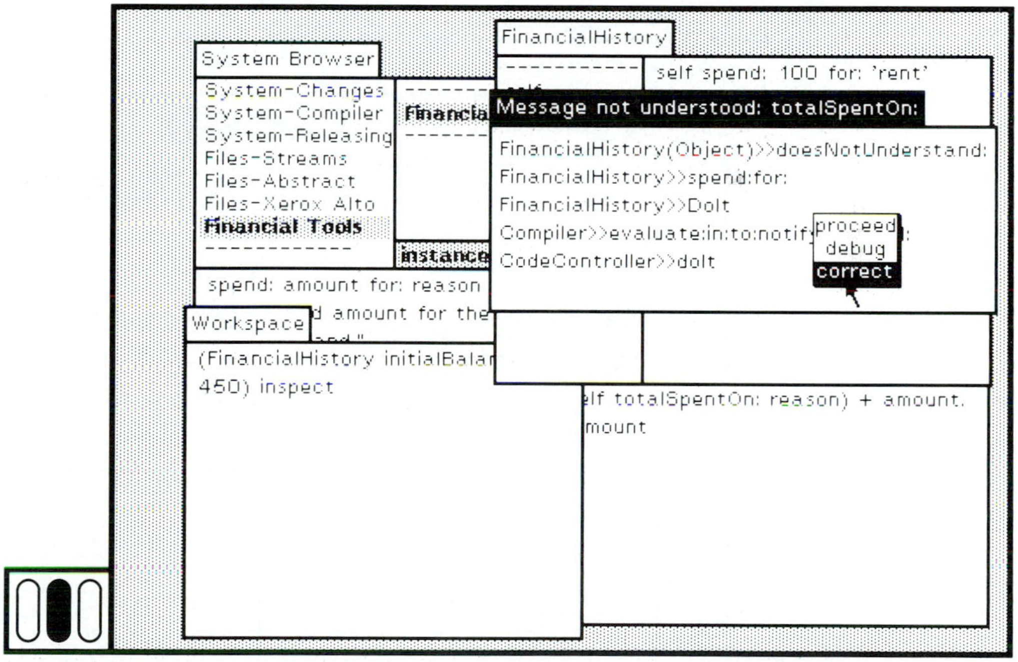

Figure 18.1e

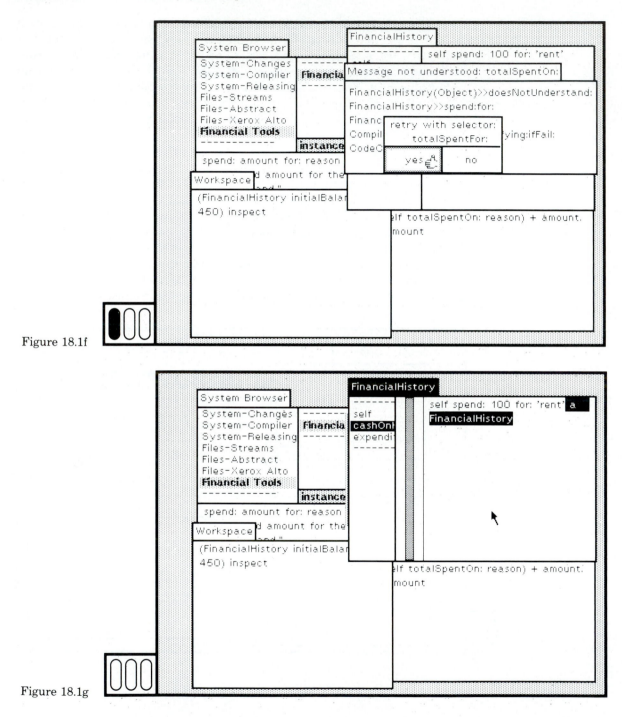

Figure 18.1f

Figure 18.1g

Unlike other uses of the spelling corrector, the correction was only temporary. You must use a system browser to find the method containing the error and to correct it (Figure 18.2). Once corrected, you can spend successfully $50 on food and $75 on a trip by evaluating the appropriate expressions in the inspector text subview (Figure 18.3). You can also choose cashOnHand and expenditures in the inspector to examine the instance variables (Figures 18.4 and 18.5).

Keep the inspector for the FinancialHistory so that you can use it in Chapter 19.

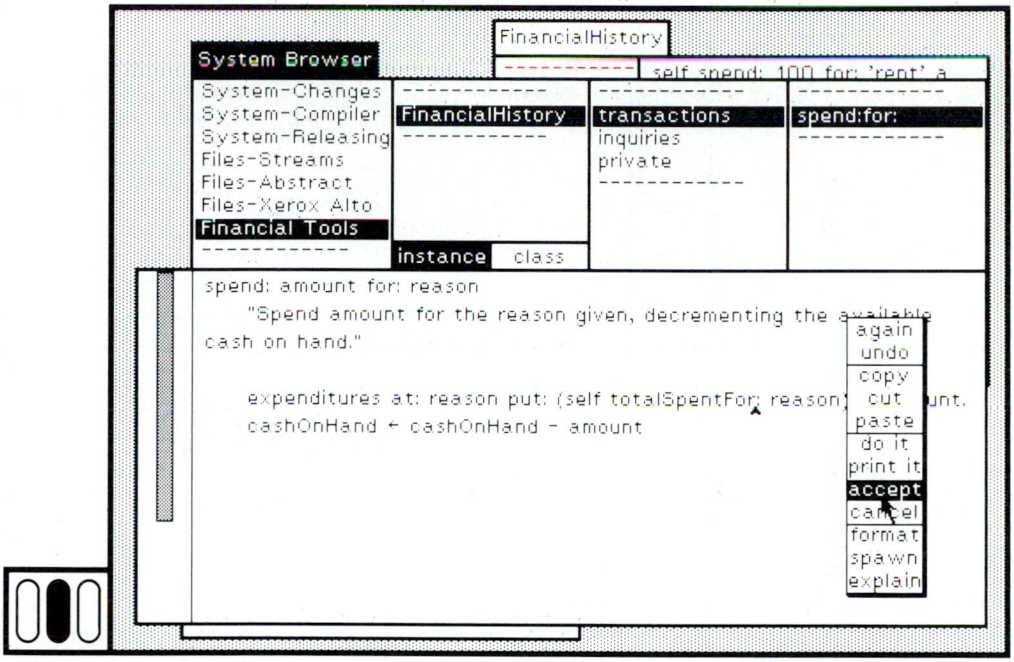

Figure 18.2

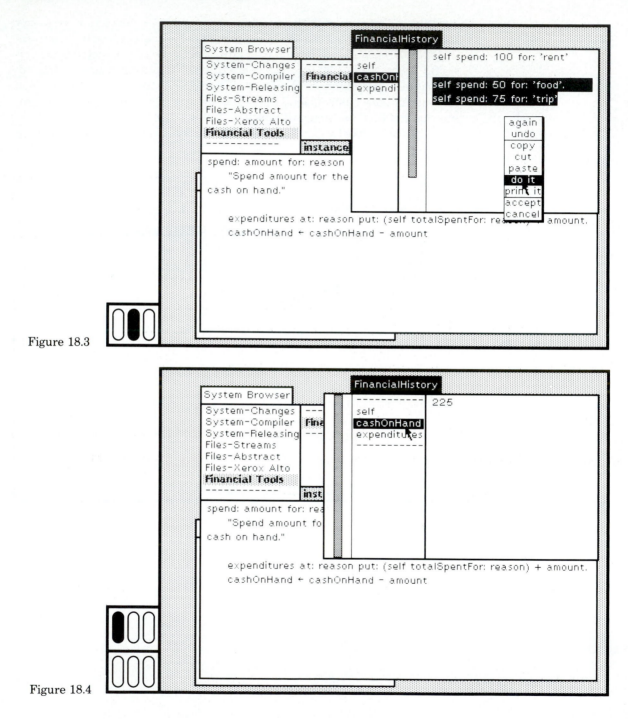

Figure 18.3

Figure 18.4

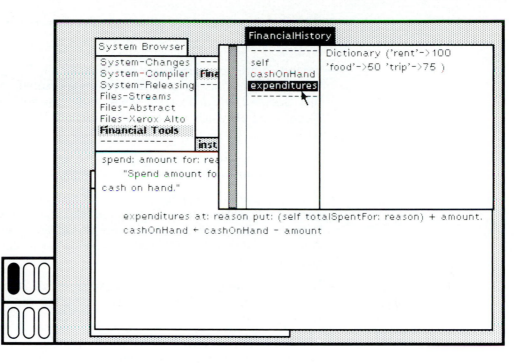

Figure 18.5

18.2

Other Runtime Errors

A notifier appears (at the center of the display screen or at the center of the active view) whenever there is an execution interrupt due to an error in running a method. These runtime errors occur for a large number of reasons. As stated earlier, most often you will encounter an error because an object is sent a message to which it cannot respond. The label of the notifer is

    Message not understood:

followed by the erroneous message selector.

    The notifier only displays the last few message-sends of the interrupted execution. You may determine that this is not enough information, either because the purpose of the interrupt was to explore further or because you do not know why the interrupt occurred. In this case, choose the yellow button command debug. The notifier is closed, and you are asked to designate a rectangular area in which a debugger will be created. The system debugger is described in Chapter 19.

Runtime errors caused by other than an incorrect message selector include:

- Trying to create an instance of Character or Boolean. All Characters are defined at the time the system is created, and are immutable. Boolean is an abstract class with two subclasses, True and False, each of which has only one instance (true and false, respectively).

- Trying to create instances with incorrect instance-creation messages (such as sending new to create a MappedCollection).

- Trying to evaluate a BlockContext with the incorrect number of arguments. For example, if the BlockContext is of the form [:i :j | i > j], then the message needed to evaluate it is of the form value: i value: j. A message to this BlockContext with any other number of value: keywords would be an error.

- In numeric computation, attempting to divide by zero, creating a Fraction with denominator of zero, or taking the square root of a negative number.

- In Collections, mismatched collection sizes for mapping operations, attempting to remove an element not in the collection, attempting to access elements of nonindexable collections using at:put:, attempting to store into an Interval or to remove elements from an Interval or an Array, using an object that is not an Integer as an index, attempting to store an object that is not a Character into a String, attempting to do a Dictionary lookup with a key or value that is not in the Dictionary, or using an index that is out of the bounds of the indexable collection.

- Sending an object an inappropriate message (one to which instances of the superclass respond, but of which the subclass blocks the use), or sending an object a message that its class should have implemented but did not (the superclass implementation is probably self subclassResponsibility).

- Sending control messages to objects that are not Booleans (ifTrue:ifFalse:, ifFalse:ifTrue:, ifTrue:, ifFalse:) nor BlockContexts (whileTrue:, whileFalse:).

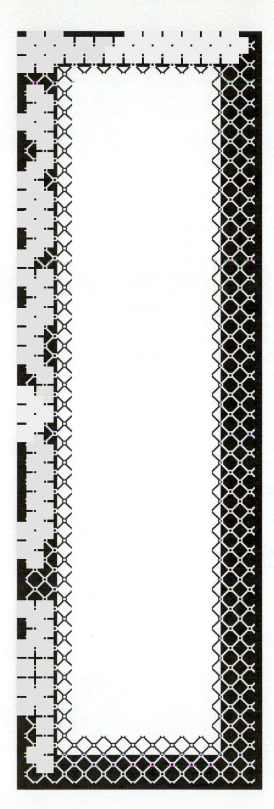

19

Examining and Debugging Execution State

To illustrate the use of the debugger, we will add another method to the class FinancialHistory which was used as an example in Chapters 17 and 18. The method will have an error in it that we can explore using a debugger.

19.1

The Activation Stack

Add the method for report, categorized under the instance protocol inquiries, as shown in Figure 19.1. Try it. Type the text self report in the text subview of the inspector for the FinancialHistory created as described in Chapter 18. Select the text and then choose the yellow button command print it (Figure 19.2).

A notifier appears indicating that the message do: was not understood (Figure 19.3). The text displayed in the notifier indicates the last few messages sent before the interrupt occurred. The methods associated with these messages have not as yet returned their values. In conventional programming language parlance, this sequence of messages represents the *activation stack* that you wish to explore to understand the source of the error.

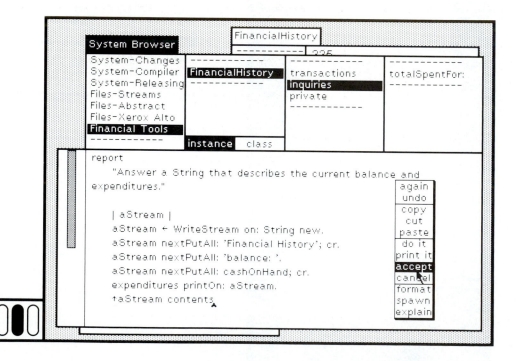

Figure 19.1

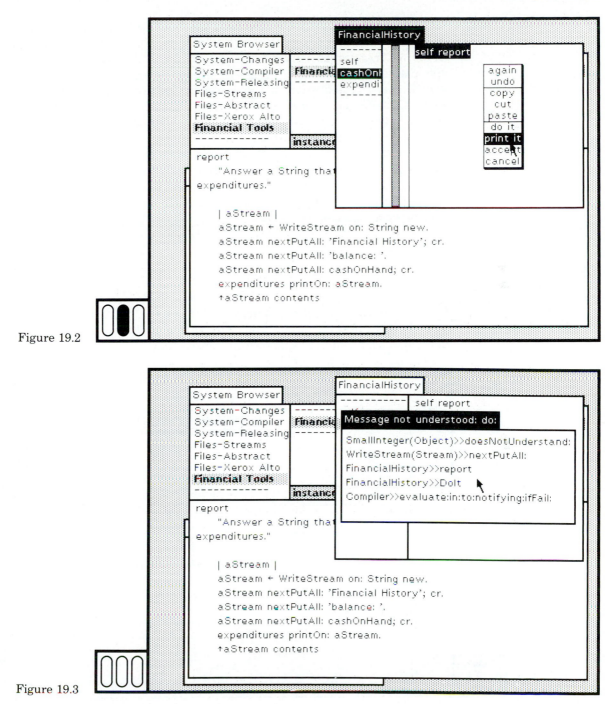

Figure 19.2

Figure 19.3

The first message-send in the example notifier indicates that the receiver of the message was a SmallInteger. There is a class name delimited by parentheses after the class name of the receiver. It denotes the class in which the message definition is specified. The example shows that the definition of the message doesNotUnderstand: is specified in Object. The second message-send indicates that the error came from sending the message nextPutAll: to an instance of WriteStream. The method associated with nextPutAll: was actually found in the description of the class Stream (a superclass of WriteStream). And the third message-send indicates that the message nextPutAll: was sent from the method associated with report that was sent to a FinancialHistory. The remaining message-sends have to do with the compilation and evaluation process, and can be ignored.

19.2

The Structure of a Debugger

Choose the yellow button command debug in the notifier (Figure 19.4). The notifier disappears and you designate a rectangular area for the debugger. The debugger is shown in Figure 19.5.

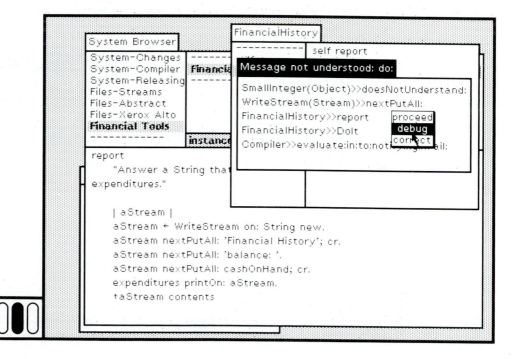

Figure 19.4

Figure 19.5

The debugger presents some or all of the sequence of message-sends that occurred prior to the interrupt. It allows you to select each one in order to see the method and to determine at which point in the method the interrupt occurred. You can choose any message-send on the stack and cause evaluation to proceed from this selected point. You can also single-step through message-sends, checking the state of the variables in order to determine the source of the error. You can change the value of variables and proceed. If you evaluate expressions within the debugger view, evaluation will be carried out in the context of the currently selected message. You can also edit and recompile (accept) a method.

A debugger view is made up of six subviews. You are already familiar with each of these subviews. The top two subviews are similar to the two subviews of a message-set browser; one is a menu of classes and messages, and the other is a text view in which the method associated with a selected message is displayed. The items in the class/message menu are the message-sends of the interrupted execution, identical in format to the message-sends displayed in a notifier. Each message-send displays the class of the receiver and the message selector of the message sent to the receiver. It also shows, in parentheses, the class in which the interpreter found the method for this message selector, if the implementation class is different from the class of the receiver. Selections in the first subview cause the corresponding methods to be displayed in the second subview. The methods can be edited, compiled, and installed (accepted), just as you are able to do in a browser.

The bottom four subviews provide two inspectors. Information appears in these inspectors only if a class/message is selected in the top view. The first inspector allows you to explore the object that was sent the interrupted message; the second inspector allows you to explore the context of the selected message-send, that is, the temporary variables of the interrupted method.

The debugger shown in Figure 19.5 illustrates the yellow button menu available when no class/message item is selected in the top subview. You can choose to ignore the problem and proceed, just as you could have done from the notifier. Or you can expand the number of class/message items in the menu.

full stack

When a debugger is first created, at most only the top nine message-sends appear. This command displays the complete stack of all the message-sends of the interrupted message-sending activity.

proceed

The debugger closes and evaluation continues just after the point of interruption. The point of interruption is a message-send that is completed with a reply that is assumed to be the value of the last expression evaluated in the method subview, or nil if no expression has been evaluated.

In order to follow the example in this chapter, do not choose a command from this menu. Instead, choose the second message-send in the top subview of the debugger (Figure 19.6a).

Three things of interest happen. First, the method associated with the selected message is displayed. In the display of this method, the message that was last sent is selected in order to focus your attention at the point at which the interrupt occurred. Second, information is displayed in the menu parts of the two inspectors at the bottom of the debugger. And third, the yellow button menu in the top subview is changed. It now contains eight commands (Figure 19.6b).

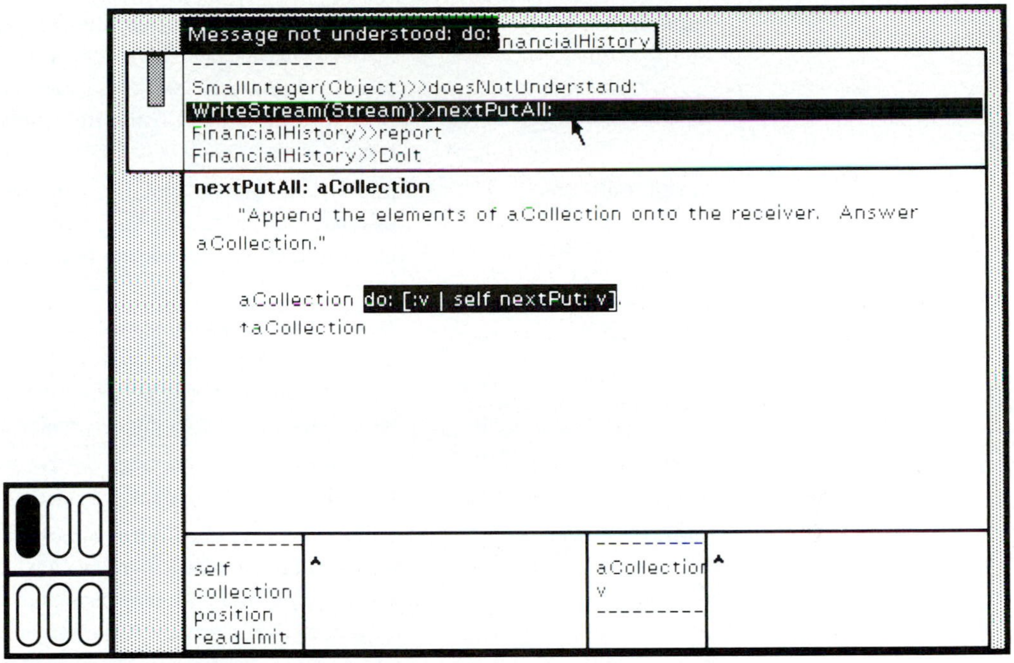

Figure 19.6a

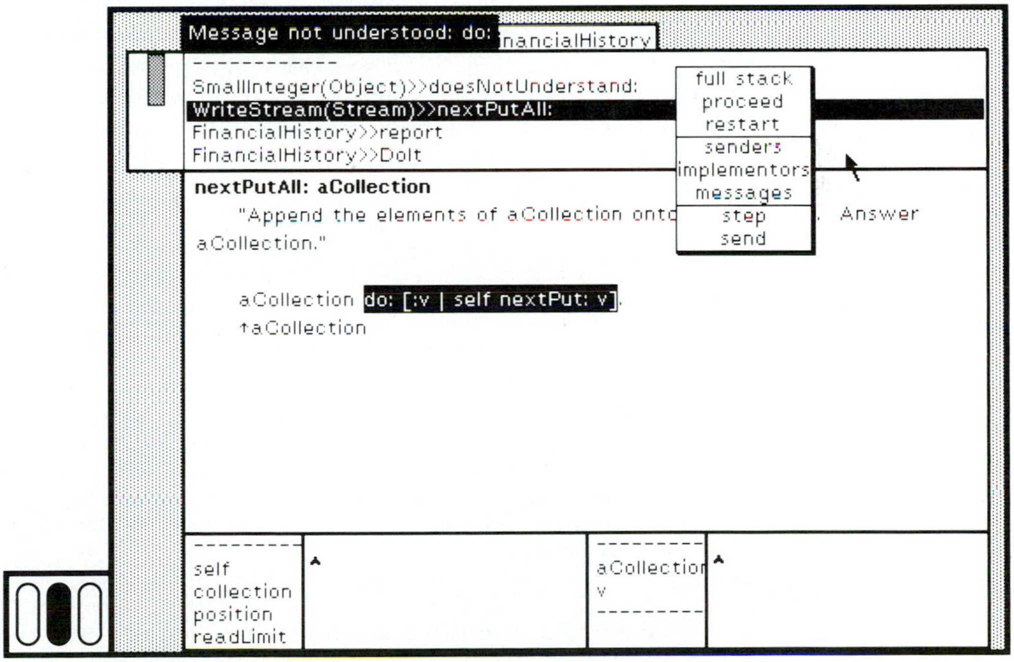

Figure 19.6b

senders   As in a class browser, creates a message-set browser on all methods that include an expression in which the currently selected message is sent. If no such methods exist, prints Nobody in the System Transcript (if the System Transcript is open on the screen).

implementors   As in a class browser, creates a message-set browser on all methods that implement the currently selected message. If no such methods exist, prints Nobody in the System Transcript (if the System Transcript is open on the screen).

messages   As in a class browser, creates a menu of all messages sent in the method associated with the currently selected message. Choosing one of these menu items creates a message-set browser on all of its implementors.

step   Evaluates the next message to be sent in the selected method (see the full explanation of step in Chapter 21).

send   This command is a refinement of the command step. If the next message to be sent were evaluated, it would consist of a sequence of messages. The command send is a request to enter that next message at the top of the activation stack and be ready to evaluate the next message in its method (see the full explanation of send in Chapter 21).

full stack   When a debugger is first created, at most only the top nine message-sends appear. This command displays the complete stack of all the message-sends of the interrupted message-sending activity.

restart   The debugger closes and evaluation starts from the beginning of the currently selected method.

proceed   The debugger closes and evaluation continues just after the point of interruption, assuming that the value of the expression forced to completion is the value of the last expression evaluated in the method text subview, or nil if no expression has been evaluated.

As described, when you make a choice in the debugger top subview, the corresponding method displays in the adjacent subview. A part of the method text is selected. This is the place at which evaluation will proceed next. Because some implementations of the Smalltalk-80 system might be too slow to allow for this selection determination, you can consider removing this selection capability from your system.

☐ *Viewing and Editing Methods*   You can edit and recompile (accept) a method that is displayed in the debugger. You do this in the same way as you edit and recompile in a class browser or in a message-set browser. All the functonality accessible from the text view of these kinds of browsers is available from the text view of the debugger, including the ability to explain tokens. The yellow button menu of the debugger text view, identical to that of the browser text view, is shown in Figure 19.7. If you recompile a method, that method becomes the top of the stack of message-sends. It is not necessary to return to the class browser, retrieve the method, and make the change. In the Smalltalk-80 system, wherever you can access a method (in any of the class browsers, message-set browsers, or the debugger), you can edit and recompile it.

Note: suppose that the method you edit is inside a block, that is, the message-send item in the top view begins with [ ]. When you recompile, then the method containing the block becomes the top of the stack of message-sends.

If the stack of message-sends contains multiple instances of a message-send, that is, a recursion exists, then you ought to make any edits to the method reference that is closest to the bottom of the stack. Suppose instead that you edit a method higher in the stack. All instances of that method lower in the stack will still refer to the old version of the method. The items in the top view change to reflect this fact; specifically, the message name changes to DoIt.

Figure 19.7

19.3

The Context of a Message Receiver

The left inspector of the debugger (bottom left pair of subviews) gives you access to the message receiver of the message selected in the top view of the debugger. The context of this message receiver is its state at the time the message was sent. In Figure 19.8a, WriteStream(Stream)>>nextPutAll: is selected; in the inspector, self refers to the instance of WriteStream. A WriteStream has four instance variables; collection refers to the String in which the description of the FinancialHistory is being collected. As shown in Figure 19.8b, collection was

'FinancialHistory Balance:'

at the point of interruption. This indicates that the next information, the cash on hand, failed to enter the WriteStream.

Inspecting the variables can give you information about the state of information in the system at the moment the method was run. You can change the values of the variables, either by

1. evaluating expressions in the text part of the inspector that consist of messages to the object self;

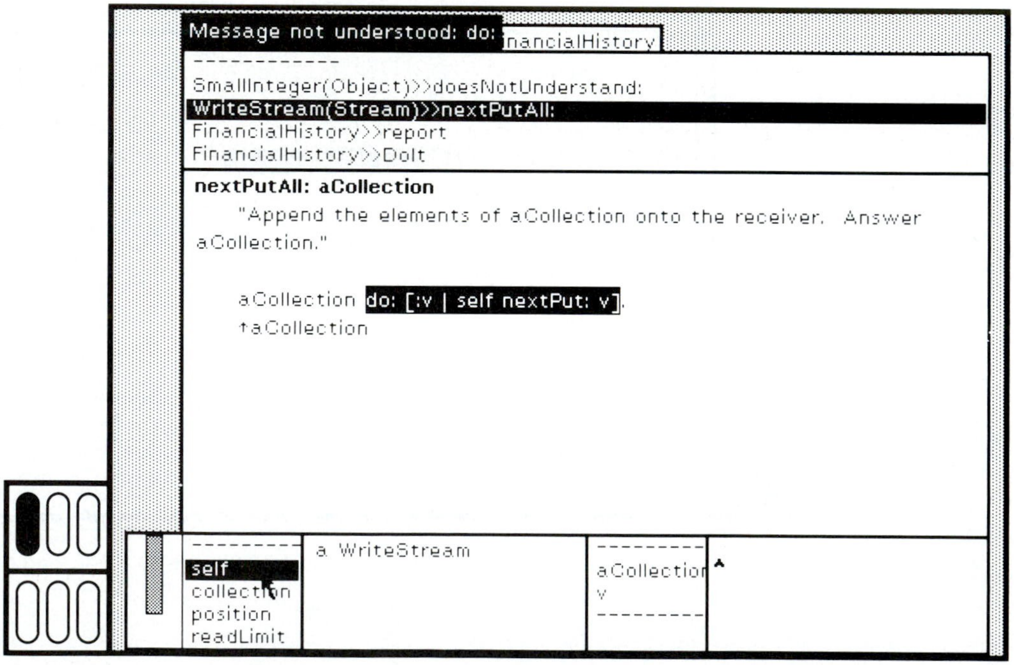

Figure 19.8a

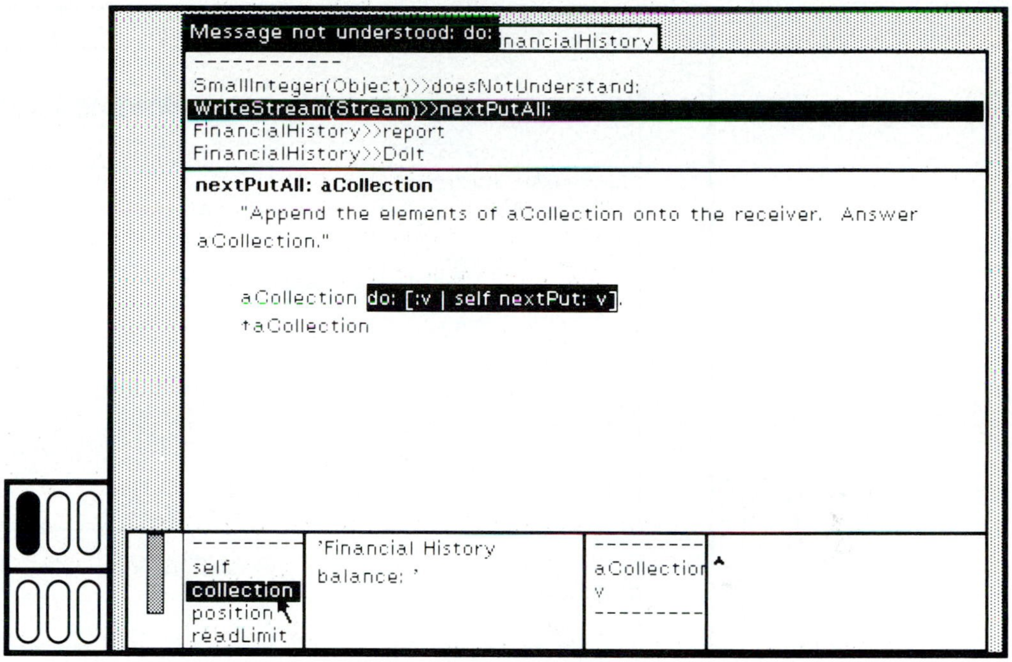

Figure 19.8b

2. evaluating assignments to the instance variables; or

3. selecting a variable, typing a new value in the text part, and then choosing the yellow button command accept.

Then you can continue evaluation from the point of the selected message, having changed these values.

19.4

The Context of an Interrupted Method

The right inspector of the debugger gives you access to the state of the method associated with the selected message, when that method was first invoked. The currently selected method shown in Figure 19.9 has one message argument, aCollection, and a block argument, v. These two names are shown in the inspector. Choose one to see its current value. Notice that aCollection is 225, which is a SmallInteger, not a Collection; hence the error.

Figure 19.9

19.5

Evaluation Within the Context of an Interrupt

Choose the next message-send, the message report to a FinancialHistory. The method text selected indicates that the error occurred when cashOnHand was to be appended to the WriteStream, aStream (Figure 19.10a). Select the text cashOnHand in the method, and choose the yellow button command print it (Figure 19.10b). The value is 225, as we expected given the result in Figure 19.9 (Figure 19.10c).

When you evaluate an expression that appears in the debugger method text, the evaluation takes place in the context of the interrupt, i.e., using the values of the receiver and the method at the time the selected method was interrupted. If you choose to proceed at this point by choosing the yellow button command proceed in the debugger top view, execution would proceed as though the value of the interrupted message send in the current method were the value of the last expression you evaluated, in this case, 225 (rather than the contents of the WriteStream as desired). If you proceed from a method without evaluating expressions, the assumed value of the method is nil.

A String representation for cashOnHand should be the argument to nextPutAll:. This representation is obtained by sending cashOnHand the message printString. (Note that the result of sending the message printString to any object is a String that describes the object.)

Figure 19.10a

Figure 19.10b

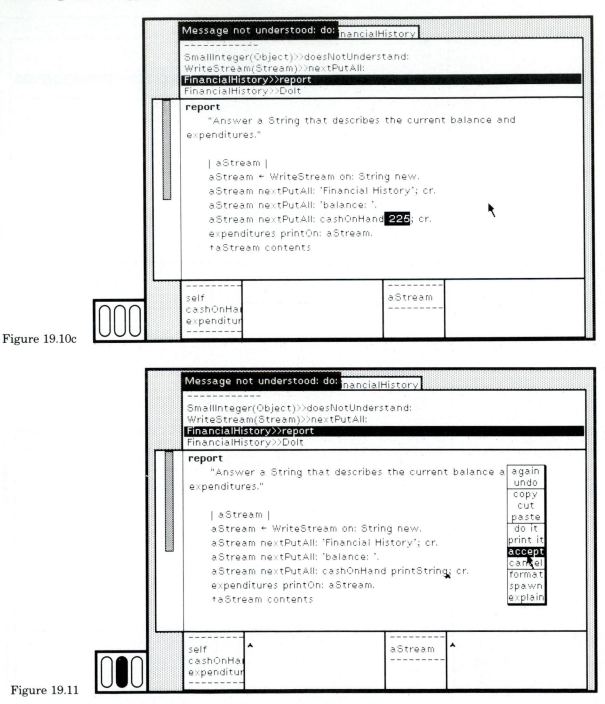

Figure 19.10c

Figure 19.11

Make the correction and choose the yellow button command accept (Figure 19.11). Notice that the method is now changed. It is placed at the top of the stack and selected in the debugger top view (Figure 19.12). Messages that had been initiated from the original form of this method have been terminated on the assumption that the change in the method may have changed the desired sequence of message sends.

Choose the yellow button command restart in the top view. The FinancialHistory is re-sent the message report, and the successful result appears in the workspace (Figure 19.13). The result could be prettier in that the Dictionary expenditures needs better formatting. We will return to this problem in Chapter 20. (Note that your browser probably had report selected at the time you were using the debugger to change the method. The updated version of the method for report is obtained by reselecting report in the browser message-selector subview.)

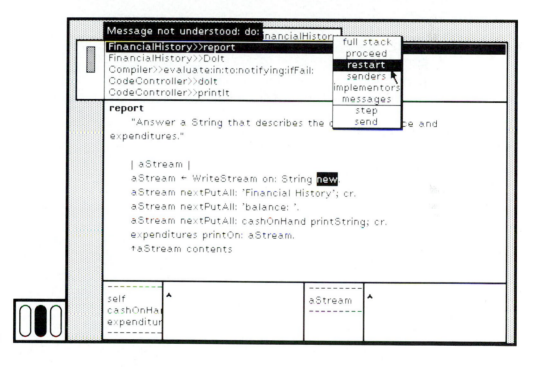

Figure 19.12

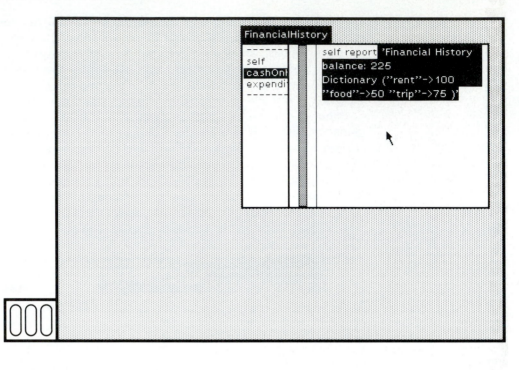

Figure 19.13

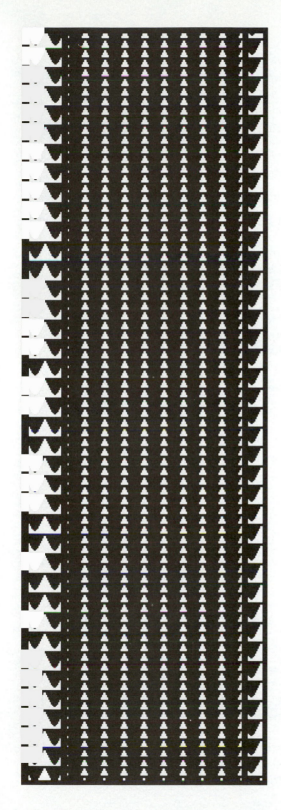

20

Kinds of Execution Interrupts

In Chapters 18 and 19, you have seen that execution interrupts can occur because of unanticipated runtime errors. It is possible to interrupt the execution of a message-send in order to examine the state of an object at the time it receives a message. There are three ways in which an interrupt can occur.

1. You set a breakpoint in a method.

2. You type the "control" and "c" keys (ctrl c) at the same time.

3. An anticipated error condition occurs while a method is running.

In the third case, the method includes a test for a possible error condition and, if found, evaluates an expression of the form

> self error: messageString

A notifier appears whose label is messageString. The label should be sufficient information to explain to the user why the error occurred.

> You can evaluate the expression Smalltalk browseAllCallsOn: #error: to see examples in the system where these tests occur.

20.1

Breakpoints

A breakpoint is set in a method by including an expression that creates a notifier. The two possible messages you can use are

> self halt

and

> self halt: messageString

In each case, a notifier appears so that you can choose to proceed or choose to create a debugger. In the first case, the label of the notifier is

> Halt encountered

In the second case, the label is the argument messageString.

An example of inserting a breakpoint is presented next. The example uses the description of class FinancialHistory presented in previous chapters.

In the method associated with report in the class FinancialHistory, insert the expression self halt just before the point at which the Dictionary expenditures is added to the WriteStream (Figure 20.1). Choose the yellow button command accept.

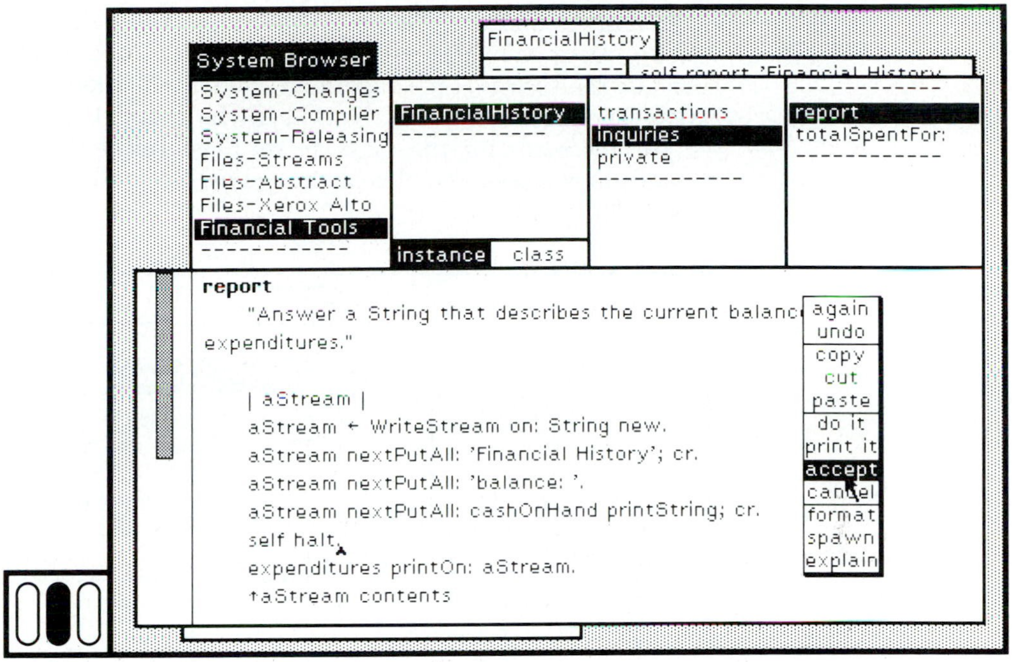

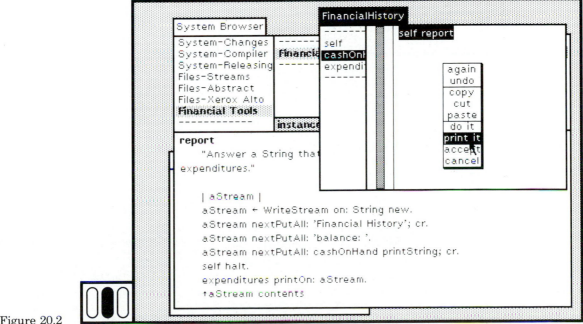

Figure 20.1

In the inspector for the FinancialHistory, type and select the expression self report (Figure 20.2). Choose the yellow button command print it.

Figure 20.2

A notifier appears (Figure 20.3). Choose the yellow button command debug. Designate the rectangular area for the debugger and then choose the second message-send (FinancialHistory > > report) (Figure 20.4). The message halt is selected in the method text in the debugger. In the inspector for the message receiver, select the instance variable name expenditures and choose the yellow button command inspect (Figure 20.5).

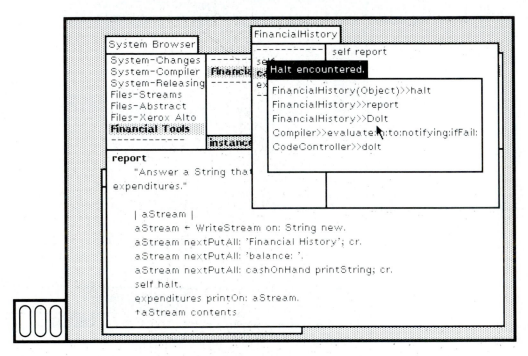

Figure 20.3

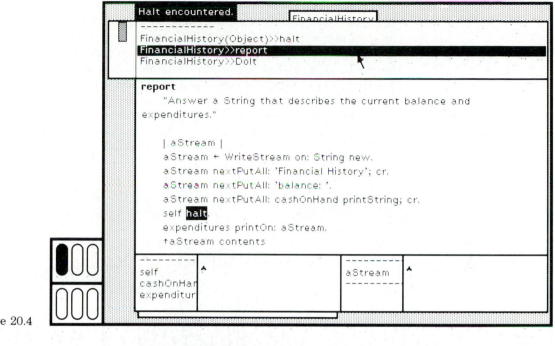

Figure 20.4

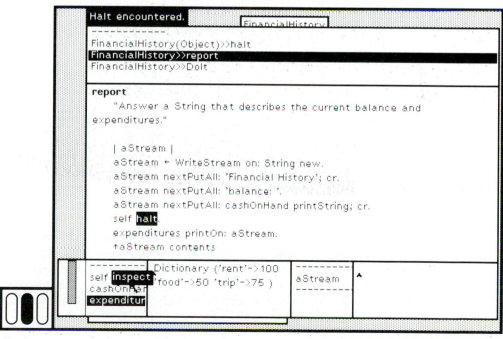

Figure 20.5

Designate the rectangular area for the inspector for the Dictionary expenditures. You can use this inspector to explore ways in which to print the keys and values of the Dictionary. In the text subview of the inspector, type, select, and evaluate the expression self keys (do the evaluation by choosing the yellow button command print it). The result is a Set of three elements, each of which is a String (Figure 20.6).

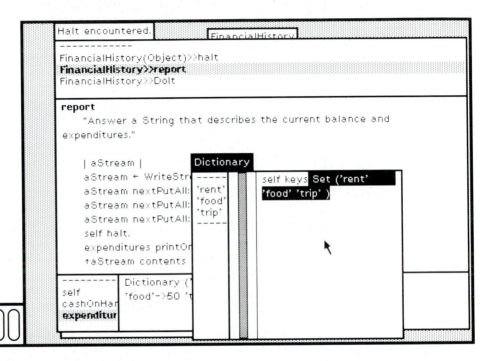

Figure 20.6

You can then try different methods for printing. An example method is shown in the inspector text subview in Figure 20.7a. The expressions format the keys and values in two columns using messages cr and tab; the text is printed in the System Transcript (Transcript) as shown in Figure 20.7b. (For this example to work, you should make certain that the System Transcript is visible on the display screen.)

Close the inspector for expenditures. In the method for report, replace the printing expression for expenditures with a version of the "practice" print expressions. Make the change shown in Figure 20.8, and choose the yellow button command accept. If you then retry evaluating self report in the inspector for the FinancialHistory, a better formatted result is displayed (remember to choose the yellow button command print it so that you can see the result) (Figure 20.9). Close the debugger.

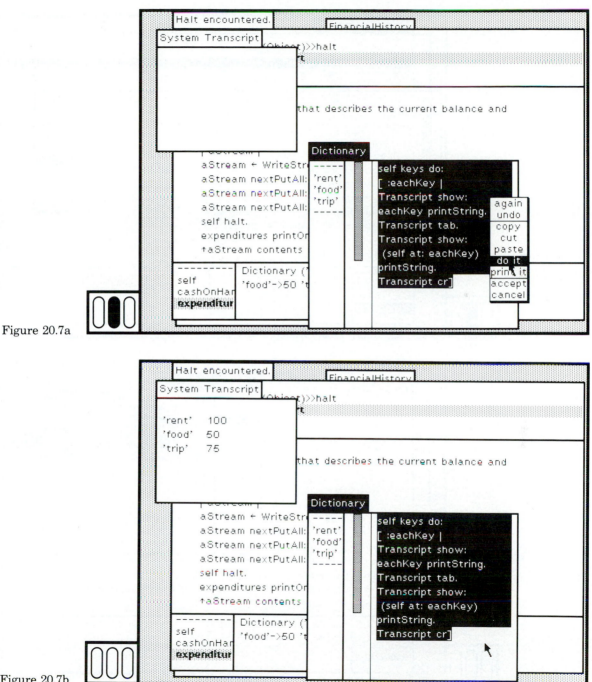

Figure 20.7a

Figure 20.7b

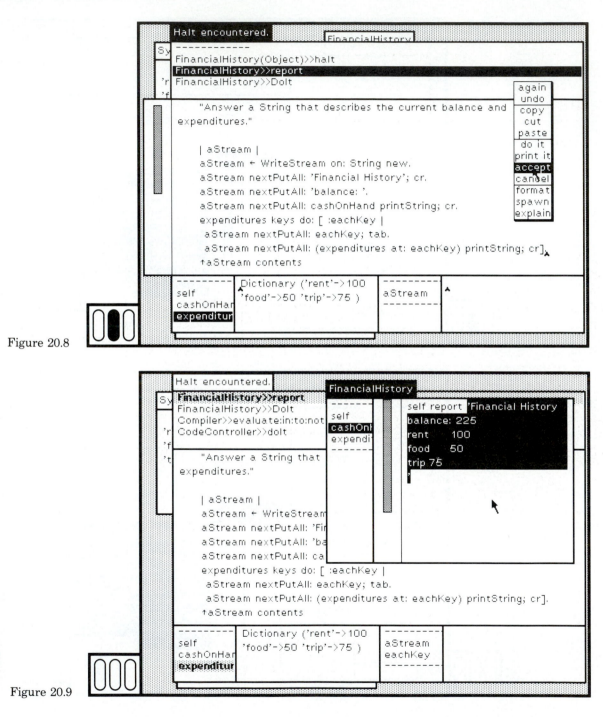

Figure 20.8

Figure 20.9

Be careful in inserting breakpoints in the system classes. Unless you understand the flow of message-sends, you might find yourself recursively creating notifiers if the code that creates the notifier, or that creates any of the views on the screen that you might select, uses the method you are interrupting.

20.2

User Interrupts

You can press the "control" key and the "c" key (ctrl c) at the same time in order to interrupt immediately the execution of any code. A notifier appears whose label is

User Interrupt

Choose the yellow button command proceed to continue the process.

Typing ctrl c is a way to interrupt a successfully running process that you wish to explore, to find out about and to possibly change the part of the system that supports the running process.

Try an example. Open a workspace as the active view. With the cursor inside the workspace, type ctrl c (Figure 20.10a). A notifier appears (Figure 20.10b). (The sequence you see in your notifier might be different than the one in the example figures due to the somewhat arbitrary timing of your typing ctrl c.)

The sequence of message-sends indicates that a SharedQueue was interrupted in its evaluation of peek. This message was sent from the method keyboardPeek to an InputState, which in turn was sent from primKbdPeek to an InputSensor. The message keyboardPressed tests to see if the user is pressing a key on the keyboard. It was sent from a StringHolderController; a StringHolderController provides the user interface to a StringHolder which is the implementation class for a workspace. Hence this is a way for you to find out which classes are involved in the implementation of the user interface. If you now open a debugger you can explore the StringHolderController and examine its instance variables and methods to learn more about the user interface objects.

20.3

Running Out of Space

A notifier appears on the screen if the system starts running out of memory space, either because you have created more objects than the system can handle, or because the objects you have created take up more space than is available. The label of this notifier is

Space is Low

You should close the low space notification (it might be hanging onto a very large activation stack if the cause of the low space was infinite re-

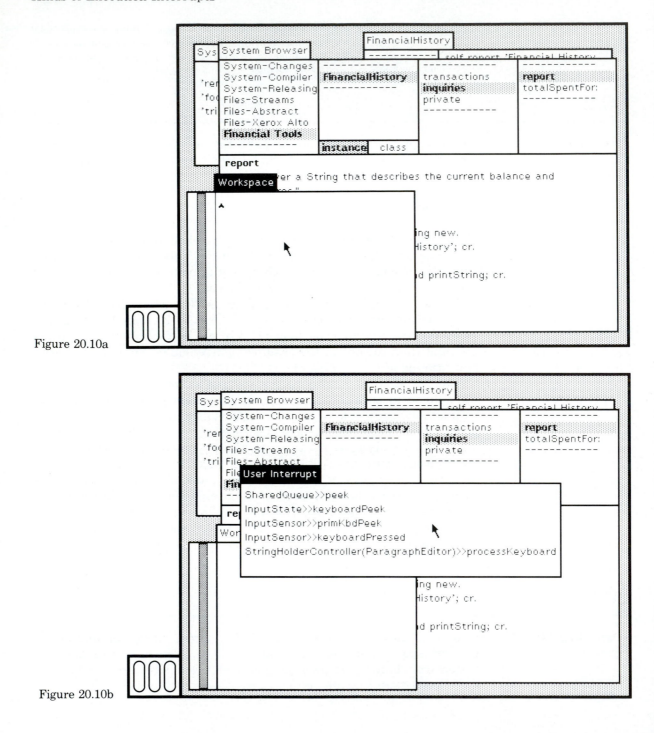

Figure 20.10a

Figure 20.10b

cursion). The low space might be due to an error in your code, such as infinite recursion, gobbling up space. Otherwise, the problem might be harder to trace, such as cyclic pointers; or the problem could be that your application needs more than the available space. In any case, protect yourself by filing out your work (as explained in Chapters 22 or 23) so that your work can be filed back into a new system image. Making a snapshot will not help you since you will simply be saving a system image that has insufficient space. If your application needs more than the space available in the initial system image, you might consider deleting other applications (sets of classes) that you do not require. You can use the system tracer to create a "clean image" (as described in Section 23.4).

At the time that the low storage notification appears, you ought to have enough time (space) in which to save your work before the system crashes. A second warning will appear if you ignore the first and continue to use the system. At this point, you will probably not have time to save your work before the system crashes.

If you want to monitor your space utilization, the System Workspace includes three expressions that you can evaluate to check on the actual space used, and to check on the number of object pointers used.

Smalltalk oopsLeft	Amount of remaining space for object.
Smalltalk coreLeft	Number of words of memory remaining.
Smalltalk core	Number of words of memory currently being used. (This computation typically takes a long time.)

The result of Smalltalk core plus the result of Smalltalk coreLeft is less than the total amount of memory available to the system. The difference is the amount of space taken up by the Smalltalk-80 interpreter and resident tables of data for the interpreter.

20.4

Recursion in the System Error Handler

When the system error handling mechanism results in a recursion calling on the messages error: or halt or halt:, then the system is not able to handle the usual user interface control. Instead, a message appears in the System Transcript (if it is open on the screen):

System Error Handling Failed

followed by the error message followed by the last three message-sends indicating the recursive call that caused the failure, and then followed by

type <s> for more stack; anything else restarts the scheduler

You have two choices. You can type the letter s on the keyboard to see some more of the activation stack (typically more indication of the recursive call), or you can type anything else in order to try to return to the usual user interface, notably to a browser to correct the problem. An example showing the appearance of the System Transcript is given in Figure 20.11.

You can test this facility by evaluating the expression

ErrorRecursion ← true

and then creating an error. ErrorRecursion is a class variable of Object and is therefore globally accessible. It is used to test for recursive calls on the primitive routines for the error handler. For example, evaluate

nil+3

If you type any key, other than s, to get the system to respond again (reschedule the ControlManager), the value of ErrorRecursion is automatically set to false.

If the System Transcript is not open on the screen, the problem still exists but you can not see the comment about the failure. Your system will appear to be "dead." In such cases, type any key other than s and see if you can get the system to respond again. Whenever the System Transcript is not open, you take a chance on losing feedback about an error.

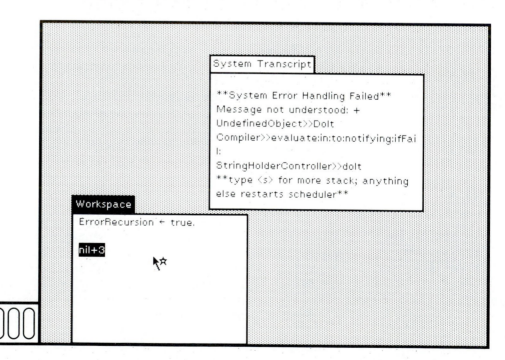

Figure 20.11

It is most likely that the reason the error handler failed is that you have modified incorrectly some critical part of the user interface. Your system is probably dead. One last resort that you can try is to type ctrl shift c (all three keys at the same time, but you should press the ctrl and shift keys first and then, while holding them down, press c). This puts you into a preemptive, teletypewriter-like interface in which you can type one expression and then evaluate it by typing the "escape" key. An image of this interface is shown in Figure 20.12. Editing in this interface is done using the "backspace" key. Only two lines are available, so if you type an expression on the second line, then the result will appear on the first line. If your user interface changes were conditional on some global flag, you can reset the flag and hope for the best. (If you are knowledgeable enough about the system, you can try to redefine the method causing the problem by evaluating the appropriate compile message to the class.) If ctrl shift c does not work, then most likely the input/output handler is locked up. There is nothing you can do except start over with a new image, and turn to Chapter 23's section on crash recovery.

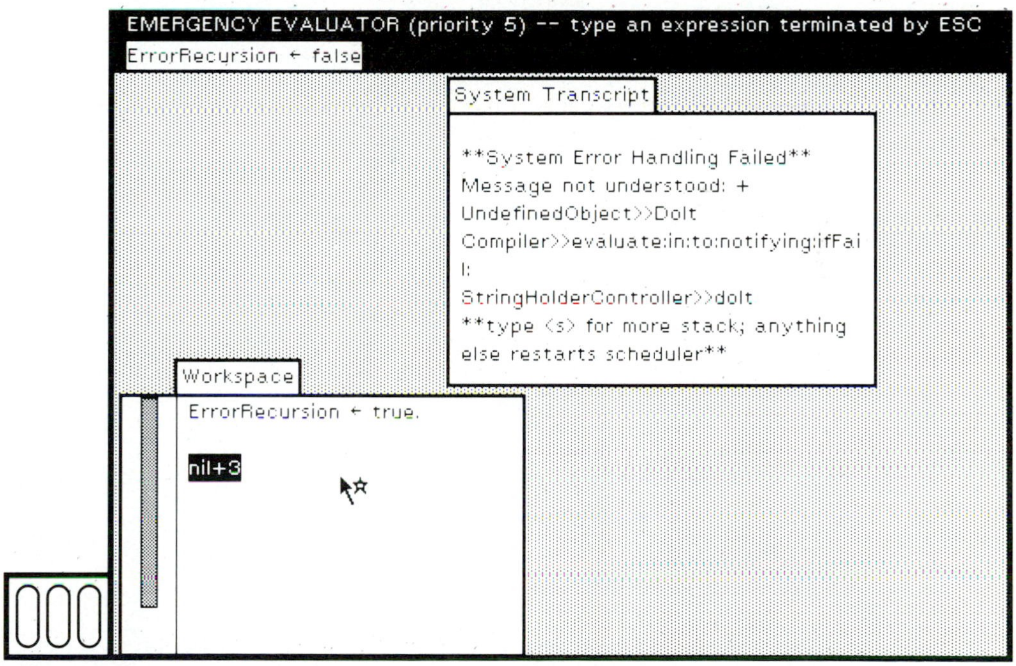

Figure 20.12

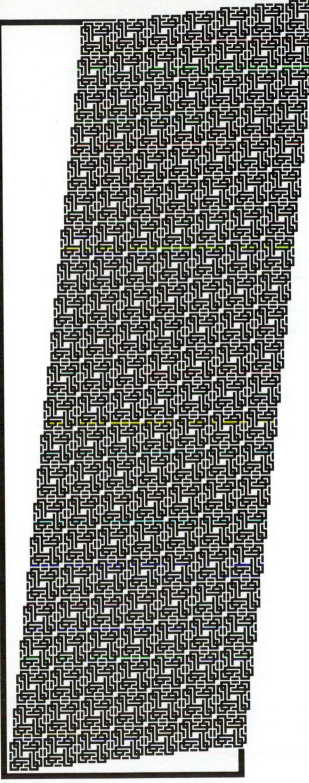

21

Single-stepping Through an Execution

Two commands in the yellow button menu of the debugger top view, step and send, make it possible to step through the execution of a method, one message-send at a time, and observe the behavior of the message receivers.

The method associated with the example for the system class Pen provides a sequence of messages that create graphical feedback so that you can observe the results as you step through the execution. In a system browser, find the method for example in the class protocol of Pen. Insert a breakpoint, self halt, at the beginning of the method, after the temporary variable declaration. Choose the yellow button command accept. The browser selections and the change to the method are shown in Figure 21.1.

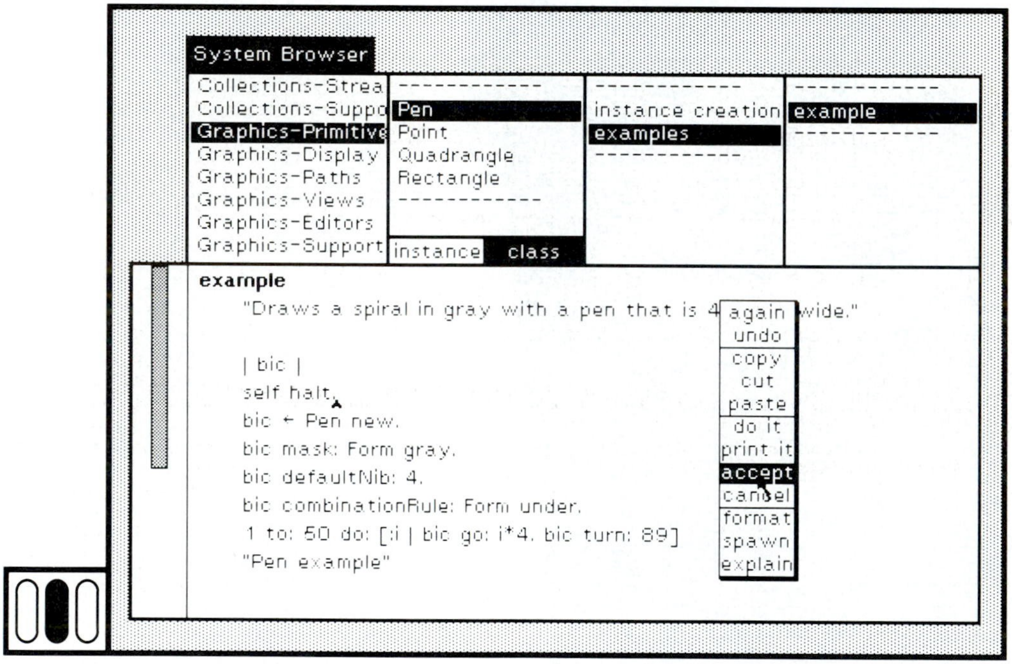

Figure 21.1

Now select the text Pen example at the end of the method and choose the yellow button command do it. A notifier appears. In it, select the yellow button command debug (Figure 21.2). Designate a fairly large rectangular area for the debugger. Then choose the second message-send; the first one is just an indicator for the message halt (Figure 21.3). Notice that the message halt is shown as the text selection in the second subview of the debugger. This selection is the next message that will be completed if you proceed (choose the yellow button command proceed), or if you choose the yellow button command step in the debugger top view.

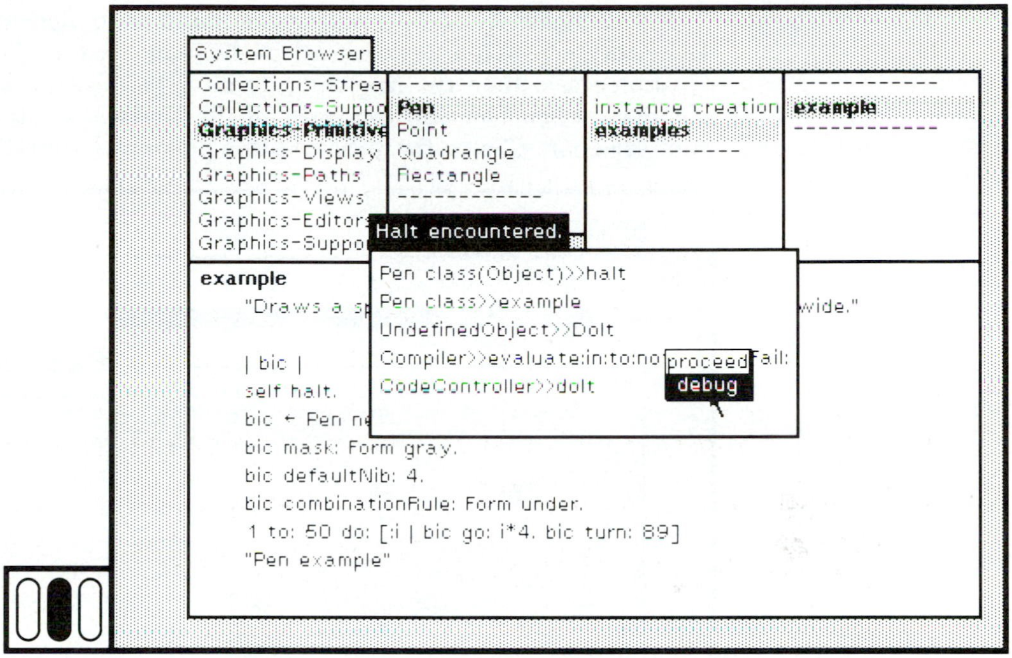

Figure 21.2

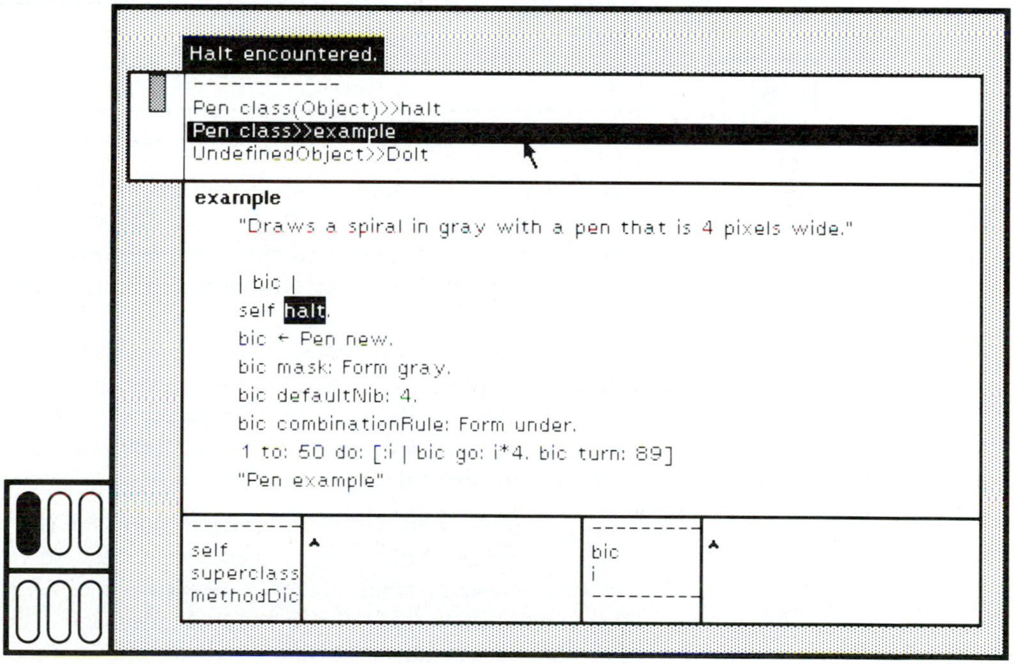

Figure 21.3

If you choose the yellow button command send, nothing will happen. Generally, when you have not selected the method at the top of the activation stack, then the first thing to do is to choose the yellow button command step. This will complete all the message-sends above the current selection. Choose the yellow button command step (Figure 21.4).

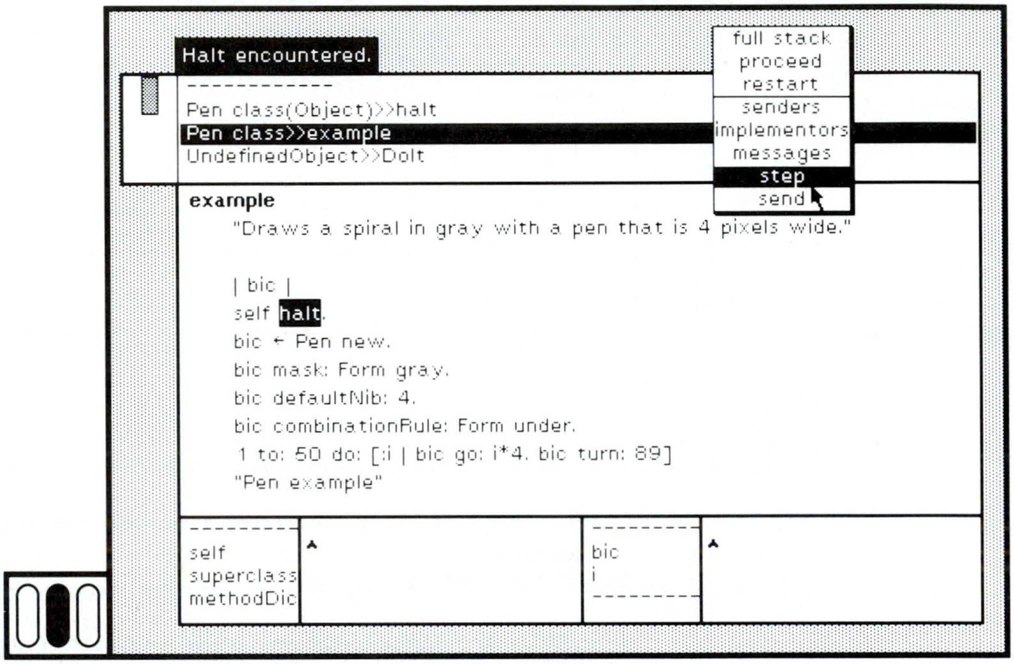

Figure 21.4

The selected message-send goes to the top of the stack and the text selection is now new (Figure 21.5). That is, the message halt was completed and execution advanced to the next message. The text selection visually shows you what send or step will do if one of them is chosen.

1. The command step does a complete message-send. If you now choose step, new will be sent to Pen and the entire method associated with new to Pen will be evaluated. Assignments are quickly passed over, so in this case, the assignment to the temporary variable bic will also take place.

2. The command send will invoke the method for the message selected, in this case, new. The message-send new to Pen will become the first message-send in the top subview of the debugger. The text selection should indicate the next message-send, the first message that is not an assignment. All assignments of the form variable ← variable or variable ← constant, up to the point indicated by the text selection, will be carried out immediately.

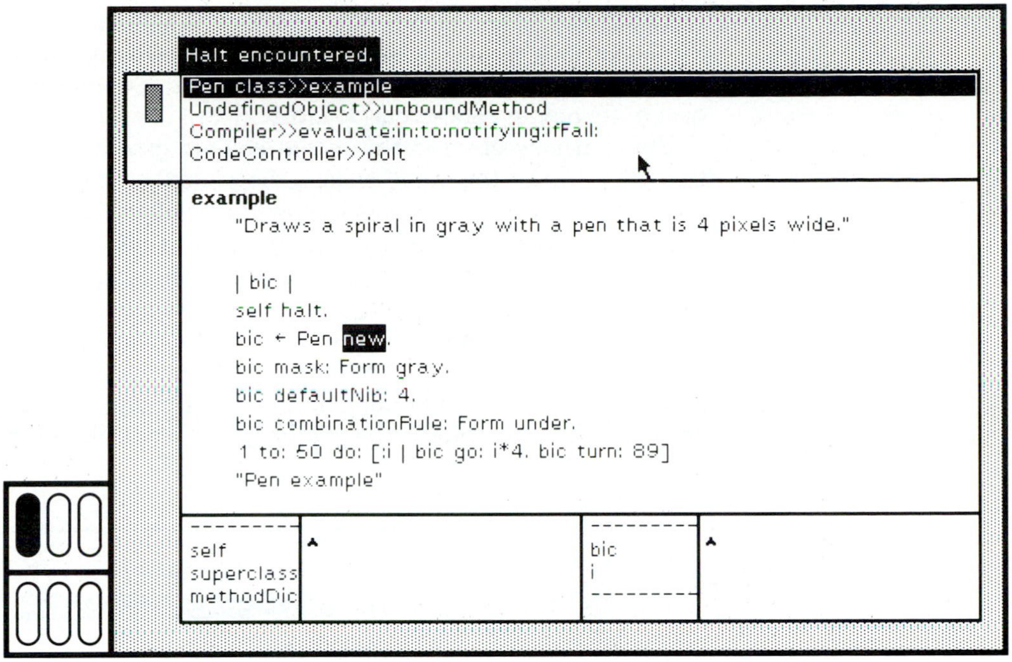

```
Halt encountered.
  ▌ Pen class>>example
    UndefinedObject>>unboundMethod
    Compiler>>evaluate:in:to:notifying:ifFail:
    CodeController>>doIt                        ▖

    example
        "Draws a spiral in gray with a pen that is 4 pixels wide."

        | bic |
        self halt.
        bic ← Pen new.
        bic mask: Form gray.
        bic defaultNib: 4.
        bic combinationRule: Form under.
        1 to: 50 do: [:i | bic go: i*4. bic turn: 89]
        "Pen example"
    -----------      ▲      -----------   ▲
    self                    bic
    superclass              i
    methodDic               -----------
```

Figure 21.5

Assuming your situation is as shown in Figure 21.5, choose the yellow button command send. The message-send Pen class> >new is entered at the top of the activation stack and displayed in the debugger (Figure 21.6).

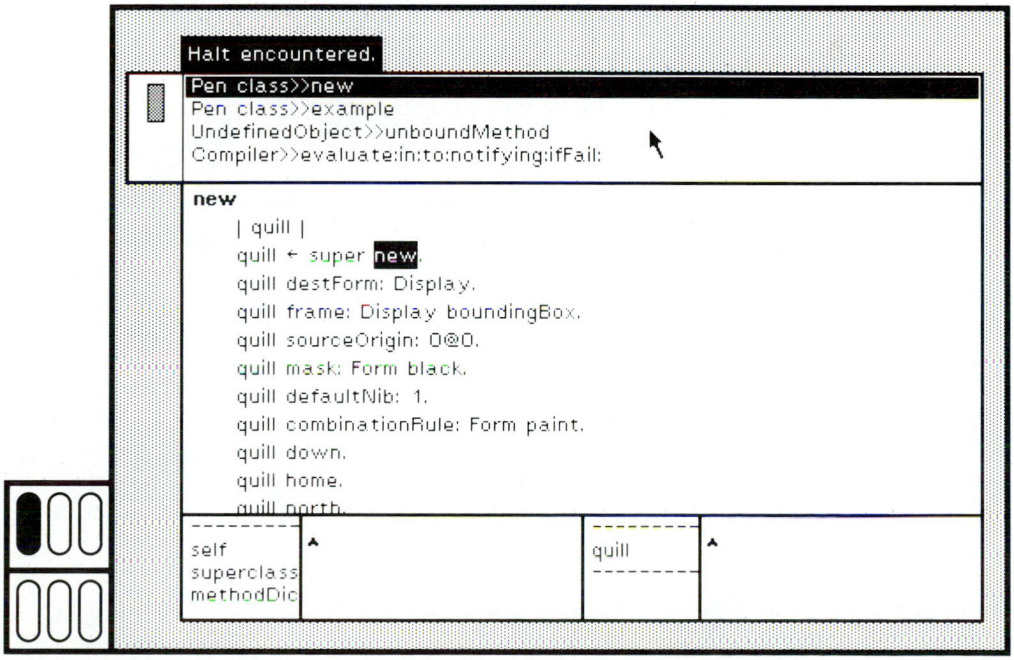

```
Halt encountered.
  ▌ Pen class>>new
    Pen class>>example
    UndefinedObject>>unboundMethod            ▖
    Compiler>>evaluate:in:to:notifying:ifFail:

    new
        | quill |
        quill ← super new.
        quill destForm: Display.
        quill frame: Display boundingBox.
        quill sourceOrigin: 0@0.
        quill mask: Form black.
        quill defaultNib: 1.
        quill combinationRule: Form paint.
        quill down.
        quill home.
        quill north.
    -----------      ▲      -----------   ▲
    self                    quill
    superclass              -----------
    methodDic
```

Figure 21.6

The first message-send, new to super, is selected. The method that is displayed is a sequence of initialization messages to the variable quill. The right inspector of the debugger shows the temporary variable name quill in its menu; choose quill (Figure 21.7).

You can now observe the initial change in the value of quill from nil to a Pen. In the top view, choose the yellow button command step and notice that the value of quill is now an instance of Pen (Figure 21.8). If you wish to see subsequent changes in the instance variables of quill, you will have to inspect quill and rechoose each variable as you step through the method.

If you just use the command step several times, you will eventually reach a point where the return expression, ↑quill, is selected (Figure 21.9). If you choose send now, nothing will happen. This last message is an action that completes the method; you must choose step in order to complete a method.

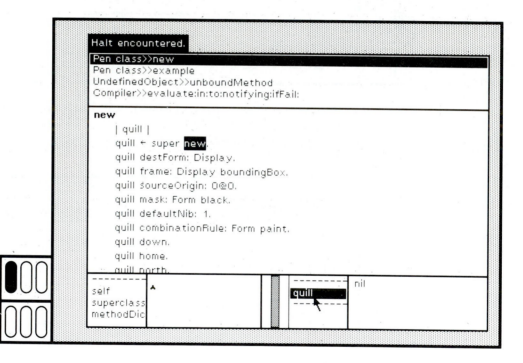

Figure 21.7

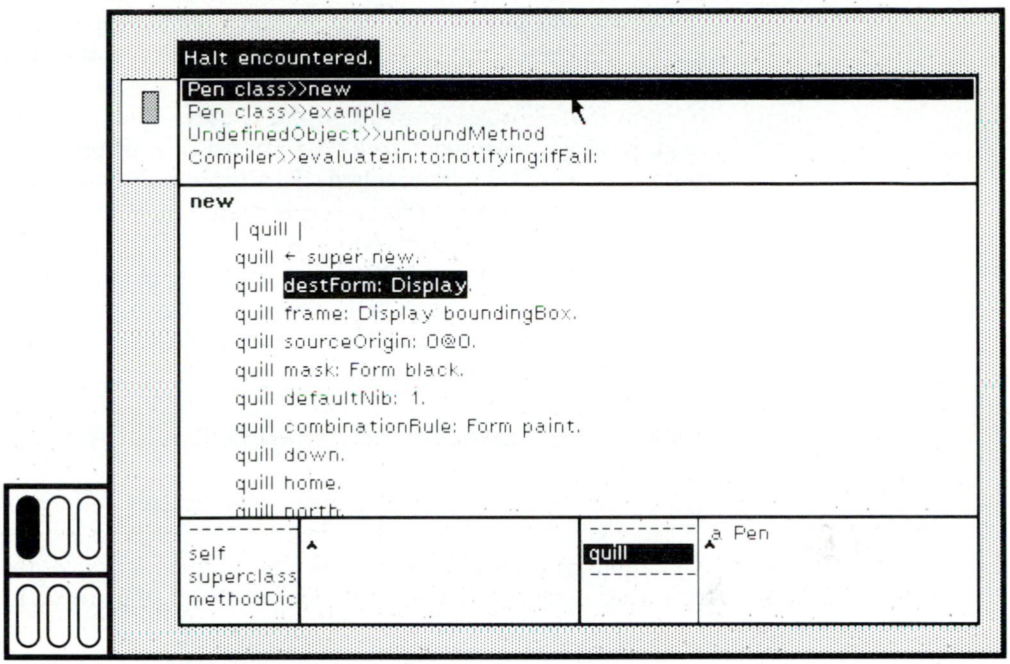

Halt encountered.

Pen class>>new
Pen class>>example
UndefinedObject>>unboundMethod
Compiler>>evaluate:in:to:notifying:ifFail:

new
    | quill |
    quill ← super new.
    quill destForm: Display.
    quill frame: Display boundingBox.
    quill sourceOrigin: 0@0.
    quill mask: Form black.
    quill defaultNib: 1.
    quill combinationRule: Form paint.
    quill down.
    quill home.
    quill north.

self
superclass
methodDic

quill | a Pen

Figure 21.8

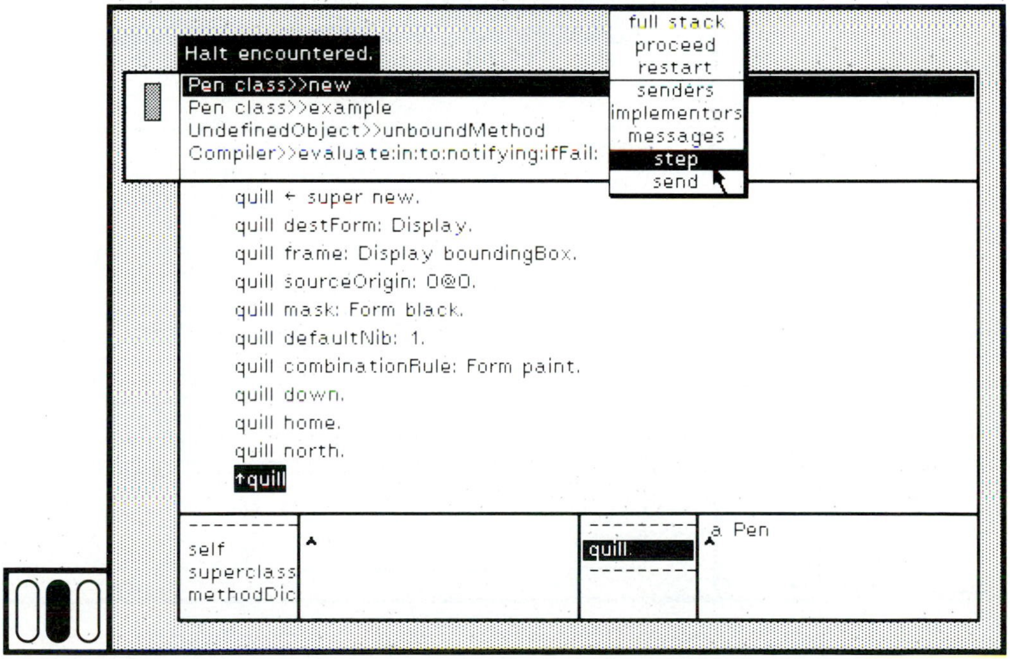

Halt encountered.

Pen class>>new
Pen class>>example
UndefinedObject>>unboundMethod
Compiler>>evaluate:in:to:notifying:ifFail:

full stack
proceed
restart
senders
implementors
messages
step
send

    quill ← super new.
    quill destForm: Display.
    quill frame: Display boundingBox.
    quill sourceOrigin: 0@0.
    quill mask: Form black.
    quill defaultNib: 1.
    quill combinationRule: Form paint.
    quill down.
    quill home.
    quill north.
    ↑quill

self
superclass
methodDic

quill. | a Pen

Figure 21.9

Choose the yellow button command step. The method is completed and is removed from the activation stack. The action is reflected in the debugger (Figure 21.10). The message new has now been sent successfully to Pen. The assignment to bic is carried out immediately, and the next message selected is gray to Form. This is precisely the state the debugger would have reached if, at the point shown in Figure 21.5 when new to Pen was the text selection, you had chosen yellow button command step instead of send.

In the inspector for temporary variables, choose the name bic in the menu; bic is an instance of Pen. In the menu of the inspector, choose the yellow button command inspect and create an inspector for bic (Figure 21.11). In the text subview of the inspector for bic, type

halftoneForm displayAt: Sensor waitButton

Select the text and choose the yellow button command do it (Figure 21.12a). Click any button somewhere on the screen where the area is clear and you will be able to see the result. A black, 16 x 16 square is displayed; this is the default mask for a Pen (Figure 21.12b).

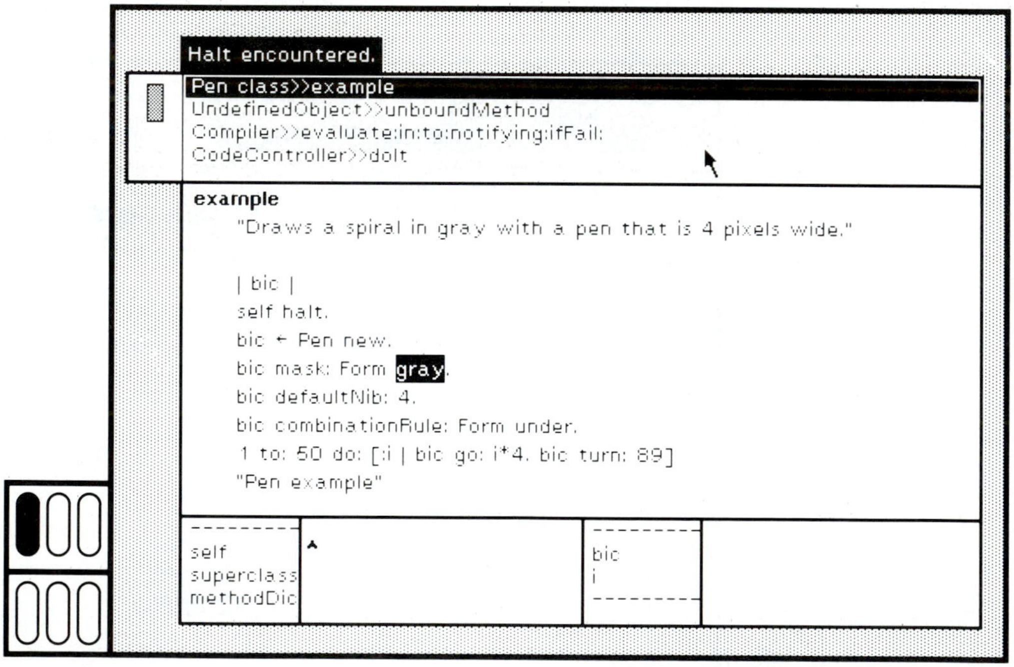

Figure 21.10

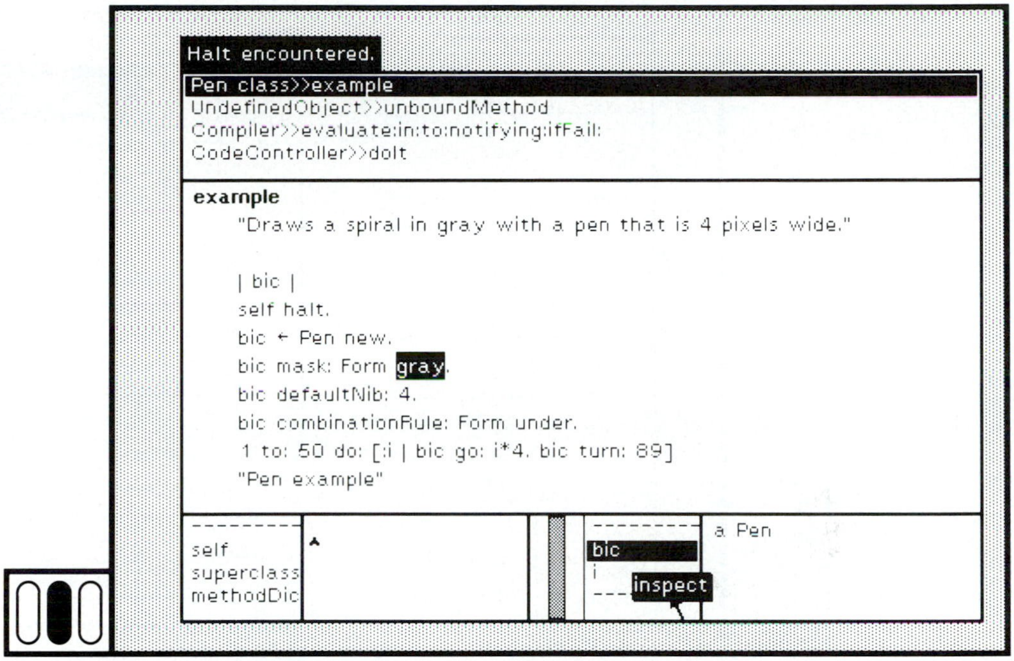

Halt encountered.

Pen class>>example
UndefinedObject>>unboundMethod
Compiler>>evaluate:in:to:notifying:ifFail:
CodeController>>doIt

example
   "Draws a spiral in gray with a pen that is 4 pixels wide."

   | bic |
   self halt.
   bic ← Pen new.
   bic mask: Form gray.
   bic defaultNib: 4.
   bic combinationRule: Form under.
   1 to: 50 do: [:i | bic go: i*4. bic turn: 89]
   "Pen example"

self   ^
superclass
methodDic

bic
i   inspect

a Pen

Figure 21.11

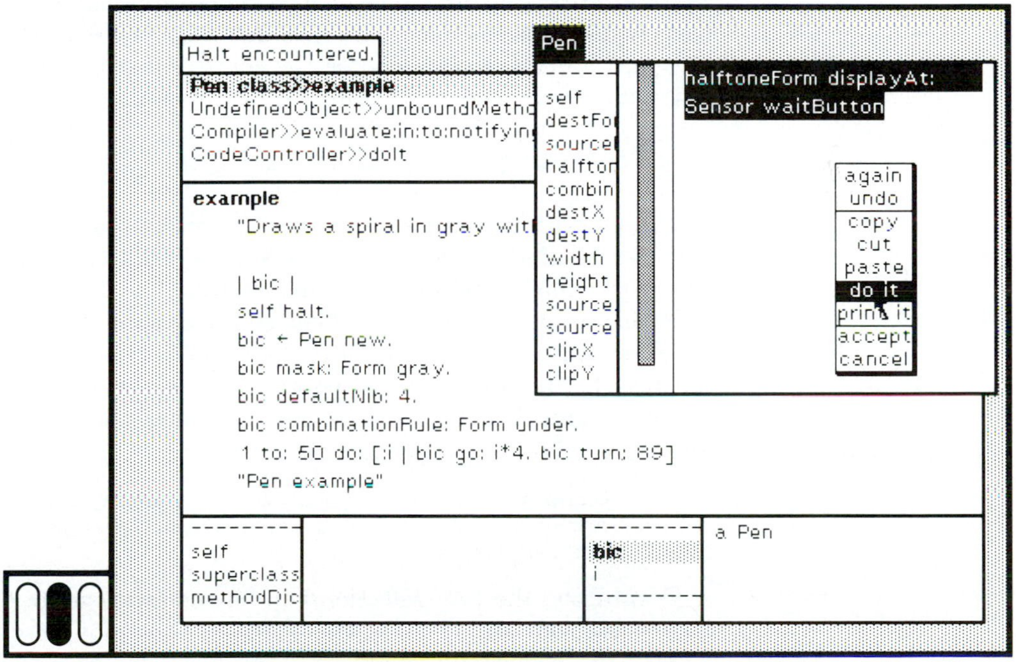

Halt encountered.

Pen class>>example
UndefinedObject>>unboundMethod
Compiler>>evaluate:in:to:notifying
CodeController>>doIt

example
   "Draws a spiral in gray wit

   | bic |
   self halt.
   bic ← Pen new.
   bic mask: Form gray.
   bic defaultNib: 4.
   bic combinationRule: Form under.
   1 to: 50 do: [:i | bic go: i*4. bic turn: 89]
   "Pen example"

Pen

self
destFo
source
halfto
combin
destX
destY
width
height
source
source
clipX
clipY

halftoneForm displayAt:
Sensor waitButton

again
undo
copy
cut
paste
do it
print it
accept
cancel

self
superclass
methodDic

bic
i

a Pen

Figure 21.12a

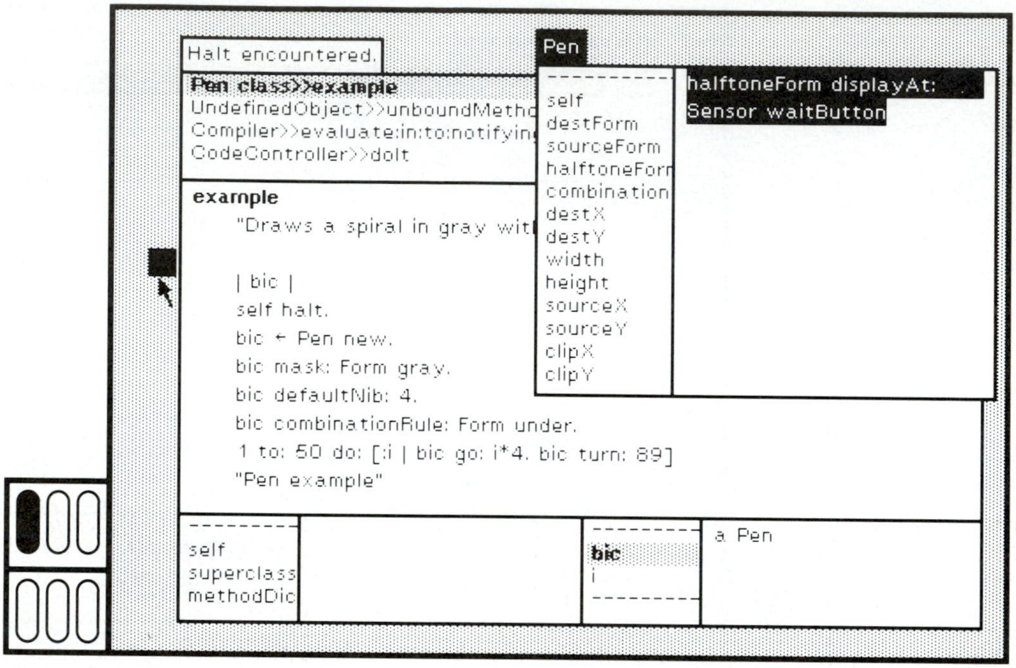

Figure 21.12b

Now return to the debugger and choose the yellow button command step in the top subview. The message gray is sent to Form. The next message is mask: to bic. Choose the command step again. Return to the inspector for bic and reevaluate the expression

halftoneForm displayAt: Sensor waitButton

Click any button somewhere on the screen where the area is clear and you will be able to see the result. A gray, 16 x 16 square is displayed; this is the new mask for bic (Figure 21.13).

Returning to the debugger, keep stepping through the method (choosing the command step); examine the variables of the Pen, bic, by choosing variable names in the inspector menu or evaluating expressions as already illustrated. You will change the size of the nib, the source Form, and the combination rule for bic.

> These evaluations will go very slowly since a simulator for the Smalltalk-80 interpreter is used. Sending defaultNib: will be especially slow, perhaps one-half minute on some machines.

Eventually, the text selection will be the message to: 50 do: [:i | bic go: i*4. bic turn: 89] (Figure 21.14). If you were now to choose the command step, you would watch the Pen draw the 50 lines that make up the spiral design; the drawing would be carried out in an excrutiatingly slow manner. Rather than choosing the command step at this point,

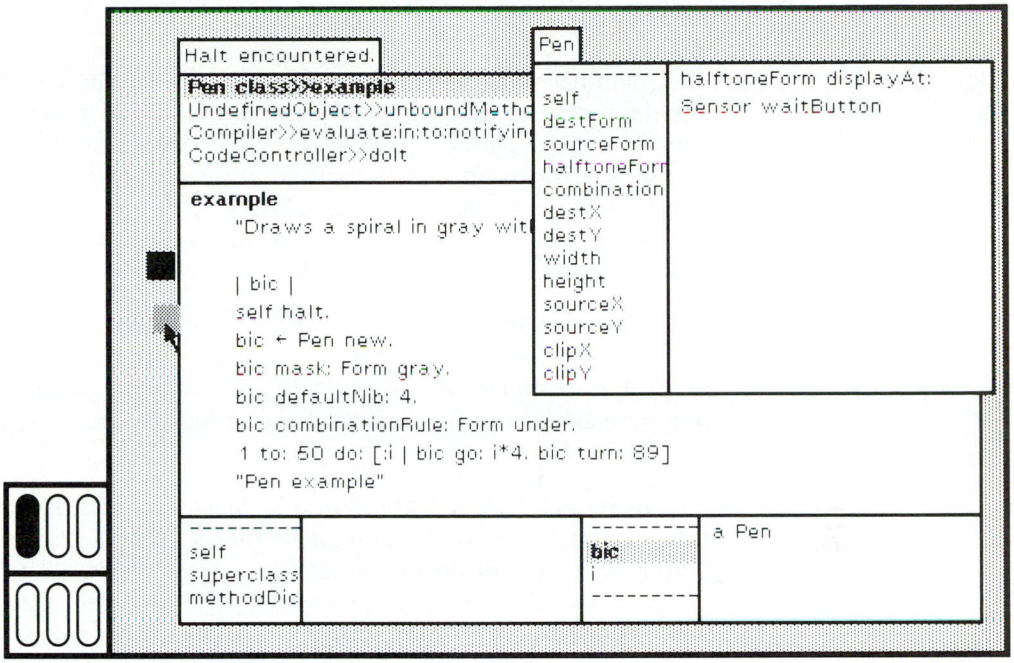

Figure 21.13

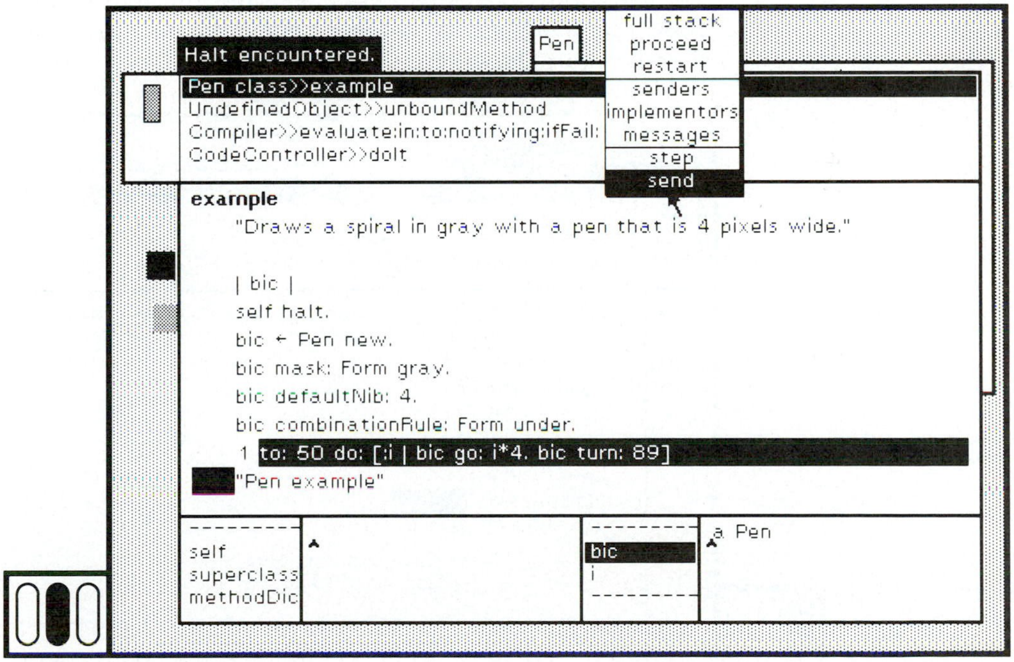

```
Halt encountered.                    Pen
Pen class>>example              ----------  halftoneForm displayAt:
UndefinedObject>>unboundMethod  self       Sensor waitButton
Compiler>>evaluate:in:to:notifying  destForm
CodeController>>doIt            sourceForm
                                halftoneForm
example                         combination
    "Draws a spiral in gray wit  destX
                                destY
    | bic |                     width
    self halt.                  height
    bic ← Pen new.              sourceX
    bic mask: Form gray.        sourceY
    bic defaultNib: 4.          clipX
    bic combinationRule: Form under.  clipY
    1 to: 50 do: [:i | bic go: i*4. bic turn: 89]
    "Pen example"
----------  ----------  ----------  a Pen
self                    bic
superclass              i
methodDic               ----------
```

Figure 21.14

```
                              full stack
                              proceed
                    Pen       restart
Halt encountered.             senders
Pen class>>example            implementors
UndefinedObject>>unboundMethod  messages
Compiler>>evaluate:in:to:notifying:ifFail:  step
CodeController>>doIt          send

example
    "Draws a spiral in gray with a pen that is 4 pixels wide."

    | bic |
    self halt.
    bic ← Pen new.
    bic mask: Form gray.
    bic defaultNib: 4.
    bic combinationRule: Form under.
    1 to: 50 do: [:i | bic go: i*4. bic turn: 89]
    "Pen example"
----------  ----------  ----------  a Pen
self                    bic
superclass              i
methodDic               ----------
```

choose the command send so that you can see, more quickly, the Pen design.

Assuming you choose the yellow button command send in the top subview of the debugger (Figure 21.14), the message to:do: to a SmallInteger is placed at the top of the activation stack (Figure 21.15). The first expression in the method associated with to:do: is an assignment, and it is carried out immediately. The text selection is at the second expression, a comparison of the temporary variable nextValue with the argument stop.

In the right inspector of the debugger, choose the temporary variable name nextValue so that you can watch the value change as the iteration proceeds; nextValue is initially 1 (Figure 21.16). Choose the yellow button command step to evaluate the test for the iteration; the next message is value:.

Choose step again. A small line is drawn, and the selection goes to +. Choose step again. The value of nextValue is now 2; the display of the change in value for nextValue is automatically updated (Figure 21.17).

Continue to choose step for awhile, say until the value of nextValue is 4, and you can see the drawing of 3 lines of the spiral design (Figure 21.18). You can now complete the example by choosing the yellow button command proceed in the top subview (Figure 21.19). Or you can close the debugger by choosing the blue button command close, and thereby abort the execution of the example.

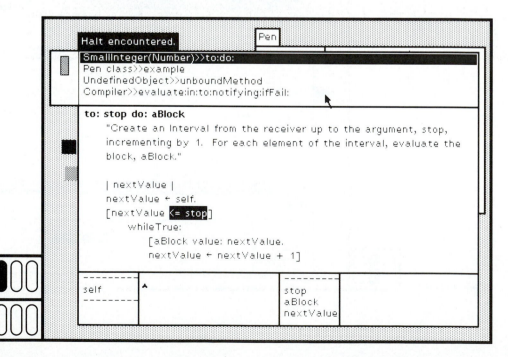

Figure 21.15

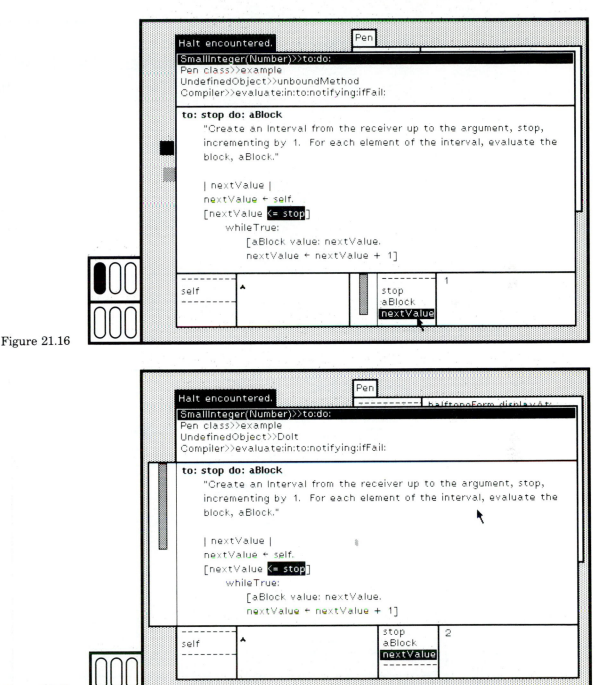

Figure 21.16

Figure 21.17

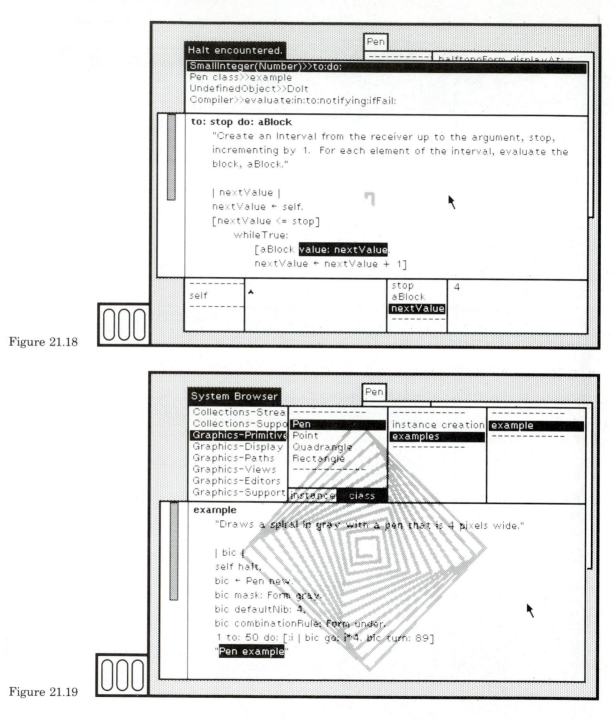

Figure 21.18

Figure 21.19

PART FIVE

External Files

Your work in developing Smalltalk-80 code can be saved in a variety of ways, all of which will be described in Part Five.

- Make a file on which new class definitions and descriptions, or parts of class descriptions are stored. This kind of a file is useful in sharing information among different users of Smalltalk-80 system images.

- Make a file on which any changes to existing class descriptions are stored. This involves filing out with respect to the system change set.

- Make a "snapshot," a file containing an executable image of the current state of the system. The system can be started up from this file.

- Make an audit trail. As you are working, a log of the changes you make to class descriptions is automatically kept on a special file. It is part of the mechanism for storing source code. This file also contains each evaluation action. It can be used for recovering from major disasters that occur before you have saved your work (with the exception, perhaps, of disk crashes).

22

The File System

The purpose of this chapter is to describe the mechanisms available in the Smalltalk-80 system for filing code in and out. In using the programming system, you should be aware of how access to the source code is handled, and how the system supports you in remembering changes you make to the system. Source code and changes are stored in files that exist on either your local disk or on a network-based file server. If the file of source code is not available to you, you can still browse the system methods by using a decompiler. The end of this chapter reviews the use of the sources and changes files and the decompiler; further details about sources and changes are given in Chapter 23.

At Xerox PARC, work in progress on an application is typically stored in personally managed snapshots. The purpose of maintaining snapshots is that they represent a collection of objects, whereas files are needed because we do not understand, as yet, how to transfer external objects, and we do understand how to transfer descriptions of objects. Files, therefore, are our primary communication medium. Periodically, files containing class descriptions and changes to system classes are made, especially when the programmer wishes to work in a new release of the system. The programmer accesses a new release and then files in the new class definitions and methods. To share additions to the system, either bug fixes or new functionality, files (rather than snapshots) are made and then stored on a shared network-based file server; an announcement of the availability of the files is made using a form of electronic mail. Throughout this chapter's discussion, it should be understood that the system makes no distinction between local disks for storing files and remote files stored on network-based file servers, other than in naming the file. (The name of a remote file includes the name of the file server and directory, and the system must request any log in identification. Smalltalk-80 systems that provide access to file servers must implement the network protocols and provide prompters for obtaining log in identification.) Because most of the computers used by the Smalltalk-80 developers are shared, files are rarely stored on local disks, with the exception of the latest system release image and changes files. All users are expected to back up their work, snapshots, or files of class descriptions, on a file server.

22.1

Writing Code onto a File

There are two ways to write code onto a file. The usual way is to select the yellow button commands in the system browsers that provide general access to class descriptions. Four layers of information can be selected for filing out from the various subviews of a system browser.

- The code that describes all the classes within a class category. Choose the yellow button command file out in the class-categories subview of the browser. The file name is the class category followed by an extension.

- The code that describes an individual class. Choose the yellow button command file out in the class-names subview of the browser. The file name is the class name followed by an extension.

- The code that describes the methods associated with a category of messages in an individual class. Choose the yellow button command file out in the message-category subview of the browser. The file name is the class name or metaclass name followed by a hyphen followed by the category name followed by an extension.

- The code associated with one method of an individual class. Choose the yellow button command file out in the message-selectors subview of the browser. The file name is the class name or metaclass name followed by a hyphen followed by the message selector followed by an extension.

In each case, the "extension" for the file name is a period followed by the characters st. The class name is inserted in front of the message-category and message-selector when creating the file name for the third and fourth subview. Any invalid file character in the selection is replaced by hyphens; invalid file characters include space, $<$, $>$, $=$, $>=$, and $<=$. Examples of file names associated with various selections is given in Figures 22.1a, 22.1b, 22.1c, and 22.1d, in which the command file out is chosen in each of the four menu subviews of a system browser.

The information written onto the files using the command file out is in the form of expressions that can be evaluated to reconstruct the class descriptions.

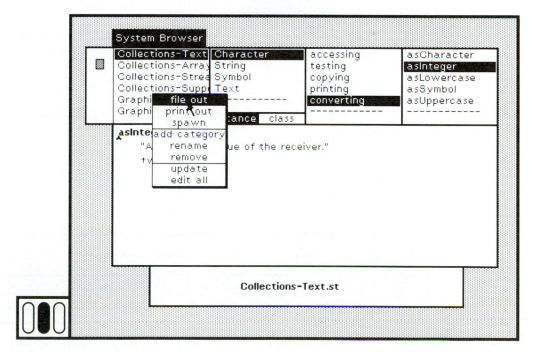

Figure 22.1a

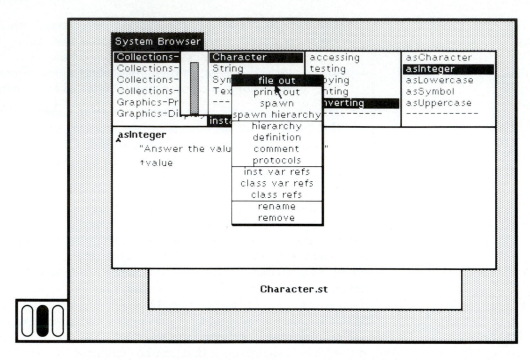

Figure 22.1b

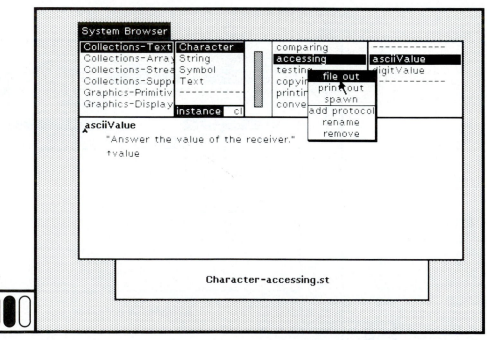

Figure 22.1c

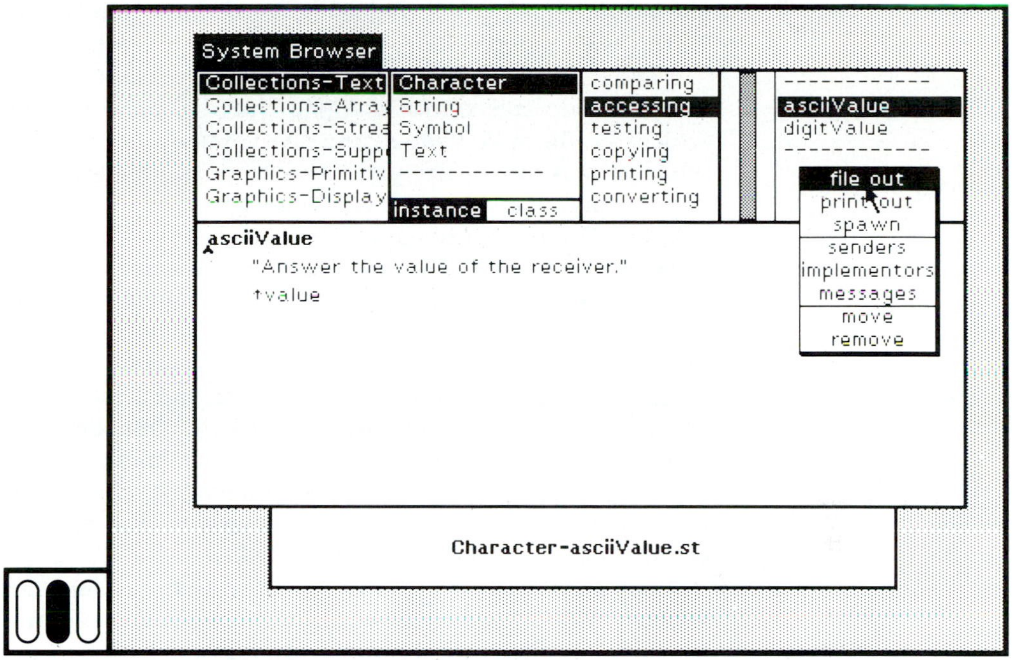

Figure 22.1d

Alternatively, choose the yellow button command print out in each of the subviews of the browser in order to obtain a "pretty printed" version of the descriptions. The file name extension is a period followed by some sequence of characters indicating the format of the contents (at Xerox PARC, the characters are press). Typically, the contents of a file created using the command print out cannot be evaluated as Smalltalk-80 expressions. The command print out is reserved as a system dependent message for creating the best possible pretty-printed version. Because printing formats differ among hardware systems, the pretty-printed version defaults to being the same as file out in the basic version of the Smalltalk-80 system.

File Formats

The format for a file created using the command file out is described in the paper by Glenn Krasner entitled "The Smalltalk-80 File Code Format" in the book he edited, *Smalltalk-80: Bits of History, Words of Advice*. A summary of that paper is given here.

The file format contains exclamation marks as special delimiters. Text up to, but not including an exclamation mark, is treated as an expression that can be evaluated. If an exclamation mark is the first character in the next chunk of text to be read, then all but this first character are treated as an expression and evaluated. The result of the evaluation is an object. This object then takes over the task of reading the file, stopping when the object determines that its task is completed. In this way, a class can read and install new methods.

Figure 22.2 shows a file out of part of the class description for Collection. The file starts with a String that indicates the date and time at which the file was created, and the version number of the system from which it was made. The exclamation mark delimits the String from the next chunk of text, which is a message to Object to create a new subclass, Collection, with no variable declarations and categorized under Collections-Abstract. The exclamation mark delimits this message from the next, which is a message to the new class Collection to store a comment about itself. The next exclamation mark is followed immediately by another. The chunk of text is a message to Collection to create a new category, accessing, and to start reading the methods for that category. The class Collection, then, becomes the file "reader." It installs a method for size. The exclamation mark after the method is followed immediately by an exclamation mark, indicating the Collection can stop reading the file. The next text chunk creates the message category testing for Collection, and the methods follow.

The "pretty printed" version for printing part of the class Collection is shown in Figure 22.3. This format can not be read by the system, but is somewhat easier for a human being to read.

22.2

Accessing the Contents of a File

Instances of external files can be created by evaluating an expression of the form

FileStream fileNamed: ′fileName′

The response to this expression is an instance of FileStream that can be sent messages for reading and writing information onto the file it accesses. Note that FileStream also responds to messages with selectors oldFileNamed: and newFileNamed: in order to open access to external files that already exist (oldFileNamed:) or do not already exist (newFileNamed:).

```
'From Smalltalk-80 of March 9, 1983 [v29] on 15 March 1983 at
9:35:22 pm'!
Object subclass: #Collection
    instanceVariableNames: ''
    classVariableNames: ''
    poolDictionaries: ''
    category: 'Collections-Abstract'!
Collection comment: 'I am the abstract class of all collection classes.'!

!Collection methodsFor: 'accessing'!

size
    "Answer how many elements the receiver contains."

    | tally |
    tally ← 0.
    self do: [ :each | tally ← tally + 1].
    ↑tally! !

!Collection methodsFor: 'testing'!

includes: anObject
    "Answer whether anObject is one of the receiver's elements."

    self do: [ :each |  anObject = each ifTrue: [↑true]].
    ↑false!

isEmpty
    "Answer whether the receiver contains any elements."

    ↑self size = 0!

occurrencesOf: anObject
    "Answer how many of the receiver's elements are equal to
    anObject."

    | tally |
    tally ← 0.
    self do: [ :each |  anObject = each ifTrue: [tally ← tally + 1]].
    ↑tally! !
```

Figure 22.2

From Smalltalk-80 of March 9, 1983 [v29] on 15 March 1983 at 9:35:22 pm

Object subclass: #Collection
    instanceVariableNames: ''
    classVariableNames: ''
    poolDictionaries: ''
    category: 'Collections-Abstract'

Collection comment: 'I am the abstract class of all collection classes.'

Collection methodsFor: 'accessing'
size
    "Answer how many elements the receiver contains."

    | tally |
    tally ← 0.
    self do: [:each | tally ← tally + 1].
    ↑tally

Collection methodsFor: 'testing'
includes: anObject
    "Answer whether anObject is one of the receiver's elements."

    self do: [:each | anObject = each ifTrue: [↑true]].
    ↑false
isEmpty
    "Answer whether the receiver contains any elements."

    ↑self size = 0
occurrencesOf: anObject
    "Answer how many of the receiver's elements are equal to anObject."

    | tally |
    tally ← 0.
    self do: [:each | anObject = each ifTrue: [tally ← tally + 1]].
    ↑tally

Figure 22.3

For example, create the file whose name is testFile, and practice writing text into it, by evaluating the following sequence of expressions.

```
| aFile |
aFile ← FileStream fileNamed: ' testFile'.
aFile nextPutAll: ' The beginning of the file. '.
aFile cr.
1 to: 50 by: 10 do:
  [ :each |
    aFile nextPutAll: each printString.
    aFile cr].
aFile nextPutAll: ' The end of the file. '.
aFile close
```

FileStream is a subclass of ReadWriteStream; the messages for writing into the file are like those of any ReadWriteStream. Using a system browser, you can explore the messages available for writing text into a file.

Note that instead of using the expression

aFile nextPutAll: each printString

in the statements for writing on the file, you could have used

each printOn: aFile

and the result would have been the same.

File List Browser

The simplest way to open a file and access its contents is to choose the System Menu command file list. You are asked to designate a rectangular area in which the file list view is displayed. This standard system view consists of three subviews. You type text in the top subview to specify file names or patterns for file names (of either existing or new files). A pattern is a sequence of characters that can contain the special characters * or #; * matches any sequence of no, one, or more characters, and # matches any one character. When you choose the yellow button command accept in the top subview, the next subview, the file-names subview, displays a list menu containing all the names of the files in the local disk that match the names you specified in the pattern subview. When you choose a file name from the menu, the contents of the selected file is displayed in the bottom text subview.

If the file system you are using allows the characters * and # in a file name, then you will want to choose other characters for pattern matching purposes, and it will be necessary to change the String matching routines. The method to be changed is String match:.

The form of the pattern subview is a sequence of file names delimited by "carriage returns," that is, each file name or pattern is placed on a separate line. Suppose you type

story

and then choose the yellow button command **accept** in the top view (Figure 22.4a). We are assuming that the file story did not exist before. The file-names menu displays one item (Figure 22.4b).

story

Choose it. The item is selected. Nothing else happens. The yellow button menu offers five commands (Figure 22.4c).

get contents	Retrieve the contents of the selected file, and display the contents in the text subview.
file in	Retrieve the entire contents of the selected file, reading and evaluating the text according to the file format for class descriptions and expressions.
copy name	Copy the text of the file name into the text editor buffer so that it can be "pasted" into other text views.

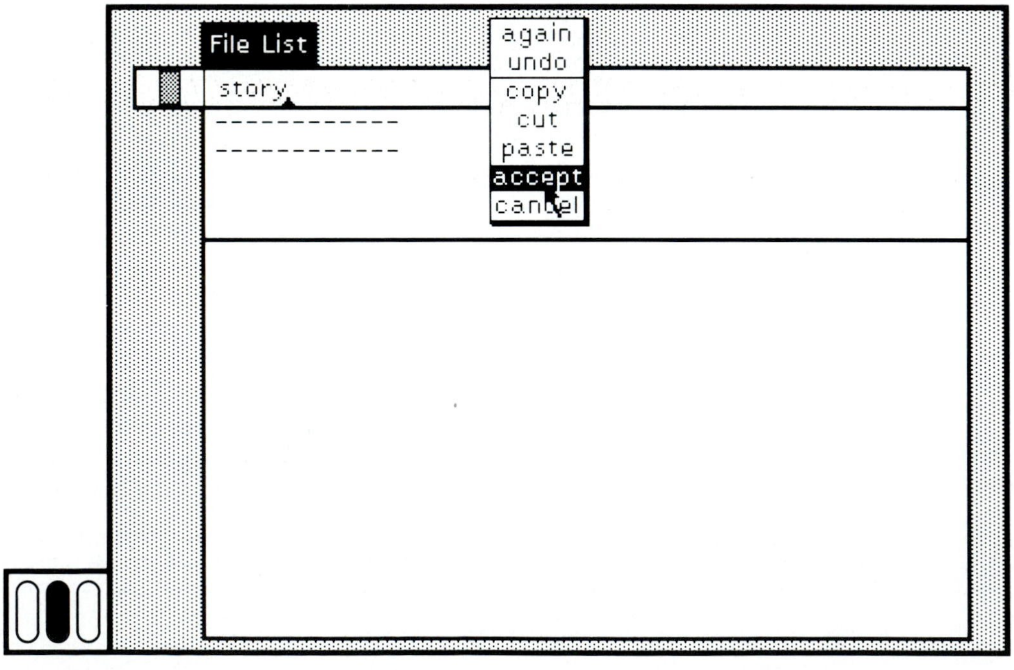

Figure 22.4a

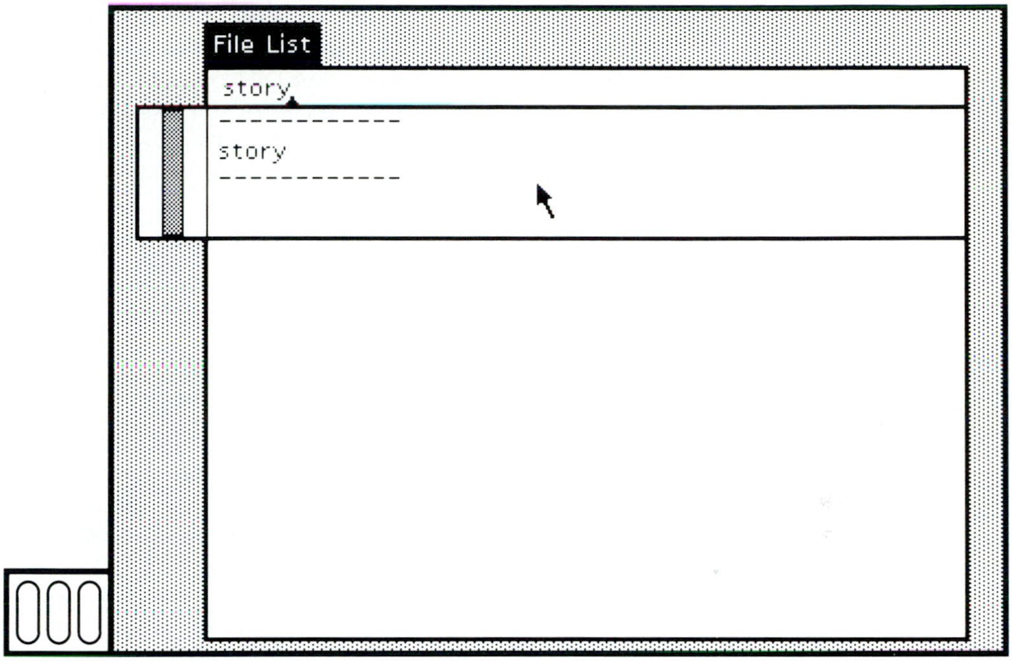

Figure 22.4b

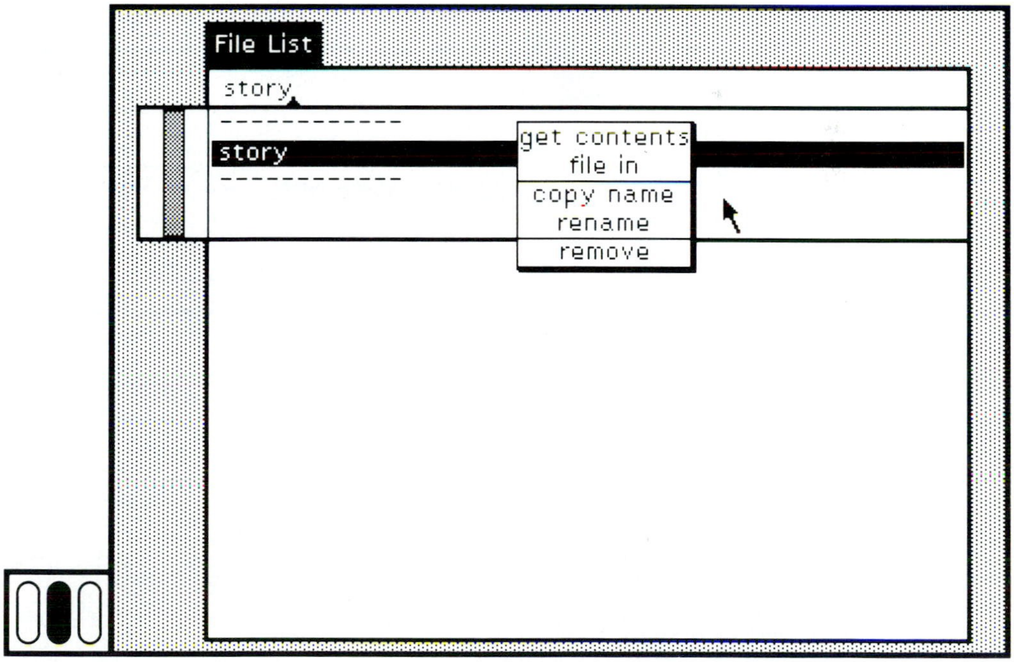

Figure 22.4c

rename	Change the name of the selected file. A prompter appears, with the name of the selected file. Edit it with the new file name. Type the "carriage return" key or choose the yellow button command accept to indicate that you have completed the file name. The menu of file names will be updated. If you type an improper file name, or no file name at all, a confirmer will appear to determine whether you want to try again to specify a file name. Examples of this command are given later in this chapter.
remove	Delete the selected file from the file directory. A confirmer appears to determine whether you really want to remove the selected file. Choose yes if you do, no if you do not.

Whenever you retrieve the contents of a file, information is presented in the System Transcript (if it is visible on the display screen). This information tells you which class and which method is currently being read and compiled. In this way, you can monitor the progress of the file retrieval.

Choose the yellow button command get contents (Figure 22.5a). The file contents is empty. The text subview displays

- new file -

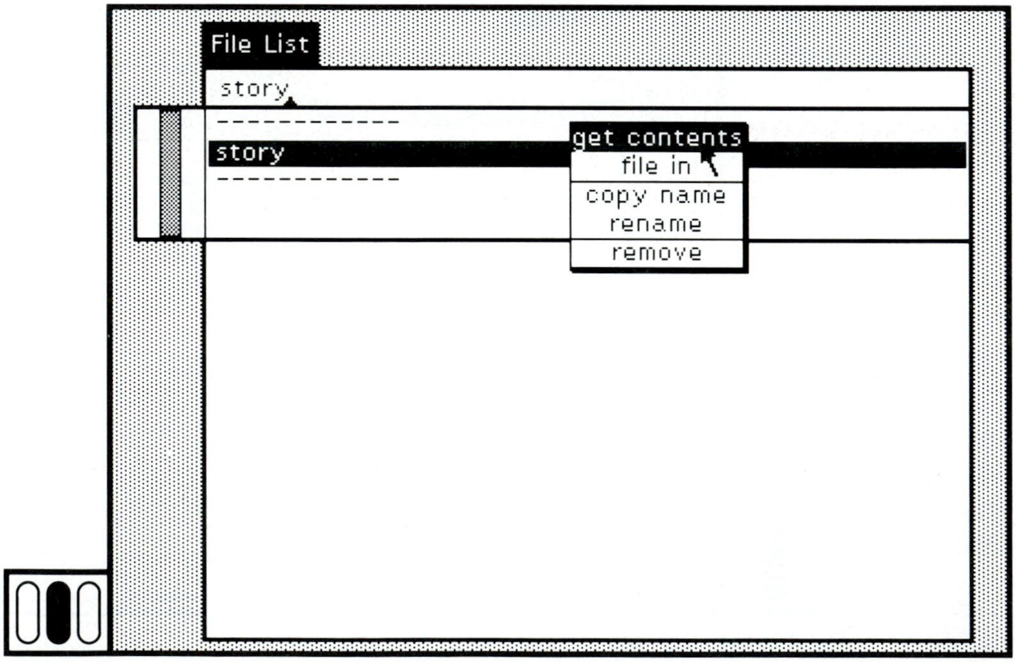

Figure 22.5a

to indicate that a new file will be created if you edit and store the contents of the text subview. Keep in mind that the new file will be created only if the contents are saved onto the file. Edit the text subview as though you were working in a regular workspace. The yellow button menu contains the text editing commands plus three additional commands, file it in, put, and get (Figure 22.5b).

file it in	Read and evaluate the text selection. This selection should be in the file-out format, which includes the exclamation mark.
put	Save the edited information onto the file. One level of back up on the file is maintained. The original version is renamed to the given file name with a trailing $ appended; the new version is stored as the currently selected file name.
get	Retrieve all the information currently in the file.

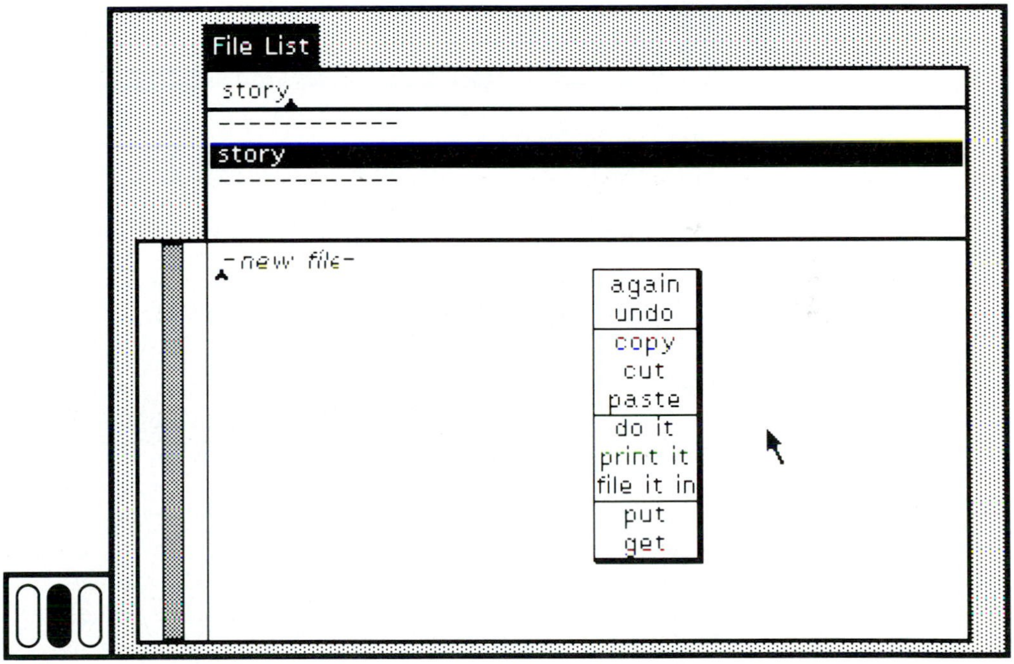

Figure 22.5b

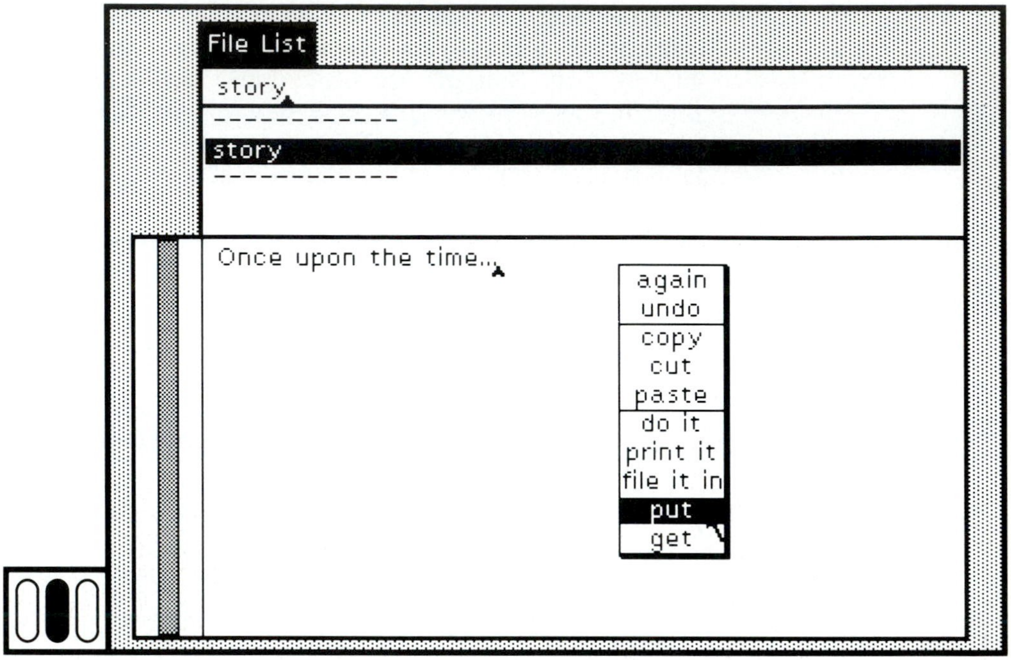

Figure 22.5c

Edit the contents and then choose the yellow button command put (Figure 22.5c).

> The cursor changes to a writing pen when a file is being written; it looks like eyeglasses when a file is being read. During the time it takes for the system to access the file, the cursor looks like an hourglass, meaning "wait" because it may take noticeable time to find the file you requested.

The commands put and get are the external file counterparts to accept and cancel. Although the contents of the file are retrieved when you select a file name, you might make changes that you later wish to throw away. In a workspace, you would choose the command cancel; in the file browser text subview, you choose the command get.

In the top subview, replace story by storage and choose the yellow button command accept. The file-names subview changes again (Figure 22.6a). Choose the single item, storage. Choose the yellow button command get contents (Figure 22.6b). Again, we are assuming that you requested a new file. Edit the text subview and then choose the yellow button command put (Figure 22.6c).

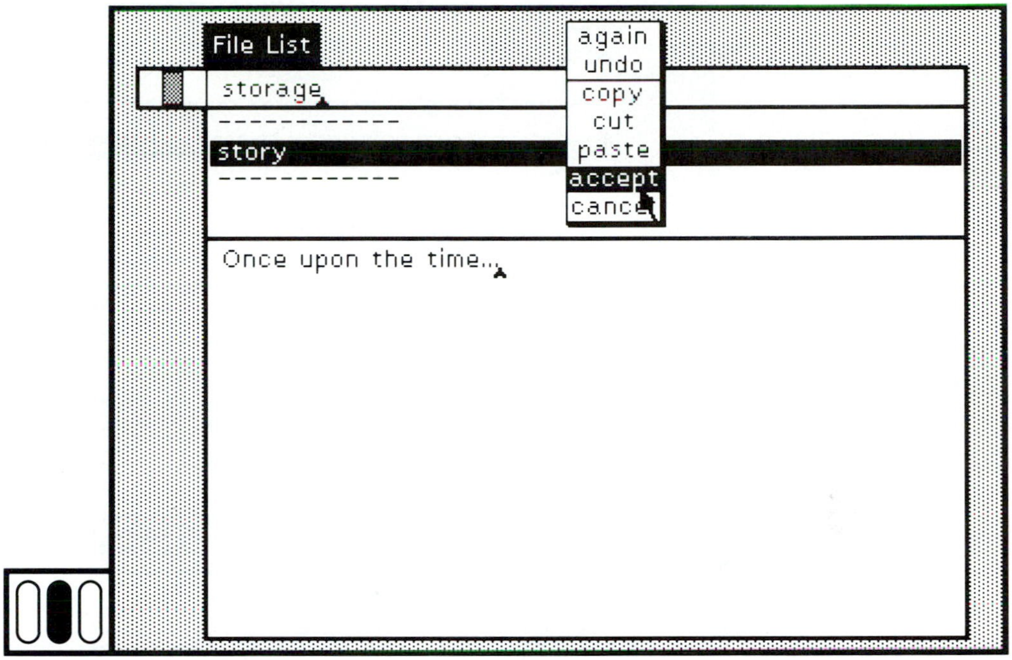

Figure 22.6a

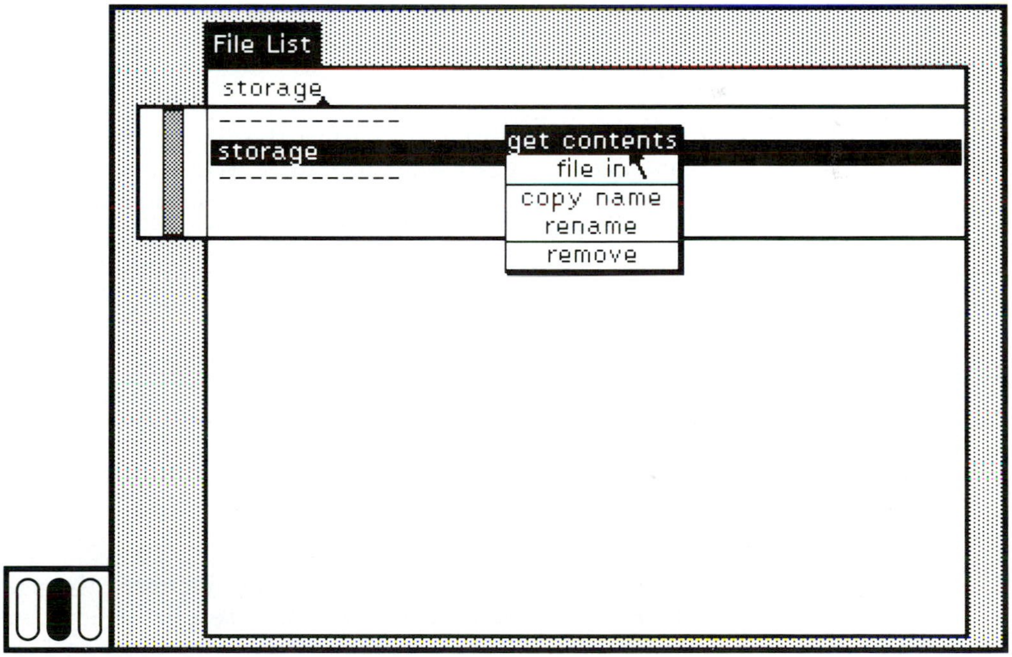

Figure 22.6b

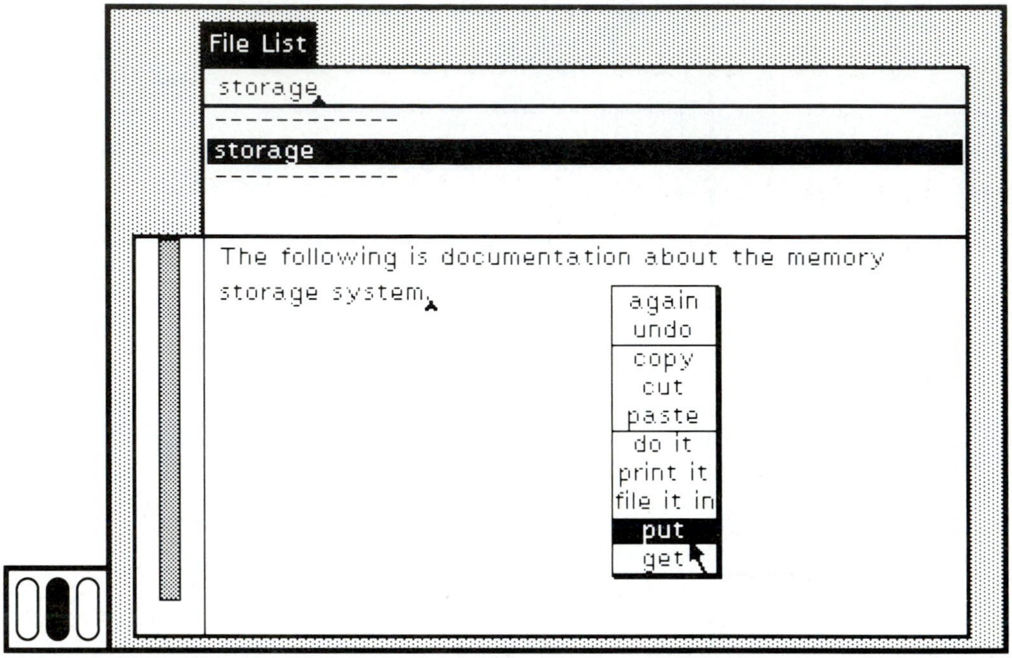

Figure 22.6c

Now in the top subview, replace all the text with the pattern

stor*

As stated earlier, the top part of the file list view can contain explicit file names or patterns for the names. String-matching provides two special notations for matching an arbitrary substring.

* match any number of characters, including none
# match exactly one character

Note that s*y matches story, as does #t*y and story*. If you type stor* in the pattern subview and then choose the yellow button command accept, then the list menu will contain (at least)

storage
story

Choosing each item and then choosing get opens the previously created file. Rename story to be tale. Choose the yellow button command rename (Figure 22.7a). A prompter appears (Figure 22.7b).

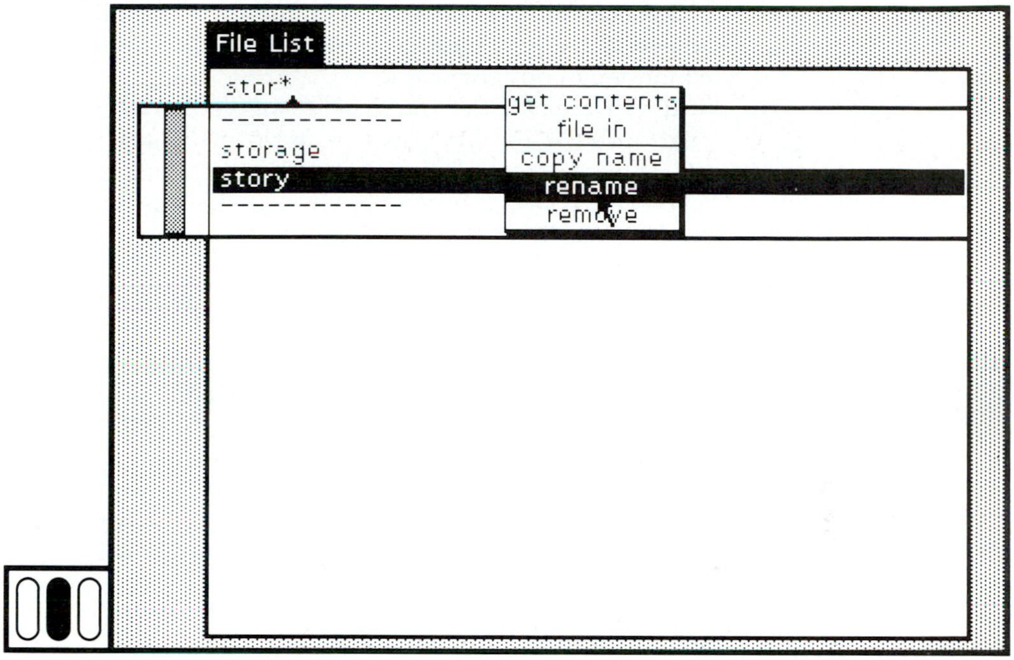

Figure 22.7a

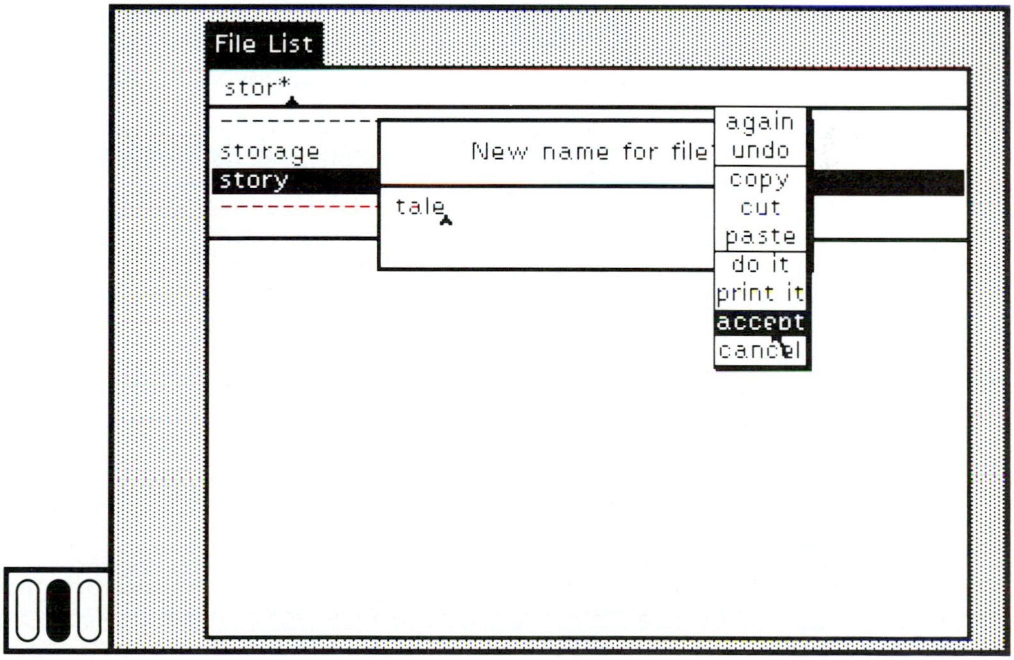

Figure 22.7b

Replace the text in the prompter with the file name tale, and then choose the yellow button command accept. The file name tale is selected automatically (Figure 22.8).

If you created the file testFile suggested earlier in this section, you might use the file list view now to see its contents. Since any number of file names or patterns, separated by a "carriage return," can be typed in the top view, you can simply add this file name to the pattern already in the view.

In addition to creating a file list view as just described, instances of external files can be accessed for editing by evaluating an expression of the form

(FileStream fileNamed: 'fileName') edit

The text subview part of the file list view, only, is created. The label of the view is the name of the file. In Figure 22.9a, the expression (FileStream fileNamed: 'tale') edit is typed, selected, and evaluated in a workspace. In Figure 22.9b, a simple view of the contents of the file is shown. The yellow button menu is like that available in the file list view.

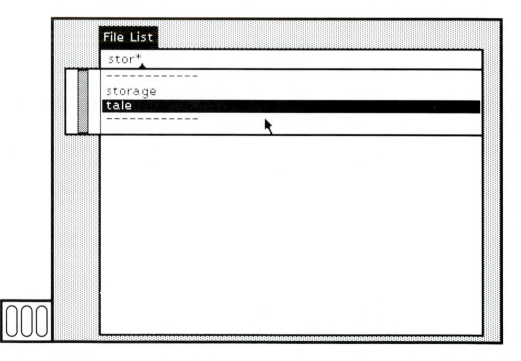

Figure 22.8

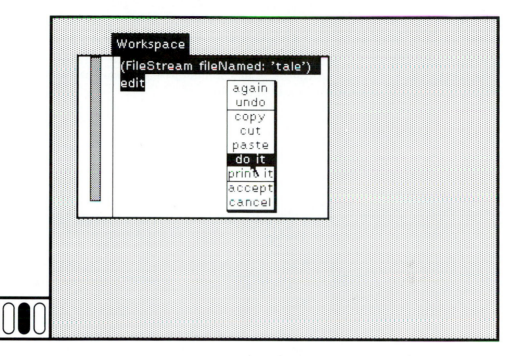

Figure 22.9a

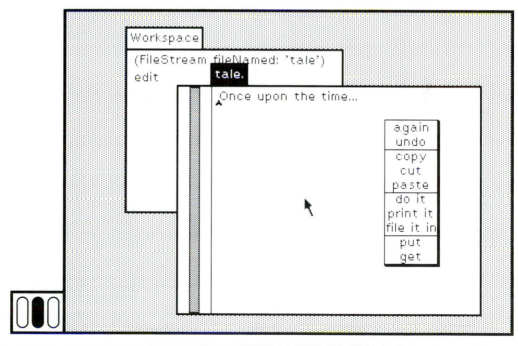

Figure 22.9b

22.3

Retrieving the Contents of a File

Class descriptions that were stored on a file whose name is fileName, using the browser command file out, can be retrieved by evaluating an expression of the form

> (FileStream oldFileNamed: 'fileName') fileIn

This expression is provided in the System Workspace for your convenience.

Whenever you read class descriptions from a file that create a new class category, any open system browsers will have to be informed of the new category. In the class-categories subview of the system browser, choose the yellow button command update.

Syntax Error View

Since files are created by choosing the file out command in a browser subview, there are three reasons why an error can exist in a file you try to read.

1. Variables or messages that had been a part of your image at the time you created the file are not in the version into which you are now filing.

2. You used a file list view and edited the text directly, creating a syntax error (which is why you should not edit class descriptions this way!).

3. You selected the text of a file and chose the yellow button command file it in, but did not select the correct sequence of characters.

As you are filing in information from a file, a status report is printed in the System Transcript (if it is open on the display screen). If, when filing in, undeclared variables are encountered, a statement showing the variable name and the fact that it is undeclared prints in the System Transcript. The system will store the method anyway, as though compilation had been successful, and you will have to use the browser to find and correct the error.

Similarly, if an unknown message selector is encountered in a method, the process of filing in will be interrupted. A notifier will appear on the screen. You can ask the spelling corrector to determine a possible new selector. If the determination is acceptable, you choose the menu item yes. This will store the right information in the system and continue reading the file. Or you can use the debugger, find and correct the error, and then proceed (choose the yellow button command proceed) to continue reading the file. Or you can simply proceed to continue reading the file, without correcting the error and, therefore, without storing the information in the system. In each case, the text in the file will not be changed.

If a syntax error exists in the expressions that are filed in from an external file, a special view will be created on the screen. It is the *Syntax Error View*. Its purpose is to report the error and give you an opportunity to edit the expression. A syntax error view consists of one text view that displays the expression to be evaluated, or the method to be compiled and stored in a class description.

To create an example of a syntax error, file out the class FinancialHistory that you had created as an example in Part Four. You do this by choosing the class name FinancialHistory in a system browser, and then choosing the yellow button command file out in the class-names subview. Use the file list view to retrieve the contents of the file you created; the file name is FinancialHistory.st (Figure 22.10).

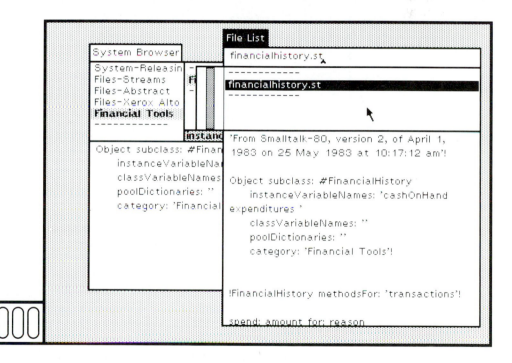

Figure 22.10

Next, create some syntax errors in this file. Find the first occurrence of an assignment expression and insert an extra left arrow, or find a keyword in a message pattern and add an extra colon. Choose the yellow button command put to store the syntax error into the file (Figure 22.11). While the text is being written on the file, the cursor changes to the shape of a pen.

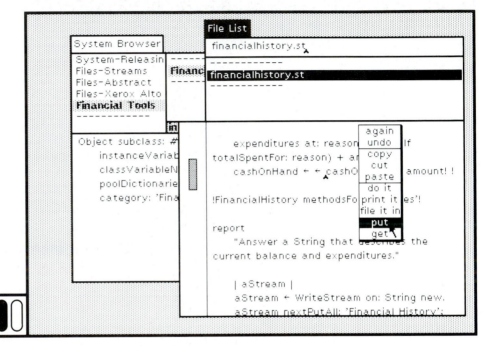

Figure 22.11

In the menu subview of the file list view, choose the yellow button command file in (Figure 22.12a). A syntax error view appears indicating that an expression is expected after the first left arrow (Figure 22.12b). Text describing the syntax error is inserted into the method at the point of the error; the text is selected. You edit the method to correct it, just as you would in a browser text subview. Choose the yellow button command accept to recompile the method (Figure 22.12c). Now choose yellow button command proceed (Figure 22.12d).

The correction you made is known to the system, but no change has been made to the text on the file itself. You either have to file out again to create a corrected file, or you have to use the file list view to access the contents of the file and make the correction.

During filing in, expressions can be evaluated. For example, an expression that creates a new class description might appear in the text in the file. If evaluating the expression generates a runtime error during the file in, then a syntax error view will appear. The poorly-formed expression will be displayed in the view. For example, suppose you

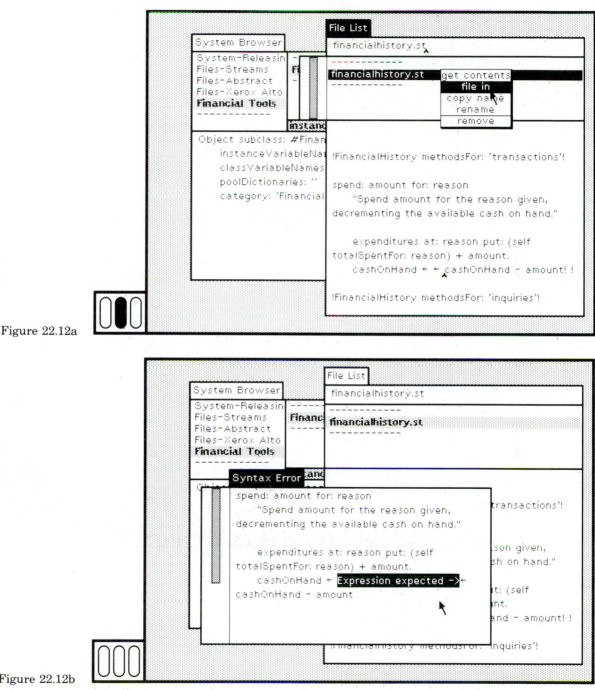

Figure 22.12a

Figure 22.12b

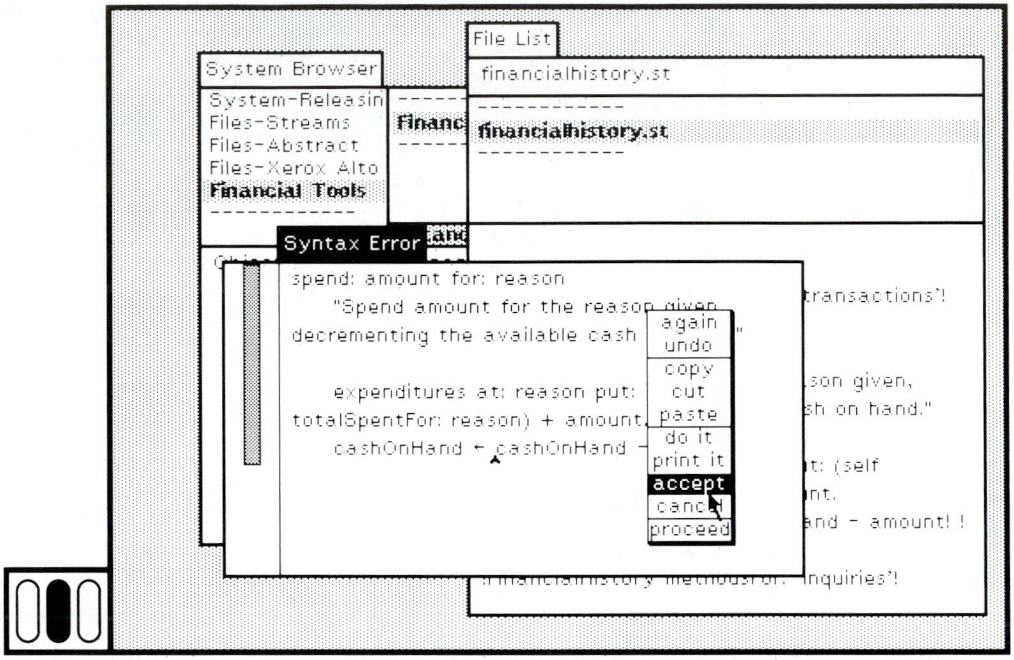

Figure 22.12c

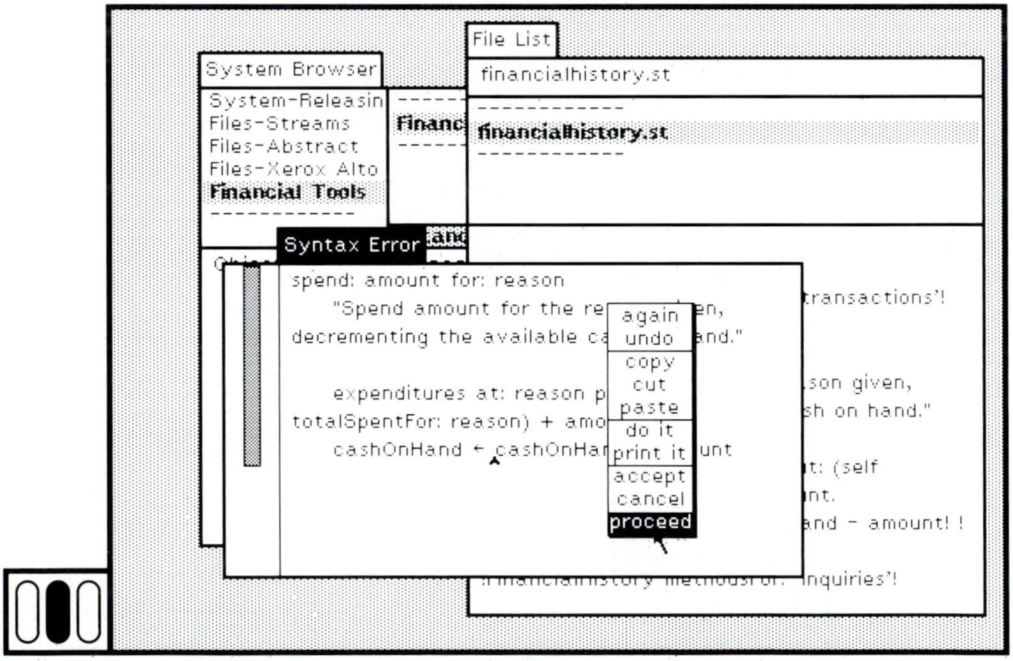

Figure 22.12d

modify the file FinancialHistory.st so that instead of trying to create FinancialHistory as a subclass of Object, the expression contains the name Oject (i.e., there is a typo) (Figure 22.13a). Choose the yellow button command put to store the change. Now choose the yellow button command file in in the menu subview of the file list. A notifier will appear (Figure 22.13b).

Open a debugger and select the message-send DoIt to see the erroneous expression. You can edit the expression and then select the yellow button command accept (Figure 22.13c). The expression is stored so that the information is now known to the debugger; the file is not corrected. To continue the process of filing in, you must choose the yellow button command proceed in the top subview (Figure 22.13d).

If, instead of correcting the error in the syntax error view, the notifier, or the debugger, you close the view by choosing the blue button command close, the process of filing in is discontinued and the file is closed.

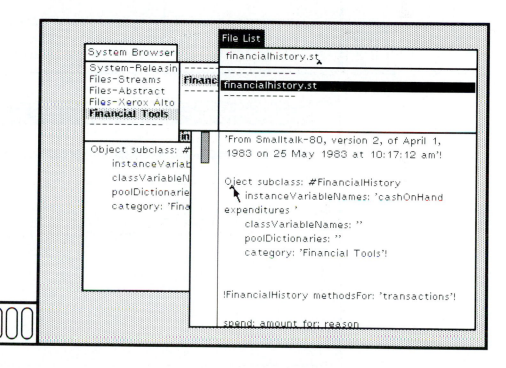

Figure 22.13a

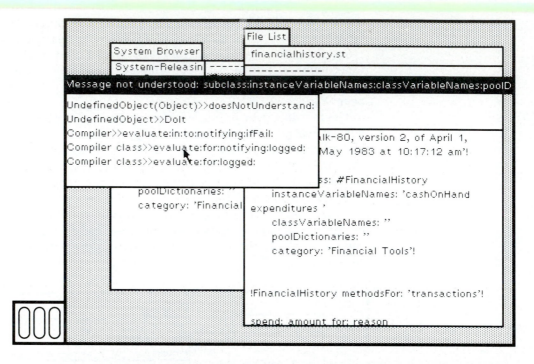

Figure 22.13b

Figure 22.13c

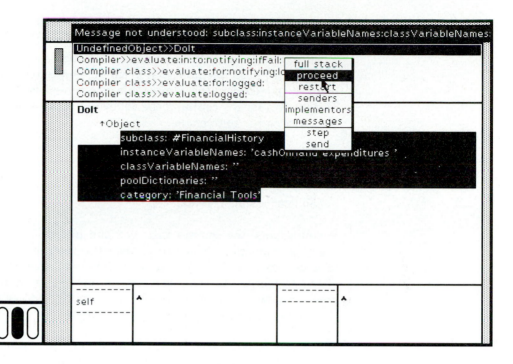

Figure 22.13d

22.4

Getting Started Revisited

Recall that in Section 1.3 you were introduced to the names of the external files needed to run the Smalltalk-80 system—the image, sources, and changes files. The sources and changes files contain text for methods stored in the format shown in Figure 22.2.

Sources and Changes Files

When you use a browser to access a method, the system has to retrieve the source code for that method. Initially all the source code is found in the file we refer to as the sources file. This file might be stored on your local disk or it might be on a network-based file server, shared among several Smalltalk-80 system users.

As you are evaluating expressions or making changes to class descriptions, your actions are logged onto an external file that we refer to as the changes file. If you change a method, the new source code is stored on the changes file, not back into the sources file. Thus the sources file is treated as shared and immutable; a private changes file must exist for each user.

The executable form of methods is compiled code (an instance of class CompiledMethod). The location of the source code corresponding to the compiled code is stored as part of the representation of a compiled method.

The sources, changes, and image files must be used in a coordinated way because of this retrieval reference in the image to one of the the two external files.

The two external files for sources and changes are referenced as elements of a global variable, the array named SourceFiles. The first element of the array is the sources file, the second is the changes file. The System Workspace contains the following expressions for changing the reference to the sources file.

```
SourceFiles
    at: 1
    put: (FileStream oldFileNamed: ' filename.sources ' ).
(SourceFiles at: 1) readOnly.
```

If you rename the sources files, you can inform the system by evaluating this expression. You can change the reference to the changes file (SourceFiles at: 2) in a similar way. Extensive access to the changes file, either to merge the work represented on two or more such files or to create a new one, is available in the Smalltalk-80 system. This access, the change manager, is presented in Chapter 23.

Decompilation

When you do not have access to the sources file, because it is not available on your local disk (perhaps there was not enough space) or you do not have access to a remote file server where it is stored, then it is not possible to browse methods in the way described in Chapter 9. Your system, however, contains the compiled version of the methods, and the system includes a decompiler. If you use the decompiler, you can obtain the text for methods, even though you can not obtain comments or the names of arguments and temporary variables.

There are two ways to inform the system to decompile, rather than to try to access the sources file.

1. Hold down the left "shift" key on the keyboard at the same time that you choose a message selector in the message-selector subview of a system browser.

2. In the System Workspace, evaluate the expression

```
SourceFiles ← nil
```

The system will notice that the global variable SourceFiles is not an array referencing two files, as expected, and will decompile methods when you try to access them in a browser. In addition, the changes file will not be maintained.

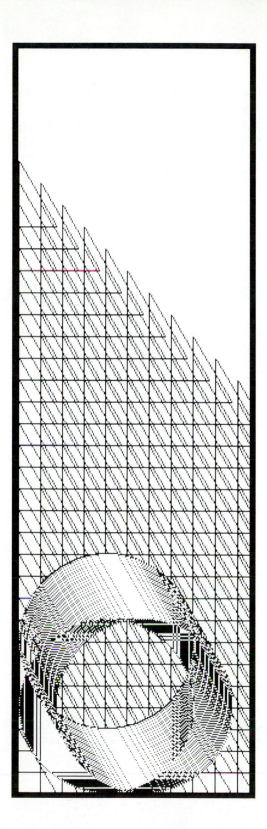

23

System Backup, Crash Recovery, and Cleanup

This chapter covers four aspects of the system that fall in the category of housecleaning support. Once again, we review the use of a snapshot as a way to save your work. We discuss the availability of the change set for monitoring the changes you make to classes and for supporting your ability to create files for sharing your work. While you are using the system, each addition or change to the system and each evaluation that you make is stored on an external file. This "audit trail" can be used by you to recover from a system crash and to merge the work of several programmers. After you work for awhile in a system image, housecleaning is needed to create new versions of the system image, changes, and sources files. This chapter includes an explanation of how to create "clean" system files. Version management is a general problem that is not directly supported by the standard system views. Research has been conducted in this area, and an experimental form of version management is used by the Smalltalk research team at Xerox PARC. A brief review of this research is provided in the last section of this chapter.

23.1

Saving Your System State

Periodically you might wish to save the current state of your work in the form of a system image. This is especially appropriate if you are going to make changes whose behavior you are not clear about, and which might, therefore, crash the system. Creating a snapshot is also appropriate if you feel that the amount of space for object storage is very low and you do not want to take a chance on losing your work. And it is important to save your work periodically if you feel that your hardware is not sufficiently reliable.

The System Menu contains the command save. Choose this command (Figure 23.1a). When you choose the command save, a prompter appears. It contains the name of the image file currently being used (Figure 23.1b). Note that the extension for the file name is not included. (Note also that this is the first part of the name found as the first element of the global array, SourceFiles.)

If you want to use this same file name, then choose the yellow button command accept, or simply type the "carriage return" key (Figure 23.1c).

> For some systems, to gain performance, part of the display screen turns white while the snapshot is being created on the file. It restores as soon as the file is completely written.

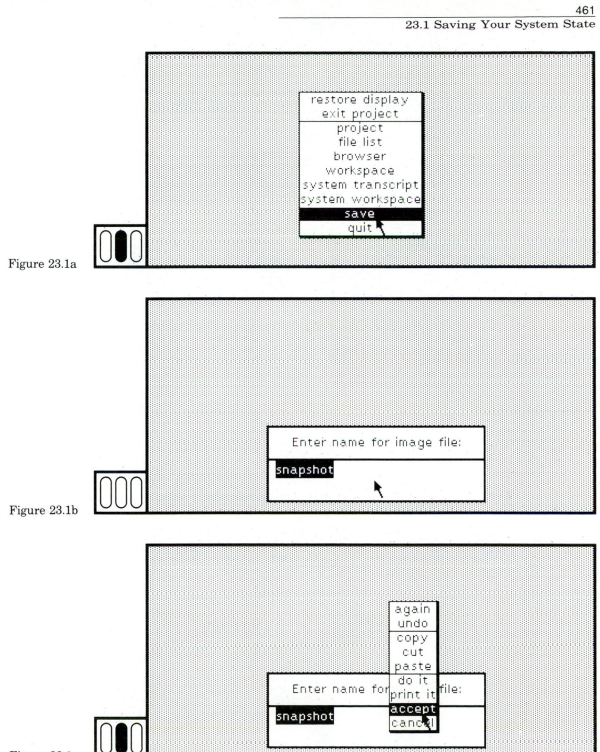

Figure 23.1a

Figure 23.1b

Figure 23.1c

If you want to use a different name than the one that appears in the prompter, then edit the text in the prompter. To terminate, choose the yellow button command accept, or type the "carriage return" key.

A new file for the image is created; the name is the name you gave in the prompter followed by a period followed by the characters im (an abbreviation for "image"). The image file must be coordinated with the file containing the changes made in this image of the system. Thus another new file is created; the name is the name you gave in the prompter followed by a period followed by the characters changes.

If you request a snapshot and then change your mind while the prompter is visible, delete all the text from the prompter. Choose the yellow button command accept, or type the "carriage return" key.

When you back up your work on another personal disk or on a network-based file server, you should save both the image file and the changes file. When you want to use these files again, you should use them with the same interpreter you used when the files were created.

Access to snapshot is also available when you choose System Menu quit. You are given the choice, then, to save, then quit.

23.2

The System Change Set

Within each project, a set of changes you make to class descriptions is maintained. (Projects are described in Chapter 4.) Using a browser view of this set of changes, you can find out what you have been doing. Also, you can use the set of changes to create an external file containing descriptions of the modifications you have made to the system so that you can share your work with other users. Sharing work, such as an application, involves sharing files of new class descriptions and sharing files of any changes you have to make to existing system classes.

Information is added to the set of changes whenever you

- change an existing method

- add a new method

- remove a method

- change the category of a message

- change an existing class definition

- change a class comment

- add a new class

- rename an existing class

- remove a class

- change the category of a class

These changes occur either by your system interactions (expression evaluations or method compilations), or by your retrieving information from a file (filing in). That is, the file contains class definitions or method definitions, and these are modifications to the system noted in the change set. If you change a method several times, there will be only one entry for that method in the change set.

Keep in mind that an independent set of changes is maintained by each project. If you want to maintain a set of changes for each activity in which you participate, you can create a project for each. The changes you make to class descriptions, and the addition of classes to the system, however, are shared among all the projects that you create.

☐ *Accessing the Set of Changes*   The set of changes can be accessed in the system by sending the single instance of SystemDictionary, Smalltalk, the message

Smalltalk changes

> Smalltalk is a global variable that is a dictionary whose keys are the names of all the other global variables in the system, notably the names of existing classes. The set of changes is an instance of class ChangeSet and is bound to a class variable of SystemDictionary named SystemChanges.

The expression

Smalltalk changes asSortedCollection

may be found in the System Workspace. If you evaluate this expression by selecting the text and then choosing the yellow button command print it, you see a description of the changes you have made so far. Try this when you first start using the system, and try it again after you have compiled some methods and/or have defined some classes. An example result of evaluating the expression is shown in Figure 23.2. The changes displayed are the ones that existed in the system after

- the class FinancialHistory was added to the system (as described in Chapter 13)

- an instance of FinancialHistory was created and inspected

- several messages were sent to the instance

- a new method was added to class Dictionary to modify printOn:

- the method for report was changed to use printOn:

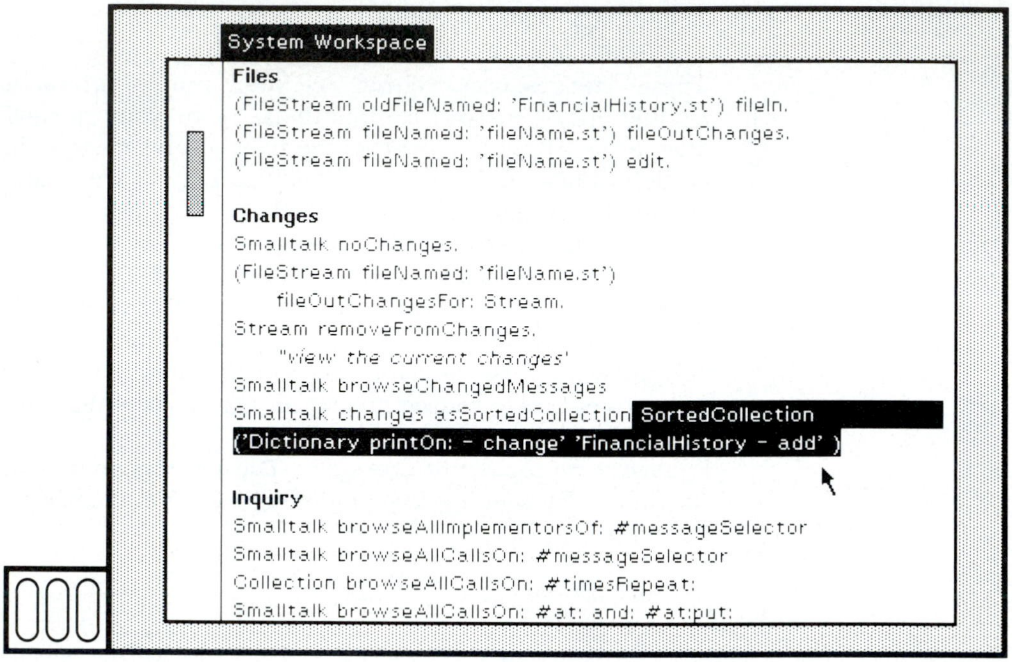

Figure 23.2

The changes show only that class FinancialHistory was added, and that a method in class Dictionary was added. The fact that expression evaluations were carried out is not stored in the set of changes.

☐ *Removing Entries From the Set of Changes*   There are three ways to remove entries from the set of changes for the current project.

1. Remove all the entries from the set of changes by evaluating the expression Smalltalk noChanges.

2. Remove all the entries that have already been saved on a file. This is automatically done whenever you file out from a system browser. For example, if you file out a class description, all entries about the class are removed from the set of changes; if you file out a particular method, any reference to the method is removed.

3. Remove all entries that refer to a particular class, ClassName, by evaluating an expression of the form

ClassName removeFromChanges

Whenever you start with a new system image and you want to make certain that the change set contains only subsequent changes, you should evaluate the expression Smalltalk noChanges; the expression appears in the System Workspace.

If you create a new class definition, the set of changes indicates that the class was added to the system. Henceforth, any changes to this class are not entered into the change set. This is because it is understood that the class is new and, therefore, everything about the class is new. If you file in a new class definition and then wish to maintain information about subsequent changes to the class, you should remove the class from changes using the message removeFromChanges or, if appropriate, sending Smalltalk the message noChanges.

A typical way in which several people can work together on a project is to maintain independent changes files. A file created by one person is filed into the system, the change set is emptied, and then all new changes logged. Then a file of the changes is created. The next person retrieves the original file and then retrieves the file of changes.

□ *Storing the Set of Changes on a File*   Changes to class descriptions (class definitions, comments, and methods) can be saved on an external file by evaluating an expression of the form

(FileStream fileNamed: ′ fileName ′) fileOutChanges

Alternatively, changes pertaining only to a specific class, ClassName, can be filed out by evaluating an expression of the form

(FileStream fileNamed: ′ fileName ′) fileOutChangesFor: ClassName

The process of filing out the changes does not modify the set of changes, so that the changes can be filed out again, especially if additional changes are made later in the working session. Rather than keeping a snapshot of your work, you might prefer to back up periodically by creating files of changes.

As noted earlier, the process of filing out a class by choosing the yellow button command file out in a system browser causes references to that class to be removed from the set of changes. One strategy to use in creating external files for sharing your work is, first, to file out any classes that you added to the system, and second, to file out the remaining contents of the set of changes. The set of changes should then contain only changes to system classes.

*Change-Set
Browser*

You can create a view of the set of changes that is like a message-set browser. This is done by evaluating the expression

Smalltalk browseChangedMessages

that appears in the System Workspace. Try it (Figure 23.3).

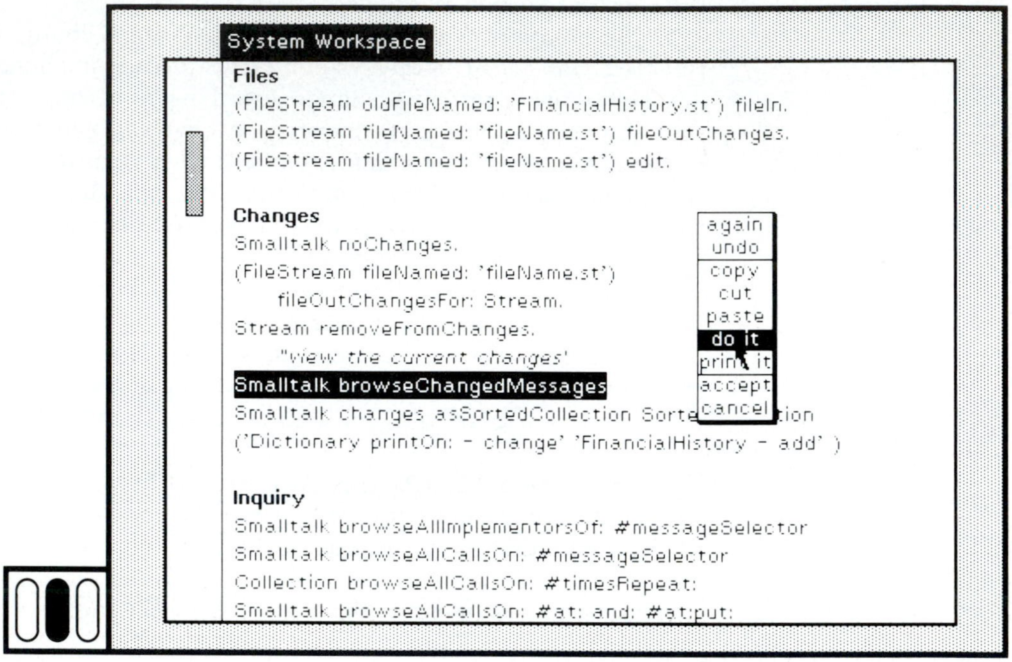

Figure 23.3

If there are no changes, then no browser is created and the word No-body appears in the System Transcript (if it is visible on the display screen).

The change-set browser shown in Figure 23.4 is a view of the same information that was printed in the workspace of Figure 23.2. The two parts of the change-set browser are identical to a message-selector browser as described in Chapter 10. The top subview is a list menu; the yellow button menu associated with it is the same as the yellow button menu associated with a message-selector subview of a browser. If you choose one of the class/message pairs, the method associated with the message appears in the text subview of the change-set browser.

You can file out or print out the method, and spawn a message-selector browser for the currently selected message. You can inquire about senders, implementors, and messages in the method. And you can move the message to a new message category, or you can remove the method from the system. You can not modify the change set using commands in the change-set browser.

Notice that the fact that a new class was added to the system does not appear in the change-set browser; only changed methods are accessed using this browser.

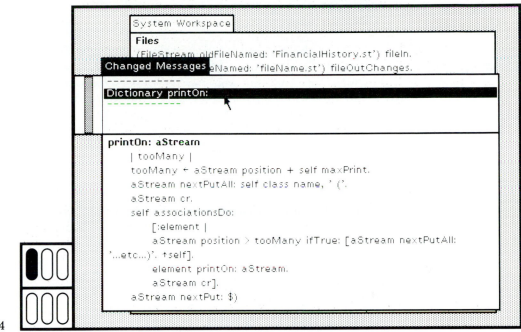

Figure 23.4

23.3

The System Audit Trail

The storage of changes in the Smalltalk-80 system takes two forms: an internal form as a set of changes (actually a set of objects describing changes), and an external form as a file on which your actions are logged while you are working (in the form of executable expressions or expressions that can be filed into a system). The previous section described a browser to access the internal form; this section describes a browser to access the external one.

All the information stored in the internal change set is also written onto the changes file. In addition, when you make a snapshot, the changes file is marked with the notation

''----SNAPSHOT----''

so that you can use a change-management browser (described later) to request a view only of the information stored in the changes file since your last snapshot. You can also look at the file and see what changes occurred between snapshots.

The changes file serves two important uses: to provide information for recovery from a crash, and to support a way of sharing code implemented by a group of programmers, including finding and resolving conflicting changes.

Crash Recovery

Because the changes file maintains a log of each of your actions, you can use it to recover from a system crash, that is, any situation in which you find that you can no longer communicate with the system and therefore can not safely save your work. Recovery can be done in two ways. After a crash, start up a previous system image that you can run (presumably the last snapshot that you successfully made and saved). Evaluate a message such as

Smalltalk recover: 5000

The argument, 5000, represents the number of characters from the end of the changes file that you wish to copy. The characters are copied onto a file named st80.recent. A view of this new file will be created on the screen. Explore it. Find the last place in the file containing the text `" ----SNAPSHOT---- "`. This is the point at which you wrote the last snapshot. If you can not find this text on the file, you will have to re-evaluate the message recover: again, this time with a larger number.

Now that you found the point at which you had previously saved your work, you can use the yellow button command file it in in the view of the file st80.recent to selectively evaluate and file in the changes you had made up to the time of the crash.

Change-Management Browser

Alternatively, you can use a browser that we refer to as the *Change-management Browser*. This browser lets you access your do it or print it evaluations, as well as method definitions, whereas the change-set browser described in Section 23.2 does not. Moreover, the order in which you made changes is retained in the changes file and presented in the change-management browser. The order of changes is not retained in the internal change set. You can use this ordering information to back up to a previous version of a method.

The change-management browser lets you

- examine the contents of one or more changes files

- examine the method changes stored in the change set

- configure a new changes file

- redo any of the changes or evaluations

- determine whether there is any conflicting implementations of a method in two or more changes files

To open a change-management browser that has no initial change content, evaluate the expression

ChangeListView open

To open a change-management browser that initially displays all the actions stored in the current changes file since your last snapshot, evaluate the expression

ChangeListView recover

Or you can specify a changes file (fileName) whose content should be displayed initially in the change-management browser. Evaluate the expression

ChangeListView openOn:
   (ChangeList new recoverFile: (FileStream oldFileNamed: ′fileName′))

All of these expressions are provided in the System Workspace. Select and evaluate the first one (Figure 23.5).

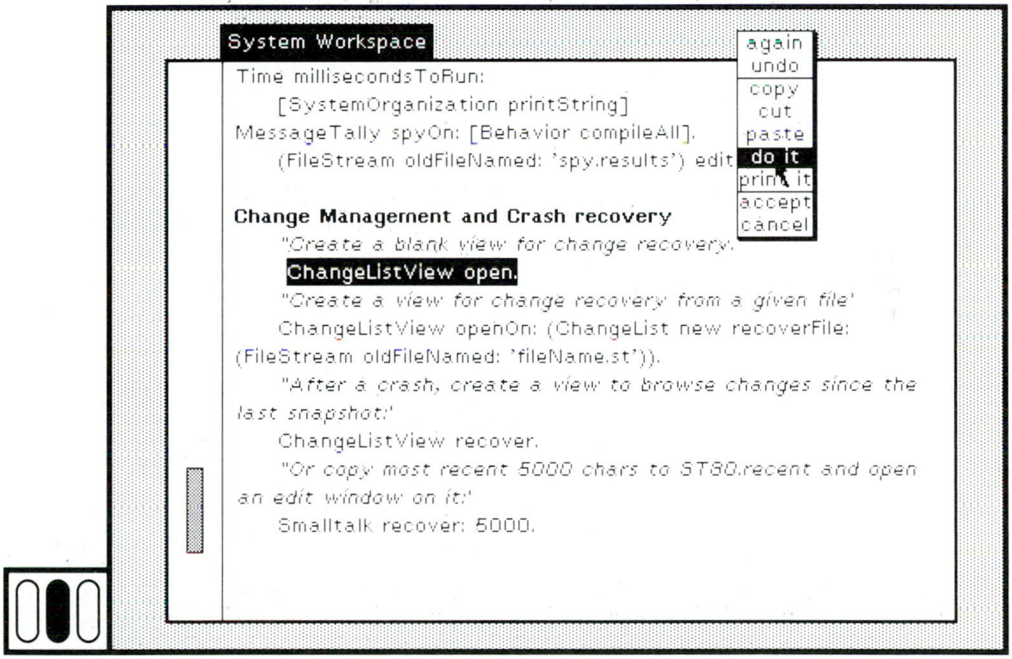

Figure 23.5

The empty change-management browser is shown in Figure 23.6. It consists of three major parts: the top part containing a list menu, the middle part containing several browser menu items that control the kind of information that will display in the menu, and the bottom part in which text is displayed and can be edited. With the cursor in the top subview, press the yellow button to observe the menu (Figure 23.7). The

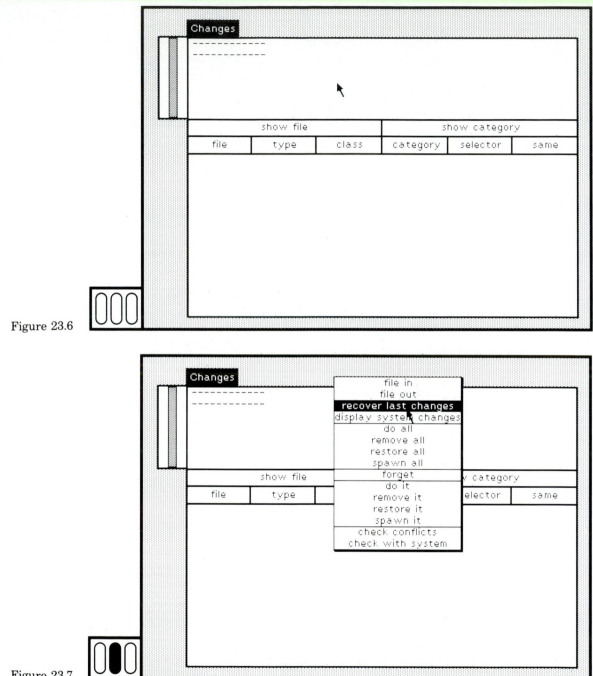

Figure 23.6

Figure 23.7

menu commands allow you to specify changes files to read or to write, and allow you to operate on a single item or on a group of items in the list menu. Two commands invoke conflict analysis on the items in the list menu.

☐ *Commands that specify changes files*

file in	A prompter appears in which you type the name of a changes file. When you choose the yellow button command accept, references to the contents of this file are added to the browser menu. If you change your mind and want to abort this command, type nothing in the prompter and choose the yellow button command accept or type the "carriage return" key.
file out	A prompter appears in which you type the name of a changes file. When you choose the yellow button command accept, the items in the browser menu that are not marked for removal are stored in the file. If you change your mind and want to abort this command, type nothing in the prompter and choose the yellow button command accept or type the "carriage return" key.
recover last changes	Adds to the browser menu references to the contents of the current changes file since the last snapshot.
display system changes	Adds to the browser menu references to the methods in the internal change set.

☐ *Commands that operate on a group of items*

do all	Evaluates each expression or new definition that is referenced in the browser menu and is not marked for removal.
remove all	Marks every item in the browser menu for removal.
restore all	Unmarks every item in the browser menu that is currently marked for removal.
spawn all	Creates another change-management browser whose menu is identical to the currently displayed menu.
forget	Deletes every item in the browser menu that is currently marked for removal.

☐ *Commands that operate on a single item*

do it	Evaluates the item that is currently selected, whether or not it is marked for removal. The item is either an expression, or a class or method definition.

remove it	Marks the item that is currently selected for removal.
restore it	Unmarks the item that is currently selected and that is marked for removal.
spawn it	Creates a message-selector browser for the current definition in the system of the item that is selected. You can then visually compare to see if the changes file specifies a different definition, and then you can decide which one you prefer to use.

☐ *Commands that check for conflicts*

check conflicts	A prompter appears in which you type the name of a changes file. When you choose the yellow button command accept, an analysis is done of all the items in the change-management browser menu to see if any of them refer to the same message selector, but specify different definitions. Any conflicts found are written on the file.
check with system	A prompter appears in which you type the name of a changes file. When you choose the yellow button command accept, an analysis is done of all the items in the change-management browser menu to see if any of them refer to the same message selector, but specify different definitions. Also checks to see if any item specifies a different definition than is currently in the system. Any conflicts found are written on the file.

If you start with an empty change-management browser, and choose the yellow button command display system changes, you access the same information that is shown in the change-set browser. If you start with an empty change-management browser, and choose the yellow button command recover last changes, you access the same information that is shown if you evaluate the expression ChangeListView recover.

Assume that the internal change set is the one displayed in Figure 23.2, and that you have not made a snapshot since you made these changes. Choose the yellow button command recover last changes in the top subview of the change-management browser. The information shown exceeds that available from the change-set browser (Figures 23.8a and 23.8b). In addition to method definitions (such as FinancialHistory spend:for:), the change-management menu contains

- class defines (for example, define FinancialHistory)
- expression executions (for example, doIt self spend: 100 for: ′rent′)
- category changes

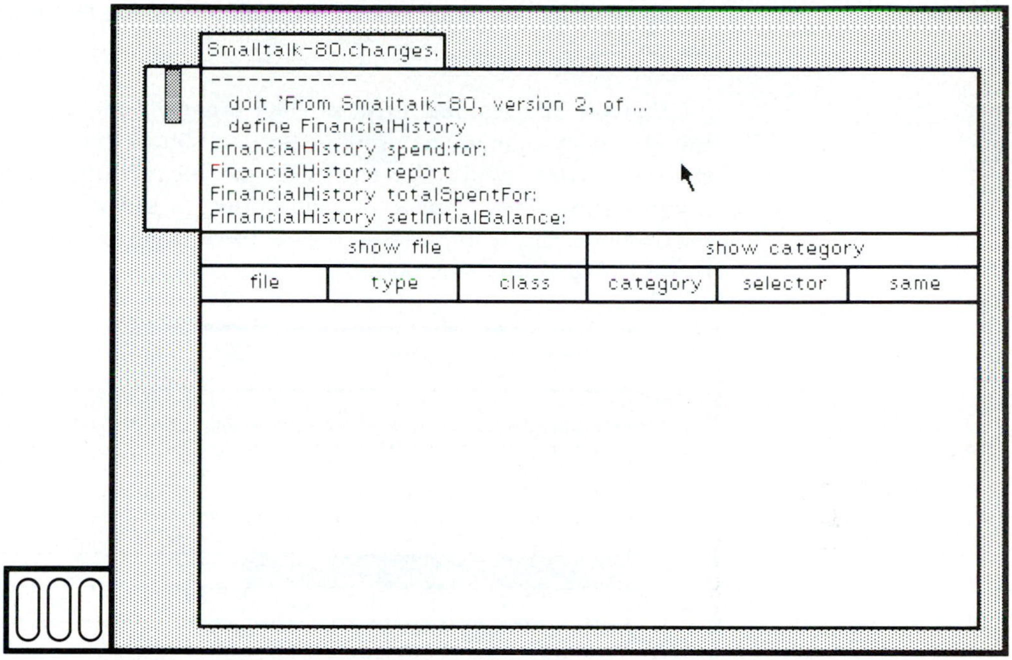

Figure 23.8a

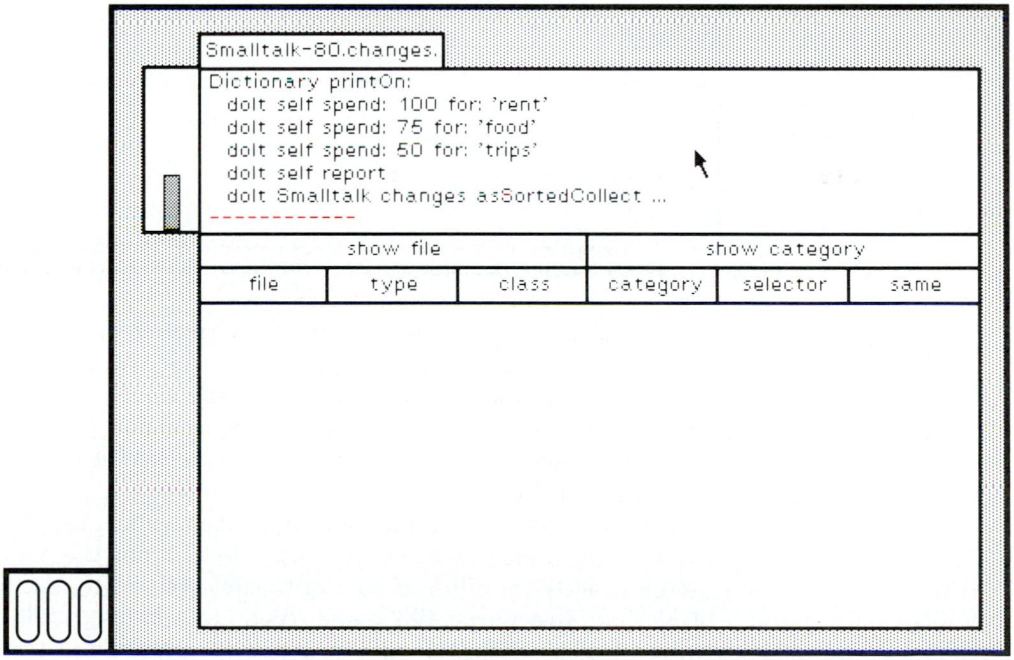

Figure 23.8b

These "special" changes are shown indented from the left margin of the list menu.

☐ *Display Options and Filters*   The menu items in the second part of the change-management browser let you obtain more information. Click the red button while the cursor is in the rectangle labeled show file (Figure 23.9). This "turns on" the option to see which changes file the list items came from, useful if you have accessed multiple files. Click again to "turn off" this option.

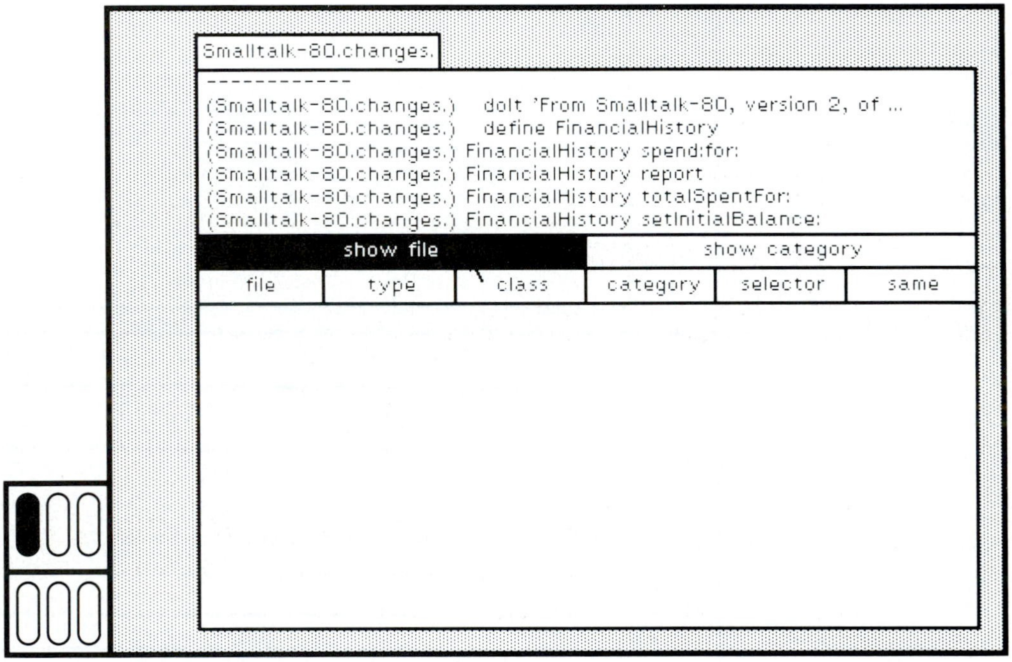

Figure 23.9

Now click the red button while the cursor is in the rectangle labeled show category (Figure 23.10). This "turns on" the option to see the category of the methods referenced in the list menu.

The remaining menu items provide a filter on what information should be shown in the list menu. Choosing one of the items "turns on" the filter indicated.

The filters only have meaning if an item in the top subview is selected. The basic idea is to remove any items from the menu that do not match exactly the filtered part of the selected item. An item is made up of at most five parts: file name, type (doIt, define, method, and so on), class, message category, and message selector. Thus the possible attributes for filtering items are

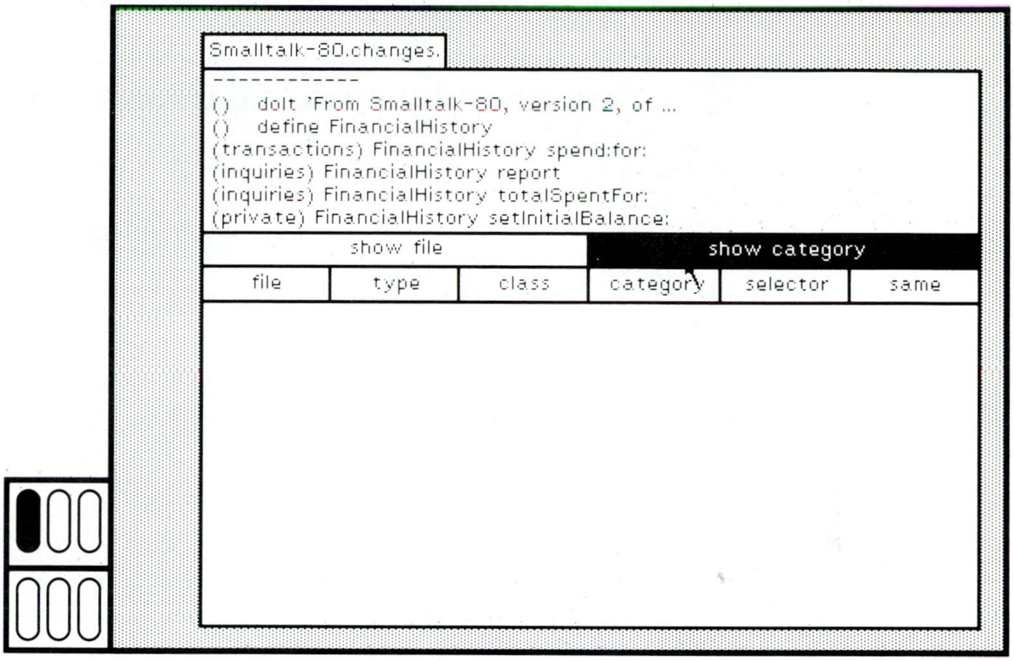

Figure 23.10

file	The changes file for all items should be the same as that of the selected item.
type	The type (evaluation, class definition, method definition) of all items should be the same as that of the selected item.
class	The class to which the items refer should be the same as that of the selected item.
category	The class category for each item should be the same as that of the selected item.
selector	The message selector of each item should be the same as that of the selected item.
same	All items should be precisely the same (this makes it possible to see multiple entries that are possibly conflicting definitions).

Suppose the menu item selected is a method definition and you choose the filter labeled type (Figure 23.11). Then the only items displayed in the menu are method definitions. Choose the filter type again, that is, "turn off" this filter. Suppose the menu item class is FinancialHistory and you choose the filter labeled class (Figure 23.12). Then the only items displayed in the menu are method definitions for FinancialHistory.

You can explore the change-management browser further by marking and unmarking items for removal, and spawning related browsers using the appropriate commands in the yellow button menu.

```
Smalltalk-80.changes.
------------
(transactions) FinancialHistory spend:for:
(inquiries) FinancialHistory report
(inquiries) FinancialHistory totalSpentFor:
(private) FinancialHistory setInitialBalance:
(instance creation) FinancialHistory class initialBalance:
(inquiries) FinancialHistory report
```

show file			show category		
file	type	class	category	selector	same

```
spend: amount for: reason
    "Spend amount for the reason given, decrementing the available
cash on hand."

    expenditures at: reason put: (self totalSpentFor: reason) +
amount.
    cashOnHand ← cashOnHand - amount
```

Figure 23.11

```
Smalltalk-80.changes.
------------
()    define FinancialHistory
(transactions) FinancialHistory spend:for:
(inquiries) FinancialHistory report
(inquiries) FinancialHistory totalSpentFor:
(private) FinancialHistory setInitialBalance:
(inquiries) FinancialHistory report
```

show file			show category		
file	type	class	category	selector	same

```
spend: amount for: reason
    "Spend amount for the reason given, decrementing the available
cash on hand."

    expenditures at: reason put: (self totalSpentFor: reason) +
amount.
    cashOnHand ← cashOnHand - amount
```

Figure 23.12

Conflict Resolution

Detecting conflicts between method definitions is described in the paper "Managing the Evolution of a Smalltalk-80 System" by Steve Putz in the Smalltalk-80 implementation considerations book, *Smalltalk-80: Bits of History, Words of Advice.* The main reason conflict checking is needed is that work done by different people can affect the same methods. When work is done in parallel by several programmers, each programmer submits a changes file. It is not possible to file-in each changes file, one at a time, since one file may undo (redo improperly) the definition provided in another file.

A conflict analysis routine is available in the system to examine code files and report the ways in which they conflict. Whenever two or more submissions define the same method, all conflicting definitions are appended to a "conflict report" file. It is then up to the programmers involved to determine how to resolve the conflicts, often by writing a new method that merges the needed functionalities.

Conflict checking is requested by choosing one of two commands in the yellow button menu of the top subview of the change-management browser, conflicts among the menu items (check conflicts) or conflicts among the menu items and the system methods (check with system). For each command, you must type a file name in a prompter and choose the yellow button command accept. The file is then created. When the analysis is completed, you can use the file list view to examine the file.

> Missing from the audit trail (changes file) is date stamping on each entry, back linking to alternative definitions, and "person" stamping (that is, associating the name of the person who made the change), all of which can be useful when multiple persons participate in a project and share the use of an image and its changes file.

23.4

Creating a "Clean" System

If you use an image long enough, modifying system methods and adding new methods, you will eventually create a very large audit trail on your changes file. Most methods will be referenced in this changes file rather than in the sources file. When you then want to create a new system release, you will want to clean up your system so that it has the following characteristics.

1. All up-to-date definitions and methods are on the sources file.

2. The changes file is empty (except for the date and version comment).

3. You are assured that there are no unreferenced objects in the system image.

Even when you are not releasing a new system, you may want to keep your changes file as short as possible. The changes file grows to include definitions for methods that override one another. That is, in the process of programming, you might try several versions of a method before settling on a definition. Each version will appear in the changes file, even though the system compiled method only refers to the last one. The most common "clean up" needed, then, is to condense your personal copy of the changes file, leaving the shared sources file untouched.

Creating a New System Image

A new system image is created by a process we call "doing a VMem-write," that is, writing a new file that contains an image of the virtual system. The idea of a VMem-write is to trace every accessible object, and write a copy of each object onto a disk image. This determines which objects are actually being used and which are occupying space unnecessarily. The end result is to release any possible free space. Moreover, the resulting clone can be started up and run, just like a snapshot.

> Some care is taken so that objects appear in the same order in the data space as they do in the system object table. This aspect of the implementation is covered in Part Four of the book *Smalltalk-80: The Language and its Implementation*.

The second purpose of a VMem-write is to allow any transformation of the system, such as changing the bytecode set or the structure of a class of objects (for example, the representation of floating-point numbers), which can not be done while you are interacting with the system. To initiate the VMem-write, evaluate the expression

    SystemTracer writeClone

In this case, no special transformations will be carried out. The result is a new image written on a file named

    clone.im

which you rename according to whatever system version naming conventions you have.

One of the common transformations done with the VMem-write is to clamp out (remove) classes. You might want to do this because your system includes some applications that you wish to remove in order to have a version of the system that takes up less space. Or you might want to do this because you have developed an alternative implementation of an application and had been using both versions until the new one was stable; now you are ready to eliminate the original version. For the most part, you do not need a VMem-write to eliminate classes from your system since you can use the command remove in the class-names subview of a system browser.

To clamp out classes, use a different message to SystemTracer.

SystemTracer writeCloneWithout: aSetOfClasses

where the argument is an instance of Set whose elements are the classes that you do want to clamp out. The method associated with SystemTracer writeCloneWithout: will do two things.

1. Remove the class references from the system dictionary, Smalltalk.

2. Remove any class categories that become empty as a result of removing the classes.

This means that the running image (the image from which you create the VMem-write) will be irreparably modified, so make sure that you have backed up your system image appropriately.

Before doing any VMem-write, you might want to clamp out some message protocols for various classes. You do this directly by using the system browser to remove the protocols from the class. Again, this means that you are irreparably modifying the source image, so make sure that you have backed up your system image.

> Included in the description of class SystemTracer is a clamping mechanism called winnowing. Its purpose is to cull out all unreferenced messages, with the exception of ones you specifically name. Then, based on these deletions, cull out more, and so on. This is basically a first attempt to understand how to drop out major parts of the system. You can explore this feature by examining the comment and the method associated with the message winnow: in class SystemTracer.

Static Checks

Before creating a new image, you will want to check for things that might be wrong with the current image. The system includes class Checker that contains many messages that support your doing static checks of the system. You can check for messages implemented but not sent by any method (this situation might be acceptable if the message is there for semantic completeness of a protocol), and messages sent but not implemented (this suggests a possible runtime error). An important thing to check for is the existence of obsolete classes. Send Checker the message obsoleteClasses. The response is an OrderedCollection of the classes in the system that have been made obsolete. A class becomes obsolete when it is removed from the system, but one or more instances exist. To remove the obsolete class, all instances must be deleted. You remove the instances by finding all references to them and setting the references to nil.

Condensing
Sources and
Changes

The purpose of condensing changes is to remove all redundancies from the changes file. Condensing also removes all logged information other than one copy of the changed method definitions. To condense your changes file, evaluate the expression

Smalltalk condenseChanges

In the System Transcript, you can observe the name of each class and message category as the source code for each is written onto the new changes file. The final name of the changes file is the name of the current one.

If you want to merge your changes file into a sources file, evaluate an expression of the form

Smalltalk newSourceFile: prefixName without: aCollectionOfClasses

where prefixName is a String representing the file name. Evaluating this expression creates two files whose names are

prefixName.sources

and

prefixName.changes

The second file is empty except for the date and version comment. Besides writing the method definitions, all class definitions are written and everything is alphabetically ordered, by class name, on the sources file.

An example of using this expression is

Smalltalk
    newSourceFile: Smalltalk versionName
    without: Array new

in which the prefix file name is the current system version name and no classes are omitted.

23.5

Version
Management

In his paper, Steve Putz also describes a special application he developed for managing the evolution of the Smalltalk-80 system. The system he describes supports users in reporting bugs and bug fixes, and in suggesting or announcing new applications (we call these "goodies"). The central feature of this development support system is a network-based database containing information about the past and proposed changes to the system, as well as bug reports and application announcements. The database also contains documentation about system changes and released system versions. This version management system is considered experimental and was not provided as a part of the standard Smalltalk-80 system. A summary of the version handler is provided here; if you are interested in more details about this area you should examine the Putz paper.

The interface to the system version handler is done using a special browser. There are actually three different browsers that filter information from the database of system changes and system release documentation: a version browser, a new feature browser, and a bug report browser.

The version browser supports you in examining the changes introduced in the currently selected version of the system, the changes submitted that were not included in the version release, remaining known bugs, and the known bugs for which fixes can be retrieved but are not as yet incorporated into the system. Figure 23.13a shows an example of a version browser. It consists of two subviews, one is a list menu and the other displays text. Each of the four kinds of information that you

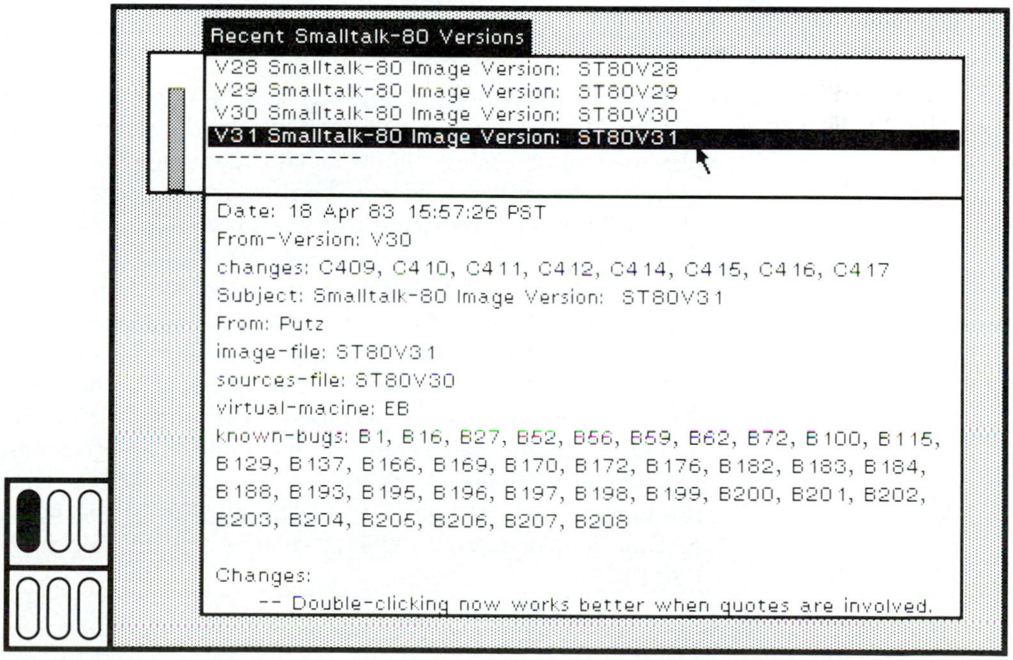

Figure 23.13a

can access is presented in a menu associated with the top subview of the version browser (Figure 23.13b). Choosing a menu item creates a browser that presents the requested information.

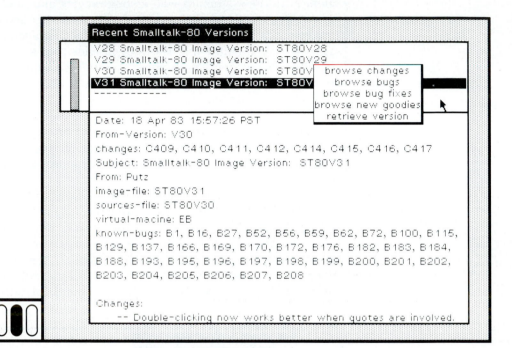

Figure 23.13b

Figure 23.14 shows a browser that was created by asking to see all the known bugs in the currently selected version of the system. It was obtained by choosing yellow button command browse bugs in the top view of the version browser. The numbers in the menu subview of the "bugs" browser correspond to those cross-referenced in the version handler.

Browsers are available that are used for submitting bug reports or fixes or goodies, and for composing a new system version. The bug report and bug fix browser is a modification of an electronic mail retrieval browser. The user can browse for a reported bug and then fill out a form that documents the proposed fix (Figure 23.15). The bug fix is then added to the database when the user selects the command accept in the yellow button menu of the browser. If a bug fix is selected in the report browser, a cross reference from the bug fix to the bug report is stored so that someone browsing bug reports will be told about the proposed bug fix.

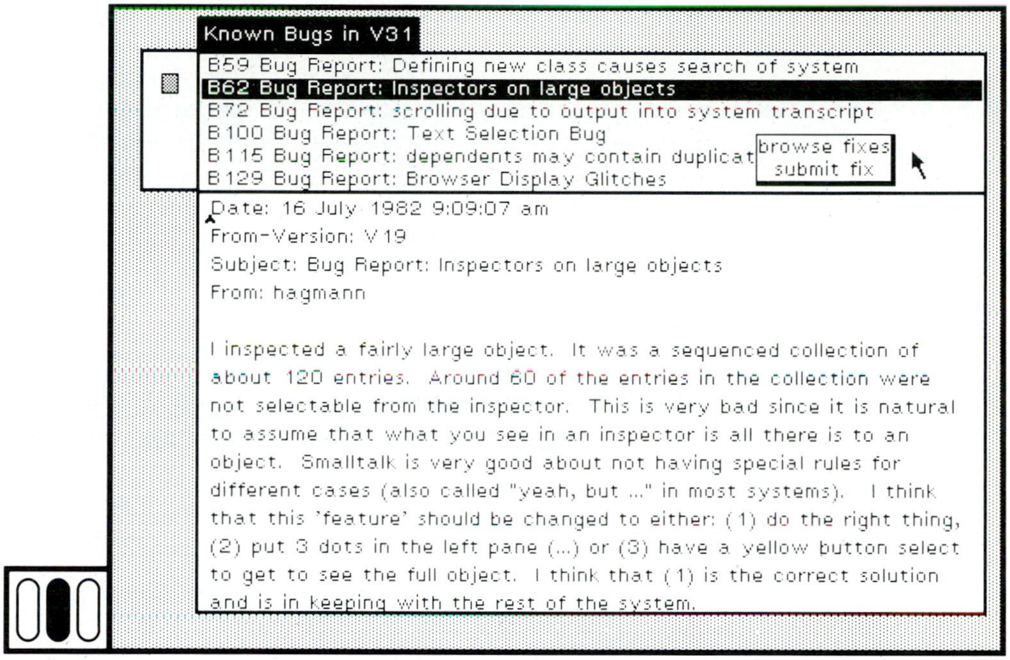

Known Bugs in V31

B59 Bug Report: Defining new class causes search of system
B62 Bug Report: Inspectors on large objects
B72 Bug Report: scrolling due to output into system transcript
B100 Bug Report: Text Selection Bug
B115 Bug Report: dependents may contain duplicat browse fixes
B129 Bug Report: Browser Display Glitches   submit fix

Date: 16 July 1982 9:09:07 am
From-Version: V19
Subject: Bug Report: Inspectors on large objects
From: hagmann

I inspected a fairly large object. It was a sequenced collection of
about 120 entries. Around 60 of the entries in the collection were
not selectable from the inspector. This is very bad since it is natural
to assume that what you see in an inspector is all there is to an
object. Smalltalk is very good about not having special rules for
different cases (also called "yeah, but ..." in most systems). I think
that this 'feature' should be changed to either: (1) do the right thing,
(2) put 3 dots in the left pane (...) or (3) have a yellow button select
to get to see the full object. I think that (1) is the correct solution
and is in keeping with the rest of the system.

Figure 23.14

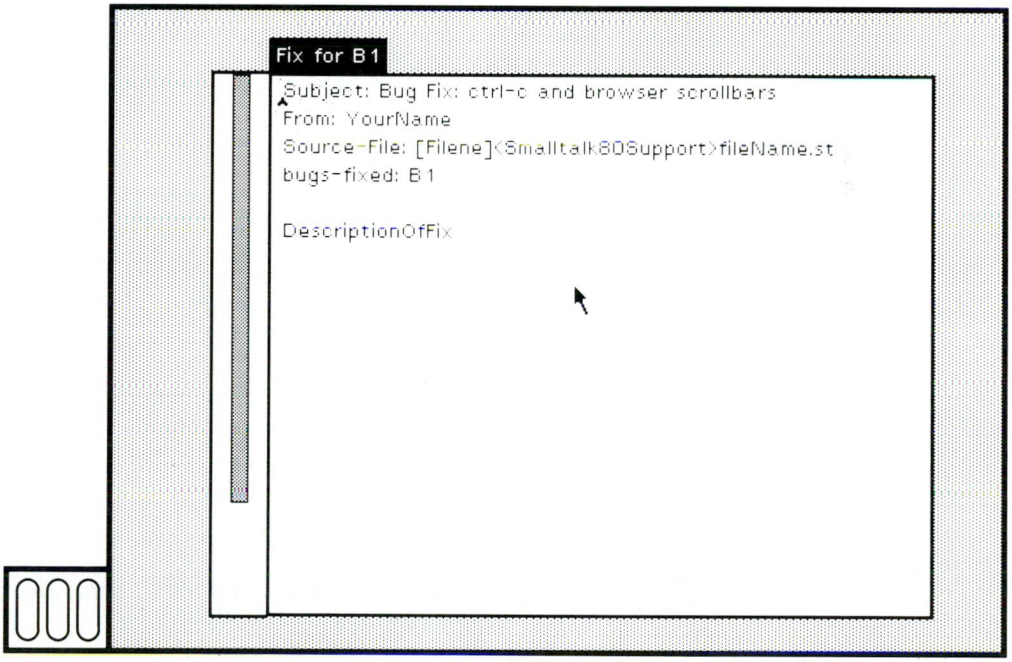

Fix for B1

Subject: Bug Fix: ctrl-c and browser scrollbars
From: YourName
Source-File: [Filene]<Smalltalk80Support>fileName.st
bugs-fixed: B1

DescriptionOfFix

Figure 23.15

Figure 23.16 is a browser for "goodies" that was obtained by choosing the yellow button command browse new goodies in the top view of the version browser. "Goodies" are new ideas for the system, new applications or user interface changes or performance improvements, that have been contributed by any user who has access to the network-based database for the Smalltalk-80 system. If you are interested in using a goodie, you choose a command from the yellow button menu of the goodie browser so that class descriptions for the goodie are filed into your system. Each goodie description is associated with a file of class descriptions that implement the goodie.

```
┌─────────────────────────────────────────────────────────┐
│  New Goodies for V31                                      │
│  ┌──────────────────────────────────────────────────┐    │
│  │ ───────────                                        │    │
│  │ C334 Goodie: Even Better Move and Collapse         │    │
│  │ C343 Goodie: five-paned browser                    │    │
│  │ C352 Goodie: Icons for collapsed views ┌──────────────────┐
│  │ C367 Goodie: Faster recompiling of clas│browse source files│
│  │ C413 Goodie: Prettier clock            │browse bugs fixed  │
│  │ ───────────────────────────────────────│ file in changes   │
│  │ date: 16 February 1983 6:04:48 pm       └──────────────────┘
│  │ from-version: V28
│  │ subject: Goodie: Even Better Move and Collapse
│  │ from: Putz
│  │ source-file: <Smalltalk80Support>EvenBetterMove-sp.st
│  │
│  │ In answer to Glenn's last two goodies, here is a version which makes
│  │ a Form out of the window and lets the user drag around the window
│  │ with the mouse.
│  │
│  │ Note that this is what Laura does in the Rehearsal World. Also note
│  │ that on memory-poor machines (e.g. Dolphin) this may excercise the
│  │ compactor or run the system out of memory. I suppose a test could
│  │ be put in which checks coreLeft first, but virtual memory would be a
│  │ much nicer solution.
│  └──────────────────────────────────────────────────┘
└─────────────────────────────────────────────────────────┘
```

Figure 23.16

New system versions are created by choosing items from a menu of submitted bug fixes and goodies in order to compose a list of changes that should be checked for conflicts and then incorporated into a running system. Bug fixes might conflict with one another in the sense that they change the same methods. The system conflict analyzer can be used to check for any such conflicts, leaving it up to you to resolve the differences.

This approach to version management was successfully used in managing the refinement of the Smalltalk-80 system.

Appendix 1

Financial History Views
and Controllers

This appendix contains a complete listing of three class descriptions: FinancialHistory, FinancialHistoryView, and FinancialHistoryController. These three classes implement a simple model for monitoring income and expenditures (FinancialHistory), viewing that model as two bar charts (BarChartView and FinancialHistoryView), and interacting with that model in order to increase income or expenditures. A sample screen image of the bar charts is shown in Figure A.1 in which the yellow button menu is showing. The menu has two items: spend and receive. Choosing either one of these brings up a prompter in which the user specifies the reason why money is being spent or received (Figure A.2). Once a reason is specified, a prompter appears in which to specify the amount of money (Figure A.3). The appropriate bar chart is then updated (Figure A.4). If the reason given is new (Figures A.5, A.6, and A.7), the bar chart is reorganized to display the new bar. The view is created as a standard system view so that the blue button menu is available (Figure A.8).

This example is given to you as another sample of how to use the classes View and Controller that are provided in the Smalltalk-80 system as basic building blocks with which to construct interactive graphical interfaces. It is unlike the examples in Chapter 15 in that a different approach to creating the yellow button menu is used. The format for presentation is that of a class implementation description as introduced in the book *Smalltalk-80: The Language and its Implementation*. The example makes use of prompters (instances of the class FillInTheBlank).

The first class, FinancialHistory, was described in Chapters 17, 18, and 19. This version of the class adds access to the instance variable incomes as well as expenditures. Note the addition of the changed mes-

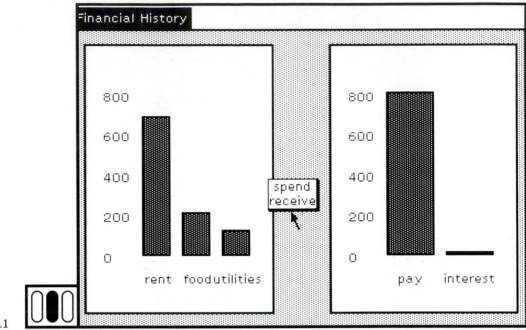

Figure A.1

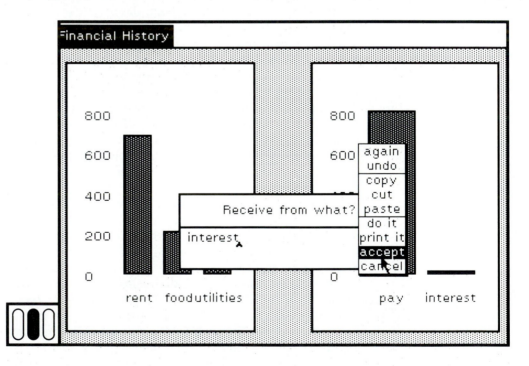

Figure A.2

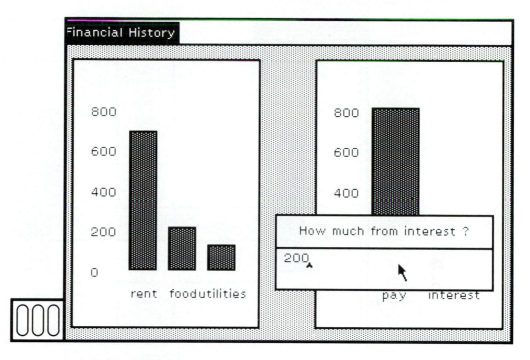

Figure A.3

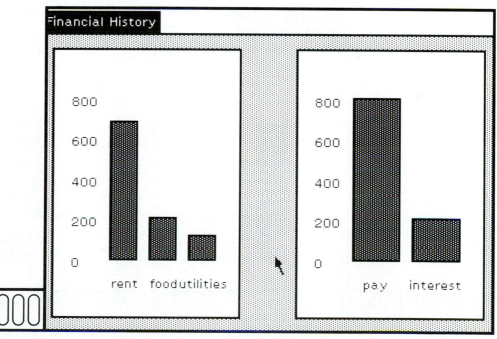

Figure A.4

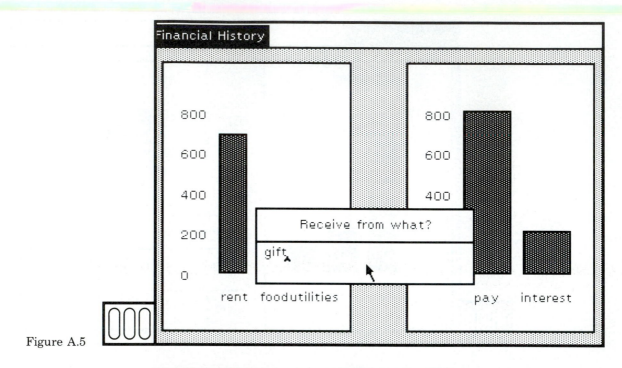

Figure A.5

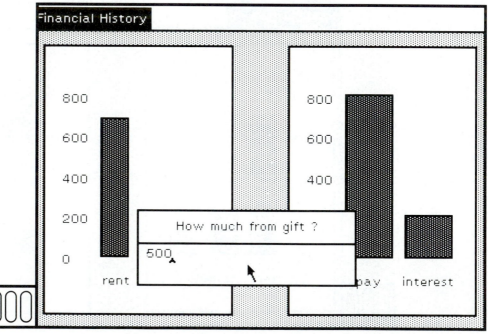

Figure A.6

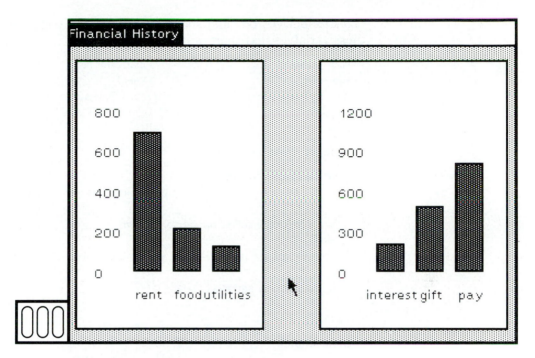

Figure A.7

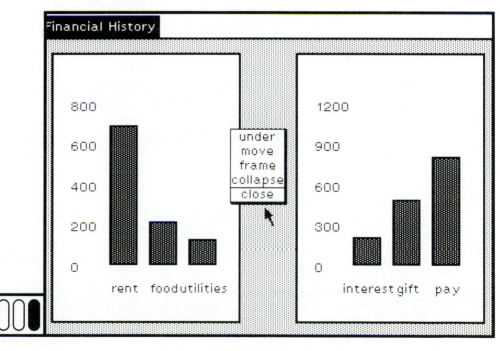

Figure A.8

sages to receive:from: and spend:for: to notify any objects dependent on these variables that there was a change.

class name	FinancialHistory
superclass	Object
instance variable names	' cashOnHand incomes expenditures '
category	' Financial Tools '
class methods	

instance creation

initialBalance: amount
" Create a FinancialHistory with amount as the initial balance. "

↑super new setInitialBalance: amount

new
" Create a FinancialHistory with 0 as the initial balance. "

↑super new setInitialBalance: 0

instance methods

transactions

receive: amount from: source
" Receive amount of money from source, and increment cash on hand by this amount. "

incomes at: source
        put: (self totalReceivedFrom: source) + amount.
cashOnHand ← cashOnHand + amount.
incomes changed

spend: amount for: reason
" Spend amount of money for reason and decrement cash on hand by this amount. "

expenditures at: reason
        put: (self totalSpentFor: reason) + amount.
cashOnHand ← cashOnHand - amount.
expenditures changed

inquiries

cashOnHand
" Answer the current balance? "

↑cashOnHand

expenditures
" Answer the Dictionary of expenditures. "
↑expenditures

incomes
" Answer the Dictionary of incomes. "

↑incomes

totalReceivedFrom: source
" Answer the total amount of money received from source. "

(incomes includesKey: source)
   ifTrue: [↑incomes at: source]
   ifFalse: [↑0]

totalSpentFor: reason
" Answer the total amount of money spent for reason. "

(expenditures includesKey: reason)
   ifTrue: [↑expenditures at: reason]
   ifFalse: [↑0]

private

   setInitialBalance: amount
     " Initialize the instance variables. "

     cashOnHand ← amount.
     incomes ← Dictionary new.
     expenditures ← Dictionary new

You can create an instance of FinancialHistory, and spend and receive money, by evaluating the following expressions.

```
Smalltalk at: #HouseholdFinances put: nil.
HouseholdFinances ← FinancialHistory initialBalance: 1560.
HouseholdFinances spend: 700 for: 'rent'.
HouseholdFinances spend: 78.53 for: 'food'.
HouseholdFinances receive: 820 from: 'pay'.
HouseholdFinances receive: 22.15 from: 'interest'.
HouseholdFinances spend: 135.65 for: 'utilities'.
HouseholdFinances spend: 146.14 for: 'food'.
```

In the above expressions, HouseholdFinances is created as a global variable. Then the instance of the class FinancialHistory is created and several messages are sent to it. At this point, if we were to view the incomes and expenditures of HouseholdFinances as two bar charts, we would see the image shown in Figure A.1.

The next step is to create a special bar-chart viewing mechanism for a Dictionary. Class BarChartView has no variables declared.

class name	BarChartView
superclass	View
category	'Financial Tools'
instance methods	

accessing

barFrame
" Answer the area available for the bars. The response to insetDisplayBox is implemented in the superclass View. "

↑self insetDisplayBox insetBy: (50 @ 10 corner: 10 @ 50)

labelCount
" Answer the number of labels needed. Although this is specified as a constant, it should probably be an instance variable. "

↑5

maximumValue
" Answer the maximum value on the y-axis. The message model, whose response must be a kind of Dictionary, is implemented in the superclass View. "

| total |
total ←
    self model values
        inject: 0
        into: [:sum :value | sum + value].
↑(total / self labelCount roundTo: self units) * self labelCount

numberOfColumns
" Answer the number of bars needed in the chart. "

↑self model size

positionFor: value
" Answer the relative position within the chart for value. "

↑self barFrame height * value / self maximumValue

units
" Answer the unit increment of values used to compute the ticks on the y-axis. Although this is a constant, it probably should be an instance variable. "

↑100

displaying

displayView
" Display the x- and y-axis labels and then the bars. This message is

sent from View's implementation of the message display, in which the View requests display of each of its subparts. "

```
self displayXLabels.
self displayYLabels.
self displayBars
```

displayXLabels
```
| corner |
corner ← self barFrame bottomLeft.
self model keys do:
    [ :key |
      key displayAt:
          corner + (self barFrame width - 20 /
                      (self numberOfColumns * 2) @ 20)
                  - (key asDisplayText boundingBox extent / 2).
      corner ←
          corner + ((self barFrame width / self numberOfColumns) @ 0)]
```

displayYLabels
```
| count label increment |
count ← self labelCount.
increment ← self maximumValue / count.
label ← 0.
count timesRepeat:
    [label printString displayAt:
        (self barFrame bottomLeft
          - (35 @ ((self positionFor: label)+7))).
      label ← label + increment]
```

displayBars
```
| height bar corner |
corner ← self barFrame bottomLeft.
self model keys do:
    [ :key |
      height ← self positionFor: (self model at: key).
      bar ←
          corner - (0 @ height) extent:
              (self barFrame width / self numberOfColumns - 10)
                  @ height.
      Display black: bar.
      Display fill: (bar insetBy: 2@2) mask: Form darkGray.
      corner ←
          corner + ((self barFrame width / self numberOfColumns) @ 0)]
```

update: aParameter
" Some values have changed, so update the view. "

```
self display
```

You can try out the bar chart viewing mechanism on any Dictionary with numeric values whose keys are instances of String or Text. In particular, try the following expressions in order to see the bar chart for the HouseholdFinances expenditures.

```
| aBarChartView |
aBarChartView ← BarChartView new.
aBarChartView model: HouseholdFinances expenditures.
aBarChartView window: Rectangle fromUser.
aBarChartView insideColor: Form white.
aBarChartView borderWidth: 2.
aBarChartView display
```

The third statement asks you to specify the screen area in which the bar chart will be displayed. The expression Rectangle fromUser means that you are to designate a rectangular area. Make it large enough to accommodate the text for all the keys in the Dictionary, HouseHold-Finances expenditures.

The definition of a BarChart is faulty in several ways. First, the units are designated as 100. If all the values of the Dictionary are less than 100, then an error (division by zero) will occur when you try to display the bar chart. Second, the number of labels (labelCount) is specified as 5, true in our example, but probably not all the time. You can improve the class description by parameterizing these values. To see the problem, try the following expressions.

```
| aDict aBarChartView |
aDict ← Dictionary new.
aDict at: ' 1 ' put: 10.
aDict at: ' 2 ' put: 20.
aDict at: ' 3 ' put: 30.
aDict at: ' 4 ' put: 40.
aDict at: ' 5 ' put: 50.
aDict at: ' 6 ' put: 60.
aBarChartView ← BarChartView new.
aBarChartView model: aDict.
aBarChartView window: Rectangle fromUser.
aBarChartView insideColor: Form white.
aBarChartView borderWidth: 2.
aBarChartView display
```

The next step is to create a viewing mechanism for FinancialHistory that groups together the bar charts for incomes and expenditures within a single view. Class FinancialHistoryView specifies a view that consists of two views, the bar charts. It is a subclass of View, and adds no new variables.

class name	FinancialHistoryView
superclass	View
category	'Financial Tools'
class methods	

instance creation

open: aFHModel

" Create a standard system view of the FinancialHistory, aFHModel, that consists of two bar charts, one for expenditures and one for income. "

| aFHView aBCView topView |
" First create the top view that is a standard system view and provides the blue button menu for moving, framing, collapsing, and closing the view. "
    topView ← StandardSystemView new.
    topView model: aFHModel.
    topView borderWidth: 2.
    topView insideColor: Form lightGray.
    topView label: 'Financial History' .

" Create the FinancialHistoryView and make it fill the top view. "
    aFHView ← self new model: aFHModel.
    topView addSubView: aFHView.

" Create the bar chart of expenditures and place it inside the FinancialHistoryView. Its interior should be white, its border 2 pixels wide, and it should have no user interaction independent of the one provided for FinancialHistoryView. "
    aBCView ← BarChartView new model: aFHModel expenditures.
    aBCView window: (10@10 extent: 35@35).
    aBCView insideColor: Form white.
    aBCView borderWidth: 2.
    aBCView controller: NoController new.
    aFHView addSubView: aBCView.

" Create the bar chart of incomes similar to that of the one for expenditures. "
    aBCView ← BarChartView new model: aFHModel incomes.
    aBCView window: (55@10 extent: 35@35).
    aBCView insideColor: Form white.
    aBCView borderWidth: 2.
    aBCView controller: NoController new.
    aFHView addSubView: aBCView.

" Standard system views have standard system controllers that respond to the message open by asking the user to designate the rectangular area in which the view will be displayed. "
    topView controller open

instance methods

controller access

defaultControllerClass
" Answer the name of the class that provides the usual user interaction for this class. "
↑FinancialHistoryController

Note that the last method, defaultControllerClass, specifies that the user interaction for a FinancialHistoryView is handled by a FinancialHistory-Controller. You will not be able to add this method to the system until you declare the class FinancialHistoryController, as follows. A Mouse-MenuController is a system controller that provides the mechanisms for storing and retrieving pop-up menus. FinancialHistoryController is like this class except it provides a particular yellow button menu for items spend and receive. When these items are chosen, the corresponding messages, spend and receive, will be sent to the FinancialHistory-Controller.

class name	FinancialHistoryController
superclass	MouseMenuController
class variable names	' FHYellowButtonMenu
	FHYellowButtonMessages '
category	' Financial Tools '
class methods	

class initialization

initialize
" Specify the yellow button menu items and actions. "

FHYellowButtonMessages ← #(spend receive).
FHYellowButtonMenu ←
    PopUpMenu
        labels:
    ' spend
receive '

instance methods

initialize-release

initialize

" Make certain that the instance knows about the menu items. "

super initialize.
self initializeYellowButtonMenu

menu messages

receive

" Ask what amount is being received for what reason, and then update the FinancialHistory accordingly. Use the prompter, a FillinTheBlank, to obtain the needed information. (Note that comma is the String concatenation operator. Also note that no special care is being taken to make sure that the number is a positive one—perhaps you might want to add this condition.) "

| spendOn amount |
spendOn ← FillInTheBlank request: ' Receive from what? ' .
spendOn isEmpty ifTrue: [↑self].
amount ← FillInTheBlank request: ' How much from ' , spendOn,' ? ' .
amount isEmpty ifTrue: [↑self].
amount ← Number readFrom: (ReadStream on: amount).
model receive: amount from: spendOn

spend

" Ask what amount is being spent for what reason, and then update the FinancialHistory accordingly. Use the prompter, a FillinTheBlank, to obtain the needed information. (Note that comma is the String concatenation operator. Also note that no special care is being taken to make sure that the number is a positive one—perhaps you might want to add this condition.). "

| spendOn amount |
spendOn ← FillInTheBlank request: ' Spend for what? ' .
spendOn isEmpty ifTrue: [↑self].
amount ← FillInTheBlank request: ' How much for ' , spendOn,' ? ' .
amount isEmpty ifTrue: [↑self].
amount ← Number readFrom: (ReadStream on: amount).
model spend: amount for: spendOn

control defaults

isControlActive

" sensor, declared as an instance variable in the superclass Controller, is an instance of InputSensor. It can determine the cursor location, and whether mouse buttons or keys on the keyboard are pressed. "

↑super isControlActive & sensor blueButtonPressed not

private

initializeYellowButtonMenu

" yellowButtonMenu:yellowButtonMessages: is specified in the superclass MouseMenuController; the response is to create the correct menu image and corresponding messages. "

self yellowButtonMenu: FHYellowButtonMenu
    yellowButtonMessages: FHYellowButtonMessages

After defining the class FinancialHistoryController, remember to define the message defaultControllerClass in FinancialHistoryView.

To initialize the menus before trying to use the class, you evaluate the expression

FinancialHistoryController initialize

You can then evaluate

FinancialHistoryView open: HouseholdFinances

in order to try out the user interface as shown in the figures.

These classes are offered as initial ideas with which you can play. There are several modifications to try. Make certain that only the part of the view that needs to redisplay does whenever there is a change. Try to change the user interface to the bar chart so that you can point to a bar and "drag" it up in order to change the value in the Dictionary (that is, instead of providing NoController as the user interface to a BarChartView, create a new controller that handles the user red button actions). Be careful that the scale on the axis of the chart is appropriate for such action. Try to create viewing mechanisms that display pie charts or graphs instead of bar charts. Make a view in which the expenditures or incomes are shown as both graphs and bar charts, and make certain that both views update correctly when the Dictionary changes.

Appendix 2

Smalltalk-80 Software Development Do's and Don'ts

As a software engineer at Xerox Special Information Systems (XSIS), I am responsible for the ongoing support of the Xerox 1100 Scientific Information Processor Smalltalk-80 System. I participate in the development of Smalltalk-80 virtual machine implementations and virtual image releases. In the past, as a member of the Publishing Systems Department, I developed an experimental interactive page make-up editor with the Smalltalk-76 programming environment (precursor to the Smalltalk-80 system). I also observed and supported the development of two major applications with the Smalltalk-80 system at XSIS. As a result of these experiences, I would like to share with you several important "do's and don'ts" for Smalltalk-80 software development.

☐ *First and foremost: Do read the documentation.* Perhaps this statement should be printed on the cover, or even emblazoned on your machine, rather than located at the end of a book that you have probably just finished reading! Early Smalltalk-76 and Smalltalk-80 development projects at XSIS began with seasoned software engineers who had no prior experience with Smalltalk programming, nor did they have off-line documentation. Their success in the beginning should be credited to their programming background, but also to the user support provided in the Smalltalk-80 environment. However, several system features and techniques that would have simplified their development efforts were not discovered until well into the projects, when early versions of this book became available. Change management, system tracing, and performance analysis were several useful tools that they had not discovered on their own.

☐ *Before embarking on your first Smalltalk-80 development project: Do
understand the basic language concepts.* The basic language concepts
are outlined in Chapter 5 of this book and summarized in Section 5.5.
This recommendation may seem obvious, but it is so easy to develop
software by copying and editing existing system code. Often the new
programmer, anxious to use the system, starts programming before
learning about the object and message-sending metaphor of the
Smalltalk-80 language.

☐ *Whether your development team consists of one person, or many: Do
understand and use the change manager.* The change manager is one
of the most important tools for software development in the
Smalltalk-80 environment. It is described in Section 23.2 "The System
Change Set" and Section 23.3 "The System Audit Trail." This facility
tracks and helps you to maintain all changes you have made to the system. It allows you to selectively browse them, remove them, incorporate
them into another version of the system, check for conflicts, and pre-
pare the changes for release to other members of the development team
or to end users. Should a system crash occur, the change manager can
recover all changes since the system's state was last saved.

☐ *At the outset of a project involving two or more programmers: Do assign a member of the team to be the version manager.* Refer to Section
23.5 "Version Management" to learn about the kinds of tools the version manager might create. The responsibilities of the version manager
consist of collecting and cataloging code files submitted by all members
of the team, periodically building a new system image incorporating all
submitted code files, and releasing the image for use by the team. The
version manager stores the current release and all code files for that release in a central place, allowing team members read access, and
disallowing write access for anyone except the version manager. Much
of this process can be automated.

☐ *In the course of software development: Do not modify system classes
when subclassing is possible.* It is more desirable to subclass an
existing system class, using multiple inheritance when appropriate,
rather than to modify system class definitions and behavior. There are
two reasons for this. The first relates to managing changes. It is more
difficult to track changes to system classes than it is to track changes
that are concentrated in a single, user-defined subclass of a system
class. The second reason involves compatibility with new system releases. It is more difficult to incorporate your software into a new version of the Smalltalk-80 image if your system changes conflict with
changes in the new version, that are needed to improve the basic system rather than a specific application. There are indeed cases when it

is appropriate to change system classes, but it is important to understand the potential impact before doing so.

☐ *Do browse the system to find existing features that can be exploited in your applications.* Refer to Part Two of this book "How to Find Information in the System." Unlike traditional programming, about 90% of Smalltalk-80 programming typically consists of making relatively small modifications and enhancements to existing code. The programmer searches the system for classes and methods that demonstrate behavior similar to the desired functionality of the new application, and then extends the behavior through the mechanism of subclassing or copying and editing. Graphical interactive applications are created by extending the existing hierarchy of classes that support viewing and controlling behaviors.

☐ *Do not be at the mercy of the system; if you do not like something, change it.* Several XSIS customers comment about various details of the system that they would prefer to have changed. Examples are the size of the system font or the functionality of a particular system view or the way a particular method is written. My response to these comments is to remind the customer that the system is designed so that they can easily and freely change it. This concept is a new one to many people because traditional programming environments carefully protect system code from modification. The Smalltalk-80 environment treats system code and user code alike. Mold the system into an environment that suits your needs. The researchers designed the system so that they could experiment with creating new systems; the changeability of all of the system parts is a necessary attribute of this research. The easy changeability of system code, of course, means that you can make changes that crash the system. Therefore, make certain you have saved your work before trying something that changes system code that you might not fully understand. For creating applications that can not be changed by the end user, you might want to try mechanisms for protecting the code—for example, hiding the existence of certain classes from your users.

☐ *Do share your creative "goodies" with a friend.* Your creativity will inevitably result in novel yet natural extensions to the environment. Michael Malcolm, an XSIS software engineer, did not like the way text selection was handled originally, so he cleverly enhanced the old technique and shared it with other Xerox Smalltalk-80 programmers. It was such a useful extension to the system that it was incorporated into all subsequent releases. This "goodie" became part of the system because he packaged it so that other programmers could easily file it into their images for experimentation, and because he announced its existence over the Xerox electronic network to ensure its broad availability.

The Smalltalk-80 environment provides such a rich set of interactive software development tools that the programmer's time shifts from finding the path of least resistance through a complex web of system utilities to actually writing code. With this system, my belief that programming is an art is at last fulfilled.

☐ *And finally: Do have fun!*

Prepared by
Evelyn Van Orden
Xerox Special Information Systems

System Workspace Index

SourceFiles ← Disk ← nil

When these variables are nil, it is assumed that no sources can be accessed so that the decompiler should be used when browsing class descriptions. In addition, no changes file (audit trail) will be maintained. See Section 22.4.

Files

Information about external files is found in Chapters 22 and 23.

(FileStream oldFileNamed: 'fileName.st') fileIn

Read the class descriptions and expressions stored on a file. See Section 22.3.

(FileStream fileNamed: 'fileName.st') fileOutChanges

The information maintained in the system change set can be stored on a file. See Section 23.2.

(FileStream fileNamed: 'fileName.st') edit

A view of the contents of a file can be created. See Section 22.2.

Changes

While you are working in a project (Chapter 4), a set of class and method changes is maintained. See Section 23.2.

Smalltalk noChanges

Initialize the set of changes. See Section 23.2.

(FileStream fileNamed: 'fileName.st') fileOutChangesFor: Stream

Changed definitions for a particular class can be filed out. See Section 23.2.

Stream removeFromChanges

References in the set of changes to a particular class can be removed. See Section 23.2.

Smalltalk browseChangedMessages

View the current changes in a browser. See Section 23.2.

Smalltalk changes asSortedCollection

View the current changes as a SortedCollection. See Section 23.2.

Inquiry	The system supports your making many inquiries about the relationships among the objects. See Chapters 8, 9, and 10.
Smalltalk browseAllImplementorsOf: #messageSelector	Like the menu item implementors in the message-selector subview of a browser. See Section 10.4.
Smalltalk browseAllCallsOn: #messageSelector	Like the menu item senders in the message-selector subview of a browser. See Sections 10.4 and 12.2.
Collection browseAllCallsOn: #timesRepeat:	Like the menu item senders in the message-selector subview of a browser, except constrained to the methods of a particular class. See Section 10.4.
Smalltalk browseAllCallsOn: #at: and: #at:put:	Like the menu item senders in the message-selector subview of a browser, except accesses information about two message selectors rather than just one. See Section 10.4.
Smalltalk browseAllCallsOn: (Smalltalk associationAt: #Transcript)	Obtain a message-set browser that provides access to all methods in the system that reference a particular literal found in Smalltalk. See Section 10.4.
Smalltalk browseAllCallsOn: (TextConstants associationAt: #Centered)	Obtain a message-set browser that provides access to all methods in the system that reference a particular literal found in the pool dictionary TextConstants. See Section 10.4.
Smalltalk browseAllCallsOn: (Object classPool associationAt: #DependentsFields)	Obtain a message-set browser that provides access to all methods in the system that reference a particular literal found in one of Object's pool dictionaries. See Section 10.4.
Smalltalk browseAllSelect: [:meth | meth numLiterals > 40]	Obtain a message-set browser on all methods such that, when the block is

	evaluated with the method as its argument, the result is true. See Section 10.4.
FileStream instanceCount	Answer the number of instances of the class that exist in the system.
FormView allInstances inspect	Create an inspector on the collection of all the instances of the class that exist in the system. Inspectors are presented in Chapter 8.
Undeclared inspect	Create an inspector on the pool of variables that the user tried to reference but that were found to be undeclared. See Section 6.1.
Dependents	Access objects that have been declared as dependents of one another (for example, a particular view is dependent on the object it views).
(Object classPool at: #DependentsFields) keys	DependentsFields is a Dictionary, a class variable of Object in which knowledge about object dependencies is stored. It is sometimes referred to as a "soft field." Its keys are the objects that have other objects dependent on them.
(Object classPool at: #DependentsFields) keysDo: [:each | (each isKindOf: TextCollector) ifTrue: [each release]]	This is a useful expression for searching for a particular kind of object, here instances of TextCollector, that may have dependents. If there are dependents, they are sent the message release, that is, break the dependency. This is needed to make certain that undesired cyclic pointers are destroyed.
Globals	Names in Smalltalk other than classes and pools.

Disk	A FileDirectory.
Sensor	An InputSensor. See example uses in Section 6.4 and Chapter 21.
Display	A DisplayScreen. See example uses in Sections 6.4 and 11.3.
ScheduledControllers	A ControlManager. See Section 2.5.
Transcript	A TextCollector. See Section 3.4.
Processor	This single instance of ProcessorScheduler coordinates the use of the physical processor by all processes requiring service.
SourceFiles	Array of FileStreams. See Section 22.4.
SystemOrganization	A SystemOrganizer, the basis of the hierarchical indexing for the system browser. See Chapter 9.

Pool Dictionaries

Smalltalk	A SystemDictionary in which reference to all global variables, especially classes, is maintained. See Sections 6.1 and 10.4.
AltoFilePool	A pool dictionary known to AltoFile, AltoFileDirectory, and AltoFilePage.
FilePool	A pool dictionary known to ExternalStream, File, FileDirectory, and FilePage.
TextConstants	A pool dictionary known to ArrayedCollection, CharacterBlock, CharacterBlockScanner, CharacterScanner, CompositionScanner, DisplayScanner, DisplayText, Paragraph, ParagraphEditor, StrikeFont, TextLineInterval, and TextStyle.

Undeclared	A global dictionary in which to store the names of variables the user improperly tries to reference. See Section 6.1.
Smalltalk removeKey: #GlobalName	Remove a particular entry from the Dictionary Smalltalk.
Smalltalk declare: #GlobalName from: Undeclared	Add a particular entry from Undeclared to Smalltalk, effectively declaring the variable. See Section 6.1.
Transcript show: (3+4) printString; cr	Display the result of evaluating $3+4$ in the System Transcript, Transcript. See Section 3.4.
Smalltalk frills: false	For slow machines, some of the automatic selection that happens in the debugger and browsers can be turned off by evaluating this expression.
Display	Evaluate expressions to Display or to DisplayScreen to change the display area used by the system.
DisplayScreen displayExtent: 1024 @808	Make the screen 1024 dots wide by 808 dots high. See Section 6.4.
DisplayScreen displayExtent: 640@480	Make the screen 640 dots wide by 480 dots high. See Section 6.4.
Measurements	Take some measurements of the amount of space being used in the system. Evaluating these expressions typically takes a long time.
Smalltalk core	Amount of memory—number of objects, number of words of data. See Section 20.3.
Smalltalk oopsLeft	Number of objects that can still be created. See Section 20.3.
Smalltalk coreLeft	Amount of memory left for your programming. See Section 20.3.

MethodContext instanceCount

Instances of MethodContext hold all the dynamic state associated with the execution of a CompiledMethod. In addition to their inherited state, this includes the receiver, a method, and temporary space in the variable part of the context. This expression is a way to determine the number of interrupted executions of a method that are known to the system.

Disk freePages

Amount of space left on your disk for files.

Time millisecondsToRun: [SystemOrganization printString]

Length of time in milliseconds it takes to evaluate the expression(s) in the block.

MessageTally spyOn: [Behavior compileAll]

Do an analysis of the performance of the expression(s) in the block. See Chapter 14.

(FileStream oldFileNamed: 'spy.results') edit

Examine the file on which a performance analysis has been stored.

Change Management and Crash Recovery

Recovering from system crashes is discussed in Chapter 23.

ChangeListView open

Create a blank view for change recovery. See Section 23.3.

ChangeListView openOn: (ChangeList new recoverFile: (FileStream oldFileNamed: 'fileName.st'))

Create a view for change recovery from a given file. See Section 23.3.

ChangeListView recover

After a crash, create a view to browse changes since the last snapshot. See Section 23.3.

Smalltalk recover: 5000

Copy the most recent 5000 characters to the file named ST80.recent and open an edit window on it. See Section 23.3.

Menu Command Index

abort   238, **355**, **358**
accept
    to compile   24, 26, 100-101, 164, 166, 174,
      179, 200, 221, 238, 242, 244, 252, 256, 280,
      284, 303, 308, 310, 320, 324, 333, 346, 364,
      369, 373, 389, 392, 399, 402, 406, 416, 452
    to store   37, 48, 134, 147, 156, 173-175, 180,
      225-227, 233, 249, 254, 265, 268, 272, 278, 284,
      303, 331, 339, 395, 439-440, 444, 448, 455, 460,
      462, 471, 477
add category   173, 272
add field   **156**
add protocol   **178**, 225-227, 278, 284, 308
again   **57**, 58-59, 61, 179
browser   **42**, 43, 162, 218
cancel   37, 131, 134, **180**, 282, 444
category   **475**
check conflicts   **472**, 477
check with system   **472**, 477
class   **163**, 168, 218, 278, 364, **475**
class refs   **175**, 213, 303, 324
class var   **355**
class var refs   **175**, 211
close   20, 40, **48**, 72, 132, 146, 238, 261, 379, 426,
    455
collapse   **48**
comment   **174**, 249, 303, 324
continue   **23**
copy   **58**, 60-61, 179
copy name   **440**
correct   **379**
correct it   **355**, 356, **358**, 367
cut   **58**, 60-62, 179

debug   160, **383**, 388, 416
definition   **174**, 252, 333
display system changes   **471**, 472
do all   **471**
do it   **106**, 107-110, 170, 179, 182, 220, 238, 258,
    260, 282, 288, 354, 364, 416, 422, **471**
edit all   **173**, 272
enter   42, **68**
exit project   **42**, 68
explain   **180**, 182
file   **475**
file in   **440**, 452, 455, **471**
file it in   **443**, 450, 468
file list   **42**, 439
file out   **172**, **173**, **177**, **178**, 292, 373, 432-433,
    451, **471**
forget   **471**
format   **179**, 244
frame   **47**, 48
full stack   390, **392**
get   **443**, 444
get contents   **440**, 442, 444
global   **355**
hierarchy   **174**, 200, 203-204
implementors   **179**, 199, 200, 204, **392**
inspect   **146**, 152, 284, 404, 422
instance   **163**, 168, 224, 284, 321
inst var refs   **174**, 211
messages   **179**, 201, 203, **392**
move   **47**, 179, 264
no   20, 36, 40, 48, 126
paste   **58**, 61, 179
put   **443**, 444, 452, 455

Subject Index

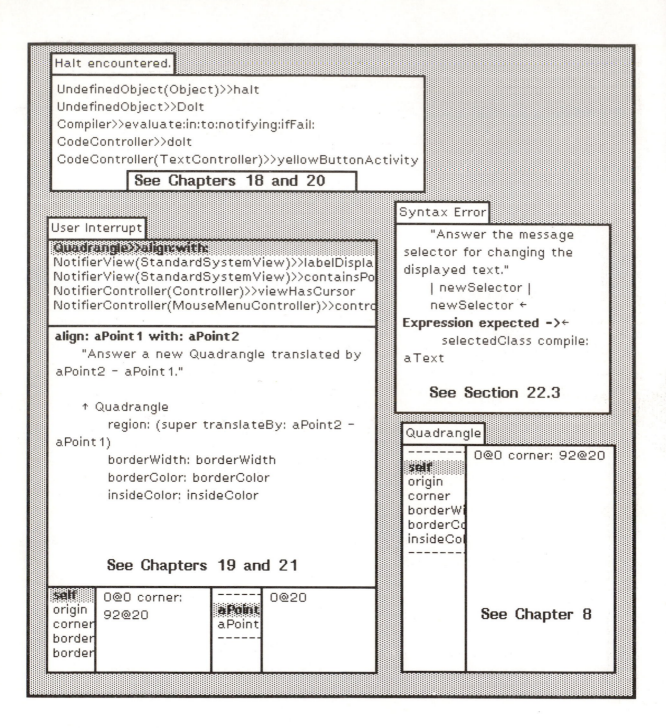

Halt encountered.

UndefinedObject(Object)>>halt
UndefinedObject>>DoIt
Compiler>>evaluate:in:to:notifying:ifFail:
CodeController>>doIt
CodeController(TextController)>>yellowButtonActivity

See Chapters 18 and 20

User Interrupt

Quadrangle>>align:with:
NotifierView(StandardSystemView)>>labelDispla
NotifierView(StandardSystemView)>>containsPo
NotifierController(Controller)>>viewHasCursor
NotifierController(MouseMenuController)>>contro

align: aPoint 1 with: aPoint 2
    "Answer a new Quadrangle translated by
aPoint2 – aPoint 1."

    ↑ Quadrangle
        region: (super translateBy: aPoint2 –
aPoint 1)
        borderWidth: borderWidth
        borderColor: borderColor
        insideColor: insideColor

See Chapters 19 and 21

self origin corner border border	0@0 corner: 92@20	------ aPoint aPoint ------	0@20

Syntax Error

    "Answer the message
selector for changing the
displayed text."
    | newSelector |
    newSelector ←
Expression expected ->←
        selectedClass compile:
aText

See Section 22.3

Quadrangle

------ self origin corner borderWi borderCo insideCo ------	0@0 corner: 92@20
	See Chapter 8